Essentials of
Health Information Systems and Technology

Jean A. Balgrosky

Lecturer

Fielding School of Public Health

University of California at Los Angeles

Los Angeles, California

Founder

Bootstrap Incubation, LLC

Solana Beach, California

Chief Information Officer

MD Revolution

La Jolla, California

JONES & BARTLETT
LEARNING

World Headquarters
Jones & Bartlett Learning
5 Wall Street
Burlington, MA 01803
978-443-5000
info@jblearning.com
www.jblearning.com

Jones & Bartlett Learning books and products are available through most bookstores and online booksellers. To contact Jones & Bartlett Learning directly, call 800-832-0034, fax 978-443-8000, or visit our website, www.jblearning.com.

Substantial discounts on bulk quantities of Jones & Bartlett Learning publications are available to corporations, professional associations, and other qualified organizations. For details and specific discount information, contact the special sales department at Jones & Bartlett Learning via the above contact information or send an email to specialsales@jblearning.com.

Production Credits
Executive Publisher: William Brottmiller
Publisher: Michael Brown
Associate Editor: Chloe Falivene
Production Editor: Sarah Bayle
Senior Marketing Manager: Sophie Fleck Teague
Art Development Editor: Joanna Lundeen
Art Development Assistant: Shannon Sheehan
Manufacturing and Inventory Control Supervisor: Amy Bacus
Composition: diacriTech
Cover Design: Kristin E. Parker
Rights and Photo Research Coordinator: Ashley Dos Santos
Cover Image: © John Swanepoel/Shutterstock, Inc.
Printing and Binding: Edwards Brothers Malloy

To order this product, use ISBN: 978-1-284-0-3611-4

Library of Congress Cataloging-in-Publication Data
Balgrosky, Jean A., author.
  Essentials of health information systems and technology / Jean A. Balgrosky.
    p. ; cm.
  Includes bibliographical references and index.
  ISBN 978-1-4496-4799-5
  I. Title.
  [DNLM: 1. Health Information Systems. 2. Medical Informatics. W 26.55.I4]
  R858
  610.285—dc23
                        2014011074
6048

Printed in the United States of America
22 21 20 19   10 9 8 7 6 5

Dedication

This book is dedicated to the information technology professionals working day after day in and on behalf of healthcare organizations across the country without whose work, nothing described in this book would be possible.

Table of Contents

Preface

We simply have to look around at our immediate surroundings to see how our world is evolving due to the introduction of disruptive technologies, practically before our very eyes. Health care, the practice of medicine, public health, and health in the lives of individuals are no different—and information technologies (IT) have a lot to do with these changes. This text addresses health information systems (HIS) and technology, and it is intended to take the mystery out of this subject, which can be daunting to even the most knowledgeable and talented around us—healthcare experts, physicians, nurses, and public health professionals alike. Why? Because unless something that appears foreign or complex or unusual has been carefully and simply explained to us, it remains a mystery, and we tend to avoid the subject, which prompts us to sidestep taking the dive into the world of health information systems and technology.

But what a loss, to avoid one of the most interesting, creative, ever-changing topics on the planet! No healthcare professional in any discipline can do her or his work without health information systems and technology. In this text, we dig in and explore together the simple truths and principles about this technical and disruptive subject. When we break it down into basics and principles that apply to any technology or any situation, suddenly what can be an intimidating, seemingly complex subject becomes much clearer.

What qualifies me to write about this topic? I have spent my career in the fields of health care, medical records science, health information systems and technology, innovation, and public health. As a chief information officer (CIO) for 20 years in two large, complex health systems, I learned tough lessons about health information technology, planning and managing systems, people, and change, and introducing disruptive technologies into healthcare organizations in a variety of markets across the United States. I learned how to develop HIS strategic plans, negotiate with and manage IT vendors, and implement new systems. In pursuing my PhD, I have learned the art and science of research; as an educator for the past 7 years, I have learned to teach graduate students pursuing their master of public health (MPH), master of science (MS), or PhD in health policy and management degrees. A good deal of my career has been spent explaining health information systems and technology to healthcare professionals, people, and students—those proficient in elements of technology as well as those completely unfamiliar with HIS and technology but expert in their chosen domain of health care such as nursing, medicine, management, quality, laboratory science, finance, or other disciplines.

My favorite discipline has always been the clinical side of health care, because, well, that is what health care is all about—caring for people who at a point in their lives find themselves vulnerable and in need of support, care, therapy, and maybe a little education about how to better take care of themselves. This is my bias. As my dear mentor, Dr. Paul Torrens, taught us at UCLA in the introductory course on the U.S. healthcare system, everyone has a bias, and it is important to state what that is at the outset of a conversation, writing, or lecture, so that people can take that perspective into consideration. The clinical side of health care is why healthcare organizations exist; the prevention of disease and harm is the mission of public health. Such organizations do not exist to provide fabulous billing services to the world or terrific strategic plans as a product. These functions in healthcare organizations are important, but they are support roles, intrinsic to success but ancillary to the real purpose of healthcare organizations and public health—namely, to provide high-quality health care to patients in the practice of medicine as well as public health services to citizens and populations in the pursuit of health.

This text, then, is about HIS and technology for health care and public health. It is also about making this complex, potentially overwhelming topic simple. Because curricula in universities and training programs for the health sciences, medicine, nursing, computer science, and other disciplines that lead to careers in health care, medicine, and public health have not included information technology courses until very recently, most people working in healthcare organizations and public health institutions today had absolutely no education or formal training in HIS. And yet, these are exactly the same people who are being asked to make the transformative change using HIS—to take the big leap into implementing disruptive technologies into their clinical and business environments, all while taking care of sick and injured people. This is a tall order, and it can be very stress inducing without proper support and clarification along the way of "what we are doing and why we are doing it." In fact, computerization of healthcare organizations and public health entities does not need to be a mystery, nor does it need to be as high risk as is it when those entering the process do so without education in the fundamentals of planning, selecting, implementing, using, and reaping the benefits of HIS and the data, information, and knowledge it can produce. My goal in this text is to give you a fundamentals playbook, thereby making HIS and technology more than the "black box" that it seems to so many otherwise highly qualified healthcare professionals or students whose goal it is to understand and work in health care, health policy and management, and public health someday.

This text is also intended for those new students who are just preparing for their careers, as they launch into whatever orbits their professional life takes them. Younger students, of course, have the advantage of having grown up with technology as part of their everyday existence, which definitely gives them a leg up in learning about it. But readers should not think that just because smart phones or laptop computers are easy and intuitive for them to use, they do not need to learn the fundamentals of planning, selecting, implementing, managing, and using the large HIS that guide organizations small and large. The disciplines of HIS, informatics, and data management are essentials of healthcare management, the new practice of medicine, and public health initiatives, and these are quite different from using personal computing devices whose applications and functions are integrated at the factory. We are counting on you! Young people starting out in their careers—along with experienced professionals broadening their perspectives, knowledge, and marketability—can carry the day into a better, more cost-effective healthcare and public health future. This future will be enabled by innovative uses of HIS and emerging health technologies that can help us take care of patients more effectively in our hospitals, clinics, and physician practices, and help people stay healthier and safer in their daily lives.

Industry by industry, segment by segment, and organization by organization, the key principles of HIS strategy, planning, management, and implementation (and key principles for computer systems) are very nearly the same, no matter which types of systems or technologies or organizations are involved. By focusing on fundamentals, guiding principles, management issues, and proven methods, you will be well equipped to deal with HIS selection and implementation projects in your department or organization. My goal is for you to feel confident with your grasp of this subject—HIS—and the health information systems and technology aspects of your professional role. Whether HIS is your primary focus or is secondary to your role, you will need it to do *any* job in health care and public health. The firmer your command of the basics of HIS and technology, the more qualified you will be for any new job or opportunity in which you find yourself and that ignites your professional passion. This is true regardless of the specialty, domain, department, function, or type of healthcare organization in which you work.

The truth is that no matter which area of healthcare practice you enter—such as project management, nursing, medicine, finance, operations, public health programs and outreach, health education and health promotion, policy, or another role— *your job will include health information systems–based and technology-related responsibilities.* It will be incumbent upon you to implement systems in your department, function, or organization throughout your career. It is much better to have a handle on the basics and key principles of HIS, so that you will be confident and proficient in those duties. By knowing these principles, you will be able to volunteer for the next HIS implementation project in your organization with conviction—and know that by understanding the basics of technology, you will be able to quickly pick up the technology specifics relevant to each new project.

Some readers may become so enamored with HIS at this level that they are spurred to go further and specialize in this area. I am here to share a simple message: You can do it! With emerging education and training programs in IT and a growing number of programs specializing in HIS, plus growing numbers and types of professional and entrepreneurial opportunities, you can make this your career if you so choose. The sky is the limit. Opportunities abound for productive, exciting, and well-paying careers in HIS for the long haul. In whatever area you choose to invest your education and training, HIS and technology will simply make you more proficient in that discipline, better able to innovate compete and reinvent yourself, more valuable to the organization, and more qualified for a wider range of opportunities and responsibilities. The more you know about HIS and technology, the better.

Now that you've had this heartfelt pep-talk, we will move on to a quick review of the key topics of *Essentials of Health Information Systems and Technology*.

ORGANIZATION OF THIS TEXT

This text is organized into sections that follow the HIS model presented in the *HIS Scope, Definition, and Conceptual Model* chapter and used throughout the text as a conceptual model for framing and organizing the materials and principles introduced. With a picture in your mind of how the various pieces and principles fit together, you will gain confidence in your overall understanding of the many facets of HIS and technology, which in turn will make a lifetime of learning about this area much easier for you from this point forward. I guarantee you will understand something that the majority of people in your organization do not, which provides you with a tremendous opportunity to be a leader in your healthcare career no matter where it takes you.

The first section, *Understanding Health Information Systems and Technology*, begins with the *Alignment: Health Information Systems and Technology and Current Challenges in Health Care* chapter, which explains why HIS and technology matter so much in health care and public health today. Topics include HIS's relationship to primary issues in health care today, health care cost and quality, motivations for today's emphasis on HIS, the role of the U.S. government in HIS in health care and public health today, changing consumer expectations, uses in other countries, opportunities for research and policy making, and relevance to the public's health. The *HIS Scope, Definition, and Conceptual Model* chapter presents the HIS model and lays out the types of settings in which HIS and technology are used.

The second section, *Systems and Management* (the first sphere of the HIS model), addresses planning, managing, and implementing HIS and technology. It begins with the *Health Information System Strategic Planning* chapter, which presents a conceptual HIS planning framework. I had the good fortune to be introduced to this planning tool early in my career, thanks to the transformative work of Jay McCutcheon and Bart Neuman, pioneers in HIS planning and strategy. I have used this HIS planning framework during my entire career, including now as I teach what I have learned over the years. It seldom fails to make the proverbial light bulb come on for my students, as I explain it and their eyes brighten and they smile, which tells me they now grasp a clarifying construct for understanding how all these different types of systems and technologies fit together, just as I did when I learned this timeless concept early in my career.

The *HIS Application Systems and Technology* chapter walks you through the basics of software systems and technology. It was written by the skillful hand of James Brady, a stellar expert in the technology and security of HIS. This chapter covering the basics of technology may seem a bit daunting but take a deep breath and jump in—you will gain so much by doing so.

The *Managing HIS and Technology Services: Delivering the Goods* chapter teaches you about managing people, projects, and processes of HIS and technology. The *Implementation* chapter introduces you to the exciting and challenging world of selecting and implementing systems—a topic essential to anyone who actually wants to put these new systems to work in an operational environment. Implementation is exciting work, but definitely not for the faint of heart; it is rewarding because you will use everything you have ever learned every single day of an implementation project.

The last chapter in this section is *Leadership and Adoption of HIS and Technology*, in which you are introduced to HIS leadership methods and roles, and the interesting tale of adoption of new technologies in health care and generally in organizations of any type.

The third section, *Understanding Health Informatics*, begins with the *Health Informatics* chapter. This chapter familiarizes you with various types of health informatics and roles for informaticists, such as in medicine and nursing; relates HIS and technology to Donabedian's health care quality framework including structure, process, and outcomes; and delves into the unsettling but important topic of unintended consequences of implementing HIS in healthcare organizations.

Penned by the pragmatic and knowledgeable Ric Speaker, the *Data* chapter explores the vital world of data, and discusses sources and characteristics of data, "Big Data," data stewardship and management, data challenges, and data security and protection. The importance of understanding and appreciating the essential topic of data when learning about HIS and technology cannot be overemphasized—at the end of the day, it is always about the data.

The *Business and Clinical Intelligence* chapter covers an area of enormous interest—the use of systems and their data for secondary uses that give us insight into the details and evidence regarding what we do clinically and in the business of health care. This exciting world of analytics—retrospective, real time, and predictive—creates new knowledge for the purpose of improving health outcomes.

The next section, *Research, Policy, and Public Health*, contains the *HIS and Research, Policy, and Public Health* chapter. It discusses uses of HIS for research, including roles of universities, government, private foundations, and reporting organizations in that worthy cause. The relationships of HIS and technology to policy and public health are examined as well.

The final section, *New Directions for HIS and Technology*, includes the *What Lies Beyond the Current State of HIS and Technology?* chapter, which explores the trajectory and potential future paths of emerging technologies and their application and use in health care and public health. eHealth, mHealth, uses of social media, personalized health care and medicine, and telemedicine are discussed, followed by an introduction to some of the issues and ethical dilemmas associated with ubiquitous use and access to data for purposes of health care and public health, including the dynamic tension between security and privacy of information versus access.

I have put my heart and soul into *Essentials of Health Information Systems and Technology*, just as I always have into the work experiences, mistakes, and lessons learned that are contained within this text. I hope you like it; but more importantly, I hope you find it useful and can apply what you learn here as you pursue the path in health care that ignites your passions. As I tell my students in the classroom, I share the mistakes I have made and the lessons learned from those experiences, so you can go into your careers equipped with that knowledge—and make new mistakes and learn a fresh set of lessons on your own!

Jean Balgrosky

Prologue

Essentials of Health Information Systems and Technology is intended as a basic but thorough introduction to a complex and intimidating topic. It is intended to take the mystery out of a subject that some people find exciting but others feel they cannot master because it is too highly technical.

Jean Balgrosky brings to health information systems (HIS) and technology her extensive experience implementing health information systems at Scripps Health and Holy Cross Health System (now Trinity Health) and her ongoing experience studying and teaching about health information systems at the University of California, Los Angeles. Her experience places her in a unique position to understand and teach both the theory and the practice of health information systems and technology. As she writes in the Preface: "A good deal of my career has been spent explaining health information systems and technology…". This will be obvious as you read the book.

Essentials of Health Information Systems and Technology is an important addition to our *Essential Public Health* series. This text emphasizes key concepts as well as many specifics about health information systems and technology. Once these concepts are understood, such as the need to match the structure of the HIS to the structure of the organization, the architecture of the HIS system becomes much easier to understand. It is then far easier to "get it" in terms of the types of technology that are a "fit" for various organizational or information scenarios.

This text provides substantial information about and clear explanations of the key technologies used to create systems and networks for healthcare and public health purposes. The concepts are presented without assuming extensive background, using an easily accessible approach. The text is ideal for use in introductory courses without prerequisites. Understanding the concepts is key because the applications are sure to change—and change rapidly—in the coming years. If you understand the essential components of technology such as hardware, software, networks, and mobile devices, you do not need to be a technical expert. You can focus on the basics, and then learn the technology specifics necessary for each project.

Therefore, the key principles are the focus of this text, which highlights HIS and technology planning and strategy, architectures, implementations, and uses, with accessible explanations and examples. Successful systems implementations are the result of cooperation and collaboration between the many different types of expertise found in any health enterprise. This is true whether one is selecting and implementing a new electronic health record system for a community clinic or a complex multihospital system, or designing and implementing new early-warning surveillance capabilities for public health agencies around the country, or using social media and smart phones to reach out with important health-related information to difficult-to-access rural areas.

The world of HIS and technology is an exciting, interesting, sometimes frustrating, and hopefully rewarding arena of possibilities and promise for making health care and public health safer, more accessible, and more effective. But it is not without its risks and unintended consequences. The proper attention is needed to determine the appropriate amount of change introduced at once. In addition, a balance must be struck between offering access to information and protecting the privacy and security of sensitive information on individuals. This text addresses these more caution-laden concepts so as to develop a realistic perspective of what it takes to implement systems and technology successfully.

New systems are not magic, and the benefits we hope to achieve from their use do not happen just by pushing a button. These systems and the data they produce must be carefully stewarded to ensure positive results and the avoidance of new problems that can result from improperly implemented or managed systems. The future of HIS and technology is unfolding, limited only by our imaginations and our will to adapt our systems and work methods carefully, creatively, and productively. *Essentials of Health Information Systems and Technology* will guide your way into this emerging world and help you cope and contribute.

Richard Riegelman MD, MPH, PhD
Series Editor

Acknowledgments

Essentials of Health Information Systems and Technology is a labor of love stemming from the challenging, exciting, complex area in which I have spent my career. As a chief information officer (CIO), educator, and bootstrap entrepreneur doing and managing information systems and technology in health care, sharing what I have learned over the years has always been a goal of mine. I have had the privilege and pleasure of teaching this subject for the past 6 years to the outstanding graduate and extension students at University of California, Los Angeles's Fielding School of Public Health, who have provided valuable feedback and input regarding ways to introduce key HIS concepts and subject matter. These students and colleagues, along with the many people with whom I had the privilege of working throughout my career at Scripps Health, Holy Cross Health System, Peat Marwick, and UCLA, have been instrumental in shaping the approach I have taken in explaining the essential elements of this complicated topic, any one of which could be a book in itself. I am grateful for these many experiences and interactions, just as I am for the encouraging words from my students, colleagues, and mentors.

I have attempted to weave connections between all types of health information, whether initially produced in a healthcare organization, for public health purposes, or by an individual. Previously separate areas of our health world are converging as we embrace use of mobile technologies, the Internet, and e-commerce in healthcare and information technology innovation. This brings hospitals, physician offices, and other healthcare delivery settings in touch with public health needs, prevention, and population health management, reflecting the true focus of our greatest needs in health care today: improving quality and health status, becoming more cost-effective, and preventing and reversing troubling trends of increasing epidemics of illness associated with behaviors, the environment, and daily lifestyle habits.

I owe my passion for connecting these two worlds to my education and training at UCLA's Fielding School of Public Health, and to several people in particular. In my early days as an undergraduate, Miss Olive Johnson, a health information leader with a vision that was well before her time, provided me with mentorship and foundational education in medical record science as an undergraduate, then welcomed me back as a graduate student during a challenging time in my life to get my master's degree in health information systems management. She gave me an opportunity that forever favorably altered my life. Dr. Ray Goodman awarded me a scholarship that sustained me and my daughter through my days as a graduate student and single parent. He had the foresight to anticipate the emerging importance of health information systems and the need to prepare qualified graduates in this area. I would also like to thank Dr. Jonathan Fielding, who sponsored me in my Masters internship into the PhD program and who has been an advocate for my studies and work ever since. Since my undergraduate days, Dr. Paul Torrens has provided me with enthusiastic encouragement in my studies and work in health information systems and technology as well. To this day, Drs. Fielding and Torrens are my mentors, colleagues, and friends. Dr. Jack Needleman has served as the chairperson of my

PhD committee and provided the guidance I have needed through the dissertation research process. Dr. Diana Hilberman has been my mentor in teaching and provided important opportunities for me to integrate the discipline of health information systems and technology into the graduate programs in health policy and management at UCLA. All these people have made huge differences in my life, education, and career, and I am eternally grateful to them. I would also like to thank Drs. Leah Vriesman, Fred Zimmerman, Robert Kaplan, Tom Rice, Paul Fu, Doug Bell, and the members of the Fielding School of Public Health's Department of Health Policy and Management faculty for their support of and interest in my PhD studies and teaching. I am grateful for their enthusiastic support of developing an HIS curriculum for the department and the opportunity to develop and teach classes on this topic, which has provided me with the testing ground for much of this text's content.

Another early lucky break in my career trajectory is owed to Sister Geraldine M. Hoyler, C.S.C. She plucked me out of a crowd of more typical candidates at the time and gave me my first job as a CIO at the age of 32. My work in those days was fueled by insights and innovations of Jay McCutcheon and Bart Neuman, inventors of the HIS planning model that I use to this day, and which provides a key framework for the concepts presented in this text. My friends and colleagues Dr. Neetu Chawla and Jessie Chatigny have provided valuable advice and encouragement, acting as expert sounding boards as I waded through the challenges of structuring and writing chapters. I'd like to thank my Bootstrap Incubation colleagues Kyle, Brandy, Sonya, Wyatt, Courtney, Melanie, Seth, CJ, Chris, Mannix, Brian, Kevin, and Bryce, who have picked up the slack and patiently waited as I went through spurts of writing and revising. Thank you for keeping my knowledge current as every day we strive to create innovations in health information technology together. I am ever so grateful for my new friends and colleagues—in particular, Dr. Samir Damani and his team, who inspire me and many others in the pursuit of digital health, population health management, and personalized medicine.

I owe special thanks to my author comrades and contributors, Jim Brady and Ric Speaker. They threw their hats willingly into the ring to help get this text written, tackling incredibly vital and challenging chapters. Bravo to their contributions and commitment to the text, among all their other responsibilities. We all have agreed: It was the hardest thing we have ever done! Jim and Ric, this text would not be here without you. I am lucky to have loyal friends and brilliant colleagues such as you. I also owe a debt of gratitude to Danny Boye Meyers, genius at the Apple Store genius bar in La Jolla, California, who rescued my raw, original Chapter 8 from the jaws of the asterisks bug in a split second, nimbly outsmarting my laptop, making it think it had crashed before it dissolved the chapter before our very eyes, ultimately and amazingly recovering the chapter at a critical time in the schedule to compose this manuscript. I am humbled by his adept brilliance. Further, I want to acknowledge all the hard-working information technology professionals I have been privileged to call my colleagues throughout my career. You have taught me everything about HIS and service to the mission of health care.

Through the several years-long process from conceptualizing through writing and revising this text, Dr. Dick Riegelman, editor of the *Essentials of Public Health* series, has provided me with the extraordinary combination of opportunity, guidance, constructive feedback, support, and enthusiasm for this volume. I hope *Essentials of Health Information Systems and Technology* matches his hopes and expectations for a topic so relevant to a complete education in public health and health management. I appreciate his vision and believe students will benefit greatly as a result.

I would like to thank Mike Brown of Jones & Bartlett Learning for his vision and excitement about adding this title to the series, and Chloe Falivene for her organized, professional, and energetic approach to getting this text from outline to manuscript to published product. Sarah Bayle has provided stalwart and focused editing leadership, along with copyeditor Jill Hobbs and permissions expert Ashley Dos Santos, whose discipline ensures a properly referenced and cited book. I always felt as if my hard work was very important to each of them and, along with Dr. Riegelman, they provided me with a fantastic, professional support team.

Last and most importantly, to my family—nothing in my life is possible without you. I am eternally grateful to you for your love and patience while I spent weeks at a time holed up writing. To my dear husband Parker, thank you for your support and encouragement to write this text, and for understanding how important it was to me to do this. (And thank you for handling family responsibilities during those days on end I was writing.) To my children Melissa, Jessica, Seth, Sarah, Wyatt, CJ, and Steven, thank you for being here—you and your families are my inspiration for everything I do. I also want to express my love and gratitude to my parents, who, although no longer with us, instilled in me the value of education and the importance of books, and provided me with unending motivation to strive to do something good with my life. This text is for you. And to my sister Wendy and brother Steve, thank you for your constant love and support, which has always provided such great comfort to me.

About the Author

Jean Balgrosky, MPH, RHIA, teaches Health Information Systems and Technology at UCLA Fielding School of Public Health, where she also received her MPH in health information management and BS in health services with a specialization in medical record science. She is currently a PhD candidate in health policy and management and is completing her dissertation, *Adoption of Health Information Technology by Physicians for Use in Their Practices*. Ms. Balgrosky's career in health information systems and technology has included the role of chief information officer (CIO) in large, complex healthcare organizations for more than 20 years, consulting, and teaching at the graduate level. More recently, she has become an entrepreneur, mentor, and board member for start-up companies in the life sciences, digital health, software-as-a-service, and healthcare analytics arenas. She is also CIO of a digital health company.

Essentials of Health Information Systems and Technology is Ms. Balgrosky's first book, for which she draws largely from her 30-year career in health information systems and technology as well as from teaching graduate courses at UCLA the past 5 years. She has authored numerous papers and articles over the course of her career, is a frequent speaker, moderator, and panelist at health information technology conferences, and plans to publish the results of her dissertation research regarding physician adoption of electronic health records.

Ms. Balgrosky has provided leadership throughout her career to the evolving health information systems and technology industry, maintaining her accreditation as a Registered Health Information Administrator as the foundation of her knowledge of medical record management and electronic health records. Her goal in writing this and subsequent books is to develop courses and resource materials for health information systems curricula, as well as to infuse necessary information technology topics into other courses taught in schools of public health and health management. Examples of courses that now require information technology components include financial and human resources management, quality, organizational behavior, strategic planning, marketing, and medical and nursing educational programs.

Ms. Balgrosky lives in Del Mar, California, with her husband Parker. They have seven children and, at current count, nine grandchildren.

Contributors

James W. Brady, MEd, PhD, CISSP, CISM, CRISC, PMP, CSM, CPHIMS, FHIMSS
Area Chief Information Officer
Kaiser Permanente Orange County
Anaheim, CA
Adjunct Faculty
National University
San Diego, CA

Ric Speaker
Entrepreneur and Health Information Systems Executive
Bear Creek Works, LLC
Heber City, UT

SECTION I

Understanding Health Information Systems and Technology

CHAPTER 1

Alignment: Health Information Systems and Current Challenges in Health Care

INTRODUCTION

Why Is HIS Getting So Much Attention Today?

It makes great sense to automate health care using modern information technology and systems, but currently an inordinate amount of attention is focused on the rapid introduction of **health information systems (HIS)**, especially **electronic health records (EHRs)**, into healthcare organizations of all shapes and sizes throughout the United States. Hospitals, clinics, physician practices of all sizes, public health organizations, and other settings in which health care is delivered have put HIS implementation high on their priority lists. This is because patients, physicians and nurses, managers of these healthcare organizations, the government, public health organizations, policy makers, and quality improvement organizations have

an extreme sense of urgency about implementing HIS as a means of improving the quality and efficiency of health care. Traditional paper-based records and work processes are inadequate for addressing the complexities of medical care and the interactions between healthcare organizations involved in the care of patients, particularly as many require a variety of care settings and services. Administrative processes in health care have also increased in volume and complexity. Done properly, computerization of these tasks relieves people of many mundane manual tasks and also improves efficiencies. Health care innovations today commonly incorporate new technologies such as mobile devices, genomic capabilities, and high-speed networks. Infrastructure spans from organizations to personal computing devices and smartphones. The field of health care seeks to improve cost and quality performance by adopting these new technologies and HIS in new ways across the care continuum. Any student preparing to work in health care in *any* capacity is compelled to understand the basics of HIS and its use in health care now and into the future. This need was the motivation for this text, the *Essentials of Health Information Systems and Technology*.

What Else Is Happening in HIS That Students Must Be Aware of?

Every student needs to be aware of the powerful roles that government and the free market play in influencing how HIS is used in health care. The government regulates and passes laws concerning proper implementation and use of HIS and **health information technology (HIT)**, while the free market encourages commercialization of HIS products and services to enhance vendor company stock prices and dividends for shareholders. Both of these forces are changing the way health care is delivered and how the U.S. health system functions, but their efforts often push in different directions or collide with opposing interests.

How Can a Student Begin to Understand HIS?

This text is designed to take the mystery out of understanding HIS. Computer systems can be complicated. This text describes how HIS is used in organizations and throughout the U.S. health system by healthcare and public health professionals—but not how such systems are built, programmed, or technically developed. Those areas are better addressed in schools of computer science and engineering. The text matches different types of HIS to different purposes within healthcare organizations and health care in general, such as to meet clinical, financial management, and public health reporting needs. It also covers the innovative ways HIS is expanding its reach through mobile devices, social networking, digital health and wellness, predictive analytics, and convergence with entire areas such as the biotechnology and pharmacology fields.

HEALTHCARE COST AND QUALITY ISSUES

In 2012, health care accounted for 17.2% of the U.S. gross domestic product (GDP); this is equal to $2.8 trillion, or $8915 per person, and with an average annual projected growth rate of 6.2% per year for 2015 through 2022, health spending could comprise 19.9% of the GDP by 2022.[1] Health care in all its related parts is undergoing massive change and experiencing numerous challenges in the process. The drivers of change are inadequate quality and the unsustainably high costs of health care. The Institute of Medicine (IOM) published two watershed reports, *To Err Is Human* (1999) and *Crossing the Quality Chasm* (2001), which provide solid evidence of alarming quality problems and make suggestions for improvement. *To Err Is Human* describes high levels of avoidable medical errors in U.S. hospitals that result in as many as 98,000 patients dying every year—patients who should have been discharged from the hospital successfully.[2] *Crossing the Quality Chasm* outlines six key aims necessary to improve the quality of care[3]:

- *Safe*: Ensuring care helps and does not harm patients.
- *Effective*: Providing services based on scientific evidence to all who could benefit, and refraining from providing services to those not likely to benefit.
- *Patient centered*: Providing respectful and responsive care according to patient preferences, needs, and values.
- *Timely*: Reducing delays for those who receive and those who give care.
- *Efficient*: Avoiding waste of materials and resources in patient care processes, including equipment, supplies, ideas, and energy.
- *Equitable*: Providing care that is consistent in quality regardless of a patient's characteristics such as gender, ethnicity, geographic location, and socioeconomic status.

Unfortunately, despite significant efforts on many individuals' and organizations' parts, the U.S. health system remains inefficient and ineffective compared to the health systems of other developed nations by the majority of standard population-based outcome measures.[4] Sadly, these numbers have not improved since the two seminal IOM reports were published more than a decade ago. An updated evidence-based analysis estimates the number of deaths due to medical errors in U.S. hospitals to be more than 400,000 per year; the same analysis cites poor incident reporting processes (only 14% of total adverse events) as contributing to this phenomenon and appeals for greater patient involvement in identifying errors and preventable harmful events.[5]

Given this background, what does HIS mean to health care? Is HIS just a collection of computers and technologies used by those practicing modern medicine and delivering healthcare services to automate their work? Or is HIS a transformative force that can radically alter and improve the work processes by which health care is delivered? The answer to both questions is "yes." HIS can both speed up existing processes *and* enable brand new ways of delivering health care to people. It is also important, as we delve into the complex world of HIS, to always ask the question, "What are the benefits and what are the risks of adopting any new technology?" New and computerized is not always better than how things have been done traditionally, if they have been done safely and in a well-organized fashion.

Another key question for understanding HIS is, "How prevalent is HIS use?" Today, we are in the midst of a growing, massively transitional phase of healthcare delivery, moving toward greater use of computers in delivering, managing, and studying health care. It is much more difficult to transition from traditional paper-based processes to computerized information processes than it is to begin a new health-related activity or process that uses automation from the beginning. The fact that our society is in the throes of such massive, disruptive change in the way we do our work in health care has added an ever-present element of risk and uncertainty to the exact end point of this journey to automate and improve health care. We can envision a better health system and enhanced health for all people through the use of technology and HIS. But getting there will be a long journey, fraught with missteps and difficulty because these changes rely on technology innovation and human behavior, and the end point of such change is not defined. In addition, the introduction of HIS into health care is creating many unintended consequences, both good and bad, that are not yet fully understood.[6]

Thus, when we move to computerize health care, we must constantly ask the question, "What are we trying to accomplish and why?" We must evaluate whether we have achieved what we set out to and make necessary adjustments along the way as we make sweeping changes throughout the U.S. health system, including computerizing our systems and processes. From the broadest perspective, the future of HIS in health care will entail the automation of processes we know and the adoption of new processes that have yet to be created. It is difficult to predict whether this transition will be truly disruptive or simply innovative, and to evaluate the difference between those two. The net effect of HIS, however, must be positive—the health of people depends on it.

MOTIVATION

The IOM's watershed report *To Err Is Human* studied 33.6 million hospitalizations in the United States. Based on the resulting data, the IOM estimated that each year an estimated 44,000 to 98,000 patient deaths occur during hospitalizations, not because of the patient's condition, but rather due to mistakes occurring in hospitals. This number was greater than the number of deaths per year due to motor vehicle accidents, breast cancer, and AIDS combined.[2] This devastating statistic translates into 1310 to 2917 deaths per 1 million hospitalizations due to medication errors every year, year after year. If the Six Sigma level of reliability is applied, that ratio translates into 114 avoidable deaths per 1 million hospitalizations due to medication errors. (Six Sigma is a quality improvement methodology that strives to eliminate errors in processes to a near-perfection level through data analysis techniques.[7]) Unfortunately, if any one of those persons included in the avoidable death statistics is you or a loved one, this is 100% of what matters to you. The *To Err Is Human* report provides all the motivation needed to improve quality and outcomes and to increase the focus on patient safety. It sheds light on the whole U.S. healthcare system, rather than focusing on any one caregiver or provider. The bottom line is that the costs of health care continue to rise, and quality problems have persisted. But what is the connection to HIS?

The answer lies in the IOM's second watershed report, *Crossing the Quality Chasm*. This report identified four key reasons for the significant gap in the U.S. health system between reality and ideal quality:

- *The growing complexity of science and technology, with delays between innovation and implementation.* Modern medicine is becoming increasingly multifaceted, with increasingly specialized areas of practice emerging. Also, new biomedical equipment and information technologies are being developed at an exponential rate, all of which make the access to complete and current information and the interaction between the various new technologies equally complex. This trend has been relentless for decades, as expressed more than 30 years ago by David Eddy: "The complexity of modern medicine exceeds the inherent limitations of the unaided human mind."[8] HIS initiatives must target this gap and help close it.

- *The increase in chronic illness burden with a system centered on acute illness.* The aging demographics of the U.S. population and the increasing incidence of chronic illnesses such as obesity, cancer, diabetes, and heart disease occurring within a health system that emphasizes the "medical model" of care have resulted in a lack of effectiveness in dealing with the majority of today's illnesses. The mismatch between an epidemic of chronic illness and settings oriented toward acute care dominates the U.S. health system, resulting in failure to successfully address these conditions. By the time a person with diabetes is sick enough to come to the hospital, it is too late to treat that condition in a way that addresses the root cause of the illness. All that can be done in a hospital setting is address the symptoms and outcomes of this condition. Such chronic illnesses require access to patients in less costly settings such as clinics and doctors' offices, and importantly, in their homes and everyday lives. The inpatient hospital setting is ill equipped to deal with these prevalent chronic conditions; hospitals are set up to cure acute illness, not manage chronic illness or prevent it in the first place.

- *The inadequate use of information technology (IT).* The IOM report asserts that IT can be instrumental in preventing or catching many types of medication errors that cause avoidable deaths and countless injuries or near misses each year. Many HIS capabilities contained within EHRs are designed with capabilities to prevent such errors, such as drug–drug interaction alerts, allergy alerts, **computerized physician order entry (CPOE)**, and others. Also, the IOM report indicates that many of the errors responsible for avoidable patient deaths occur in "hand-offs" of patient information between caregivers, between departments of the hospital or clinics such as the laboratory and nursing, or between physicians in their offices and the hospital settings. These paper or verbal hand-offs can be eliminated or reduced through the use of computer systems such as EHRs that transmit information electronically, greatly reducing the risk of errors in the information as it is transmitted.

- *A payment system that provides conflicting incentives and does not reward quality improvement.* For decades, doctors and hospitals have not been paid based on the quality of their services or on patient outcomes. Instead, they are paid just for providing those services and properly documenting this care. Thus there is a low correlation between how well patients do and how well the provider is paid. This translates into a lack of financial incentives for quality outcomes and instead provides incentives for utilization of services, regardless of the outcome for the patient. Quality improvement is not "baked into" the processes surrounding patient care, but rather is seen as occurring at additional effort and expense to the physician and hospital organizations (providers). This results in quality improvement being viewed as an add-on or separate activity in these organizations and discourages efforts to interweave quality improvement into the fabric of the care provided.[2]

HIS AND THE U.S. GOVERNMENT'S ROLE AND GOALS IN HEALTH CARE

Several seminal laws and research reports have marked the U.S. government's current involvement in the evolution of HIS activities and in response to the unsustainable escalation of healthcare costs. These important elements include the following:

- The **Health Insurance Portability and Accountability Act (HIPAA)**
- The IOM reports *To Err Is Human* and *Crossing the Quality Chasm*
- The IOM report *Health IT and Patient Safety: Building Safer Systems for Better Care*

- President George W. Bush's and President Barack Obama's healthcare initiatives
  - The **American Recovery and Reinvestment Act (ARRA)** of 2009: Title IV—**Health Information Technology for Economic and Clinical Health (HITECH) Act**
  - The **Affordable Care Act (ACA)** of 2010

The Health Insurance Portability and Accountability Act

Initially introduced to ensure that individuals' insurance would be portable across states and jobs, HIPAA had far greater impact through its "administrative simplification" (Title II) elements. HIPAA requirements for **electronic data interchange (EDI)** anticipated the need for data standards for electronic claims in health care, in addition to seeing that electronic records required standards for privacy and security. These standards, originally targeting the Medicare claims processes, introduced far-reaching administrative simplification attributes, including the following:

- Standards (the first mandate for electronic HIS standards for data transmission protocols)
- Requirement that providers and health plans participating in Medicare participate
- Privacy and security of **protected health information (PHI)**
- Preempted state laws, thus reducing fragmentation across the United States
- Imposed penalties for noncompliance, giving these regulations and laws teeth[9]

Title II Administrative Simplification Act

The Title II Administrative Simplification Act aimed to improve the U.S. health system's efficiency by introducing standards governing the use and communication of healthcare information. The rules include protection of identifiable PHI and apply to all provider and payer organizations, called "covered entities" by the legislation. Covered entities include health plans, healthcare billing services, and healthcare providers (hospitals, clinics, and physician practices) that transmit healthcare data, submit claims, and receive reimbursement from Medicare. While the scope of these regulations refers to organizations participating in Medicare, the impact reaches far beyond Medicare to virtually all healthcare entities, because Medicare standards and practices set the benchmark standards for all payers. HIPAA's administrative simplification rules include the following:

- *Privacy Rule*: Regulates the use and disclosure of PHI, laws implemented in 2003. It mandates that a person's medical information with identifying information attached to it cannot be used, viewed, or shared by anyone in a healthcare organization other than a healthcare professional or public health practitioner who has the need to look at that information for the purposes of taking care of or addressing the business needs of that person. The privacy rule applies to PHI on any medium—electronic or paper.
- *Transactions and Code Sets Rule*: Establishes EDI standards for healthcare claims. Claims sent to payers for reimbursement, and subsequent reimbursement to the providers, must be sent electronically in a certain technical format, standardizing electronic claims processing and thus making it more efficient.
- *Security Rule*: Defines administrative, physical, and technical security safeguards. This rule establishes specifics for ensuring secure transmission of data through systems and over the Internet, so that even though HIS and the Internet are used, the data traveling on these networks and in these systems are secure.
- *Unique Identifiers Rule*: Establishes **National Provider Identifier** (**NPI**) standards for providers. This rule establishes unique identifiers for providers, ensuring accuracy of electronic provider payments.
- *Enforcement Rule*: Defines civil financial penalties for HIPAA violations. This rule provides the teeth of the HIPAA regulations. If providers violate HIPAA rules, they face significant financial and other penalties.[9]

HIPAA rules and regulations have set a new bar for government participation in defining the way forward in automating healthcare administrative and clinical processes while protecting individuals' privacy and allowing for public health issues to be addressed to prevent disease, injury, or disability. Driven initially by the need to ensure portability by establishing standards for electronic claims transactions for Medicare, HIPAA standards for electronic data transmission, privacy, and security of PHI have redefined HIS's and the U.S. healthcare system's norms and practices.

THE QUALITY CRISIS FURTHERS U.S. GOVERNMENT INVOLVEMENT IN HIS

Responding to the findings outlined in the *To Err Is Human* and *Crossing the Quality Chasm* reports, the federal government established two waves of policies intended to encourage the implementation of HIS in the U.S. health system. With added emphasis on improving quality and cost-effectiveness in health care, the federal government identified the implementation of HIS initiatives as a priority, particularly the implementation of EHRs for all U.S. patients by 2014, first by President George W. Bush and then by President Barack Obama.[10]

President Bush signed several initiatives into law to provide "seed grants" to fund pilot projects testing various uses of IT in healthcare settings. One of these initiatives was the Medicare Prescription Drug Improvement and Modernization Act of 2003; it included provisions for the development of standards for electronic prescribing, an initial step in the implementation of EHRs. This move precipitated the establishment of a Commission on Systemic Interoperability to plan the establishment of technical interoperability standards for e-prescribing systems.[11] Also under executive authority of President Bush, the Office of the National Coordinator of Health Information Technology within the Department of Health and Human Services (HHS) was established.

Next, also under the administration of President Bush, came Executive Order 13335 of April 27, 2004, titled "Incentives for the Use of Health Information Technology and Establishing the Position of the National Health Information Technology Coordinator," as well as the "President's Health Information Technology Plan," calling for a 10-year plan to get EHRs online for all Americans.[12,13] These national policy interventions built upon other major national initiatives, including the Consolidated Health Informatics initiative in 2003 involving HHS, the Department of Defense, and Veterans Affairs, which established the goal of uniform standards for electronic exchange of clinical health information across all federal healthcare entities.[14]

While these national and presidential initiatives provided encouragement and incentives for hospital and physician providers to invest the money and time in the daunting task of automating their organizations and practices using HIS, the stimulus with the greatest impact has been ARRA, the legislation that includes the HITECH Act. This act greatly expanded the resources available for HITECH activities. First, it created a strategic plan for a nationwide interoperable HIS, a plan that is required by this act to be updated annually. Second, it called for a leadership structure consisting of two committees to advise the coordinator: a Health Information Policy Committee and a Health Information Standards Committee. As part of the $787 billion ARRA stimulus package, the HITECH Act requires the government to lead the development of standards that allow for nationwide electronic exchange and use of health information to improve the quality and coordination of care.[15]

Through the HITECH Act, the government is investing about $30 billion in HIT infrastructure and Medicare and Medicaid incentives to encourage doctors and hospitals to use

HIS to electronically exchange patients' health information.[16] The Congressional Budget Office calculated that this investment will save the government $10 billion and will generate additional savings throughout the health sector through improvements in quality of care and care coordination, reductions in medical errors, and duplicative care. The HITECH Act also strengthens federal privacy and security laws to protect identifiable health information from misuse as the healthcare sector increases the use of HIS. The Congressional Budget Office estimates that as a result of this legislation, approximately 90% of physicians and 70% of hospitals will be using comprehensive EHRs by 2020.[17] These standards are having a seismic effect on vendor products for EHRs and other HIS software, which must now meet these standards or else face quick elimination from the marketplace because they will not qualify organizations to receive their incentives based on meeting these standards.

HITECH establishes "meaningful use" criteria for EHR implementations that must be met for hospitals and physicians (provider organizations) to receive incentive payments (for Medicare patients). **Meaningful Use** criteria are features, functions, and capabilities of EHRs shown to improve care (**Table 1.1**). The meaningful use criteria measure EHR adoption of these capabilities, such as the percentage use within an organization of EHR capabilities such as CPOE, as a way of encouraging EHR adoption. Although many specifics are laid out in the Stages 1 and 2 criteria (followed by Stage 3, the criteria and dates of which are being set), generally speaking, through 2016, if a provider organization meets these criteria for implementing specified levels of EHR system functionality, that qualifying provider receives an incentive payment through a slight increase in payment for Medicare patients. After 2016, if these criteria are *not* met, a penalty is levied in the form of reduced Medicare reimbursement for services provided by those noncompliant hospitals and physicians. Financial penalties for physicians not using EHRs meaningfully by 2016 include a loss of 1% of their Medicare payments, a loss of 2% in 2017, and a loss of 3% in 2018. Hospitals will lose percentages of their annual updated reimbursements from Medicare under the **diagnosis related groups (DRGs)** system (which is used for calculating payments for various conditions and treatments) if they do not meet the meaningful use criteria by 2017.[18] These increases (incentives) or reductions (penalties) in Medicare payments will significantly impact the financial well-being of these provider organizations, as Medicare patients account for a major proportion of patients and participation in Medicare is the only realistic course for the vast majority of provider organizations to remain viable.

TABLE 1.1 Summary of Meaningful Use Criteria Stages 1, 2, and 3

The meaningful use criteria, objectives, and measures will evolve in three stages over the next 5 years:
1. **Stage 1, 2011–2013:** Data capture and sharing
2. **Stage 2, 2014–2015:** Advance clinical processes
3. **Stage 3, 2016–2017:** Improved outcomes

Stage 1: Meaningful Use Criteria Focus on...	Stage 2: Meaningful Use Criteria Focus on...	Stage 3: Meaningful Use Criteria Focus on...
Electronically capturing health information in a standardized format	More rigorous HIE	Improving quality, safety, and efficiency, leading to improved health outcomes
Using that information to track key clinical conditions	Increased requirements for e-prescribing and incorporating lab results	Decision support for national high-priority conditions
Communicating that information for care coordination processes	Electronic transmission of patient care summaries across multiple settings	Patient access to self-management tools
Initiating the reporting of clinical quality measures and public health information	More patient-controlled data	Access to comprehensive patient data through patient-centered HIE
Using information to engage patients and their families in their care		Improving population health

HIE, health information exchange.
Reproduced from healthit.gov. (n.d.). EHR incentives & certification: How to attain meaningful use. http://www.healthit.gov/providers-professionals/how-attain-meaningful-use

The HITECH Act paves the way for increased demand associated with the ACA, making available major training grants to stimulate the establishment of university- and community college–based HIS training programs as a means of addressing the current shortage of approximately 60,000 HIS professionals needed to support implementation of EHR systems and other HIS activities called for in the HITECH program.

CONSUMER EXPECTATIONS AND ENGAGEMENT

Emerging research and common sense tell us that if patients—people—are more engaged in their healthcare processes and in maintaining their health, their health status outcomes will improve. Of course, personal responsibility is a strong determinant of health and well-being, and the more attention paid to one's health and the health of one's family members, the better. Clinicians are adapting their practice of medicine and healthcare services in ways that engage and involve patients in the process. HIS in its many forms—including the Internet, secure email, smart devices, machine-to-machine (M2M), and social media—will play a part in the integration of people and providers in the care process. In addition to information being available to caregivers and providers through components of HIS such as EHRs and other robust capabilities such as clinical decision support, direct interaction between patients and clinicians is now becoming the norm. While the infrastructure necessary to accomplish this communication between organization-based providers and patients in their homes is not available everywhere, healthcare delivery organizations are earnestly building out these systems and connectivity in a wave of innovation characteristic of today's evolving healthcare landscape. If you do not yet communicate with your doctor using computer technology, you soon will.

These new uses of intersecting HIS and social media are also placing new demands on HIS in healthcare organizations, because any transmission of PHI (as defined by HIPAA) must take place securely and in ways that ensure privacy and the confidentiality of that information. As you will recall, providers who violate HIPAA face stiff penalties. Organizational models are also changing rapidly in response to the evolution of technology. Through IT, families can now be connected to their loved ones who may be in the hospital. Likewise, care settings can be connected across the continuum of care, from the hospital, to the physician's office, to the imaging center, to home health, to the workplace, and to schools, to name a few of the various settings in which health care happens. Myriad new devices have been devised to facilitate this connection: In addition to mainframe computers, desktops and laptops, tablets, iPads, smartphones and smart, mobile, biomedical devices can be used by people wherever they are to test blood sugar or capture other important health symptom data. Clearly, paper medical records will no longer suffice—they do not have the capacity to house the data and information that originate far and wide about a patient who traverses this range of care settings in the normal course of care and life, let alone genomic data and customized cancer care, and medical home frameworks. These new types of data, care, and organizational structures require new ways of handling information. People must be connected to their healthcare providers and medical information in new ways. All this means healthcare providers must learn to think "horizontally" in terms of clinical workflows and the movement of important information about patients among all these cross-continuum settings; they must collaborate across and between vertical settings (e.g., different offices, specialties) to optimize the new flows; and they must provide increasingly efficient patient care processes and better outcomes, improved patient experiences and involvement, and improved satisfaction for providers as well.

USES OF HIS IN OTHER COUNTRIES

HIS activity is an international affair, with many countries engaged in activities of information infrastructure establishment, especially EHRs and **health information exchange (HIE)** initiatives (efforts to automate, streamline, and innovate within their unique healthcare systems). In a recent study funded by the Commonwealth Fund, HIS and technology plans and projects in Australia, Canada, Germany, the Netherlands, New Zealand, the United Kingdom, and the United States were examined. More than 90% of general practitioners in Australia, New Zealand, the Netherlands, and the United Kingdom reportedly used EHRs, whereas only 10% to 30% of practitioners in ambulatory settings in the United States and Canada used EHRs. A striking finding of this study is that only 10% of hospitals in the seven countries studied met the criteria for major elements of an EHR.[19] Massive but varied investments of financial resources and organizational energy are being made country by country, and the results are largely the same internationally—HIS adoption is slow and painstaking work.

While national systems that are based on a single payer—that is, "closed" health systems in which providers, hospitals, and the payer are all part of the same unified health system, such as in the United Kingdom—have a shot at pulling together a consistent effort to implement HIS initiatives nationwide, this is still incredibly difficult work for many reasons. First, the financial resources required to both start up and then maintain EHRs and HIS infrastructure are of such magnitude that if other major priorities such as economic crises or changes in national leadership emerge at the same time, progress can be slowed. Also, as in the United States, political, popular, and professional energy and will must align to muster the resources and commitment to initiate and implement the HIS infrastructure required to support a health system nationally. Unfortunately, sometimes one of these pillars of progress may falter. For instance, in Germany, a setting in which EHRs and "smart cards" for 80 million citizens' personal health records made major headway in the past decade, more recent times have seen mounting concerns about privacy on the part of the citizenry, slowing momentum and progress toward EHR adoption in that country.[20] The United Kingdom, Denmark, Australia, the Netherlands, and Taiwan also have encountered major difficulties in adopting electronic systems for health care. Major transformational systems such as EHRs and the infrastructure they require are accomplished slowly, and while such change is desired, the obstacles associated with their implementation are felt in all types of health systems, whether national or free market in philosophy.[21] In addition to the software, hardware, and network infrastructures needed to support these systems, the difficulties of other changes such as the establishment of technical standards and discipline in the management of data have proved enormously challenging to health systems in countries around the world.

PROTECTING THE PUBLIC'S HEALTH

All of these HIS initiatives on the part of healthcare organizations, the government, consumers, and health IT professionals have an additional purpose: to make data available, using appropriate safeguards to ensure data integrity and protect citizens' privacy, for purposes of protecting the public's health. Public health officials and organizations can benefit from HIS data made available by healthcare providers; such data may provide alerts to outbreaks of disease, aid in preventing injury, or provide tip-offs to bioterrorism.

These data may also be used to conduct comparative studies of the effectiveness of different types of therapies across groups or populations and thereby determine which might be better to use under various circumstances. It is most efficient, from the entire health system's perspective, for healthcare data to be coordinated, protected, consistent, and used for multiple purposes, each with the intent of providing health care, improving the public's health, and improving the overall quality of health services in the United States. This understanding is reflected in the HIS model that forms the conceptual foundation for this text.

SUMMARY

Motivation for recent significant increases in HIS initiatives in the United States centers largely on deepening concerns regarding the cost and quality of health care. HIS initiatives, including EHRs and health information exchanges, are seen as key ingredients in improving the efficiency and effectiveness of health care. The U.S. federal government has included HIS initiatives in its economic stimulus legislation, intended to update the nation's aging infrastructure and elevate the technical sophistication of the healthcare system. Major regulations and policy interventions by the federal government include HIPAA and ARRA, which established the HITECH Act. Consumers of healthcare services have come to expect the same level of automation and convenience in health care as they experience in other segments of the U.S. economy and consumer services. The United States is one of many countries internationally that are striving to implement comprehensive HIS to improve the efficiency and effectiveness of their health systems.

KEY TERMS

Affordable Care Act (ACA)   6

American Recovery and Reinvestment Act (ARRA)   6

Computerized physician order entry (CPOE)   6

Diagnosis related groups (DRGs)   8

Electronic data interchange (EDI)   6

Electronic health record (EHR)   3

Health information exchange (HIE)   8

Health information systems (HIS)   3

Health information technology (HIT)   3

Health Information Technology for Economic and Clinical Health (HITECH)   6

Health Insurance Portability and Accountability Act (HIPAA)   6

Meaningful Use   8

National Provider Identifier (NPI)   7

Protected health information (PHI)   6

© Johan Swanepoel/
Shutterstock, Inc.

Discussion Questions

1. Which current challenges in health care are primary drivers of HIS adoption in the United States? How might HIS initiatives help the U.S. health system address these issues?

2. Do you think that the federal government needed to establish regulations and enforce laws regarding privacy, security, and confidentiality of PHI? What about policies and regulations intended to stimulate adoption of HIS, including EHRs? Why or why not?

3. Should the government mandate capabilities of EHRs intended to improve quality of care or should quality initiatives be left to providers and provider organizations? Explain your response.

4. Are consumer expectations capable of influencing HIS adoption in the United States? In which ways should patients/consumers engage in their care using HIS?

5. Which lessons can U.S. providers draw from the experiences of other countries in implementing HIS?

6. What are a few of the many ways that HIS data can be used not only for supporting the delivery of healthcare services, but for additional purposes such as protecting the public's health?

REFERENCES

1. Centers for Medicare & Medicaid. (2012). National health expenditure projections 2012–2022 Forecast Summary. (2012). http://www.cms.gov/Research-Statistics-Data-and-Systems/Statistics-Trends-and-Reports/NationalHealthExpendData/downloads/proj2012.pdf

2. Committee on Quality of Health Care in America, Institute of Medicine. (1999). *To err is human.* L. Kohn, J. Corrigan, & M. Donaldson, Eds. Washington, DC: National Academy Press.

3. Committee on Quality of Health Care in America, Institute of Medicine (IOM). (2001). *Crossing the quality chasm: A new health system for the 21st century.* Washington, DC: National Academy Press.

4. McCullough, J. C., Zimmerman, F., Fielding, J. E., & Teutsch, S. M. (2012). A health dividend for America: The opportunity cost of excess medical expenditures. *American Journal of Preventive Medicine, 43*(6), 650–654.

5. James, John T. (2013, September). A new, evidence-based estimate of patient harms associated with hospital care. *Journal of Patient Safety, 9*(3), 122–128.

6. Committee on Patient Safety and Health Information Technology, Institute of Medicine. (2012). *Health IT and patient safety: Building safer systems for better care.* Washington, DC: National Academy Press.

7. Definition: Six Sigma. (2006). http://searchcio.techtarget.com/definition/Six-Sigma

8. Congressional Budget Office. (n.d.). Evidence on the costs and benefits of health information technology. http://www.cbo.gov/sites/default/files/cbofiles/ftpdocs/91xx/doc9168/maintext.3.1.shtml

9. HIPAA privacy rule and public health guidance from CDC and the U.S. Department of Health and Human Services. (2003). http://www.cdc.gov/mmwr/preview/mmwrhtml/m2e411a1.htm

10. Bush, G. (2004). http://www.whitehouse.gov/news/release/2004/04/20040427-4.html

11. O'Sullivan, J., Chaikind, H., Tilson, S., Boulanger, J., & Morgan, P. (2004). Overview of the Medicare Prescription Drug, Improvement, and Modernization Act of 2003 (2004). http://royce.house.gov/uploadedfiles/overview%20of%20medicare.pdf

12. Executive Order: Incentives for the use of health information technology and establishing the position of the National Health Information Technology Coordinator. (2004). http://georgewbush-whitehouse.archives.gov/news/releases/2004/04/20040427-4.html

13. Thompson, T. G., & Brailer, D. J. (2004). The decade of health information technology: Delivering consumer-centric and information-rich health care: Framework for strategic action. http://www.providersedge.com/ehdocs/ehr_articles/The_Decade_of_HIT-Delivering_Customer-centric_and_Info-rich_HC.pdf

14. SearchHealthIT. (2010). Consolidated health informatics http://searchhealthit.techtarget.com/definition/Consolidated-Health-Informatics-CHI

15. Health Information Technology for Economic and Clinical Health Act or HITECH Act. (2009). http://waysandmeans.house.gov/media/pdf/110/hit2.pdf

16. Blumenthal, D., & Tavenner, M. (2010). The "Meaningful Use" regulation for electronic health records. *New England Journal of Medicine, 363,* 501–504. http://www.nejm.org/doi/full/10.1056/NEJMp1006114

17. CBO letter estimating federal direct spending and revenues of HITECH to Honorable Charles B. Rangel Chairman Committee on Ways and Means U.S. House of Representatives. (2009). http://www.cbo.gov/sites/default/files/cbofiles/ftpdocs/99xx/doc9966/hitechrangelltr.pdf

18. HITECH Answers. (n.d.). EP meaningful use objectives. http://www.hitechanswers.net/ehr-adoption-2/meaningful-use/ep-meaningful-use-objectives

19. Jha, A. K., Doolan, D., Grandt, D., et al. (2008, December). The use of health information technology in seven nations. *International Journal of Medical Informatics, 77*(12), 848–854.

20. Versel, N. (2010). Germany halts smart card program for security review. *Fierce Mobile Healthcare.* http://www.fiercemobilehealthcare.com/story/germany-halts-smart-card-program-security-review/2010-01-26

21. Anderson, G. F., Frogner, B. K., Johns, R. A., & Reinhardt, U. E. (2006, May). Health care spending and use of information technology in OECD countries. *Health Affairs, 25*(4), 819–831. http://content.healthaffairs.org/content/25/3/819.fullDiscussion Questions

CHAPTER **2**

HIS Scope, Definition, and Conceptual Model

INTRODUCTION

Before delving into the depths of health information systems (HIS), it is important to lock in some key concepts regarding the scope of HIS and take the mystery out of computer systems by reviewing the overall structure of how systems and their uses fit together. The conceptual model adopted in this text provides an understanding of the relationships among the major elements of HIS—not just the "systems" of HIS, but also the art and science of making use of systems and information (informatics), the data created and captured in these systems, and the variety of uses that the data can be put to work to do, such as research, policy, and public health. Each of these uses of data depends on the foundational HIS that create and capture data through the applied use of systems to

do clinical and administrative work in healthcare organizations of all types, shapes, and sizes. This chapter describes and builds the layers that comprise the entire HIS model.

Definition of Health Information Systems

In this text, we will define the scope of HIS as including all computer systems (including hardware, software, operating systems, and end-user devices connecting people to the systems), networks (the electronic connectivity between systems, people, and organizations), and the data those systems create and capture through the use of software. Each key layer of this progression through the totality of HIS relies on the foundation of core systems, and requires professionals who specialize in that layer's work. Next, we look at the various layers of HIS one at a time—systems; health informatics; data and analytics; and research, policy, and public health.

Systems and Their Management

Well-architected, properly managed computer systems are the foundation of the ability to create, transmit, and use information. As obvious as this sounds, with availability of the Internet, development of cool new devices such as iPhones and Androids, and advertisements everywhere from vendors touting the ease of "cloud computing," it is sometimes tempting to think that access to high-quality, useful systems and information is as easy as 1-2-3—that all that is necessary is to "plug into" one of these devices or some other easily accessible computing modality. The hard truth is that the myth of "plug-and-play" simply delays the realization that meaningful health information and data—whether available via the Internet, over a secure internal network, or through the use of an iPad or another innovative device—are only as good as the HIS platform that serves as the data source. In other words, the access devices and networks do not actually create data; instead, **data** are created and captured by painstakingly and properly implemented HIS that provide features and functions to support the workflow (sequence of common tasks) and processes (end-to-end methods) of healthcare providers and organizations, patients, and public health professionals.

These HIS that create and capture data (which can then be coalesced into meaningful information) serve as the *foundation* upon which all other information- and data-related capabilities depend. It might seem old-fashioned, but the source systems and devices that support the work of providers and healthcare organizations remain the essential building blocks of all other advanced uses of data and information and computerized workflow support modalities such as health informatics, data analytics and outcomes analysis, research and public health data surveillance, and predictive modeling techniques.[1] We will talk more about these source systems and their management in the *HIS Strategic Planning*, *HIS Application Systems and Technology*, and *Managing HIS and Technology Services* chapters.

The HIS model in **Figure 2.1** depicts this relationship: HIS and their management form the footing for health informatics, data and analytics, and research, policy, and public

health uses of HIS. These components of the total scope of HIS, in turn, rely on the fundamental HIS for the capabilities and data the HIS create and capture so that these spheres can exist. For example, without the foundational HIS, informatics would have no systems capabilities and features and functions to work with in redesigning workflows and calculating rules and alerts, or clinical decision support and artificial intelligence aids to help in the advancement of the practice of medical, nursing, or other health-related professions.

Likewise, without well-managed HIS used to support key work processes such as clinical care and administrative functions (e.g., billing and payroll), no data would be created and captured for use in databases for analytical and business intelligence purposes. In addition, without these HIS, no data would be created and captured for research, policy, and population-based public health purposes.[2] Data to be used for research, policy analysis, and public health surveillance need to come from somewhere—they need to be *real* data values, emanating from *real* healthcare processes and patients, which are then made available for these secondary purposes on any large scale.

Health Informatics

Informatics is the use of information systems and technology to redesign, improve, and recreate the way work is done in disciplines such as the practice of medicine, nursing, medical imaging, and public health. In most cases, informatics focuses on certain quality or process improvement objectives, but this varies based on the setting in which the informatics activities take place. Informatics comprises the "use" of the computer capabilities that HIS provide to end users. In health care, this includes the activities of physicians, nurses, and other clinicians in the various settings in which they do their work, as well as professionals working in public health in its various environs, such as community settings, public health clinics, and other public health organizations. HIS are expected to enable improvements in the efficient delivery of health care, the quality of services provided, and health outcomes across the U.S. population.

Data and Analytics

Much of the value of systems is locked up in their data—a resource created only as systems are used and data captured in those systems' databases. Creating this resource can yield additional value, the rewards of which are reaped at an exponential scale through secondary uses of this data treasure trove. While primary uses of data involve the transactions that support day-to-day activities of professionals and

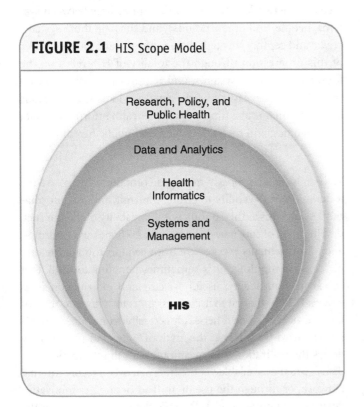

FIGURE 2.1 HIS Scope Model

Research, Policy, and Public Health

Data and Analytics

Health Informatics

Systems and Management

HIS

organizations, the only way to create *information* is through the **aggregation** and compilation of these data to create something greater than the single units of data—in other words, to create meaningful information that is relevant to someone who is doing the work of health and health care. Thus the creation of information and the ability to conduct analysis and gain knowledge are completely dependent upon the creation and capture of the data in the first place.

If someone attempts to create information out of proxied, extrapolated, or estimated data for a certain purpose, the only fruit of those data will be educated guesses. With real data, emanating from real activities conducted in real organizations through real processes, real analysis and research drawing real inferences, associations, outcomes, and evidence can be accomplished. Data created and captured in systems represent a treasure trove to be carefully stewarded and valued every step of the way. Everything else in the conceptual model displaying the progression of information from HIS relies on these data.

The importance assigned to real data is not unique to the healthcare field. "Business intelligence" is a popular term for the value realized by flexibly analyzing comprehensive stores of data representing the totality of an organization or provider's scope of activity. In other words, data from various systems that support clinical and financial transactions can be combined to enable analysis that reveals insights into the entirety of the activities within the scope of that entity. In health care, this concept leads to the notion of "clinical intelligence."

Research, Policy, and Public Health

At the pinnacle, data created and captured in HIS become available for research. These data fuel the work of university researchers—with their inherent expertise, curiosity, and desire for insight—and they enable analysts to measure the health of patient populations and provide evidence for improving efficiency and effectiveness of healthcare processes and outcomes. Policy makers rely on research that predicts the long-term implications of steps taken in the delivery of health care and implementation of healthcare laws and regulations; that is, they rely on researchers' findings, such as studies carried out in university settings, or analyses performed by governmental agencies and organizations dedicated to health care and public health.[3–5] The simple data captured, one patient at a time, in EHRs designed to support individual workflows at separate organizations are ultimately aggregated into databases that can be made available to researchers and analysts. These aggregated data for research and analysis—the proverbial acorn—ultimately guide the work of policy makers and public health professionals responsible for governmental, political, and legal

decisions about healthcare directions, policies, programs, and investments—the mighty oak tree (see **Figure 2.2**).

Public health officials are in a position to harvest the bounty of the entire HIS data chain, as the scope of their work expands from the purview of a person, an organization, or group of patients, to the entire country, ultimately reflecting an international scope. As data are aggregated from systems that support clinical care or business activities across organizations and geographies, they can be analyzed according to many dimensions, such as demographic characteristics (e.g., female versus male, age groups, or race or ethnicity), pathogen (e.g., tuberculosis or anthrax), disease (e.g., cancer, heart disease, or acute illnesses), providers (e.g., hospitals, primary care physicians, or specialists), payment mechanisms (e.g., fee-for-service, health maintenance organization [HMO], preferred provider organization [PPO], Medicare, Medicaid, or uninsured), or other characteristics to better understand trends across an entire population. Such analysis of population-wide characteristics and activities is not confined to the boundaries of an organization (e.g., a hospital) or a segment of the population (e.g., patients insured by a certain carrier or analyses pre- and post-healthcare reform). Rather, inquiries and reports of interest to public health officials reflect the full expanse of their responsibility or perspective, such as a county, region, nation, or the world, as opposed to a subset consisting of those persons who are covered by insurance, are cared for at a particular institution, or live in certain geographies that may be over-represented by the available data. The options or variations available for a particular scope are completely determined by the data available for such analyses and the generalizability of those data to an appropriate population. Elsewhere in this text, we consider the types and sources of data that can be used for these analyses.

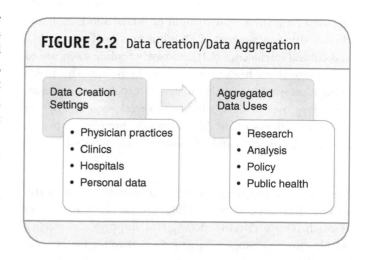

FIGURE 2.2 Data Creation/Data Aggregation

Data Creation Settings
- Physician practices
- Clinics
- Hospitals
- Personal data

Aggregated Data Uses
- Research
- Analysis
- Policy
- Public health

Progression and Maturation of HIS Through the HIS Conceptual Model

We can outline the steps in the progression of the use of HIS and HIS data according to the HIS conceptual model.

1. Foundation (HIS)

The progression begins with core HIS and their effective and proper management. None of the subsequent layers of HIS can exist without the foundational, core systems and infrastructure.

2. Use (Informatics)

HIS software system capabilities support clinical and business transactions, and enable redesign and improvement of healthcare workflow and processes, a discipline referred to as health informatics. The automated support of daily activities carried out in a healthcare organization—and use of HIS by the professions of medicine, nursing, and public health to develop new, streamlined, and more effective workflows in the care of patients, with the intention of improving health care—is the unique discipline of informatics. The term "informaticist" has emerged as our world has become automated; this role is found at the intersection of computers and the work of professionals using those systems, such as physicians, nurses, and public health officers, and the work of IT professionals designing, building, and implementing those systems, such as computer systems engineers, systems analysts, programmers, trainers, and testers.

3. Learning/Knowledge (Business/Clinical Intelligence, Data, and Analytics)

The use of data for learning and gaining new knowledge begins when transactional data are created and captured in HIS through the use of HIS software, then coalesced into databases and **analytics** platforms. Subsequently, these data are used for analysis and creation of information, including clinical decision support (CDS), business intelligence (BI), and clinical intelligence (CI), ultimately leading to enhanced knowledge about health care and public health. This newly gained knowledge and the analytical capabilities represent secondary uses of data, which can reveal ways to improve healthcare processes, health outcomes, population health, and overall efficiency and effectiveness in health care.[6]

4. Change

Eventually the progression and maturation of the use of HIS and the data they produce will improve our ability to conduct research, create effective policy, and improve the public's health through change. The path to change for the better is illuminated by evidence produced through use of systems, analytics, and research using data created and captured in HIS.

HIS USES IN ORGANIZATIONAL AND COMMUNITY SETTINGS

With so many different types of organizations and players using health data, the answer to the question "What does this organization or entity use HIS for?" will differ for each type of organization or entity. Likewise, the mission, vision, and goals of each organization will drive the types of systems that are "core" to its purpose. In each instance, one must answer the question "What is the fundamental reason for using HIS?". This requires thinking through the types of systems that different kinds of providers will need to deliver care to their patients and measure outcomes of that care, as well as the types of HIS needed by different types of payers, patients/consumers, public health agencies, or research organizations.

Inpatient, Outpatient, and Ambulatory Healthcare Provider Organizations

Provider organizations are found in any setting in which healthcare services are delivered by healthcare professionals, including hospitals (e.g., free-standing community hospitals, academic medical centers, specialty hospitals, rural hospitals, and multihospital systems), integrated delivery networks, physician offices, physician groups and multispecialty practices, home health agencies, and outpatient clinics of all types (e.g., free-standing surgical centers, community clinics, imaging centers, and urgent care clinics, to name a few). Anywhere care is delivered, HIS are playing an increasingly essential role.

Hospitals began gradual, widespread development of HIS many years ago. The first systems implemented by these organizations supported financial accounting and patient billing functions, with occasional specialized niche clinical or research applications being developed by innovative clinicians with a special knack for technology and access to technical professionals such as programmers. In the 1970s, hospitals began rolling out HIS supporting processes in clinical settings, with the nascent systems including features such as order entry or results reporting. Generally speaking, these early HIS in the clinical areas of hospitals were geared more toward capturing charges for purposes of providing data to patient accounting systems, which then used these data to populate claims to insurers and bills to patients. Most of these systems were developed in hospital data processing departments, where the early HIS innovators invested in hardware platforms, operating systems, and programming packages, and hired programmers and systems analysts to define HIS requirements for various areas in the hospitals and create the programs and systems based on those requirements. Those in-house systems would then be implemented gradually throughout the sponsoring hospital with the support of in-house development teams. Team members collaborated with end users, who helped define the requirements based on their own ideas for uses of computers; they also took advantage of ideas generated in collaboration with colleagues from other hospitals who might also be working on in-house computer systems for their areas.

In the 1970s, early HIS software vendors emerged. Some of these vendors acquired software from the hospitals, doing in-house development, and then commercialized this software into products for which hospitals could purchase licenses to use in their organizations. Others developed their own software, which was then commercialized and licensed to hospitals on a multiyear basis. Thus the HIS software industry was born. These early HIS software products initially focused on financial and patient accounting/billing functions; later, during the 1980s, clinical systems supporting the automation of specific departmental areas in hospitals (e.g., laboratory, radiology, and pharmacy) began to emerge, as did order communications and results reporting systems for use in hospitals and a few large multispecialty physician practices.

The market for commercial HIS products, along with consulting services to help an increasing number of hospitals, clinics, and physician practices implement them, grew steadily throughout the 1990s, with sales of these products and services totaling hundreds of millions of dollars. Also in the 1990s, with the work of a few forward-thinking, pioneering organizations serving as examples, and the presence of a few software vendors that were able to make the leap and develop commercial software products to support a broad range of integrated clinical functions, electronic health records (EHRs) emerged. The introduction of EHRs spurred a massive wave of automation of hospitals that continues today. The current norm in U.S. health care is for hospital and clinical processes in all areas of financial, administrative, and clinical activity to be automated. The HIS products and services supporting the entire highly diverse collection of organizations providing health care and patient health services are the basis of a multibillion-dollar industry.

Patients'/Consumers' Homes

Consistent with the spread of mobile computing throughout our society and world, patients being cared for by providers and people in their homes or places of work can increasingly access their patient records and providers, as well as monitor their personalized health data. Additionally, vast sources of health-related information are accessible through the Internet, from mobile devices, and via electronic sources to consumers of healthcare services or those interested in learning about various health or medical conditions, services, and products. The age of patient engagement is upon us—increasingly CEOs of healthcare institutions and providers working in healthcare organizations have realized that they can achieve the best outcomes in organizational performance and clinical care by enlisting patients in the process. Likewise, many people now expect to be part of their own healthcare process, consistent with how they drive participation in other types of commerce and consumption of goods and services.

While this sounds quite logical, it is a far stretch from the not-too-distant era of the "passive patient," a time in which physicians were seen as almost god-like figures and providers were reluctant to share the contents of a patient's medical record with the patient or family. In fact, part of the author's education in medical records science in the 1970s consisted of learning how to carefully manage the situation in which patients asked to see the contents of their medical records: Legally patients have always had a right to that information, but providers actively avoided showing them the information for fear they would not understand it or could not handle knowing what was going on inside their own bodies. The language and values of health care reflect this traditional expectation of the obedient patient as being either "compliant" or "not compliant" with the instructions or prescriptions of the expert, superior clinician. Patients who do not "follow doctor's orders" are seen as deviant or irrational, and are blamed for poor outcomes.[7] In fact, the term "patient" linguistically derives from the passive voice in the English language and implies the entity receiving something, in an inferior position, from someone or something (in this case, the clinician or physician who prescribes a regimen of treatment and therapy) from a superior, dominant position.[8]

Modern-day patients and people (meaning individuals before they become sick or injured and who are in the mode of maintaining their health) are playing an increasing role in their care by taking advantage of the connectivity and empowerment of access to information—a role inherent to the information age. Just as we use computers to research and obtain services and products in retail, food, and entertainment, so we now *expect* to be able to access our personal health information from providers and interact electronically in the care process from our homes or places of work. A growing body of evidence is now emerging in the literature showing that clinical outcomes, patient satisfaction, and cost performance improve when patients are engaged and activated in the processes of their care. HIS is a powerful facilitator of such engagement.[9,10] Plus, as the tipping point is within our collective sight vis-à-vis the adoption of EHRs in most hospitals and physician practices, innovators are enthusiastically embracing new means of personal connectivity and engagement in the healthcare arena using IT tools widely applied in other industries.[11,12]

Payers, Insurance Companies, and Government Programs and Agencies

The mechanism by which hospitals, physicians, clinics, and all other healthcare providers are paid for the healthcare services provided to their patients involves insurance companies or payers of one type or another. Several types of payers are found in the United States: private insurance companies, government programs that pay for healthcare services for various groups of citizens based on age or income, military programs that pay for these services for military personnel and their families, and other special insurance programs. Private payers or health insurance companies include companies such as United Health, Aetna, Blue Cross/Blue Shield, Cigna, and others. Government-funded health coverage programs include Medicare (health insurance for people age 65 or older or with certain illnesses such as permanent kidney failure and those with certain disabilities), Medicaid/MediCal (state-specific health insurance for people and families with low incomes), State Children's Health Insurance Plan (SCHIP; state-administered programs using federal money for uninsured children younger than 19 years of age from low-income families), TriCare (health insurance for active and retired members of the military and their families), and Department of Veterans Affairs (government-sponsored programs for military veterans, covering the care they receive from doctors, hospitals, emergency rooms, and immunizations).[13,14]

Military Healthcare Organizations

TriCare is a program that provides for health insurance and coverage of healthcare services, available to all active and retired members of the military and their families (referred to as "dependents" in military vernacular). The Department of Veterans Affairs (VA) offers additional medical care to retired military personnel when needed, which is either fully covered if the veteran is totally disabled, or partially covered if the veteran is partially disabled as a result of military service. CHAMPVA (Civilian Health and Medical Program of the Department of Veterans Affairs) is a health benefits program that helps retired military and their families.[15]

In the 1980s and 1990s, some of the pioneering work that led to the development of EHRs was done in military healthcare settings. For example, the Veterans Health Information Systems and Technology Architecture, commonly referred to as the VistA system, provided an early and shining example of the benefit and power of a comprehensive, integrated EHR. The VistA system was enormously important to the development of EHRs because it supports not only care delivered in inpatient hospital settings, but care for ambulatory patients as well. A predecessor of the VistA system was developed in the early 1980s in a joint venture between the giant government contractor Science Applications International Corporation (SAIC) and the VA, and was a more basic form of a clinical information system that was used extensively throughout the system of VA hospitals and clinics. The VA ultimately replaced this earlier, simpler version of a core clinical system with the more comprehensive, sophisticated VistA system. Not only was great progress made in the evolution of HIS through these efforts, but over the years the thousands of VA hospitals and clinics have served as training grounds in which numerous medical students and clinicians learned to care for patients using computers to support the care and administrative processes. In fact, this system is so widespread that nearly 70% of all physicians practicing medicine in the United States today have used it as part of their medical training.

Public Health Organizations

Public health organizations are entities that exist to protect and enhance the public's health. Among other roles, they serve as a "safety net" by providing health care for patients who are uninsured or underinsured (e.g., through county hospitals and community clinics). In addition, public health services include preventive programs operated by municipal or county Departments of Public Health, such as free clinics, school-based immunizations, health-related and nutrition educational programs, birth control education, distribution of condoms, inspection and safety ratings of restaurants, violence prevention programs, environmental health alerts, and a host of other services aimed at maintaining and preserving the health of a population of people within a certain region, state, or locale. Put simply, the role of these public health organizations and initiatives is to attend to the "public's health." In other words, public health organizations always think in terms of the populations whom they serve; they are *not* invested in the for-profit or medical care business of health care. Such organizations are typically funded by government programs at the federal, state, county, or local level, and they exist to keep the entire community of people in their jurisdiction or community protected from environmental risks and able to maintain their health to the degree feasible. A public health organization measures its target population's health by collecting and examining statistics such as infant mortality; mortality and morbidity rates; biological surveillance; immunization rates; rates of communicable diseases such as tuberculosis, HIV/AIDS, and meningitis; deaths and injuries due to violence; air quality; and a variety of other metrics that tell public health officials about the status of and threats to the population's health.[16]

Public health organizations whose primary goal is to measure, monitor, and report key public health statistics nationally are another type of entity whose mission it is to maintain, monitor, and improve the public's health. These organizations depend on a variety of data sources to create such public health information:

- Data from hospitals, clinics, and physician practices gathered through the claims administration processes for Medicare, Medicaid, SCHIP, and other government-sponsored health insurance programs
- Data from laboratories across the nation set up specifically for bio-surveillance and homeland security
- Data voluntarily provided to federal or research organizations that are committed to the study and evaluation of healthcare quality and cost issues

Examples of national organizations of this type include the following[17]:

- Centers for Disease Control and Prevention (CDC): Provides online resources for dependable health information
- Public Health Institute: Promotes health, well-being, and quality of life for people across the nation and around the world
- Rural Assistance Center: Provides health services-related information for rural America

Health Information Exchanges and Regional Health Information Organizations

Since the early 2000s, provider organizations in some regions have been entering into collaborative arrangements of varying scopes and business models with the goal of sharing patient-related health information, securely, between providers organized into not-for-profit, collaborative "data sharing" organizations in that region. Examples of regional organizations that might participate in these consortia include hospitals and hospital systems, clinics, physician practices, emergency responders such as paramedics, tumor registries, imaging centers, community clinics, public health institutions, and others. The idea is that these providers seek

to make patient data that they have in their own systems available to other providers if needed to support care for the same patient. The aim is to improve the timeliness of data availability, support clinicians in emergency situations when patients need care at an organization where they typically do not receive care, make existing data available in an emergency to help speed diagnosis and treatment, reduce the need to repeat tests that have been performed at another clinical setting for which the results are stored and readily available within that organization's EHR, save the patient the discomfort and inconvenience of repeated care and testing, facilitate cross-continuum care models such as accountable care organizations (ACOs) and medical homes, and reduce costs and waste when possible.

These pioneering cooperative, collaborative efforts have met with mixed success, but have sprouted (such as the Rhode Island statewide information network) and in some cases taken root (such as the Michiana Health Information Network) across the United States. Many of these initiatives have struggled mightily and then failed due to lack of a sustainable business model, unworkable technical models, lack of cooperation on the part of member organizations, difficulties extracting data from member organizations' systems, or lack of cooperation between competitor providers and vendors. Despite these challenges to forerunners in health information exchange (HIE), progress continues and is beginning to show signs of sustainability. As EHRs become more commonplace, integrative technologies that enable extraction and sharing of data securely have also become more robust: EHR vendors are now enhancing their products' capabilities and providing the technology and software capabilities necessary to share patient data securely as a standard part of their software. Each of these factors may facilitate sharing this information among regional providers.

In addition to today's rapid advancement of ubiquitous technological capabilities in the private sector, a federal mandate related to HIE, included as part of the American Recovery and Reinvestment Act (ARRA) of 2009, is contained in the Health Information Technology for Economic and Clinical Health (HITECH) Act. This act has allocated funding of $27 billion in incentives for hospital and physician providers to adopt EHRs and achieve meaningful use criteria (**Exhibit 2.1**), including, among many types of EHR capabilities, electronic HIE.[18] Thus organizations designed to accomplish HIE—often called **regional health information organizations (RHIOs)**—have gained significant momentum as a result of the HITECH Act; RHIOs enable participating provider organizations to securely exchange patient care-related data and achieve

Meaningful Use criteria in their quest to reap the rewards of HITECH's financial incentives. By sharing patient data securely according to the requirements set out by HITECH and Meaningful Use criteria, RHIOs and other forms of HIE move us slowly but surely closer to a more integrated, less wasteful U.S. health system. Examples of successful RHIOs include Rhode Island Health Network, Michiana Regional Health Information Network, Delaware Health Information Network, and others. Examples of failed RHIOs include Santa Barbara RHIO, early iterations of California Health Information Network, and others. Thus far, smaller regions have achieved the best early results. Owing to their more cohesive, less competitive provider environment and smaller scale, these less complex regions have improved chances of connecting a more manageable scope of organizations, data, and patients for whom data are exchanged.[19,20] Providers participating in these HIEs and taking advantage of their interoperability capabilities vary widely, and widespread use of such capabilities will likely take many years to realize.

External Regulatory, Reporting, Research, and Public Health Organizations

The primary purpose of HIS is to support patient care and administrative processes of healthcare providers and organizations devoted to patient care and the provision of health-related activities and public health services. Each type of organization engaged in such efforts is accountable to its community and board constituents as well as to regulatory oversight bodies, and each collaborates with myriad third-party organizations ("third party" means an organization or agency external to the provider organization). Some third-party or external organizations set standards (metrics) for healthcare providers to use when measuring the quality and cost of the services they provide. The third-party organizations then collect the reported measures from participating health providers and create statistical benchmarks from the aggregate data for those providers to use when evaluating their performance against the performance of other like organizations and implementing quality-improvement and cost-control initiatives. Examples of such third-party or external organizations include The Leapfrog Group, whose mission is to promote improvements in the safety of health care by giving consumers data to make more informed hospitals choices, and state organizations such as the California Health Care Foundation's report cards on hospitals and long-term care facilities, among others. These external organizations may also be state or federal regulatory agencies given the responsibility of monitoring the safety and compliance of provider organizations serving certain constituents (e.g., state or county populations, cardiology patients, children, or aged patients); their responsibilities are typically outlined by governmental regulations that are often funded by a governmental agency.

A third-party external reporting agency may also monitor key metrics regarding quality of care for a particular state or the country as a whole. For instance, the Department of Health Services (DHS) and Office of Statewide Health Planning and Development of the California Health and Human Services Agency (OSHPOD) are state-based agencies charged with ensuring safety in hospitals and other healthcare settings. Provider organizations are required to report data to those state agencies on a regular basis about

---

EXHIBIT 2.1 HIE-Related Meaningful Use Criteria

Meaningful Use Stage 2 and Health Information Exchange (HIE) Highlights

- **Common Standards and Implementation Specifications for Electronic Exchange of Information:** The Meaningful Use Stage 2 final rules define a common data set for all summary of care records, including an impressive array of structured and coded data to be formatted uniformly and sent securely during transitions of care and, upon discharge, and to be shared with the patient themselves. These include:
  - Patient name and demographic information
  - Vital signs
  - Diagnosis
  - Procedures
  - Medications and allergies
  - Laboratory test results
  - Immunizations
  - Functional status, including activities of daily living and cognitive and disability status
  - Care plan field, including goals and instructions
  - Care team, including primary care provider of record
  - Reason for referral
  - Discharge instructions

Modified from healthit.gov. (n.d.). EHR incentives & certification: How to attain meaningful use. http://www.healthit.gov/providers-professionals/how-attain-meaningful-use

all services provided to their patients and communities, as well as any untoward events, such as wrong-site surgeries or hospital-acquired infections, that occur to patients. The *Health Informatics* chapter discusses external reporting organizations in more detail.

Other examples of external organizations to which healthcare providers submit vast amounts of data and reports reflecting services provided, safety practices, costs, and outcomes of care include **The Joint Commission**, a quasi-regulatory organization that inspects and accredits hospitals based on their ability to meet a rigorous set of scored criteria (**Figure 2.3**), and the Cardiac Reporting Organization, which was established to monitor cardiac mortality rates nationally.[21,22] Regulatory requirements are mandatory and failure to provide required data and reports—or submission of data reflecting poor performance such as

too many medical or patient care errors that could harm patients—may result in the hospital or provider being reprimanded and monitored, fined, subjected to a temporarily suspended or revoked license, or closed. Other, more voluntary third-party reporting relationships may have to do with a provider organization voluntarily providing data and reports to an external reporting group so that it can be compared to similar organizations regionally or nationally in an effort to continually improve participants' cost performance, clinical quality of care, and transparency to their communities. Examples of these types of relationships include the Institute for Health Care Improvement (IHI), The Advisory Board, The Leapfrog Group, and the California Hospital Assessment and Reporting Taskforce (CHART).[23–25] CHART, for example, is a voluntary program in which 86% of California hospitals are participating; it provides report-card–type evaluation and peer-comparative data that hospitals can use to assess, benchmark, and improve their quality and cost performance.

To support this kind of reporting, the third-party organization's reporting databases must be able to create a compilation of clinical and cost-related data from hospitals, clinics, and physician practices—that is, data originating in these providers' own smaller-scale HIS that support their clinical and business processes and activities. Data submitted to the third-party organizations come directly from the multiple HIS supporting patient care and reporting capabilities at the provider organizations; none of these external organizations is the original source of the data. Rather, these external entities review, report, aggregate, and consolidate data from many provider organizations; then benchmarks or report cards on the provider organizations' performance can be compared to the benchmarks or report cards for all other organizations that submit data and reports to that same third-party reporting organization. Whether such reporting is voluntary or mandatory, it is the job of all provider organizations to responsibly, promptly, and transparently report the numbers, types, mishaps, costs, and quality associated with the services they provide to interested parties, such as quality monitoring groups, payers, government, communities, and patient populations. Such reporting relationships represent **secondary uses of data** that originate in provider organizations as a direct result of patient care and business support activities, data originally created and captured in the clinical and administrative transaction systems of health provider organizations. In contrast, the original patient care and administrative transactions represent the **primary use of data** created and housed in these providers' HIS. **Figure 2.4** is an overview of the primary and secondary uses of HIS data and systems by providers of care and others in the healthcare ecosystem.[26]

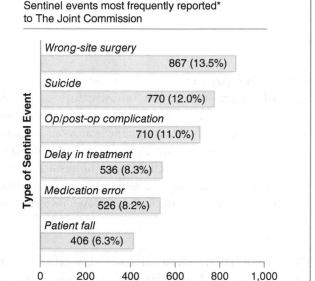

FIGURE 2.3 Sentinel Events Most Frequently Reported to The Joint Commission*

A sentinel event is an unexpected occurrence involving death or serious physical or psychological injury, or the risk thereof. Such events are called "sentinel" because they signal the need for immediate investigation and response.

Sentinel events most frequently reported* to The Joint Commission

Type of Sentinel Event

- Wrong-site surgery — 867 (13.5%)
- Suicide — 770 (12.0%)
- Op/post-op complication — 710 (11.0%)
- Delay in treatment — 536 (8.3%)
- Medication error — 526 (8.2%)
- Patient fall — 406 (6.3%)

Number of Reports
*6428 total reports as of september 30, 2009

Reproduced from DYK (Did You Know?). Sentinel events most frequently reported to The Joint Commission. Available at http://webmm.ahrq.gov/dykarchivecase.aspx?dykID=40. Reprinted with permission of AHRQ WebM&M.

FIGURE 2.4 Primary and Secondary Uses of HIS Data

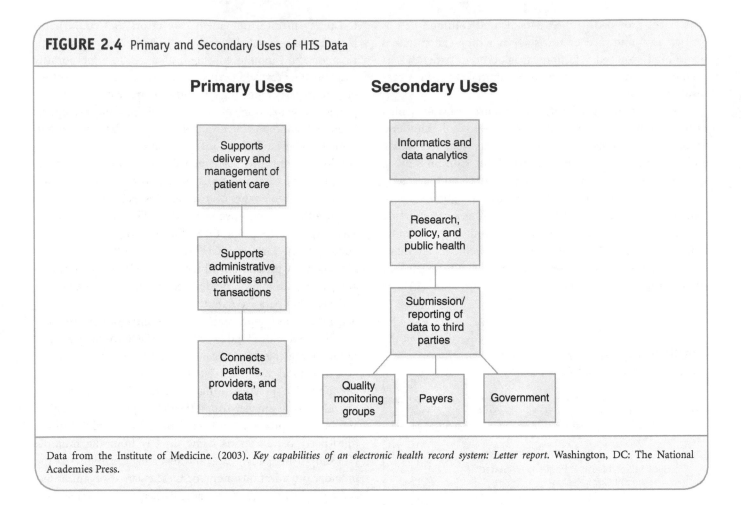

Data from the Institute of Medicine. (2003). *Key capabilities of an electronic health record system: Letter report.* Washington, DC: The National Academies Press.

Public Health Reporting Systems

Local, county, state, and national public health organizations and reporting agencies exist to monitor and protect the public's health for the citizens living within their purview. Just as healthcare provider organizations must automate their clinical and administrative processes using HIS, so public health organizations must design, implement, and use computer systems to collect and analyze data reflecting the health of a population. This paves the way for implementation of effective programs to support that population's health status and create initiatives for the management of chronic disease.[27] Examples of such HIS reporting systems for public health purposes include systems for detection and monitoring of public health problems; analysis of public health–related data; and public health knowledge management, alerting, and response. The Public Health Information Network (PHIN) initiative

of the federal government works in conjunction with the National Health Information Infrastructure to establish standards (Consolidated Health Information) for automation of clinical health data for public health reporting purposes. Timely access to such clinical data and connectivity between laboratories to facilitate sharing results data will improve the opportunities for responding to public health issues such as outbreaks of disease, disaster, or terrorism.[28]

SUMMARY

The scope of HIS includes a universe of data-related systems, activities, and new knowledge developed from using those systems. The ability to maximize the depth and breadth of HIS utility for achieving the ultimate goals of improving outcomes and developing knowledge depends on the progressive development and maturation of systems and their use as reflected in the HIS conceptual model. The layers of this model provide a comprehensive view of the total scope of HIS activity:

- *HIS:* Building the foundation of HIS and their management.
- *Health Informatics*: Enhancing the use of those systems to improve how work is done and meaning can be derived from data.
- *Business Intelligence/Clinical Intelligence*: Using data and creating information from which to learn and build knowledge, which leads to further creation of relevant information and new uses of data for analytics, including clinical decision support, business intelligence, and clinical intelligence.

- *Research, Policy, and Public Health*: Eventually improving the health of populations through evidence-based change driven by well-informed research, policy, and public health.

HIS supporting clinical, administrative, and research/reporting activities are used extensively in a wide variety of organizational and community settings, including inpatient and outpatient healthcare provider organizations; patients' and consumers' homes and places of work or livelihood; payers, insurance companies, and government programs and agencies; public health organizations; health information exchanges and regional health information organizations; and regulatory, reporting, and research organizations.

KEY TERMS

Aggregation   15

Analytics   16

Data   14

Informatics 14

Primary uses of data   21

Public health   18

Regional health information
    organization (RHIO)   19

Secondary uses of data   21

The Joint Commission 21

Discussion Questions

1. What are the key steps in the progression of HIS according to the HIS conceptual model? What is the relationship between the various layers?

2. Why do you think it is necessary to be attentive in entering data elements that may not have a clear relationship to the work you are doing? How does the information use or data collection of a laboratory technician in a hospital differ from that of a public health administrator at a county agency or a specialist physician at an outpatient facility?

3. As more healthcare provider organizations adopt EHRs, what do you think will be the effect on healthcare-related research? On public health issues?

4. Why are healthcare organizations just in the beginning stages of engaging patients in their care? Do you think HIS has anything to do with this change? Do you think this will have a beneficial effect for the organizations? For the patients? Explain.

5. Insurance companies use a lot of data from provider organizations' HIS to process claims and calculate reimbursement. How important is this practice to the overall healthcare process? Given that this process involves money for the provider organizations, which is more important: HIS for patient care or HIS for gaining reimbursement for that care?

6. Military personnel and veterans often get their care from military or VA healthcare providers, but some of their care is received in non-military settings. How might clinical data from one setting be sent to another for purposes of caring for these military patients?

7. What are *primary* uses of HIS? What are *secondary* uses of HIS? Which of these can best help the U.S. healthcare system improve?

8. Public health reporting and surveillance systems have gotten much more attention since the terrorist attacks on the United States on September 11, 2001. Do you think this is justified? Who do you think should be responsible for surveillance locally or nationally—healthcare providers like hospitals and physician offices or the government?

REFERENCES

1. Restuccia, J. D., Cohen, A. B., Horwitt, J. N., et al. (2012, September 27). Hospital implementation of health information technology and quality of care: Are they related? *BMC Medical Informatics and Decision Making, 12,* 109.

2. Kern, L. M., Wilcox, A. B., Shapiro, J., et al. (2011, April). Community-based health information technology alliances: Potential predictors of early sustainability. *American Journal of Managed Care, 17*(4), 290–295.

3. Fryer, A. K., Doty, M. M., & Audet, A. M. J. for the Commonwealth Fund. (2011, March). Sharing resources: Opportunities for smaller primary care practices to increase their capacity for patient care. http://www.commonwealthfund.org/Publications/Issue-Briefs/2011/Mar/Sharing-Resources.aspx

4. O'Malley, A. S., Grossman, J. M., Cohen, G. R., et al. (2009, December 29). Are electronic medical records helpful for care coordination? Experiences of physician practices. *Journal of General Internal Medicine.* http://www.commonwealthfund.org/Publications/In-the-Literature/2009/Dec/Are-Electronic-Medical-Records-Helpful-for-Care-Coordination-Experiences-of-Physician-Practices.aspx

5. Davis, K., Doty, M. M., Shea, K., & Stremikis, K. (2008, November 25). Health information technology and physician perceptions of quality of care and satisfaction. *Health Policy, 90*(2–3), 239–246. http://www.ncbi.nlm.nih.gov/pubmed/19038472

6. Committee on Data Standards for Patient Safety. (2003). *Key capabilities of an electronic health record system: Letter report.* Washington, DC: National Academies Press.

7. Euromed Info. (n.d.). The patient as a passive recipient of care. http://www.euromedinfo.eu/the-patient-as-a-passive-recipient-of-care.html/

8. Wanner, A. (2009). *Deconstructing the English passive.* Berlin/Boston, MA: De Gruyter Mouton. http://www.degruyter.com/view/product/40717

9. Hibbard, J. H., & Greene, J. (2013, February). What the evidence shows about patient activation: Better health outcomes and care experiences; fewer data on costs. *Health Affairs, 32,* 2207–2214.

10. Courneya, P. T., Palattao, K. J., & Gallagher, J. M. (2013, February). Innovation profile: HealthPartners' online clinic for simple conditions delivers savings of $88 per episode and high patient approval. *Health Affairs, 32,* 2385–2392.

11. Office of the National Coordinator for Health IT. (2013). ONC releases data on hospital EHR adoption, meaningful use. http://www.ihealthbeat.org/articles/2013/3/7/onc-releases-data-on-hospital-ehr-adoption-meaningful-use.aspx

12. Health care industry moves slowly onto the Internet. (2009, April 5). *New York Times.* http://bits.blogs.nytimes.com/2009/04/05/health-care-industry-moves-slowly-onto-the-internet/

13. Healthcare.gov. (n.d.). Health insurance basics. http://www.healthcare.gov/using-insurance/understanding/basics/

14. Brigham Young University. (n.d.). Government-sponsored healthcare programs. http://personalfinance.byu.edu/?q=node/533

15. Military.com. (n.d.). Transition health care programs (TAMP). http://www.military.com/benefits/tricare/transitional-health-care-programs.html

16. World Health Organization. (n.d.). Public health surveillance. http://www.who.int/topics/public_health_surveillance/en/

17. Medical College of Wisconsin, MPH Program. (n.d.). National public health organizations. http://www.mcw.edu/mphprogram/Resources/PublicHealthOrganizations.htm

18. Blumenthal, D., & Tavenner, M. (2010). The "Meaningful Use" regulation for electronic health records. *New England Journal of Medicine, 363,* 501–504. http://www.nejm.org/doi/full/10.1056/NEJMp1006114

19. Adler-Milstein, J., Bates, D. W., & Jha, A. K. (2009, March/April). U.S. regional health information organizations: Progress and challenges. *Health Affairs, 28*(2), 483–492.

20. Adler-Milstein, J., Bates, D. W., & Jha, A. K. (2011, May). A survey of health information exchange organizations in the United States: Implications for meaningful use. *Annals of Internal Medicine, 154*(10), 666–671.

21. The Joint Commission. (n.d.). About the Joint Commission. http://www.jointcommission.org/about_us/about_the_joint_commission_main.aspx

22. Shahian, D. M., Edwards, F. H., Jacobs, J. P., et al. (2011). Public reporting of cardiac surgery performance: Part 1—history, rationale, consequences. *Annals of Thoracic Surgery, 92*(3), S2–S11.

23. Agency for Healthcare Research and Quality. (n.d.). About us. http://www.ahrq.gov/index.html

24. Leapfrog Group. (n.d.). About Leapfrog. http://www.leapfroggroup.org/about_leapfrog

25. California Hospital Assessment and Reporting Taskforce. (n.d.). http://www.chcf.org/projects/2009/california-hospital-assessment-and-reporting-taskforce-chart

26. Committee on Data Standards for Patient Safety. (2003). *Key capabilities of an electronic health record system: Letter report.* Washington, DC: National Academies Press.

27. O'Carroll, P. W., Yasnoff, W. A., Ward, M. E., et al. (Eds.). (2003). *Public health informatics and information systems.* Series: Health Informatics. New York, NY: Springer-Verlag.

28. Public Health Informatics Institute. (n.d.). http://www.phii.org/blog/new-health-it-framework-available-acos

SECTION II

Systems and Management

CHAPTER **3**

HIS Strategic Planning

INTRODUCTION

To kick off this chapter, and before we examine the process of strategic planning for health information systems (HIS), we will cover some terminology basics to form a foundation for understanding this chapter's topic. First, let us consider the key ideas of "strategy." Although it may seem obvious what these mean, we will explain these ideas in the context of health care and establish a common understanding as a precursor to applying these concepts to HIS. This will give us a working set of assumptions that apply to the concepts in this chapter and throughout the entire text.

HIS STRATEGY: ORGANIZATIONAL STRATEGY AS ITS ROADMAP

The term "strategy" is a word we often hear, readily applied to many different arenas, especially when discussing organizations and their work or important activities. It is easy to dilute the meaning of this term into something amorphous or general, so that the term "strategies" is often used interchangeably (and erroneously) with terms such as "goals," "tactics," "policies," "schemes," "agendas," "plans," or "objectives." At the uppermost levels of an organization's agenda are directional statements or overarching plans directly tied to mission and vision, the ways that the organization will be able to successfully move itself forward toward its purpose. These are strategies.

Strategies are defined and developed by first reflecting on the organization's reason for existing (its mission) and examining the organization in the context of its market; outlining a long-term and maybe changing view of its place in that environment or market in the future (its vision); and then understanding the ways it wants to behave, the philosophies it wants to support, its guiding principles, and the ways it wants to do its work (its values). The organization's mission, vision, and values are communicated widely throughout the organization and to its constituents at all levels. These guideposts are written down, placed on posters on the walls of employees' offices, discussed and dissected at great depth, published on the website, and established as official resolutions by the organization's highest level—the board of directors or trustees—as well as communicated to customers, clarified to management, reviewed with employees, and so on. Every action the organization takes should be consistent with these pillars of the organization's purpose (**Figure 3.1**).

Note that we have not defined anything yet, named any strategy, or outlined any specific actions: All effort up to this point is spent fully engaging with clarifying and defining the mission, vision, values, and hoped-for future of the organization. These are the "why" questions that must come ahead of the "what" questions.

Steps in Determining Strategy

The first step in understanding where an organization needs to put its efforts and resources, and which types of efforts or strategies those might be, is for the organization to define its mission, vision, and values. When these overarching and most essential statements of purpose and principle are agreed upon, they become the beacons that guide the organization through its many decisions and challenges. The mission, vision, and values are essentially the compass by which the organization sets its direction for long-term growth and adaptation to ever-changing environmental and market conditions. Once these tenets are defined, and then collectively and officially embraced, the organization knows the direction in which it should be trying to go. The next step is to determine how the organization should go about doing so and which activities will get it moving in that direction.

Determining the course for the organization and criteria for decisions about where it invests its precious resources involves framing a vision for the organization (answering the question, "What does this organization look like in 10 years?") and drawing a migration path between the *current state* of the organization and the desired *"vision"* or *future state* (**Figure 3.2**). The organization can then describe major directional strategies and enterprise-wide actions that will move the organization in the desired direction.

For instance, if the vision for the organization is to meet the needs of an aging community that includes significant numbers of people with cardiovascular conditions, it may decide to become the number one provider of heart health care in its community or region, providing such care to all patients regardless of their ability to pay. Key strategies to accomplish this might include the following: (1) within 10 years, build a new, comprehensive, state-of-the-art heart care hospital; (2) create a charitable foundation to fund care for the uninsured or underinsured on a needs-based system; (3) negotiate a partnership with health plans to provide incentives for preventive population-based or chronic illness management initiatives and good heart care outcomes; and (4) initiate grant proposal efforts to create funding opportunities to draw researchers and key physicians to the hospital to provide excellent heart care, conduct research, and develop new knowledge around the care and prevention of heart disease. These four strategies might then be further broken down into initiatives and projects, which are the actual work that the organization must do to move itself toward its desired future state, always in accordance with its mission, vision, and values. In

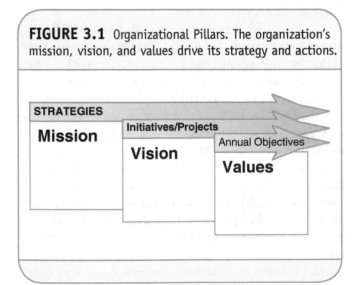

FIGURE 3.1 Organizational Pillars. The organization's mission, vision, and values drive its strategy and actions.

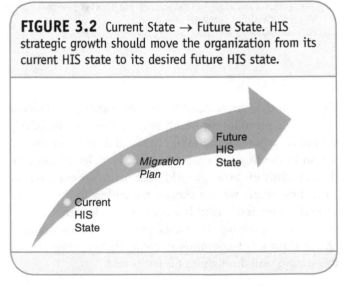

FIGURE 3.2 Current State → Future State. HIS strategic growth should move the organization from its current HIS state to its desired future HIS state.

this way, the organization can accomplish what it sees as its purpose and reason for existence: It assures that the finite resources and energies of the organization are used to move the organization toward its desired future. These initiatives and projects can be described in the form of multiyear goals for the organization. To ensure that the goals are accomplished, the organization must build them into strategic capital budgets; annual operating budgets; and specific, assignable, actionable, annual objectives—the measurable steps and assigned tasks by which each goal is pursued and accomplished and to which people in the organization are held accountable.

Relationship Between Organizational Strategy and HIS Strategy

Why is this discussion about organizational mission, vision, values, strategies, goals, and objectives important to **HIS strategy** development? The answer to that question is an easy one: The HIS strategy should be to build the information technology (IT) capabilities and systems necessary to enable the organization's strategies and support these business and clinical goals and objectives. The HIS strategy will encompass its own set of HIS strategies, projects, goals, and objectives, all of which directly tie back into the organization's overall strategies and goals. The HIS strategy is the interpretation of the organization's strategic plan into the IT language of systems, infrastructure, data, expertise, information, and connectivity. To build systems and HIS infrastructure that do not align in this way—or, worse yet, that run counter to these forward-thinking evolutionary steps—hinders the capacity and forward movement of any organization and threatens to waylay the organization on its trajectory toward its vision state.

The organization's strategic plan thus serves as the roadmap for its HIS strategic plan. The HIS strategic plan should directly reflect the strategies of the organization and should not stray one iota from enabling the organization to move in its desired direction. It should be absolutely focused on supporting the accomplishment of those organizational strategies and initiatives. In other words, the HIS strategy is a mirror image of the organizational strategy. There is no need for a separate or isolated HIS strategy: That would be meaningless, wasteful, and counterproductive. Rather, the HIS strategy requires the availability of an organizational direction and strategic plan—otherwise, the HIS strategy could be based on something as random as the last conference someone attended, inertia, what the organization across town is doing, or the influence

of a convincing software salesperson (think snake oil). If this happens, the expensive investment of time, resources, and energy put into building the organization's HIS and technology infrastructure would be a wasted or misguided effort that does not help the organization reach its desired state. Clearly, then, it is important to make time for organization strategic planning and for HIS strategic planning. Do not skip or short-change these highly related processes. To do so will result in costly HIS misalignment, which *will* be (not *can* be) devastating to the accomplishment of the organization's strategic plans, in spite of all of its worthy effort.

One last question: What happens if your organization does not have a strategic plan and you need to develop a strategic HIS plan and make major HIS decisions and investments? Take charge and create the strategic organizational plan as best you can before launching off to develop and implement the HIS strategy. The strategic organizational planning *must* come first. Document everything you can about what people are thinking about the future directions and plans of the organization. Be a leader. Pull a group of people together, interview people from all disciplines and levels of the organization, and write down everything you learn according to the outline provided in **Exhibit 3.1**. Circulate what you document and get people's reactions—and then adjust your documentation based on this feedback. In addition to getting guidance from executive management, ask entry-level employees, grass-roots workers, nurses, physicians, process experts in a variety of departments, senior leaders, people in the community, board members (might want to get permission on that one first), and administrative assistants (especially!) what they think. You will likely be pleasantly surprised at what you learn: Thoughtful people know the truth about what is going on; they know how to make things work more efficiently and effectively. Everything you learn in this process will be important input for your work of HIS strategy development. Be organized as you go about this process: Systematically interview a subset of the people in each category and all others you think have a perspective on the work of the organization. This research will paint a picture of what is important to various constituents in the organization and in the community, whose interests all need to be served by the organization and, therefore, by its computer systems and information capabilities. The bottom line is that the HIS strategy should be like a reflection in the pool of the organization's future—it should contemplate the present and lay a path to its desired future.

EXHIBIT 3.1 Outline of a Strategic Plan for a Healthcare Organization—Greentown Community Clinic

Strategic Plan

This document lays out a thorough and thoughtful analysis of the long-term future plans for an organization, taking its environmental conditions and community into consideration.

Example: The Strategic Plan for Greentown Community Clinic contemplates the future of the community and defines the plans and funding necessary to address the community's future healthcare needs over the next 10 to 20 years.

- ***Executive Summary:*** This section summarizes the essential points contained within each section of a strategic plan, with the intention that decision makers who are asked to consider approving a strategic plan, such as members of a board of directors, can quickly and easily access the primary considerations and issues contained in the plan. (The executive summary is typically 1 to 2 pages long and single-spaced.) The executive summary for the Greentown Community Clinic concisely summarizes the main points from each section of its strategic plan for each element listed.

Sample text:
Greentown Community Clinic plans to grow to at least twice its current size over the next 5 years to meet the growing and unmet needs of its community, which has doubled its population in the last decade.

- ***Organization History:*** This section describes the organization's background, including any relevant themes that set the backdrop for the strategic direction for the organization.

Sample text:
The Greentown Community Clinic was established in 1969, at a time when funding from Medicaid provided the means to begin to address the healthcare needs of Greentown's growing numbers of migrant worker citizens, many of whose family incomes were below the federal poverty line. These citizens also were often uninsured or underinsured.

- ***Vision Statement:*** This section expresses the long-term vision of the organization.

Sample text:
Greentown aims to provide for the comprehensive healthcare and wellness needs of its community, especially targeting those who cannot pay for those services, in a manner that sustains and enables these people and families to thrive.

- ***Mission Statement:*** This section describes the organization's purpose and way that its vision will be carried out.

Sample text:
Greentown Commuity Clinic is committed to high-quality, compassionate, and sustaining care that meets the healthcare and wellness needs of all members of its community, regardless of their ability to pay.

- ***Target Population:*** This section defines the people whom the organization intends to serve within the scope of this strategic plan, which may be a different or expanded population than the one it currently serves.

Sample text:
Greenfield Community Clinic serves the citizens of Greenfield and all new inhabitants within a 50-mile radius of the town.

- ***Community Served:*** This section defines the characteristics and demographics of the population and community served by the organization.

Sample text:
Greentown Community Clinic serves members of its target population who come to the clinic for care, regardless of financial or demographic status. Greentown's patients and community consist of a diverse combination of people who represent all major ethnic groups, with the low-income population comprising a growing segment of the community and one that is particularly in need because many are displaced from areas nearby where economic conditions have worsened in recent years. This population is predominantly in professional service, agricultural, and educational occupations.

- ***Future Issues:*** This section describes characteristics and considerations that influence the direction of the organization.

Sample text:
Greentown Community Clinic faces significant challenges inherent as a result of its rapidly growing population and reduced levels of reimbursement based on the decreasing percentage of its population that has health insurance, due to an expanding low-income demographic.

- ***SWOT Analysis:*** The Strengths, Weaknesses, Opportunities, and Threats section of the strategic plan describes each of these possibilities as they relate to the organization's market share, competition, facilities, programs, services, medical staff, operations, finances, and other key elements.

Sample text:
In market share, Greentown Community Clinic's strengths include a growing population that needs the types of services

EXHIBIT 3.1 Outline of a Strategic Plan for a Healthcare Organization—Greentown Community Clinic

it offers; a weakness in terms of market share is its vulnerability to insufficient revenues if Medicaid reimbursement is not achieved for all those who are eligible for it based on their family income. There is an opportunity for more people from Greentown's socioeconomic demographic segments to obtain health insurance through health reform in addition to Medicaid. However a threat exists in the potential shift of those newly insured citizens obtaining care in settings other than the Greentown Community Clinic, thus reducing volume below planned-for levels.

- **Assumptions:** This section lists the key assumptions that inform and potentially drive strategic decisions and plans, which are estimations of future charactristics and thus will vary to some degree as reality unfolds and must be watched closely as time progresses.

Sample text:
Greentown Community Clinic will be one of three community clinics in Greentown for the foreseeable future.

- **Goals and Objectives:** This section identifies multiyear goals and a process for establishing annual objectives that form the basis of annual operating budgets.

Sample text:
Goals for Greentown Community Clinic include the implementation of a comprehensive electronic health record (EHR) system to enable communication between departments and engagement of patients through a patient portal that connects them from their homes and places of work. Objectives would be to define the requirements for the EHR and send an RFP to vendors in year 1, select and plan the impementation of the EHR in year 2, and go live with a new EHR system in year 3.

- **Implementation Strategies:** This section describes potential strategies for execution of the contents of the strategic plan, including approaches to key goals.

Sample text:
In accomplishing the goal of remodeling its interior and updating the exterior of its buildings, Greentown Community Clinic will establish focus groups from the community that participate in the remodeling and renovation design and plans.

- **Organizational Structure Future Plans:** This section describes changes to the organization that will need to

accompany and enable the strategies contained in the strategic plan.

Sample text:
To support the implementation of the HIS plan including an EHR system, Greentown Community Clinic will recruit key IT professionals and create a robust HIS department.

- **Plans–Buildings, Technology, Renovation:** This section describes the changes and developments necessary for the physicial plant and buildings to meet the needs described in the strategic plan.

Sample text:
Greentown Community Clinic will add three new satallite clinics over the next 10 to 15 years to provide access to its growing patient population.

- **Marketing Plans:** This section establishes a brand in accordance with the mission, vision, and values of the organization and identifies the approach to marketing its services and capabilities to its community.

Sample text:
Greentown Community Clinic will establish its brand as "the peoples' clinic" and communicate this message and the services that reflect it to the various locales and segments of its patient population and community.

- **Key Relationships:** This section describes key organizational and community relationships necessary for the organization to succeed in accomplishing its strategic plan.

Sample text:
Greentown Community Clinic seeks to develop relationships with the primary employers, churches, and schools within its service area as a means of connecting with the people in its patient population and engaging them in managing their health and wellness.

- **Future Organizational Polices:** This section describes key policies that the organization must adopt in order to successfully meet its strategic plan and future vision.

Sample text:
Human resources policies will be adapted to allow for flexibility in hiring practices to provide maximum employment opportunities for Greentown citizens, in concert with its vision of becoming "the peoples' clinic."

- **Governing Board Plans—Structure, Role, Responsibilities:** This section defines the governance structure and

(Continued)

EXHIBIT 3.1 Outline of a Strategic Plan for a Healthcare Organization—Greentown Community Clinic (*Continued*)

responsibilities, identifying key roles and types of expertise and representation needed to properly guide the organization through the opportunities and challenges of its future development.

Sample text:

The Greentown Community Clinic Board of Directors will be comprised of 15 to 20 members who possess expertise in key disciplines reflecting the needs of the organization. The Board of Directors will form subcommittees for closely overseeing plan execution, such as in the areas of finance, information technology, strategic planning, operations management, human resources, and clinical leadership.

- **Feasibility Plan/Pro Forma:** This section estimates the financial, human, and other resource requirements needed to accomplish the strategic plan.

Sample text:

A 5-year financial pro forma estimating revenues, capital requirements, and operating expenses for the 5- to 10-year

time horizon contemplated in the Greentown Community Clinic strategic plan.

- **Contingency Plans:** This section describes possible directional changes from the expressed strategic plan and its assumptions, including changes in that plan based on those deviations as reality unfolds over the planning time horizon.

Sample text:

The Greentown Community Clinic plans to hold 15% of all revenues in reserve to provide for changes in reimbursement, its economic condition, and the financial well-being of its citizens.

Data from Washington State Hospital Association. Importance of strategic planning. http://www.wsha.org/files/62/Gov_Board_Manual_strategic _planning.pdf

HIS STRATEGY: WHERE DO WE BEGIN?

Four essential themes feed into a solid understanding of HIS strategy: (1) the organizational strategy, which serves as the foundation for **HIS planning**; (2) the HIS planning framework; (3) HIS decision-making processes; and (4) the context of the changing national HIS strategy, consumer expectations, and the realities of the HIS marketplace for products and services. These four themes underlie all HIS strategy development and planning.

Organizational Strategy Provides the Foundation for HIS Planning

The HIS plan should be a direct reflection of the organization's strategic plan. How is this accomplished? First, as described earlier, for the HIS computer systems, networks, and automation of processes to have a beneficial effect on the organization and be a cost-effective investment of financial, human, and physical resources, the HIS and technology plan must support and enable the organizational plan, from both business and clinical perspectives, and in consideration of internal and external drivers. The previous section explained this relationship in terms of strategy and planning, but we emphasize here

that the development of the HIS strategic plan must be based on that organizational plan. The HIS plan serves its purpose when it supports and enables the organization to achieve its strategies according to its mission, vision, and values.

How does the organization know its desired future state and proper forward direction? How does it improve its processes to achieve new, streamlined ways of delivering services to its customers and supporting its business and administrative functions? It knows these things—or rather, it discovers them—by taking the time, energy, and expense to produce a strategic business plan that is then used to formulate a consistent HIS plan. This planning process consists of a systematic examination of the organization's current state or condition, as well as the changing internal and external dynamics and conditions. The planning process defines a 5- to 10-year desired future state based on the organization's mission, vision, and values (sound familiar?), identifying which strategies will move the organization in this desired direction, setting specific goals based on those strategies, and then breaking those multiyear goals into measurable annual objectives against which organizational performance can be measured and budgets set. The strategic business plan guides annual goals, objectives, budgets, and projects—these can be specified at a great level of detail yet still understood in terms of how they relate to the higher-level strategy. As the old Irish saying goes, "Keep your head in the clouds, and your feet on the ground."

Because the HIS strategy uses this organizational strategic plan as its roadmap as well, it logically devises projects that establish information technologies and computerization aligned with the strategic direction of the overall organizational plan. Thus investments in HIS, set upon this foundation, are guaranteed to not only automate the organization, but also focus that automation in ways that propel the organization gradually and surely toward its desired future state (**Figure 3.3**).

Many system strategies focus primarily on selecting a software vendor to provide whatever solutions an organization seeks. This is a mistake. While picking good vendors to provide **software** and **hardware** products is paramount to creating a successful HIS portfolio for an organization, it is much less important than determining whether and how the implementation of that vendor's software product will address the right types of IT capabilities for the organization's needs at that time and into the future. In other words, are the ways a vendor's products can be applied to the structure, functions, and connections of the organization relevant to the structures, functions, and connections that will take the organization into the future successfully? Will the vendor be able to work collaboratively with the people in the organization to design and build specific workflows that meet the organization's needs? Will they support effective and efficient business and clinical processes? The answers to all these questions should be "yes." Even an only moderately impressive or semi-sophisticated set of software capabilities that is properly placed—in alignment with the

organization's strategy—will be vastly more helpful than an elegant, high-capability software package that is misplaced or inadequately tailored to the needs and preferences of your organization's **knowledge workers**. Poorly applied software, no matter how impressive or fancy, hinders an organization's forward movement. If the vendor software products purchased and implemented are sophisticated but misaligned with the future design and direction of the organization, they will hamper the organization's progress in meeting its strategies and goals because the hefty investment of the organization's time, talent, and resources will be spent pushing the organization against its grain, and the yield from those misapplied resources will produce low value results and potential harm. Be careful when a vendor proposes replicating a solution that it developed for another client—that may be easier for the vendor, but it may not be the best bet for your organization. And remember, there are no shortcuts to good HIS implementations—they are slow and painstaking projects that involve the attention, commitment, and hard work of everyone in the organization.

Now that the organization has a sense of its future direction through the development of its strategic business plan, how does the HIS plan get defined and created? Those responsible for the HIS planning process now have what they need to create the HIS roadmap and strategies that marry up with that strategic business plan and help propel the organization in the right direction. HIS planning should be synchronized with the strategic business planning undertaken by the organization. Using the organization's business plan as its guide, the HIS plan then documents the current state of its computer systems and IT infrastructure, contemplates a 5- to 10-year desired future state of HIS and technology (**HIS architecture**), and lays out a path of HIS initiatives and projects that will migrate the organization's systems from "where we are" (current state) to "where we want to be in 5 to 10 years" (future state). These HIS initiatives and projects must be accomplished in the right order (the organization should put the foundational IT infrastructure in place first before implementing new software systems that rely on that infrastructure, for example). At that point, the systematic implementation of new HIS should follow the roadmap laid out by the strategic HIS plan to migrate the organization's systems to a new set of systems and capabilities that help the organization evolve, innovate, and grow.

It may be overwhelming to think about the entirety of the HIS that an organization needs now and in the future and about how all those systems will fit together into a unified whole. At any given time within any healthcare organization, many different constituencies are sure to

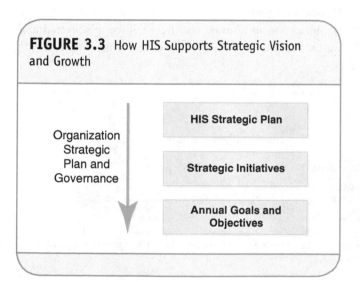

FIGURE 3.3 How HIS Supports Strategic Vision and Growth

request and create demand for their functions, departments, or processes to be automated with new computer systems. Typically, the demand for new systems serving various areas of the organization is enormous—exceeding the capacity for change within the organization at any one time. Thus, HIS strategic planning must prioritize the introduction of new systems carefully. Further, the demands and requests often deal with functionality oriented to a certain department or service, such as cardiology or billing. The key is to get those requesting the new systems for their areas to see the larger picture and understand the opportunities to integrate systems. The benefits of implementing enterprise-wide systems rather than creating silos of information—isolated systems that address the work of only one department or function of the organization—are profound. Enterprise systems help the organization move forward in a coordinated, comprehensive fashion—silos do not.

How does HIS leadership manage these many needs and organize the computer system implementations in ways that balance the needs that must be addressed with the resources required for these implementations in a way that makes sense from a computerization perspective? The answer lies in thoughtful HIS planning, working collaboratively in multidisciplinary groups according to a disciplined methodology, and documenting and then prioritizing all the information and computerization needs of the organization's many constituents. This work is done according to an HIS architectural framework, the subject of the next section of this chapter and the second pillar in HIS planning. The HIS planning process involves first a top-down view of the organization as seen through the eyes of its senior leadership, who establish the vision, set the direction, determine the resources available, and develop structures and responsibilities for the HIS planning process. It then assumes a bottom-up, grass-roots perspective

to contemplate how work can be done better and what is actually necessary to get the new HIS in place at a very detailed level. It is this combination of "top-down" and "bottom-up" perspectives that makes for a realistic, comprehensive, and forward-thinking HIS plan.

HIS Planning Framework: An Aligned, Architectural Approach

As described in the previous section, sound HIS strategy is a direct reflection of the organization's strategic plan and, as such, will be an enabler of the organization's strategic evolution. Thus the planned HIS must support all business and clinical strategies, as well as enable some business and clinical strategies that would not be feasible using paper-based processes. An example of this type of enabling HIS is the use of wireless technologies and social media platforms for engaging patients and the community in wellness initiatives and population-based health strategies, as well as for giving researchers and analysts helpful data and insights into population-based ways to help manage chronic conditions and health promotion[1] (**Figure 3.4**).

A good HIS plan also advances the organization's performance—for example, by reducing costs, reducing waste, improving revenues, enhancing service, improving the quality of care, and increasing patient, employee, and provider satisfaction. When the HIS strategies and systems support the organization in doing all these things, they are "aligned" with the strategic and operational needs of the organization.[2] To do *all* these things and not just *some* of these things, the HIS plan should be designed using a systematic approach to planning a "balanced" HIS architecture. If the HIS strategy does only a few of these things, the organization may be partly—but not fully—successful in achieving its future state vision. If the HIS agenda is misaligned, or even partially incorrect, significant organizational resources will be misdirected and wasted because the resources consumed while implementing

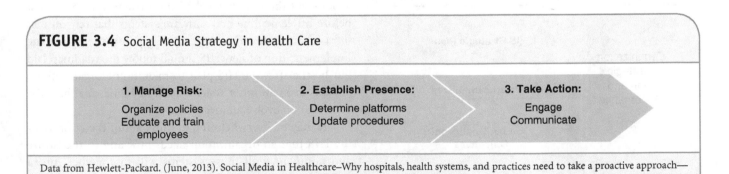

FIGURE 3.4 Social Media Strategy in Health Care

1. **Manage Risk:**
Organize policies
Educate and train
employees

2. **Establish Presence:**
Determine platforms
Update procedures

3. **Take Action:**
Engage
Communicate

Data from Hewlett-Packard. (June, 2013). Social Media in Healthcare—Why hospitals, health systems, and practices need to take a proactive approach—now. HP Whitepaper. http://h20195.www2.hp.com/V2/GetPDF.aspx%2F4AA4-7062ENUS.pdf

the HIS will not further the organization's strategies. This is true regardless of which type of healthcare organization it is. Perhaps most serious of all, without an effective, aligned HIS plan, the organization might cease to exist in the future, given the cost of HIS and the evolution of all commerce and interaction to electronic forms. These principles apply to creating HIS plans for physician practices, hospitals, hospital systems, long-term care organizations, home healthcare agencies, and public health organizations alike.

Next, we present a generic HIS conceptual planning framework that can be adapted for use in any type of healthcare organization. This framework, which was developed in the 1980s in a consulting and teaching context, offers a nontechnical method for thinking about HIS. It lays out the types and categories of software systems needed by a healthcare organization on a two-by-two, four-quadrant grid, based on the functional area or analytical purpose each system serves (**Figure 3.5**). We will walk through this HIS planning framework and define each quadrant into which various types of software systems fit.

The diagram's left-hand column represents transactions, or day-to-day activities and repeatable tasks necessary to conduct the clinical and business work of the organization.

These activities embody the "real-time," transaction-based production work of the organization, when efficiency and consistency are essential to productivity of employees and high-quality clinical and administrative work. The right-hand column represents the information based on "post-production" or retrospective reporting and analysis necessary to manage clinical and business aspects of the organization, including the following types of capabilities:

- Managerial and clinical reporting
- Analytical activities assessing the efficiency and effectiveness of processes and tasks taking place on the "production" or functional side of the organization
- Decision support systems for planning and evaluating clinical services and outcomes, financial performance, and operational effectiveness

The top row of the framework refers to the clinical or healthcare services aspects of the organization, in accordance with the mission and purpose of the organization. The bottom row refers to those elements of the organization having to do with the "business" or institutional administration of the organization.

FIGURE 3.5 HIS Planning Framework: Quadrants

	Transaction/Functional Support Systems	Management/Decision Support Systems (BI/CI)
Clinical	Quadrant I (Clinical Transaction Systems)	Quadrant III (Clinical Management/Clinical Intelligence Systems)
Administrative	Quadrant II (Administrative Transaction Systems)	Quadrant IV (Administrative Management/ Business Intelligence Systems)

Key: BI, business intelligence; CI, clinical intelligence.

Modified from Jay McCutcheon's Systems Planning Framework.

Thus Quadrant I (the top left box in Figure 3.5) represents the transactional activities having to do with patient care and the organization's core service mission. Quadrant II represents the day-to-day transactions having to do with running the business activities and institutional processes of the organization. Quadrant III represents reporting and analytical capabilities associated with the clinical activities and outcomes of the organization. Quadrant IV represents the management reporting and analytical capabilities associated with the business and administrative aspects of the organization.

What do these quadrants and categories have to do with HIS planning and computer systems for the organization in question? Answering this question leads us to connect the types of functions and processes that can be supported with automation with the types of computer systems and software that provide that "functionality." Certain types of computer system software applications are built to support certain functional areas, departments, or types of transactions or processes required to either deliver clinical care or support the business processes of a healthcare organization. For instance, an electronic medical record supports the processes essential to taking care of patients, such as registering a patient, placing an order for a treatment, delivering the results of a laboratory test to the provider, and writing a prescription for a patient.

Examples of business processes supported by computer software applications include populating a bill with claims data and electronically submitting that claim to a payer, and using computer software to keep track of inventory and reordering of medical supplies used within the organization. More categories of these types of functions are shown in **Figure 3.6**.

Other types of software help analysts, researchers, and other knowledge workers in healthcare organizations understand the costs or clinical outcomes associated with various types of patients with certain conditions, or tally the most frequently seen types of patients in a physician office or hospital or clinic, for example. When using this generic HIS planning framework, these types of software and computer systems would reside in Quadrant III (management information and analytics associated with evaluating the clinical effectiveness of care provided within the organization). Use of an analytical software tool to evaluate budgeted expenditures versus actual expenditures would reside in Quadrant IV (management information and **business intelligence** associated with managing the business side of the organization). In this manner, we can trace our way from the functions or processes of an organization that reside in each quadrant to the types of computer systems and software applications needed to automate those processes and functions. The planning framework shown in Figure 3.6 helps us see the

---

FIGURE 3.6 HIS Planning Framework: Scope of Quadrants

	Transaction/Functional Support Systems	Management/Decision Support Systems (BI/CI)
Clinical	I Patient/Provider/Clinical Care Activities	III Clinical Reporting, Data Analytics, Outcomes Analysis
Administrative	II Institutional Business Activities	IV Business Reporting, Data Analytics, Key Performance Indicators Analysis

Key: BI, business intelligence; CI, clinical intelligence.

Modified from Jay McCutcheon's Systems Planning Framework.

balance needed in the architecture of an entire portfolio of HIS used by an organization to support all the functions, processes, and information needs of that organization.

What types of clinical and business-related computer systems and software packages or applications support healthcare organizations? **Figure 3.7** shows the same HIS planning framework with examples of the types of computer software applications that fit into each of the four quadrants, identifying which types of processes are supported by these computer system capabilities.

What is relevant about this categorization schema is not just a listing of computer systems and software applications, but groupings and relationships between these systems and applications. Most of each quadrant's software systems are related—software written to support functionality and processes within each quadrant—and tend to make use of many of the same data elements. For instance, a software application supporting laboratory test processes and functions needs patient name and medical record number, diagnosis, physician order, correct location of the patient for gathering specimens,

which test should be performed, and ordering physician(s) to whom to deliver the lab test result. These same data elements (i.e., patient ID, patient diagnosis, physician order, patient location, physician names and orders) are needed for other clinical therapies and processes, such as medication administration and dispensation, radiology exams, physical therapy, and other patient care activities. Thus there is a high degree of overlap between the numerous clinical HIS applications and the data elements and functions they deploy. Additionally, such clinically related software applications are typically supplied by software vendors that specialize in software systems residing in a particular quadrant—for instance, as part of a comprehensive electronic health record (EHR). Such systems are identified in Quadrant I of the framework.

When data elements are shared by more than one application, and these applications operate using data stored in the same database, they are *integrated*. Software applications that share data from separate databases are *interfaced*. (We will talk more about integrated versus interfaced systems in the *HIS Application Systems and Technology* chapter.) For

FIGURE 3.7 HIS Planning Framework with Examples of Software Applications in Each Quadrant

	Transaction/Functional Support Systems	Management/Decision Support Systems (BI/CI)
Clinical	I • EHR, EMR, PHR, medical intranet • Outpatient systems • Radiology, laboratory, pharmacy • Transcription/dictation • Cardiology, ECG, ECHO • Maternity monitoring • Home health • PACS for imaging • Surgery • ICU systems, monitors, devices	III • Case mix analysis • Decision support systems • Quality analysis and reporting • Outcomes analysis • Clinical intelligence • Data warehouse • External reporting: » Joint Commission, Leapfrog, CHART, other
Administrative	II • General financials • Patient accounting • Contracts management • HRMS/payroll • Materials management/supply chain • Credentialing	IV • Financial, supply chain, HR management reporting • Cost accounting • Business intelligence, analytics • Financial decision support • Enterprise data warehouse • Budgeting, financial modeling, and forecasting

Key: BI, business intelligence; CI, clinical intelligence; ECHO, echocardiogram; EHR, electronic health record; EMR, electronic medical record; ECG, electrocardiogram; HR, human resources; HRMS, human resources management system; ICU, intensive care unit; PACS, picture and archiving communication system; PHR, personal health record.

Modified from Jay McCutcheon's Systems Planning Framework.

our purposes now, note that this is an extremely important distinction that needs to be taken into account in planning HIS architectures. Due to the sharing of many common data elements between systems and applications residing in the same quadrant, *integrated* systems within a quadrant are highly preferable to interfaced systems.

The planning framework depicted in Figure 3.6 is very helpful in categorizing systems according to the other applications they relate to and share data with frequently; and, therefore, should be integrated (sharing the same database) and not interfaced (functionality bridged between different databases). Software applications, when they will share large amounts of data, should be planned together to maximize opportunities for integration. This is especially true for functions that reside in the same quadrant, as vendors tend to provide systems related to one quadrant or another, such as clinical care (Quadrant I) or business-related financial and administrative systems (Quadrant II). Decision processes for system selection need to prioritize integration between like applications, due to the value this brings in terms of data integrity and the quality of the information produced by these systems.

The HIS planning framework discussed here provides a nontechnical way to discuss, visualize, and document the software application systems needed by an organization to do its work and provide the services to its patient population. It can be used to ensure that the HIS application architecture is "balanced"—that is, provides computerized support evenly to the various clinical and financial departments and workers whose work processes are being automated. This HIS planning framework provides a visual, nontechnical means of documenting the HIS that align with organizational strategy and support organizational activities.

Summary of HIS Alignment and Strategic Planning

Good HIS strategy and planning rely on and require a linkage to the overall strategies and activities of the organization. In fact, today all business strategies and clinical initiatives the organization might consider must be addressed from an HIS perspective. Sometimes HIS will operate in a support or process-improvement mode (i.e., providing streamlined and improved processes); at other times HIS is the enabler (in other words, the strategy is not doable without HIS technology). The organization is able, through the planning process, to identify new strategic and operational opportunities that are facilitated by HIS.

For example, the organization might have a strategic objective of growing its outpatient cancer care services. With HIS enabling technology, it can integrate its hospital services with its outpatient imaging and cancer care services, making

for a more complete and seamless care experience for patients. Alternatively, the organization might use HIS to integrate operations in hospital and university research settings, thereby connecting the "bench to the bed" in ways that help scientific advancements reach patient care settings more quickly. An opportunity to use HIS to enable new efficiency-oriented organizational strategies might apply HIS to improve supplies management by shifting this operation to "just-in-time" inventory control. Each of these three strategies would be implemented very differently if the organization did not have available modern, streamlined HIS and technology that support new streamlined processes or enable brand new models of care.

But this essential alignment—between the strategic plan and the HIS plan—extends beyond HIS supporting and enabling previously known strategies. Some strategies can be imagined only when systems and technology planning is integrated with organizational planning: When synergies between these two forces occur, brand new ideas can be conceived. For this reason, *all* strategic discussions should include an HIS element, and vice versa. That is, all HIS projects should include a calibration with strategy, to assure proper strategic alignment as well as tactical objectives associated with the HIS project. This effort should include, for example, a process redesign initiative to streamline workflow and develop new processes through automation.

During this planning process, the aligned organizational and HIS strategies can be developed into detailed tactical HIS plans including HIS initiatives, project descriptions with timetables, capital and operating budgets, staffing plans, and metrics for achieving the desired benefits and mitigating inherent risks. These detailed plans and budgets then become the organizational fodder for organization-wide communication and cultural support for the demanding teamwork associated with HIS implementations and projects.

WHY HIS STRATEGY MATTERS
Emergence of the Knowledge-Based Economy in the Context of National, Local, and Consumer Perspectives

Our world has changed. No longer are assembly-line processes with specialized workers isolated into workgroups performing one type of task sufficient or functional in today's world. A knowledge-based, connected economy has emerged in other industries, and expectations are fully upon us that health care should follow suit. This is true for both the conduct of commerce and consumer expectations.

Similarly, we think differently about assets now—a value migration from visible assets including financial and physical capital to intangible knowledge resources has occurred.[3]

Organizations are valuing, managing, and nurturing their knowledge and human assets with a different view: These human assets should be rightly recognized as the source of creating and delivering the services that result in financial and physical resources—services much needed to compete successfully in the marketplace with excellent services and products. Intellectual capital is gaining importance as the means of improving organizational performance and market position.[4] Attaining talent and allowing it to thrive is the imperative now. This is based on the creation of a work environment dependent on state-of-the-art HIS and technology that acknowledges and allows knowledge workers to create new solutions and activities that improve the ability of the organization to adapt to its new environment and meet increasing demands for improved quality and efficiency. This is a much different mind-set than a traditional strict set of known methods, rules, and benchmarks against which worker performance and productivity are measured. This is not to say that performance and productivity are not important—they most certainly are as part of good management. But they alone are not enough. The problems and capabilities of today's modern world insist on improvements based on human creativity, process enhancement, and new solutions to problems.

HIS and technology will most certainly play a central role in the emergence of the knowledge-based economy, and especially in health care as it finds its way through this developmental, evolutionary phase. What does this trend mean for health care? Patients will no longer be passive recipients of medical services; rather, they must be active participants in achieving the mutual goal held by those working in health care and those consuming healthcare services. This goes beyond the mere hope for the absence of disease or injury, but extends to achieving and maintaining optimal health and well-being.

Additionally, HIS and technology have changed the format of information itself. Digital technology is **"dematerializing" information** (eliminating paper, having paper stored out in the "cloud") and enabling separation of information from the physical structures and objects used to carry it.[5] In essence, this trend is "taking geography out of the equation." In other words, whether it pertains to a patient or a testing or therapeutic facility, essential information is no longer isolated to a physical location, but rather can be shared at the speed of light to any professionals or people who need or should have access to that piece of information simultaneously. This is an enormous change from the days of the "central records room" or the "corporate office" mentality that implied, "All the important information resides within a central office of an organization, and so does all the real intelligence." Now, within the constraints of the roles-based

security and access mandated HIPAA, information can be anywhere we desire it to be with the help of computerization. Geography, then, is no longer a primary issue. With the aid of systems and technology, information sharing and collaboration can take place across a large building, a city, a country, or even internationally. Traditional work clusters and assembly-line–based processes can be decoupled with the right types of systems support, in terms of place, time, and performance of the work.

The idea that HIS and technology "take geography out of the equation" or that information or connection between humans or machines is no longer confined to a physical space makes revolutionary changes possible for organizations and their structures. Organizational configurations are free to transition from strict, defined, hierarchical structures designed to control and facilitate the flow of information from bottom to top, to fluid, social, adaptable networks and organizational forms that can move and adapt to changing circumstances with greater ease.[3] Organizations can now be what is called "flat," meaning information sharing and collaboration occur between any and all "team members" who need to interact to achieve the work of the organization. In the case of health care, that means work on behalf of the patient and the mission of the organization. This fluidity (all with proper roles-based security and confidentiality, of course) represents a sea change from the restrictive, power-based availability of information inherent in traditional, hierarchical structures. This is not to say that hierarchy does not have its place: Many, if not most, organizations today are structured this way, and without structure, roles, and responsibilities, chaos would prevail. Nevertheless, within this discipline of hierarchy, function, and process, the ready access to information and connection between the humans working in those organizations is changing due to the automation of information—and changing for the better. Greater ease of sharing of ideas and information between knowledge workers within a trusted, secure environment can create a greater synergy between the work and ideas of those workers. It is recognized that not all good ideas must come from the top layers of an organization—in fact, generation of actionable ideas are encouraged from every part of an organization. This empowers individuals through access to information and enables the development and implementation of processes and systems that can lead to greater effectiveness and productivity for the organization overall.

What does this mean for health care? Imagine patient care in a traditional, hierarchical organization, where power—through access to information—exists predominantly with those at the top of the hierarchy (think physician leaders and administrators) but patient care (the product) is delivered at the ground level, through other knowledge workers (think nurses, technicians, and therapists) who handle the day-to-day, hands-on work of caring for the patients (in other words, delivering the product and determining its quality). Before automation could connect the various roles and players on this knowledge train, the hierarchy served this purpose. But along with that rigid discipline and restricted access of information came a certain required, measured pace of process and progress. When health care was simpler, and fewer professionals and therapies were involved, this schema worked well in well-run organizations. In today's complex healthcare environment, where multiple parties may need access to patient and business information regarding a patient simultaneously, a single thread of information passed along from person to person via paper or word-of-mouth cannot possibly keep up. Adaptability, prompt action based on real-time feedback, and fluidity are crucial elements in the interactions taking place between the many different professionals charged with responsibilities in today's healthcare organizations. Systems and technology can boost positive interaction, enabling healthcare organizations to become more adaptable and responsive to changing requirements of patient care and administration responsibilities.

Will this transformation magically take place simply as a result of buying and installing new computer systems and software? Not at all. It is a painstaking process involving thorough planning and a careful analysis of workflow, where all these activities maintain a close connection to the purpose and meaning of care in that organization. In addition to streamlining and redesigning work processes, we must successfully build systems and technology to support those improved processes that span across organizational structures to create new connections, openness of communication, and access to information to support the knowledge workers involved.

In summary, the evolution of healthcare organizations requires greater focus on systems thinking as we move from sequential, assembly-line passing of information to integrated collaboration between professionals. HIS and technology allow and necessitate that the center of attention be systems, processes, workflow, and the core mission of patient care, rather than structures, power, and upholding traditional ways of working that are dependent upon paper to record and transmit information. Automation creates opportunities for streamlining workflow to gain efficiencies, focus on service, enhance communication, and improve timeliness and quality of care. What is revolutionary about this chance is we have the chance in health care to

consider the impact of process and workflow on efficiency, effectiveness, and quality in ways that have not been imaginable heretofore.

For instance, an earlier way of working on quality assurance and process improvement relied on figuring out how to make sure the paper documents with the most up-to-date guidelines for care were printed and kept in binders on each and every nursing unit in a hospital, accompanied by regular in-service training to review these ever-changing guidelines that each and every worker must follow to be effective (and somehow this activity must be tracked to see if, in fact, the guidelines were followed). Now, patient care can be supported by computerized prompts that guide caregivers as they use these systems to use evidence-based processes of care and document these activities along the way. Of course, successful use of such a system requires close collaboration between the IT professionals who build and support these computer systems, individuals familiar with current clinical guidelines, and the clinicians who use the systems in providing care. That close collaboration is the hallmark of successful systems implementations.

Realizing the possibilities of automating processes and functions in healthcare organizations begins in the planning process. When the overarching strategies of the organization are tied directly to the HIS and technology plans of the organization, and those computer systems are subsequently implemented and put into action, they support the forward movement and desired improvements in patient care that the dedicated professionals of the organization value most. In the author's experience, 99.9% of healthcare workers are well-intentioned, caring, knowledgeable, highly trained professionals who come to work every day to do their absolute best for the patients they serve. The rewarding part about working on challenging HIS and technology projects is that—when well conceived and implemented—those efforts allow a new vision of excellent patient care and service to the community to be realized.

Facilitating Organizational Evolution

Despite being absolutely essential to communities, hospitals can no longer be treated as the center of the healthcare universe. With changing demographics, including an aging population and skyrocketing rates of chronic illness such as diabetes, obesity, cancer, Alzheimer's disease, and heart disease, increased focus is being placed on primary, personalized care. This type of care fits with *prevention*, while hospitals are intended for *acute care needs*. Innovations such as medical homes and **accountable care organizations (ACOs)** take to heart the need for coordination across the continuum of a person's life (the medical home) and the continuum of care; ACOs coordinate care ranging from primary to acute care, depending on the needs of the patient. These innovations rely on, among other things, "geography being taken out of the equation"—that is, using HIS and technology to connect clinicians, care settings, patients, and administrators involved in that continuum. The long-term integration and aggregation of patient information into a lifetime patient record enables the medical home scenario to become reality, and careful integration using HIS and technology facilitates a patient-centric view of information across various healthcare settings along the continuum of care. This continuum reaches from the hospital to the doctor's office to the patient in his or her home or workplace; it involves managing risk factors associated with a chronic illness as well as taking great care of patients in the hospital or clinical settings. Neither the medical home concept nor the ACO model would be feasible without computerized patient care records and networks connecting these settings of care.

Such scenarios become particularly vivid when one considers the integration of chronic care into the continuum to the degree necessary today. This integration responds to the demographic trends and the wide-scale shift from acute to chronic illnesses that have swept the United States in the past few decades. The effectiveness of care depends on the appropriateness of that setting for the type of care or treatment needed. If a chronically ill patient—such as someone with diabetes—arrives at the hospital for the first episode of care, it is too late for effective control of the disease; the condition by that time has become severe and expensive to treat. It is clear that both the patient and the healthcare organization are in losing situations. Of course, healthcare organizations will always approach each patient as he or she presents under the circumstances, but it is far better for the patient and far more cost-effective for the organization to address the care of a patient with a chronic condition early in the progression of that chronic condition. At this stage, it may be possible to reverse that progression or keep it from occurring by treating it early, before devastating effects take place. By the time a chronic disease manifests and reaches the later stages, more aggressive and expensive forms of care are required, which often are directed at controlling symptoms, rather than effecting a cure.

These types of patient care settings (medical homes, ACOs) are intended to create fully coordinated clinical care methods in which doctors, nurses, and therapists provide healthcare services in the appropriate venues. Claims for this care are submitted to insurance providers, and the entire process of healthcare services delivery and business dealings takes place as cost-effectively as can be managed. Traditional methods of care and reimbursement are evolving rapidly, with new arrangements between hospitals, clinics, and physicians emerging to support these new models of care and chronic disease management. The new business relationships and clinical models should be designed to support shared objectives of improving patients' and populations' health, rather than simply seeking reimbursement for an approved set of services according the rules of an insurer-based healthcare system.[6]

The payer-driven healthcare system currently found in the United States does not begin to address the true determinants of health that exist in a person's community, environment, and home. These health determinants—such as education, diet, stress levels, exercise habits, exposure to pollution and violence, and other lifestyle characteristics—factor mightily into a person's total health and wellness picture, along with access to healthcare services. These more personal touch points along the "continuum of care" do not occur primarily in traditional bricks-and-mortar healthcare services settings, but they have everything to do with the personalized behaviors, care, and health of individuals. So how do caring healthcare organizations begin to integrate these settings—from home, to school, to places of entertainment, worship, work, and community—to support the pursuit of health, by minimizing the development and effect of factors that lead to chronic conditions in the first place? HIS and technology, organized into "digital health" platforms through social media, mobile devices, and other means, can provide gateways to more integrated care that is "nearer" to the patient. Lifestyle, determinants of health, environmental conditions, and social context all matter here.

What is the role of HIS and technology in these considerations? Answering this question requires a shift in our thinking—from the inpatient, hierarchical organizations of the past as the "centers of medical care" (think hospitals), to flexible, diverse networks of community and organizational settings, many of which are "healthcare related" in the traditional sense, but others of which are not. All of these "nodes" on the network of community, health, and healing can play a vital role in the long-term health and well-being of the people who live in those communities and frequent these environments. The types of networks and platforms found in this model will be just as different as they are similar, and will include a diversity of participants, community settings, customers, educators, recreational facilities, food sources, governmental participants, suppliers, retailers, and all the relationships between them. In addition, each of these nodes on this type of network will have its own systems and connectivity to the ultimate social network, the Internet. Such a connected "community" network can be local, regional, national, or international in scope. It will be supported by a combination of organizationally based systems, personal digital assistants (PDAs), smartphones, and other mobile devices, all of which can connect to digital health platforms and to one another, to provide real-time feedback to the people using them and to create personalized health-related information.[7] Some might call this a "non-system," but as our society adapts to the ubiquitous use and availability of information technology, it will become obvious that this network of social connections that ebbs and flows with the very fabric of our lives is, in fact, a digitally enabled social system that has many variations and a powerful effect on the quality of our lives and health. Lifestyle, environmental context, and social determinants of health begin and end here.

All of these current realities, ideas, and possibilities will require and inspire a shift from a sole focus on traditional inpatient, hierarchical, bricks-and-mortar organizations to the inclusion of diverse networks between intra- and inter-organizational settings, suppliers, customers, relationships, and communities where people live, work, and play. Empowered consumers in this type of social milieu of health will be enabled by information technology. Although some of this technology—such as social media—is often excluded when defining "health information systems and technology," the empowered consumers who use it are more directly participating in their health and health care. Taking part in this evolution of healthcare delivery and information sharing represents a generational shift, a radical shift in disease trends, and a shift of the burden of coordinating and integrating care from the patient and family to an inter-organizational and personal collaboration. This collaboration will include physicians, patients, families, and the holistic combination of emotional, wellness, nutritional, exercise, social, and education services. Empowered HIS- and technology-enabled knowledge workers become active collaborators in this process as well. This evolution of health care is part of the greater societal revolution fueled by systems and technology experienced by each of us, each and every day. Where it leads us is up to us.

Extending this concept a step further, we are entering the era of personalization of health care, in which medicines, treatments, wellness regimens, prevention strategies, and therapies can be personally customized based on genetics, evidence-based practices, personal desires, and clinical characteristics of an individual's conditions. HIS and technology are intrinsic to this evolution; these HIS are the engines that bring together the predictive, individual and diverse data sets to support the **clinical intelligence** necessary to unleash the focus and creativity of well-minded clinicians, working in concert with patients and families, to develop customized preventive and therapeutic programs specifically tailored to the needs of each patient. Individuals receiving care wish to shape their care experiences. Doing so not only gives patients a voice in the process, but also leads to their full engagement with caregivers and active participation in their care, which evidence tells us leads to improved outcomes.[8]

This HIS- and technology-powered personalization is essential to helping people manage and alter risk-inducing behaviors that might lead to chronic illnesses such as diabetes, heart disease, Alzheimer's disease, and cancer. Such digital health solutions will become commonplace, because health care today requires coordination across institutions, professionals, services, and communities, and direct engagement by patients in their care and health preservation. Stated another way, the chronic conditions that will plague the majority of us will be prevented, controlled, and managed only when people modify their behaviors leading to diseases caused by those behaviors. The view that therapies (e.g., drugs and surgeries) targeting acute infections, illnesses, or injuries can also be used to treat chronic, behavior-induced illnesses is a misconception. Moreover, the only way to change a person's behavior is to involve that individual directly in the information feedback loop associated with the behavior—such as a person's nutrition, levels of physical activity (exercise), and sleep habits.

HIS strategy must take these new clinical and organizational directions into account if healthcare organizations are to cope successfully with the new reality. At this time, health care is in a state of major flux, as healthcare organizations adopt the transformative strategy of moving away from paper to electronic processes and strive to shift from a purely medical model to one that sustains health. This is challenging work, all done while the everyday important work of healthcare providers continues in a complex world of providers, payers, patients, and medical advancement. One can envision a new future state in which IT-enabled organizations and empowered knowledge workers and patients are able to collaborate using the best of medical science, patient–provider engagement, and clinical intelligence to support their efforts. Unfortunately, some organizations will never get there: The transition will require a larger step than they are able to sustain or afford by themselves, and they will have to either become part of a larger health provider organization or gradually become less relevant to the changing complexion of health care and chronic disease processes. This is not a good outcome for the communities those organizations serve; the preferred outcome is for organizations to learn to adapt and integrate HIS and technology into the evolutionary processes that healthcare and public health organizations and communities are navigating today.

Knowledge management—the strategic management of information resources—is an essential part of this evolutionary process, which depends on HIS and technology strategy as an enabling factor. Quadrants III and IV of the HIS planning framework discussed here comprise clinical and business intelligence systems, respectively (see Figure 3.6). These systems, and the data and information that are housed and produced within them for use by clinical and business knowledge workers, add an entire layer of HIS and technology to the architectures and mix of systems supporting healthcare management. Health care comprises an information-intensive set of activities. It encompasses interactions between highly trained experts such as physicians and nurses, as well as the information these knowledge workers need to ensure the best treatment for people who happen to be particularly vulnerable at this point in their lives.

In addition to creating information system capabilities within the organization, healthcare organizations must conduct environmental or market analyses, an essential component of the strategic management of knowledge resources. This type of analysis challenges existing assumptions about providers and consumers of health care based on traditional usage (i.e., the current state of the market) to predict and plan for its future status. It enables business analysts to make new assumptions about the possible future states of the patients and community that the organization will serve; these states cannot be perfectly predicted, of course, but they can be estimated or modeled using these assumptions. This type of anticipatory analysis helps healthcare organizations understand the possibilities associated with their futures, and plan and manage their services and processes to produce desired outcomes.

Clearly, HIS and technology involve much more than just automated support: They are an integral part of the care process and part of organizational evolution in communities. HIS- and technology-enabled information and knowledge provide the bases for continuous innovation and organizational adaptation as the healthcare landscape evolves. Such information and knowledge facilitate new inter-organizational connections and provide the underpinnings of competitive and collaborative advantage—namely power in the marketplace and support to the community.

HIS AND TECHNOLOGY STRATEGY: ADVANCING PUBLIC HEALTH

The use of HIS and technology, especially the area of reporting capabilities and communications networks, can have a remarkable effect on public health, the scope of which extends to the next level of the "continuum of care" when thinking about the relationship between health and access to providers or information emanating from the provider community. Care-providing entities such as hospitals, clinics, and physician practices are striving to reach patients as closely as possible to their homes and places of work—wherever people are every day—so that they may engage in their care, maintain their health, or be cared for and monitored for chronic illness outside of institutional settings. Public health extends beyond the reaches of these healthcare organizations to educate, address, intervene, promote health, and prevent illnesses such as diabetes, heart disease, and cancer, while simultaneously seeking to address conditions, habits, or lifestyle choices that impact health such as behavioral issues related to violence, sexual behaviors, eating, sleep habits, and stress management. Additionally, public health extends to all people, whether healthy or ill, insured or uninsured—striving to keep healthy people healthy and helping people who are not well retain the good aspects of their health that they have and manage their illnesses. For people who are ill, public health's aims are to provide education and support to them and their families, slow the progression of negative health-related behaviors, and prevent the adoption of habits, exposures, or behaviors that might exacerbate their conditions.

The elements of HIS and technology such as planning, systems and their management, software applications, informatics, data and analytics, and opportunities for research have important implications for public health (**Table 3.1**). Public health goes well beyond provider organizations' scopes, with access to public health initiatives being extended into rural regions, statewide, national, continent-wide, and global settings.

How we think about public health HIS and technology is a variation of how we think about HIS and technology strategy and planning for organizations as described earlier in this chapter. Public health HIS and technology have several facets that influence the ways these systems and technology are planned and implemented. Stated another way, the impact of networks and connectivity is profound in HIS and technology uses in all types of healthcare settings, but connectivity provides new means to access needed data and information for purposes of public health HIS and technology. For example, thinking about heath care as a physical, organizational construct, a person can walk across the street to the hospital

TABLE 3.1 Organizations Typically Participating in Different Spheres of the HIS Model

Spheres of HIS Model	Organizational Setting				
	Primary Care (Physician Practices, Clinics)	Community Hospitals	Academic Medical Centers, Health Systems	Public Health Organizations	Policy, Research, and Quality Reporting Organizations
HIS Systems and Management	X	X	X	X	
Health Informatics	X	X	X	X	X
Data and Business/Clinical Intelligence			X	X	X
Research, Policy, and Public Health			X	X	X

emergency room or to a doctor's office or clinic to get his or her healthcare needs met. HIS planned and designed in support of public health, in contrast, means building awareness and providing access to information about health-related issues, immunization clinics, safe water, outbreaks of infection, and other major public health concerns in remote areas and undeveloped regions or countries, to uninsured or underinsured segments of the population, across states, or through global initiatives. Without enabling HIS and technology, these far-reaching elements of public health cannot be achieved.

We are living in a time of convergence of these previously divided worlds—that is, healthcare provider organizations for acute and long-term medical care, and public health for prevention and safety net care. These two worlds are converging because of the nature of disease: Much of disease today is chronic and originates from lifestyle considerations, and medical care cannot reach people in time to prevent these diseases. Chronic, lifestyle-influenced diseases are now rampant in our society and are occurring both more frequently and to such a degree that they require institutional care. The worlds of public health and healthcare provider organizations are converging due to the attention they are both devoting to diseases related to lifestyle and behavioral choices made by people in their everyday lives. Information technology is now a ubiquitous part of how we live, how we conduct business, and how we provide healthcare and public health services. Systems, networks, and technology are merging, connecting, and integrating information and all of us, within our homes, across our towns, between our cities, and across continents. Thanks to the Internet, the global economy has become a reality. As in other industries,

the impact of these trends on the delivery and business of health care is profound. How HIS and technology are used in health care requires a great deal of planning, because these systems, networks, and technologies are very expensive and time-consuming to purchase, implement, and support over the long haul.

Next, we take a deeper look into HIS and technology planning—into an architectural approach for thinking about and planning HIS and technology for healthcare provider organizations and public health purposes.

HIS AND TECHNOLOGY STRATEGY: ARCHITECTURE BUILDS A STRONG HOUSE

Just like planning and building a strong, purposeful house that meets the needs of the people living in it, HIS and technology strategy can be thought of and expressed architecturally. It can be designed to support and enable the functions essential to the purpose, strategy, and structure of the healthcare organization, and support its own services, functions, and relationships.

The first step in creating a strong, useful house is to spend time planning and thinking through the activities and needs of those living in the house. One must then draw up detailed plans, blueprints, specifications, and cost estimates, which are reviewed and approved by all interested parties, before one shovel is shoved into the ground and construction begins. The same architectural approach applies to developing HIS and technology plans for a healthcare organization or for public health needs.

Once an HIS and technology plan is devised and approved, construction commences. The first step in the construction process is preparing the land and laying a good foundation. It is no different with HIS and technology plans: Once the overall plans are approved and funded, the first step is to lay the foundation, consisting of a robust HIS and technology infrastructure. The systems and networks rely on a strong foundation or infrastructure. **Infrastructure** is the "electronic highway" or network technology that carries data, images, voice, and information traffic between the myriad users of the systems and technology, all at the speed of light. Clearly, there is nothing more important than a reliable, robust network infrastructure as the foundation of an organization's HIS and technology plan.

An adequate infrastructure must be in place (and constantly maintained) to support the data communications, software, devices, and hardware used to automate all organizational services and functions, and to create and collect all the essential data and information as outlined in the HIS and technology plans. Riding upon this infrastructure are data and images communicated between users of the systems and the data centers where the hardware servers and network monitoring systems reside. Infrastructure also supports the communications between software systems used by clinicians and business people responsible for day-to-day services and management of the organization.

In health care, nothing is more important than having reliable systems that are up to the task of supporting processes and workflows associated with caring for patients and their families, and meeting the needs of busy employees and clinicians. In other industries, and even on the business side of healthcare organizations, if a billing system or human resources management system goes down for a few hours, the organization can quickly adapt and recover. The worst that happens may be that an extra day's work is added to the accounts receivable function, or a recruiting report is not available for a management meeting that can be rescheduled for tomorrow. In health care, however, if a system supporting a clinical function such as the laboratory, the surgical suite, or the EHR goes down for a few hours, not only the *active processes of care but patients' lives can hang in the balance.* When this happens, clinicians must be well trained in immediately turning to temporary manual systems until the computers are back up and running. Such system failures can be harrowing experiences for all involved and are to be avoided at all costs. Computer systems supporting business functions must be accurate, robust, and available 10 to 15 hours per day; computer systems supporting patient care must be accurate, robust, and 100% reliable on a 24 × 7 × 365 basis. They cannot go down! In turn, HIS and technology—especially that supporting clinical care—must be well funded, robust,

reliable, and well supported by internal HIS staff and software and hardware vendors. The number one priority is system "up-time"; the clinical system must always be up and running.

What does this mean for HIS and technology plans and budgets? It means they must be practical, realistic, rooted in good stewardship, and not based on "projections" or wished-for budget commitments. It means that the totality of all the systems running in the organization must be balanced in such a way that sufficient resources are assured not only for their building and implementation, but also for ongoing support of the systems in all essential areas. Investment in one system should be in balance with others. The HIS plans must provide a detailed and realistic accounting of what it will take to meet the HIS and technology needs of the entire organization and all of its strategies, projects, and workers over the long haul. In other words, returning to the house metaphor, you cannot talk about getting the marble bathtub with waterjets on the second floor of the house until you are sure you can afford running water. Then you must establish plumbing and electrical systems, lay out adequate space, and consult with the family to ascertain its needs. Such is the nature of HIS and technology planning: The plans for the total organization must be laid out and collectively agreed upon before becoming super-specialized or esoteric and directed toward any one department or function. Such too early specialization often comes at a price—namely, the neglect of other areas that need automated systems to support their work as well. HIS planning must take a balanced, holistic approach so that the total effort and costs to build and maintain all the needed systems and technologies are understood and approved on a feasibility basis *before* the first projects are approved and under way. This is an HIS planning cardinal rule.

Other key facets of an HIS and technology plan are mapping out the data plan—that is, who needs to share data with whom among the various functions and departments within the organization, and who inside the organization needs to share data with which outside business and clinical partners and suppliers. The data interactions between departments and systems within a healthcare organization are often likened to a bowl of spaghetti, and rightly so. With so many interrelationships within the complex and multidisciplinary nature of healthcare processes and clinical workflow, sharing and communicating cross-divisionally are key. (There is more discussion of this topic elsewhere in the text.)

Balanced Application Portfolio

When thinking about the types of systems that a healthcare organization should have, remember the bottom-line principle: No essential part can be left out. If the household cannot fully function, the people living in the house will not be happy! When considering the various types of systems that must be implemented to support a healthcare organization, the agile HIS planning framework presented in this chapter provides a straightforward approach: Systems in all four quadrants must be considered and built into the plan as needed. Major categories of HIS include the following:

- *Clinical care*: Supports day-to-day activities involving patients, providers, ancillary support services, and families (Quadrant I).
- *Institutional business*: Supports day-to-day transactions for financial, billing, administrative, human resources, and supply and inventory functions (Quadrant II).
- *Clinical intelligence and quality*: Supports clinical analytics, reporting, and measurement of clinical outcomes and quality improvement (Quadrant III).
- *Business intelligence and management*: Supports business analytics, reporting, management controls, and measurement of budgetary and cost outcomes (Quadrant IV).
- *Infrastructure*: Includes the networks, technology, devices, interface engines, Internet- and web-based systems, and machine environment necessary to housing and supporting all four quadrants of application software systems and services supporting the organization's end users.

A balanced HIS and technology plan and portfolio address the needs of all these areas in a judicious, even-handed manner.

Staffing Plan

In addition to the systems and technology portfolio outlined previously, the HIS and technology plan must identify the IT staffing and talent needed to properly design, build, and support the wide variety of systems and myriad end users of those systems throughout the organization. Each of these systems and technologies requires information systems and technology professionals who possess the highly specialized expertise required for planning, building, implementing, and supporting these systems and end users. A common misconception is that software vendors or consultants can come into the organization and provide all the necessary services to design, build, and implement new systems for the organization. That is just not so. While these external players are a very important piece of the puzzle, there is no substitute for in-house experts in the areas of HIS and technology who know *both* the technology *and* the organization, including its people, culture, and processes. It is through these relationships between HIS experts and clinicians and business people of the organization that successful implementations and ongoing support of these systems and their end users take place.

Additional HIS and technology staffing includes people from various disciplines who are recruited to serve on HIS project teams, task forces (charged with accomplishing a single initiative or objective), and steering committees (charged with overall decision making for a major aspect of HIS and technology topics). Their time is essential for interdisciplinary collaboration on the teams and groups that work together to plan, select, design, develop, implement, and evaluate systems and technologies in the organization. The membership of these groups will vary based on the area each system addresses. For instance, a clinical system project, such as a project to select a new software system for the healthcare organization's laboratory, would require participation by individuals with recognized expertise in IT as well as laboratory disciplines such as pathology, blood bank, cytology, and laboratory management. It would also be important to have representation from functions that use the services of the laboratory, such as nursing, medicine, patient billing, inpatient and ambulatory clinical settings, and others. The time spent on these types of initiatives varies, but such efforts can consume a significant portion of a person's full-time-equivalent availability for a period of many months or even years on larger projects, such as projects for an EHR system or new financial systems for the organization. These experts' careers can ultimately shift completely to HIS implementation and support.

Sometimes the addition of HIS expertise and know-how to a healthcare professional's skills set opens up an exciting branch on that person's career path. Many people who have significant experience in various areas in health care (from any of the many clinical or administrative departments such as nursing or finance) truly enjoy the new challenges associated with implementing HIS and technology. Some people just seem to have an affinity for HIS and technology, even if they have worked in other areas for their entire career and have no formal HIS education. They may make the complete transition to specializing in HIS and technology for their functional area (e.g., laboratory systems) and embrace the professional development and stimulation associated with that growth.

Data Plan

In addition to the software, hardware, and technology associated with HIS and technology, an essential consideration in HIS and technology planning is data. It is critical to develop a data plan that becomes as active a part of managing HIS and technology as keeping the systems and devices up and running. After all, the many systems and expensive technology investments are all for naught if the data being created, stored, and transmitted throughout the organization for patient care and business purposes are inaccurate. A data plan establishes principles and policies by which data will be managed and stewarded by the organization as part of the implementation and use of its HIS and technology. It consists of these agreed-upon principles, such as identified, single sources sanctioned for each type of data (e.g., an EHR system for clinical data). Also needed are data standards, a data dictionary, and a data model/map, showing the relationship between the various data elements created and captured by all the systems on the HIS plan and in the organization's HIS portfolio.

Documenting and communicating the data plan makes everyone in the organization aware of and part of proper data stewardship, which is the careful and responsible management of something entrusted to one's care.[9] Data ownership is an important part of data stewardship; the responsibilities associated with the quality and consistency of the data elements emanating from a particular system are assigned to the individuals who use that system. For instance, the quality and consistency (collective data characteristics constituting what is thought of as "data integrity") of laboratory data are the responsibility of those managing and working in the laboratory, who use the system every day to do their work. If a problem arises with laboratory reports or laboratory billing claims, then, the laboratory professionals who "own" the responsibility for laboratory data (in other words, the individuals who are the data stewards for that area) are the ones who, with the assistance of the IT professionals who support the lab system, investigate the causes of the data integrity issues and assure the problem is corrected. This is the case whether the data integrity problem was due to technical issues, a faulty interface, user training needs, or another factor. Whatever steps are necessary to correct the issues and satisfy both the organization as a whole and those who rely on absolute accuracy of these life-essential laboratory data are treated as the number one priority until the problem is resolved. (This also involves going back into the system and correcting flawed data and double-checking everything that system touches to make sure there are no "collated" data errors.)

Let's describe these data-related terms briefly. (Refer to the *Data* chapter for further discussion of the uses and attributes of data.) **Data structures** are the methods and formats used to organize data in a computer, often described in terms of records, files, and arrays.[10] IT professionals such as programmers, interface analysts, systems analysts, database analysts, and systems engineers rely heavily on data structures to do their work. The ability to move a data element from one computer system to another, or combine like data elements from source systems with different data structures, relies on properly managing and programming the commands to accurately take these data structures into account.

The **data dictionary** is a directory or database that contains data about the data elements in the systems of an organization, also referred to as metadata ("data about data"). Maintaining the data dictionary is an important way that an organization's IT department does its part for data stewardship. Knowing which data elements exist in all the various systems, where the data elements are located in those systems' databases, what the data elements' structures are, and other key "data about data" is essential to being able to manage, combine, transmit, and accurately steward data in an organization. Otherwise, confusion and error prevail.

A **data model** is a map or visual representation showing the way data are organized according to their relationship to key elements of a process. In healthcare organizations, these key elements would include patients, providers, employees, and suppliers, among other. A data model is helpful in the systems engineering and programming processes to show the branches on the tree-like structure of the data layout.

Each of these data terms is key to proper data management and stewardship, which is one of the essential parts of an HIS and technology plan. Another key part is the practice of keeping all systems up-to-date in terms of the version of that system that is being used at any point in time. If allowed to lag behind vendor updates, the software and technology will not work properly, which can lead to major problems not only in that one system, but also in any other system with which that system interacts or shares data. Keeping HIS current is akin to what users of personal computers and word programs call "updates and version control," including the essential habit of making sure you stay current with software and apply updates to your personal computer and its applications when they become available. In personal computing, sometimes the new versions or updates work very well and add needed or desired functionality. At other times, however, they seem to add features that do not make sense or, worse yet, do not work correctly. In such a case, the vendor must then send out another update or "patch" to correct the problems introduced by the problematic update or version of the software program. It is no different with the large software systems that organizations rely on for clinical and business applications and processes—the only thing that changes is the scale!

Keeping up to date with vendor software versions and updates is part of good HIS and technology management and stewardship; this requires open communication and a good working relationship with the vendor. It is one of the ways that healthcare organizations rely on their suppliers of software, hardware, devices, and services related to HIS and technology, and one of the reasons why having high-quality providers of these products and services is so very important to successful HIS and technology efforts within healthcare organizations.

HIS AND TECHNOLOGY SUPPORT OF ORGANIZATIONAL GOALS

Figure 3.7 shows the foundational HIS planning framework populated with the types of processes and functions that the organization needs to support clinical transactions, administrative transactions, clinical intelligence and analytics, and business intelligence and analytics. When thinking about HIS and technology strategy, the key to making sure the investment in those plans takes the organization in the desired direction clinically, administratively, and strategically is to connect the types of systems with their ability to support organizational goals. Consider the following examples of organizational goals common to healthcare organizations and types of systems that would support those goals.

The organizational goal of enhanced patient care processes can be supported through the implementation of a master patient/person index (MPI), or unique patient identifier, for identifying positively and pulling together data for a patient from multiple disparate systems such as hospitals, physician practices, clinics, and other points across the continuum of care, or even from multiple silo systems within the same organization. Another system that supports the goal of patient care would be the clinical data repository for combining the data together from these disparate systems and ensuring secure access by clinicians from those organizations, creating a more patient-centric view of the clinical processes involved in caring for them. Another HIS and technology capability that can support the goal of improved patient care in this scenario is an integrated, high-speed network infrastructure, providing a robust electronic highway to carry the data across divisional and organizational lines to accomplish the implementation of the first two systems. Another system capability that could support this goal of improved patient-centric care processes is the implementation of inpatient and outpatient connectivity and integration, connecting between the often distant worlds of inpatient and outpatient care processes. These HIS and technology initiatives would be identified in Quadrant I of the generic HIS planning framework,

and a proper network infrastructure would be necessary to support all of these systems.

Next, we turn to the goal of improving the quality of patient care processes within the organization. HIS and technology initiatives that would support this goal would include additional Quadrant I systems, associated with day-to-day clinical transactions such as the EHR, making data available to caregivers in a patient-centric format electronically and securely. Computerized physician or provider order entry (CPOE) is another type of system capability that can be used to improve patient care by reducing errors in data transmission and avoiding the process of manually transcribing handwritten doctor's orders, which has been shown to be associated with errors.[11]

Another type of system that can be identified for the HIS and technology plan is a quality measurement database and software system. Such **quality management systems** reside in Quadrant II and combine data from several different systems (such as EHR, laboratory, and patient accounting systems). They give the organization a platform for developing and tracking desired quality metrics by which it will measure its performance. The organization thus creates the ability to set and achieve quantifiable objectives for quality improvement, as well as to report evidence of data-driven performance to those involved in these initiatives. This type of quality management system draws data from all corners of the organization and allows the organization to move from silo-based views of quality improvement efforts to organization-wide quality initiatives with broad participation from all those involved in the many steps inherent in patient care processes.

A final example of an HIS that can be planned to support the organization's goal of improving the quality of patient care is "closed-loop medication administration." Such a system automates, documents, and tracks the processes and steps taken to order medications, transmit those orders to the pharmacy, dispense and transport the medicine to the correct patient, verify and record the correct administration of the medication to the patient in the nursing documentation, and tie that documentation back to the original order in the EHR. Closing this loop is viewed as a key method for reducing medication errors by allowing clinicians to check whether the order for a medication is correct and by ensuring that the medication administration process takes place in a timely, safe fashion, thereby contributing to the overarching goal of improving patient care quality.

Obviously, many more steps can be taken to improve patient care quality. These examples are intended to show how systems and technology can be intentionally planned to push the organization in the direction of its stated goal of improving patient care quality. In this fashion, the relationship between HIS and organizational goals can be established and built right into the HIS plans.

HIS and technology plans can also be aligned with goals geared toward increasing the financial strength and administrative capacity of the organization. Some examples of these types of administrative systems that populate Quadrants II and IV of the generic HIS planning framework follow. An integrated **enterprise resource planning (ERP)** system can enhance efficiencies and effective stewardship of finances, human resources, and materials management in support of the organization's goal of increasing its financial strength and capacity. An integrated ERP system would probably replace a number of silos systems supporting these areas of finance, human resources, and materials management and thereby improve the organization's ability to pull together administrative and financial information across these departmental disciplines. Ideally, this would result in an improved ability to manage and control the organization's finances, personnel, and supplies.

Another example of an HIS that can support the goal of enhanced organizational revenue would be an upgrade to the patient accounting system. Increasing functionality, streamlining billing and collections, and focusing on specific objectives for improvement within the patient financial services department can all contribute to improved service and revenues.

The addition of a cost accounting system to the HIS and technology plan could contribute to two goals: enhancing the financial strength of the organization and improving its revenue stream. A cost accounting capability would challenge the organization to calculate the actual costs of care versus the allowed reimbursement and reveal opportunities for trimming unnecessary costs or improving the efficiency of processes.

HIS could also be planned to enable automated charge capture. In other words, clinical systems might be introduced that can automatically capture and send data about chargeable items to the patient billing system, thereby reducing the need for manual entry of billable charges. Such systems would significantly improve and support the organization's ability to capture charges and improve revenues. Business intelligence systems (Quadrant IV) could also be added to the HIS plan to support the retrospective analysis of financial and administrative information, enabling the organization to find opportunities to meet its goals pertaining to financial strength and revenue enhancement.

Goals pertaining to the clinical improvements, research, and education can be supported with HIS and technology as well. The HIS and technology plan can include systems such as patient data registries for logging immunizations and occurrences of cancer, diabetes, and other chronic diseases, allowing researchers to gather data over time about the progression and incidence of these conditions. Systems to enable the inclusion of personalized genetics data in other analyses can be included in the HIS plan. In some cases, genetics data might eventually be added to an existing clinical database, such as an EHR.

The list of system opportunities to support organizational goals could go on and on. The point here is simply to show the importance of documenting the systems in the HIS plan in connection to a goal of the organization. The means by which each system's capability is added to the overall HIS portfolio is a matter of detailed planning that will take place in subsequent steps of the HIS planning process. The organization may pursue a goal to identify more patients for clinical trials and enhance its research capacity, for example; the HIS plan, in turn, can identify and pursue systems capabilities such as a clinical trials website and database, and research support systems to provide HIS assistance for these goals.

HIS AND TECHNOLOGY STRATEGY AND PLANS: FOLLOW-UP WITH TACTICAL DETAILS

Once the HIS and technology strategy is documented, based on the supporting and enabling goals of the organization, the detailed planning process commences, leading to systems specifications, requirements definition, systems selection, procurement, and implementations. Often participants in organizational planning processes and HIS and technology projects want to jump ahead to system selection or procurement prior to the thoughtful planning process that carefully connects HIS and technology decisions to the goals of the organization. *This is a mistake.* Ben Franklin said, "If you fail to plan, you are planning to fail." This warning certainly applies to HIS and technology. If the care and discipline of planning are neglected, the immense investments in HIS and technology that follow likely will not help the organization in the strategic and goals-based ways that are intended. Conversely, if the HIS and technology plans are aligned with the strategic goals of the organization, the tactical HIS plans and implementations that follow will have a synergistic and potentially profound positive effect on the progress of the organization toward its goals and desired future state for many years to come. This latter scenario is how the true return on investment in systems is accomplished.

The work to be done between the planning phase and the achievement of those desired outcomes is long and hard, but the effort is well worth it if done carefully and correctly. Once the HIS and technology *strategic* plans are in place, HIS and technology *tactical* plans are developed in great detail. A good deal of preparation then occurs before those tactical plans can be carried out. Capital and operating budgets for each project must be established. Project teams and specialized task forces for the HIS and technology initiatives are formed. These teams consist of IT staff, clinical and administrative knowledge workers, and often external resources such as vendor experts and consultants who have familiarity not only with the computer systems but also with the functional areas of the organization being automated. Under the leadership of an experienced IT project manager, each group creates a detailed tactical plan for each new system to be implemented. This tactical plan documents requirements for the new system, analyzes current workflows, and designs new workflows and processes intended to streamline how work is performed. Ways of caring for patients or conducting administrative functions are analyzed, identifying strengths, weaknesses, opportunities, and threats vis-à-vis current methods (SWOT analysis). New paths that streamline clinical and administrative workflows are designed and documented as part of the requirements for the new systems. Many ideas for improvement will be readily available from those employees who have been working in those areas and are painfully aware of areas of inefficiency, ineffectiveness, or risk. They are usually eager to participate in the design and implementation of a new computer system intended to improve those areas of weakness or inefficiency and often become the project's greatest supporters and assets.

Once the requirements for a new system are developed, a business plan including budgetary requirements is prepared for the new project's preliminary approval and committee presentations take place. Only when the project is approved internally does it move forward through the detailed, tactical planning phase, and interaction with the outside providers of these systems and technologies—and then only under very controlled circumstances. These activities lay the groundwork for the future decision about which vendor and system will carry the organization into the future.

All of this work is guided by interdisciplinary steering committees that oversee HIS and technology project efforts, help with staffing decisions about internal and external project resources, and provide communication and budgetary support. Once plans for the HIS initiatives coalesce and gain momentum, they motivate the organization to coordinate capabilities, expertise, points of innovation, and energies to begin the process of change through the implementation of new systems. Changes start to occur not only through the acquisition of new systems, but also in the ways people think

and envision doing their work—and the culture and mindset of the organization are never the same again. The transformation into the digital age has begun at this point, despite the fact that no new system has been selected as yet. What *has* changed are people's expectations of how they will do their work and care for patients: A new vision begins to take hold among those who work in and care deeply about the organization, the quality of care delivered in the institution, and the role it plays in serving the needs of the community now and well into the future.

ISSUES OF CHANGE AND THE NEED FOR GOVERNANCE

In addition to HIS strategic planning, HIS governance and decision making must be taken very seriously and properly managed—a feat requiring a whole new level of discipline and self-control in the organization. HIS and technology planning and implementation are expensive, time-consuming, and mission-critical processes through which the organization seeks to achieve its long-term vision and strategies. They are also highly disruptive. For reasons and in ways that are never fully clear or predictable, when ideas about changes in how people work start to occur and gain momentum, it can be a trying time in even the most forward-thinking organizations. This shift in expectations creates stress in the organization, and there will always be some who react negatively to proposed changes.

Even when the majority of the group agrees that new systems are needed and there is growing enthusiasm around a new vision for the future, many choices exist in how to approach this process. Tough decisions must be made and priorities set throughout the implementation of the countless changes that a strategic HIS and technology plan suggests and implementations require. In turn, the organization must prepare itself for structured guidance through all these decisions. **HIS Governance**—the process of thoughtful, balanced decision making for these projects and arbitration of issues that arise during the processes of change—is essential to success. Without effective and timely decisions on issues that arise during the course of these projects—decisions that have significant impact clinically, financially, and operationally—the strategic goals that the HIS plan envisions and supports may never be realized. Thus disciplined, active HIS governance is a crucial part of successful implementation of the HIS and technology plan.

HIS governance focuses on (1) the stewardship of organizational and HIS resources on behalf of the stakeholders who expect a return on their investment and (2) protection of the organization from excessive risk. Governance is conducted at the highest levels of decision making in the organization: at the board level for major expenditures and strategic changes, and at senior management and clinical leadership levels for establishing priorities, selecting software systems, resolving conflicts, communicating throughout the organization, and overseeing significant modifications to the ways that administrative and clinical work is conducted. In the case of the board of trustees or directors, "A board needs to understand the overall architecture of its company's IT application portfolio. . . . The board must ensure that management knows what information resources are out there, what condition they are in, and what role they play in generating revenue."[12] The governance structure must also specify *decision rights* and outline the accountabilities to establish the guideposts needed to boost forward progress and appropriate performance in the use of IT.[13] In addition, governance encompasses the decision mechanisms throughout the organization needed to weigh in and oversee the many decisions that need to be made throughout an HIS and technology project. HIS governance includes the leadership and organizational structures and processes to make sure the organization's HIS and technology plans and projects sustain and extend the organization's strategies and objectives.[14]

Thus HIS governance occurs at the board level *and* within organizational executive management and committee structures. It includes internal capital allocation and project prioritization committees. It is highly interdisciplinary, because HIS and technology touch every corner of the organization. No detail is too small to overlook in this type of work. The interdisciplinary aspect of governance is important because the education, decision making, and orientation about which types of changes are about to commence need to be embedded in the minds and skills sets of those people who are charged with managing the organization on an ongoing basis. This is not to say that additional expertise should not be brought in to assist in that process. Ultimately, however, this change is not just about computer systems: It includes how the organization does its work and delivers its services, and those are the responsibilities of the core leadership, management, and clinical personnel of the organization.

Effective governance, then, serves four purposes:

- Provides assurance that the HIS and technology plans align with the strategic goals of the organization
- Protects the organization from taking on too much risk with the HIS and technology projects
- Ensures adequate personnel resources and skills sets are available to these disruptive initiatives
- Ensures itself that the job is getting done properly and in a timely fashion[15]

In addition to the board of trustees (in not-for-profit organizations) or board of directors (in for-profit organizations), an essential governance group is an interdisciplinary and enterprise-wide HIS and technology steering group. This committee consists of leaders from management, medical staff, nursing, finance, human resources, strategy and marketing, ancillary clinical departments, facilities, and other disciplines. It is typically chaired by the chief information officer (CIO) of the organization (or whatever the lead IT position in the organization is called, such as IT Director or Manager of HIS). The purpose of this committee is to develop and oversee adherence to guiding HIS principles and to steer or make key interdisciplinary decisions that the project requires. These guiding principles are essential—they are the overarching ideas that, when push comes to shove, will help the group discern and find its way through difficult decisions and debates on a timely basis. Although these decisions often seem unresolvable, the organization must deal with them if the project is to move forward.

One important principle that will guide the organization through numerous tough spots is the recognition that integrated systems are superior to interfacing disparate applications. At this point in our society's automation evolution, many healthcare organizations are facing a thorny problem: They are chock full of disparate systems and silos of information that must be integrated to streamline processes and improve efficiency and effectiveness. In such a case, the principle of integration is paramount to guide systems decisions and rethink processes.

The other purview of the HIS steering group is establishing and upholding HIS policies in areas of data security, privacy, and confidentiality of information; acquisition of hardware, software, infrastructure, and devices; use of the Internet; and other key aspects of HIS and technology plans, decisions, and implementations. Standards must be established as well for software and hardware platforms, infrastructure, and data.

Perhaps the most important and difficult role of the steering committee is, once those standards are established, enforcing adherence to them. The HIS steering group must establish and exert the discipline needed to manage the organization's information systems and technology in accordance with integration versus interfacing, internal controls, and organizational integrity, all in a fashion that advances the organization toward its strategies. This work always goes against the grain of progress's primary enemy: inertia.[16]

SUMMARY

HIS and technology strategy and governance are both essential to achieving stable, successful HIS and technology that support and enable the organization in achieving its mission and vision. HIS planning and governance are highly disciplined processes that involve representatives of all major functional units of the organization. Both rely on the leadership of the CIO and senior management, including the CEO and the board of directors, as well as the leadership and collaboration of medical staff, nursing, and other clinical disciplines. The work of strategy and governance must be collaborative, cooperative, and rooted in a willingness to uphold HIS planning principles on an equitable basis to properly steward the systems, data, and information resources of the organization. It is only when HIS and technology efforts are well planned, governed, and implemented *within* organizations that a *national* HIS and technology strategy can hope to succeed *between* and *among* organizations.

External drivers such as government initiatives (e.g., the HITECH Act and meaningful use criteria), consumer expectations and engagement, and general societal progress are exerting considerable pressure on healthcare organizations to develop and implement advanced HIS and technology plans that will advance the strategic position and digital capabilities of those organizations. Once HIS strategies are in place, they can be broken down into a rolling set of strategic initiatives that are executable as manageable projects. No more than five of these strategic initiatives should be under way at any one time. These initiatives give rise to process redesign, systems projects and implementations, specific detailed requirements of functionality to support new electronic capabilities connections and roles, integration, and HIS-supported processes. From these efforts, data are created and captured and the organization begins to pull itself into a world of improved processes and knowledge. Let the change begin!

KEY TERMS

Accountable care
    organization (ACO) 42
Business intelligence 38
Clinical intelligence 44
Data dictionary 49
Data model 49
Data structures 49

"Dematerialized" information 41
Enterprise resource
    planning (ERP) 51
Hardware 35
HIS architecture 35
HIS governance 52
HIS planning 34

HIS strategy 31
Infrastructure 47
Knowledge worker 35
Quality management system 50
Software 35

Discussion Questions

1. What is the difference between strategic planning and tactical planning?

2. Why is it important to HIS and technology planning for a healthcare organization to have developed its strategic business plan? If the organization or business does not have a strategic business plan, what should HIS planners do?

3. What do the four quadrants of the conceptual HIS planning framework presented in this chapter represent? Why are the quadrants organized as they are, and what does it mean to have a balanced HIS architecture?

4. In which ways do the basic principles of architecture, such as those applied when building a house, apply to HIS architectures and planning?

5. Identify the key HIS and technology elements that need to be contemplated as part of HIS and technology planning.

6. What is the purpose of HIS and technology governance? What are the key groups responsible for HIS and technology governance in healthcare organizations and who comprises their ranks?

REFERENCES

1. Social media data could boost population health research, study finds. (2013, April 26). *iHealthBeat*. http://www.ihealthbeat.org/articles/2013/4/26/social-media-data-could-boost-population-health-research-study-finds

2. Glandon, G. L., Smaltz, D. H, & Slovensky, D. J. (2010). *Austin and Boxerman's information systems for healthcare management* (7th ed.). Chicago, IL: Health Administration Press.

3. Bradburn, A., & Coakes, B. (n.d.) Intangible assets and social, intellectual and cultural capital: Origins, functions and value. http://www2.warwick.ac.uk/fac/soc/wbs/conf/olkc/archive/oklc5/papers/k-2_bradburn.pdf

4. Leibold, M., Probst, G. J. B., & Gibbert, M. (2005). *Strategic management in the knowledge economy*. Publicus. http://www.amazon.com/Strategic-Management-Knowledge-Economy-Leibold/dp/3895782572/ref=sr_1_1?s=books&ie=UTF8&qid=1373434513&sr=1-1&keywords=Leibold%2C+Probst%2C+Gibbert%2C+2002

5. Normann, R. (2001). *Reframing business: When the map changes the landscape*. West Sussex, UK: John Wiley & Sons.

6. Nguyen, T., & Jhaveri, V. Physician compensation models and metrics under population-based reimbursement. (2013). http://www.healthleadersmedia.com/content/HOM-293313/Webcast-Physician-Compensation-Models-and-Metrics-Under-PopulationBased-Reimbursement##

7. Wu, S. J., & Raghupathi, W. (2012). A panel analysis of the strategic association between information and communication technology and public health delivery. *Journal of Medical Research*.. http://www.jmir.org/2012/5/e147/

8. Group health's participation in a shared decision-making demonstration yielded lesson, such as role of culture change. (2013). *Health Affairs, 32*, 2294–2302. http://content.healthaffairs.org/content/32/2/294.full?ijkey=zedtXaeCmz9ns&keytype=ref&siteid=healthaff

9. *Merriam Webster Dictionary*. (n.d.). www.merriam-webster.com/dictionary/stewardship

10. *Merriam Webster Dictionary*. (n.d.). www.merriam-webster.com/distionary/datastructure.

11. Agrawal, A. (2009, June). CPOE improves patient care by reducing medical errors. *British Journal of Clinical Pharmacology, 67*(6), 681–686. http://www.ncbi.nlm.nih.gov/pmc/articles/PMC2723209/

12. Nolan, R., & McFarlan, F. W. (2005). Information technology and the board of directors. *Harvard Business Review*. http://hbr.org/2005/10/information-technology-and-the-board-of-directors/ar/1

13. Weill, P., & Ross, J. (2004). *IT governance: How top performers manage IT for superior results*. Boston, MA: Harvard Business School Press.

14. IT Governance Institute. (2003). *Board briefing on IT governance* (2nd ed.). http://www.itgi.org/Template_ITGIc9a4.html?Section=About

15. Smaltz, D. H., Carpenter, R., & Saltz, J. (2007). Effective IT governance in healthcare organisations: A tale of two organisations. *International Journal of Healthcare Technology and Management, 8*(1/2), 20–41. http://www.inderscience.com/info/inarticle.php?artid=12106

16. Kouzes, J. M., & Posner, B. Z. (2007). *The leadership challenge* (4th ed.). San Francisco, CA: Jossey-Bass. http://www.nclp.umd.edu/resources/bookreviews/BookReview-The%20_Leadership_Challenge-Truesdell-2011.pdf

CHAPTER 4

HIS Application Systems and Technology

INTRODUCTION

In this chapter, we examine the applications and technology requirements needed to support the health information systems (HIS) and technology environment. There is little

doubt that healthcare delivery is complex and that HIS can deliver considerable value in improving the quality of care and reducing the costs of care. However, the technology being used to support HIS has been viewed as complicated and, in many instances, well beyond the understanding of nontechnical individuals. As sophisticated as HIS applications and technology may appear to be, when they are examined at their more fundamental levels, HIS can be readily understood.

Understanding how HIS applications are developed is essential to ensuring they produce the desired functionality. In this chapter, we review one of the primary HIS application development methods in use today—the software development life cycle. We also look at the relationships between HIS programming languages, applications, and databases. The benefits of application integration over application interfaces are also reviewed. To clearly understand HIS, we discuss the clinical and administrative HIS applications being used by healthcare organizations today.

HIS applications require a robust, high-performing, and highly available underlying technical infrastructure. Unless this technology is deployed correctly, HIS users will not be able to access their systems to perform their work—the HIS applications will perform slowly, be inaccessible, or experience data corruption. In this chapter, we examine how computer networks work, consider their importance in supporting HIS applications, and outline the different network architectures in use today. We review emerging technologies that are affecting HIS applications, such as Voice over Internet Protocol, unified communications, and video/web conferencing. Data center infrastructure, cloud computing, backups, and disaster recovery—all aspects that are critical to properly maintain HIS applications—are discussed as well. The essential components of modern server computing, including unified computing systems, server virtualization, and single sign-on, are analyzed, along with other key client, device, and mobile technologies. Finally, this chapter highlights the importance of technologies that deliver privacy and security benefits to HIS applications.

HIS APPLICATIONS

An important concept to understand is that all HIS applications are developed using a programming language, which allows them to operate by executing programming code. Data can be created or modified by programs based on input received from end-user input devices or other software programs and are stored in computer-based files. Large instances of data are normally stored in a database, which offers distinct advantages over other file types, such as documents, spreadsheets, and various forms of graphic and multimedia files. Some of these benefits include support for very large file sizes, the ability of multiple users to edit data at the same time, advanced data recoverability security, and data normalization (i.e., organizing and distilling data). While responsibilities for process redesign and implementation depend on resources within organizations, in healthcare environments, the technical work of developing and maintaining application programming is most often delegated to the vendors who own the application product or to consultants who focus specifically on application programming. Relying on the software vendor to manage software application development, upgrades, and customization allows healthcare organizations to focus on their core business objective of delivering quality health care.

Traditionally, healthcare organizations have purchased licenses for many of these vendor applications, or **commercial off-the-shelf (COTS)** products, causing healthcare data centers to be filled with many "best of breed" applications. Although best-of-breed applications provide healthcare organizations with advanced application functionality for specific service lines or departments, they are generally not developed to integrate or interoperate with other applications. Today, application integration is one way to eliminate application and data silos, and to help organizations achieve efficiencies and healthcare reform criteria. For those healthcare environments large enough to require their own customized application development, programmers are typically added to the internal information technology (IT) department to build customized applications that are specific to their organizations. Web services, Microsoft's .NET, and Sun's

Java development platform are three prevalent programming languages in use at many health systems today.

Regardless of the programming platform used to develop application programs, one of the standard development frameworks in use today is the **software development life cycle (SDLC)** methodology. When applied to the development of HIS applications, the SDLC process is designed to ensure end-state solutions meet user requirements in support of the healthcare organization's strategic goals and objectives. The SDLC methodology includes seven stages (**Figure 4.1**)[1]:

1. *Conceptual Planning.* This phase involves the identification and assessment of the system requirements and enhancements, feasibility, costs, and risks.
2. *Planning and Requirements Definition.* This phase involves identifying functional, support, and training requirements, as well as developing the initial life-cycle management plans, the project plans, and other operations requirements.
3. *Design.* This phase comprises developing the preliminary and detailed designs, including how the system will meet functional requirements.
4. *Development and Testing.* This phase includes the system development, testing, and validation activities, which are designed to ensure the system works as expected and that the project sponsor's (i.e., customer's) requirements are satisfied.
5. *Implementation.* In this phase, the system is installed in the production environment, the training of users is completed, data conversions and system issues are resolved, and the newly designed system is turned over to the project sponsor.
6. *Operations and Maintenance.* During this phase, the new or upgraded system is operationalized, with routine maintenance, upgrades, feature enhancements, and bug fixes completed.
7. *Disposition.* This phase represents the end of the system's life cycle, when the system is scheduled to be decommissioned and retired. The emphasis of this phase is to ensure that the system is disposed of in accordance with proper procedures.

HIS applications are software programs of similar functionality that are used to support and facilitate work in a given area within a healthcare setting. HIS applications have historically been developed according to the healthcare organization's functional departments, divisional areas, or service lines, as opposed to being developed for the organization as a whole. Some of these applications include laboratory systems, nursing systems, patient billing and accounting

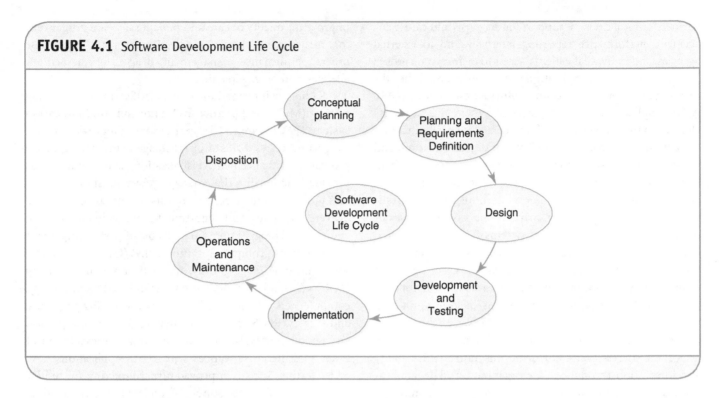

FIGURE 4.1 Software Development Life Cycle

systems, payroll and time and attendance systems, and human resources information systems. As a result, most of the early HIS applications were specific to the functional unit for which they were developed, causing the proliferation of many non-integrated systems operating within the same organization.

The development of application **interfaces** was the initial attempt to bridge these various systems in hopes that common data sets could be leveraged by multiple departments and functional areas. However, maintaining interfaces—essentially data-translation programs—between disparate applications proved to be expensive, time consuming, and inefficient. System developers soon found that application **integration**, the process that brings data or functions from different application programs together at the point when the applications themselves are first being developed so that they share common data elements and use a common data base, is much more efficient. Essentially, integration avoids building applications in silos, which in turn eliminates the need to build and maintain interfaces on a regular basis after the initial development. Application programs that are integrated use data from the same shared data repository, whereas application programs that are interfaced exchange and maintain data repositories between separate databases for each application using one- or two-way data transfers. Middleware is a type of software that is designed to provide application integration by interfacing between two existing

application programs that are already fully developed and in use.

Clinical Applications

One of the most important types of applications in healthcare organizations is clinical applications. A clinical application can be defined as any system that supports clinical care (e.g., electronic health record systems), ancillary clinical support processes (e.g., laboratory testing, radiology), clinicians (e.g., computerized physician order entry, clinical decision support), and patient flow (e.g., registration, scheduling). Clinical applications are designed to improve the quality of care; increase efficiency; provide better patient services; reduce medical record transportation costs; and improve a number of processes, including workflow, patient communications, accuracy for coding evaluation and management, drug refill capabilities, charge capture, and claims submissions.

An electronic health record (EHR) application is an example of a clinical application that supports clinical care. EHR applications enhance communication and enable the computerized documentation of patient care activities and health services from myriad settings. Key functions supported by EHR applications include electronic capture of data for subsequent storage in a data repository, real-time order entry and results reporting, administrative processes linked with clinical activities, **electronic data interchange (EDI)** with agencies and partners, clinical decision support for diagnosis and care management, performance reporting internally and to external agencies, and individual patients' access to their own records.[2,3]

Another clinical application commonly found in healthcare organizations is a **clinical information system (CIS)**. A CIS application is a computerized system that supports clinical diagnosis, treatment planning, and medical outcomes evaluations. This computerized system organizes, stores, and double-checks all of a patient's medical information. Such an application keeps health history, prescriptions, doctor's notes and dictation, and all other information together electronically, and replaces the paper charts of the past. Examples of departmental and service lines systems that are considered CIS applications include quality management, laboratory testing, radiology, endoscopy, nursing, surgery, operating room, and pharmacy. Nursing and physician documentation are also CIS applications. CIS systems include embedded clinical guidelines and treatment protocols, establish rules and alerts, and provide evidence-based treatment plans. An important success factor for achieving future CIS viability and integration throughout the organization's HIS applications is the need for enterprise-wide strategic HIS planning.

A laboratory information system (LIS) is a CIS application that supports chemistry, pathology, blood bank, instrumentation, calculations, calibrations, and results management areas within clinical settings. Core functions of a lab system include test requisition processing, scheduling and cataloging specimen collection, and test processing; delivering results of completed tests that have been verified and recorded, and results reporting directly into patient records; identifying abnormal results and alerts; providing statistical reports for lab management and patient summary reports; performing quality control and charge capture functions; and supporting lab operations management.

A pharmacy information system (PIS) is a complex CIS application that is tightly integrated with clinical care, particularly with nursing personnel and workflows. Because medication errors are always a concern with pharmacy systems, integration to ensure the proper delivery of care is a high priority. Workflow redesign is especially important when implementing medication administration management processes; pharmacy system automation requires a different approach than automation of paper-based processes. It is critical that pharmacy applications are tightly integrated with nursing **medication administration records (MARs)** and other order processes such as computerized physician order entry (CPOE) to ensure patient safety. Additional areas that pharmacy systems automate as part of their effort to

improve the quality of care and patient safety are drug inventory management, charges, medication error tracking, profile orders, performance management, drug–drug interactions, allergies, and other screenings.

Radiology information systems (RISs), medical imaging systems (MISs), and **picture archiving and communication systems (PACSs)** are all CIS applications that provide clinical support processes. MISs support image management, image processing, enhancement, visualization, and storage. RISs provide functionality that manages test requisitions, schedules procedures, manages test results, identifies charges, and delivers patient test and department management reports. In addition, radiology systems are capable of performing image enhancements, computed tomography (CT) scans, ultrasound imaging, angiography, magnetic resonance imaging (MRI) scans, nuclear medicine functions, radiation therapy, computerized patient-specific treatment planning programs, and surgery. PACS applications manage image storage, local and remote retrievals, and distribution and presentation of PACS files. Recent advances with PACS applications have added features such as improved turnaround time for results, elimination of film loss, support for teleradiology, and reduction of physical space requirements for storage.

Outpatient systems are CIS applications designed to assist in the delivery of care for patients who are hospitalized for less than 24 hours. These ambulatory care systems are CIS applications that assist caregivers in performing consultations, treatments, or interventions in an outpatient setting, such as a medical clinic. Examples of the types of procedures that are performed in this environment include minor surgical and medical procedures, dental services, dermatology services, and diagnostic procedures such as blood tests and X-rays. Ambulatory care settings have needs similar to those served by inpatient clinical and business applications, but slightly different priorities. Two important areas of emphasis in ambulatory care settings are financial and administrative systems—which include billing, eligibility determinations and authorizations, claims processing, general financial, human resources, and materials management applications—and clinical systems—which support scheduling, appointment reminders, EHRs and **personal health records (PHRs)**, transcription, prescription management, disease management, and patient communications.

Long-term care (LTC) systems are CIS applications designed to aid in the delivery of care for patients who are older than age 65 or who have a chronic or disabling condition that needs constant supervision. LTC facilities can provide nursing home care, home health care, and personal or adult day care for individuals. LTC systems include clinical, financial, and administrative management functionality that is designed to address the unique requirements of the LTC environment. Adoption of CIS applications in LTC settings has been slow to date, but transitioning to computerized systems in these environments has been shown to improve care delivery. Two special challenges are encountered in LTC environments: (1) They are not tightly integrated with health systems and (2) physicians are not routinely present at LTC facilities.

CPOE systems are CIS applications that directly support clinician workflow requirements. CPOE comprises the electronic entry of medical practitioner instructions, referred to as "orders," for the treatment of patients under that practitioner's care. Typically, these orders are communicated within and through an EHR application to departments such as pharmacy, laboratory testing, or radiology, where they will then be filled. CPOE applications have the benefit of decreasing delays in order completion, reducing errors related to handwriting translation or transcription, allowing order entry at the point of care or off-site, enabling error checking for incorrect or duplicate doses or tests, and streamlining the posting of charges and inventory management.

CIS applications have many benefits for both healthcare organizations and patients. These advantages include reduction of staffing requirements over the long term, attaining eligibility for pay-for-performance payments, recruiting and retaining physicians, enhancing the legibility of clinical documentation notes, reducing spelling errors within CIS applications, improving access to medical charts, reducing costs associated with transcription and facilities used for storing paper, and improved recovery of medical data following a disaster. Additional benefits include allowing multiple clinicians to simultaneously access medical charts, having lab and X-ray results returned automatically, checking for drug–drug and drug–allergy interactions, integrating physician dispensing software, and improving patient safety. **Figure 4.2** summarizes the key CIS applications that healthcare organizations are seeking to deploy in their efforts to achieve technology adoption and meaningful use of EHRs.[4]

Administrative Applications

Historically, health care has lagged behind other industries in the development of robust administrative and financial systems. Healthcare reform has brought increased pressure on healthcare organizations to take a more strategic approach to managing these systems. In response, healthcare providers and payers are now deploying systems that integrate administrative and financial systems. These include EHRs, along with enterprise resources planning (ERP) systems, **customer resource management (CRM)** systems, and **supply chain management (SCM)** systems. Patient accounting is an administrative application that manages billing and accounts receivable, and is often integrated into a health provider EHR application. ERP systems are bundled applications that manage a healthcare organization's financial and accounting

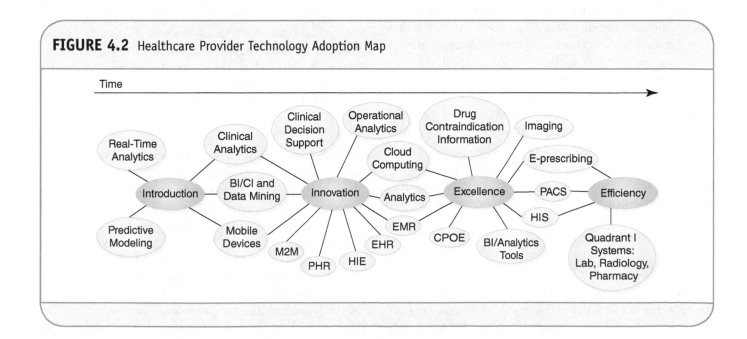

FIGURE 4.2 Healthcare Provider Technology Adoption Map

applications. They can include general ledger, accounts payable, material management, human resources management, and facilities management applications, which have been traditionally installed at healthcare organizations as separate or "point" solutions (silos).

In the Robert Wood Johnson Foundation's annual report, *Health Information Technology in the United States: Better Information Systems for Better Care* (2013), 44% of hospitals reported having a basic EHR system as of 2012.[5] This was a 17% increase from 2011, demonstrating that hospitals, physicians, and other providers have made significant strides in the adoption of health information technology and the integration of healthcare data. Physicians were reported to have also made substantial progress, with 38.2% having adopted basic EHR functionalities by 2012. Despite these advances, many organizations have not taken steps to achieve an integrated ERP solution and, therefore, may face challenges in generating comprehensive reports due to the existence of data silos and data integrity issues.

Home health care is an evolving method of care delivery that is increasingly using administrative applications of HIS. With the advent of healthcare reform and technology advances, including mobile devices that are being used by nurses in the field, delivery of care outside of traditional hospitals and clinics is becoming more feasible and widespread. With a laptop computer and broadband card, a nurse can make home visits, enter updates into his or her laptop, and automatically update central medical office systems. Home healthcare organizations require the same types of administrative, financial management, and clinical applications as other healthcare organizations. The only difference is that home health HIS applications need to be customized to meet the unique requirements found in the home health environment. This functionality includes monitoring patients for specific conditions, developing treatment plans, identifying measures that can be taken and communicated to the home health site, and communicating with caregivers in homes between visits using mobile technology. Home health care is a highly regulated arena of healthcare delivery, so automation saves caregivers the time associated with filling out the many required forms by hand, leaving more opportunity for caregiver–patient interaction, an outcome that is satisfactory for caregivers and patients alike.

TECHNOLOGY

Essential to the success of an HIS deployment is first ensuring that the basic building blocks of data communication are architected and maintained properly. Many HIS implementations risk failure or high user dissatisfaction if the infrastructure supporting the transfer of voice and data is outdated, unstable, or not managed efficiently. Two related important areas that we will cover are telecommunications and networking. Each of these technology areas is one of the most complex topics in the computer-related field.

Telecommunications and Networking

Telecommunications is defined as the electrical transmission of data among systems, whether through analog, digital, or wireless media. Data transmissions can occur across a variety of media types, such as copper wires, coaxial cable, fiber, or airwaves. Both large and small healthcare organizations today utilize these data transmission types and mediums. Data communication networks consist of three basic hardware components: servers, clients, and circuits. A **server** is a host computer that stores data or software and is accessed by clients. While a server resides at one end of a communication circuit, a **client** is the input/output hardware device at the user's end of a communication circuit. A client typically provides end users with access to the network and a server. A **circuit** is the pathway by which messages between servers and/or clients travel. Copper wire, fiberoptic cable, and wireless transmissions are three of the most common circuit types deployed today, with switches, routers, and gateways being three of the many devices used to enable circuits to transmit information.

An example of these three components in a healthcare setting can be seen with an LIS. The LIS servers hosting the data and providing the application processing will be located in the organization's data center. The doctors and nurses who need to access the LIS information will use their client computers—usually a personal computer (PC) or mobile device. The hospital or clinic's wireless or wired network, along with the Internet, can be considered the circuit that is used to transfer data between the client and the server.

Types of Networks

Networks are commonly categorized into four different types: **local area networks (LANs)**, backbone networks (BNs), metropolitan area networks (MANs), and **wide area networks (WANs)**. LANs are groups of devices located within the same geographical area, such as one or more floors within a building, or multiple buildings in close proximity to each other. BNs are designed to connect LANs, WANs, and other BNs at high data transfer speeds and typically span several miles. MANs connect LANs, BNs, and WANs that are usually located within 3 to 30 miles of each other, and are often referred to as campus networks. WANs connect BNs and MANs and can connect devices that are located around the world. Whereas healthcare organizations can create and maintain their own LAN, BN, and MAN infrastructure, commercial carriers are the primary providers of WAN infrastructure, which consists of fiber-optic cable, switching equipment, and microwave towers or satellite equipment. LANs, BNs, MANs, and WANs support data transmission speeds of up to 10 gigabits per second (Gbps) between each other, with higher speeds currently being developed. Data transfer rates via devices connected to LANs can range from 10 megabits per second (Mbps) or 10 million bits per second to 1 Gbps or 1 billion bits per second.

Networks may also be classified as intranets or extranets. **Intranets** are LANs that function similar to the Internet, providing web-based technologies that are accessible only to internal users of an organization. Vendor-developed and internally customized web-based applications can be found on an intranet. Examples of web-based applications that are often found in healthcare organization intranets include company directories, user account request systems, collaboration and file sharing sites, human resources information systems, purchasing systems, and help desk ticketing systems. **Extranets** are similar to Intranets but provide web-based content and access to applications and databases for users who are outside of the organization—for example, business partners, patients, vendors, and students/faculty.

Both intranet and extranet content are most efficiently maintained using enterprise web content management (EWCM) systems, which allow individual departments to easily update their content made available on the network without knowledge of HTML programming or use of web-design skills. In many cases, health organizations are leveraging **remote hosting** by engaging a third-party web-hosting company to manage their external web content. This is often done by entering into a contract with a professional EWCM vendor, which then supplies all the necessary hardware, software, website address information, and website development. The healthcare customer simply needs to provide the Internet connectivity to the external website, along with supplying the web content.

Network Models

Networks perform the basic function of transferring data from a sending device to a receiving device. To make this process efficient and modular, the various functions necessary to complete the data transfer operation are divided into network layers. The two most important network models useful to describe these network layers are the **Open Systems**

Interconnection model (OSI) and the Internet model. The OSI model was developed in 1984 and defines seven network layers (**Figure 4.3(a)**)[6]:

- *Layer 1: Physical Layer.* The physical layer is designed primarily to transmit data bits (0s and 1s signifying positive and negative electrical charges) over a communication circuit.
- *Layer 2: Data Link Layer.* The data link layer is responsible for the physical transmission circuit in layer 1 and converts it into a circuit, ensuring the transmission is error free.
- *Layer 3: Network Layer.* The network layer is responsible for routing—that is, identifying the best path through which to send the data—and ensuring the message arrives to the destination address.
- *Layer 4: Transport Layer.* The transport layer manages end-to-end network issues, such as procedures for entering and departing from the network. This layer establishes and manages the logical connections between the sending device and the receiving device, performs error checking, and, if necessary, breaks up the data packet into smaller packets for more efficient transmission.
- *Layer 5: Session Layer.* The session layer is responsible for initiating, maintaining, and terminating the logical sessions between end users. These functions can be best explained by considering how a telephone call is made: A phone generates a dial tone, a number

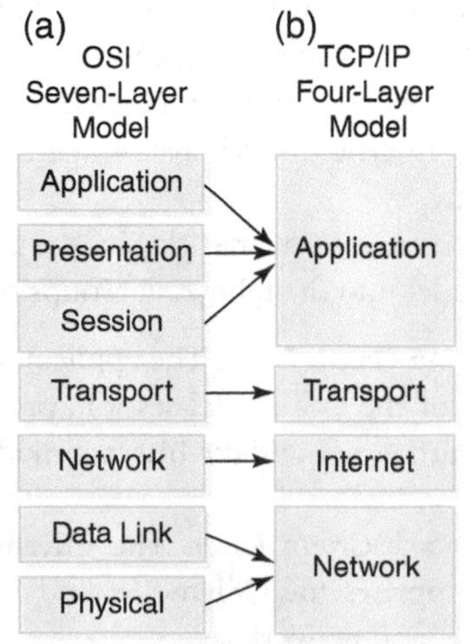

FIGURE 4.3 (a) The Seven Layers of the OSI Model (b) The Four Layers of the Internet Model

is dialed, and the receiving phone answers the call, creating the logical call session where both parties can talk to each other. The session layer also manages security checks and file transfers. Again, this can be best explained by comparing the process to a telephone call: Picking up the phone and dialing to connect to another phone initiates the session; the session is then maintained until it is terminated by one of the parties hanging up.

- *Layer 6: Presentation Layer.* The presentation layer manages the formatting of the data being transferred so that it can be presented to the end user, regardless of the type of device the end user is using. Layer 6 is also responsible for compressing the data, if necessary.
- *Layer 7: Application Layer.* The application layer is designed to manage the end user's access to the network. This includes the applications and programs used by the end user. In addition, network monitoring and network management are two important functions that are performed at the application layer. Both of these functions keep track of how the network is operating and allow network administrators to ensure that the network is working optimally.

Although the OSI model is the primary model used to describe how networks work, the **Transmission Control Protocol/Internet Protocol (TCP/IP)** or Internet model is a simpler model that is used with today's hardware and software; it is also the model that defines the Internet. Understanding both the OSI and Internet models is important for healthcare professionals, as they are wonderful examples of how complex HIS are made of multiple independent layers or modules, each functioning autonomously within their own context, yet working together with other self-contained modules to create a fully functional, multifaceted HIS. The Internet model (**Figure 4.3(b)**) keeps the same OSI model for layers 1–4, but combines the OSI model layers 5–7 into the Internet model layer 4, which is labeled the application layer.

It is also common to further classify the OSI model and the Internet model into the following groups of layers[7]:

- *Application Group Layer.* The application group layer consists of the OSI model session, presentation, and application layers, and the Internet model application layer.
- *Internetwork Group Layer.* The internetwork group layer comprises the OSI model and Internet model transport and network layers.

- *Hardware Group Layer.* The hardware group layer includes the OSI model and Internet model data link and physical layers.

Finally, it is important to understand how each network layer communicates with the other layers. When two computers are transmitting data to each other, both the sending computer and the receiving computer will use software to perform different functions at each network layer. As such, each network layer uses a formal language or protocol that defines how it will operate at each layer.

To see how this works, imagine an end user creates a message (an email, for example) using a web browser and sends that message to another user, who will also receive and read the message using a web browser. In this example and using the Internet model, the Hypertext Transfer Protocol (HTTP) is used at the application layer to create an HTTP request packet, which includes the message from the sender. The Transmission Control Protocol (TCP) is used at the transport layer to break the HTTP packet into one or more smaller-sized HTTP packets, place each of these smaller HTTP packets into TCP packets, determine the destination server address, and then open a connection to the destination server for the transfer of the TCP packets. The Internet Protocol (IP) at the network layer then determines the next stop on the way to the destination server, packages the TCP packet into an IP packet, and sends the IP packet to the next stop. The Ethernet protocol is used at the data link layer to format the message, provide error checking, add the IP packet into an Ethernet packet, and then instruct the physical hardware to transmit the Ethernet packet to the next stop. The physical layer takes the Ethernet packet and transmits it over the network cable as a series of positive and negative electrical impulses.

When the destination server receives these electrical impulses, the preceding steps are carried out in reverse order: The physical layer translates the electrical impulses into Ethernet packets, the data link layer converts the Ethernet packets into IP packets and checks for errors, the network layer converts the IP packets into TCP packets, the transport layer converts the TCP packets into HTTP packets, and finally the application layer presents the request (or webpage) from the HTTP packet to the end user.

This example demonstrates both the complexity and the elegance involved in sending a simple message between computers over a network. On the one hand, many different software programs and languages are used at the various layers, which allows applications to be built in a modular fashion. Such an approach requires that software and hardware vendors use the same standards when developing their products. On the other hand, the different and multiple layers of the protocol stack can create a level of inefficiency that slows down the transmission of data. This example also highlights the importance of *technical standards* that ensure common protocols for transmitting data along the various steps between layers.

Local Area Networks

Local area networks are the primary networks used by desktops, servers, and network and other devices to communicate when they are in close proximity with each other. LANs are used for two reasons: *information sharing*, which enables users to exchange data, files, emails, and other types of information; and *resource sharing*, which refers to a computer sharing an attached device or software application such as a printer or fax application. LANs can be set up to operate in a client–server or peer-to-peer configuration. In a peer-to-peer network, computers share information and resources equally, and there are no dedicated network servers in place. In a client–server network, one or more dedicated servers provide the client computers with various types of network services, such as web services, application services, and database services.

LANs are composed of a number of components. A network interface card (NIC) is a hardware component in each computer that enables that computer to physically connect to the network and transfer data over a network cable. Network cables connect the NIC to a wall jack or directly to a network switch using a copper or fiber-optic cable. Desktop computers typically connect using a Category 5 (CAT5) or higher copper cable, and server computers or other networking devices can be connected with either copper or fiber-optic cables. Copper cables, as the name implies, are constructed with universal twisted pair (UTP) or standard twisted pair (STP) copper wires, can be twisted or bent, and support transmission speeds between 10 Mbps and 100 Mbps. Fiber-optic cables are made of very fine layers of glass and use light to transmit data at speeds of 10 Gbps and higher; unfortunately, they are more apt to malfunction if bent or twisted. Due to cabling length restrictions, LANs must be interconnected by using hubs or switches.

LANs are the basic building blocks that interconnect desktops, servers, and other devices. When setting up a new LAN, it is important to ensure that the LAN is designed to operate at high speeds, the network traffic is optimized and controlled, and redundancy and high availability are built into the architecture. Having an unstable or slow-performing LAN will negatively affect end-user computer performance.

When designing a new LAN, attention should be given to assessing and remediating any shortcomings with how the LAN is configured. This is vital to healthcare organizations, as end-user satisfaction with HIS application depends on the network connectivity being robust and available on a 24/7 basis. Several areas to consider in this regard include replacing old, legacy network hubs with modern network switches, installing network patch panels to reduce lengthy cabling runs, eliminating "daisy-chained" network switches, replacing slower copper network cabling with higher-speed fiber-optic cabling between intermediate distribution frame (IDF) and main distribution frame (MDF) network closets, upgrading desktop computer network connections from 10 Mbps or 100 Mbps speeds to 1 Gbps speeds, replacing "flat" or statically addressed network segments with virtual local area networks (VLANs) using dynamic addressing, and implementing advanced LAN management and monitoring tools.

Wireless LANs

Wireless local area networks (WLANs) are perhaps one of the fastest-growing network technologies in today's healthcare environment. Clinicians and other healthcare workers are increasingly seeking to use mobile workstations on wheels (WOWs), laptop computers, tablet computers, smart phones, and other wireless devices to do their jobs faster, more efficiently, and with greater flexibility. WLANs operate by transmitting data from a wireless access point (WAP) through the medium of air using radio frequencies. WAPs are typically distributed on or inside the rooms and hallway ceilings requiring wireless coverage, but are physically connected to network switches using CAT5 or higher cabling. Of the various wireless technologies in use today, the Institute of Electrical and Electronics Engineers (IEEE) technologies known as IEEE 802.11a, IEEE 802.11b, IEEE 802.11g, and IEEE 802.11n are four of the most widely adopted WLAN technologies, with IEEE 802.11n being the most recent technology developed that supports the highest speeds and the largest ranges.

WLANs have the benefits of faster, easier, and less costly deployment requirements, as there is no need to go through the time-consuming and expensive process of deploying cabling to each computer. Important WLAN implementation considerations include replacing old and legacy IDF switches with power-over-Ethernet (POE) switches; ensuring POE switches have ample available and unused ports to support future growth; resisting the temptation to configure stationary computers for wireless access, thereby avoiding the additional performance limitations and complexities involved with wireless protocols; performing WLAN site surveys and staggered WAP placement to eliminate dropped- or low-coverage areas, as well as WAP contention; deploying redundant and properly distributed wireless access controllers; and implementing wireless network access control technology to support the increasing demand for guest, physician group, vendor, patient, and other non-employee access.

Wide Area Networks

Wide area networks connect users on LANs to other LANs or other WANs. As healthcare reform continues to drive healthcare organizations toward greater reliance on EHR and other computerized HIS, various configurations are increasingly necessary to connect with other computers over greater distances. Many healthcare organizations encompass facilities at multiple locations. A WAN is used to connect the LANs at this disparate locations to each other. If an organization is large enough to have multiple WANs, these can also be linked together to form an even larger WAN. The largest WAN in existence today is the Internet. WANs are interconnected using high-speed fiber-optic cabling and typically support data transmission rates of 10 Gbps or higher. They utilize network devices called routers to connect or route data traffic from one LAN or WAN to another LAN or WAN. Routers send information through network devices called gateways.

A reliable WAN with sufficient bandwidth or capacity to handle end-user network traffic is critical for the successful operation of HIS implementations. Important areas to review to attain a high-performing WAN include replacing slower, legacy WAN circuits, such as T1 lines (also referred to T-carrier lines), asynchronous transfer mode (ATM) lines, or other copper-wire point-to-point telecommunications with high-speed fiber-optic multiprotocol label switching (MPLS) circuits[8]; using multiple commercial carriers and redundant pairs of networking devices for high availability; eliminating all single points of failure along the WAN physical path; and implementing network link-load balancing (NLLB) and WAN optimization technology.

Wireless Wide Area Networks

Another wireless technology increasingly used within healthcare environments is **wireless wide area networks (WWANs)**, often referred to as broadband or cellular network technology. WWANs are wide area networks that provide service to large geographic areas through separate areas of coverage, referred to as cells. Cell phones, smart phones, tablet computers, and hot spots are mobile devices commonly used to connect to WWANs. Three families of WWAN technologies are prevalent today: (1) Global System for Mobile Communications (GSM) and Universal Mobile Telecommunications System (UMTS); (2) Code-Division Multiple Access (CDMA) One, CDMA2000, and Wideband CDMA (WCDMA); and (3) Worldwide Interoperability for Microwave Access (WiMAX) and Long-Term Evolution (LTE). The GSM/UMTS and CDMA One/CDMA 2000/WCDMA standards are referred to as second-generation (2G) and third-generation (3G) technologies, as they were designed to replace the slower, more limited analog cellular networks with higher-speed, digital cellular networks. The WiMAX and LTE standards are high-speed fourth-generation (4G) technologies that are now gaining increasing market share on a global scale. T-Mobile, AT&T, Sprint, and Verizon are four major WWAN service providers.

The consumerization of IT has given rise to the bring-your-own-device (BYOD) phenomenon, in which increasing numbers of end users seek to use their personal smart phones and/or tablets for both personal and work use.[9] Many healthcare organizations have responded to the complexities involved in supporting both personal and corporate data on a personally owned mobile device by deciding to officially support only corporate-owned mobile devices. Other organizations have developed appropriate BYOD policies and deployed mobile device management technology. Many organizations have recognized the need to provide uninterrupted cellular network coverage to doctors, nurses, and other healthcare workers for functions such as voice, texting, web browsing, and other mobile applications; for those organizations, **distributed antennae system (DAS)** technology can eliminate dead spots and other areas of poor cellular signal coverage within hospital buildings.

Storage Area Networks

Storage area networks (SANs) are dedicated back-end computer systems designed to efficiently and cost-effectively store and transfer a healthcare organization's server data. These high-speed networks are dedicated to centrally storing and providing access to data from multiple server systems. They have the distinct benefit of providing high availability, with no one single hardware component (a so-called single point of failure) being able to disrupt access to data. Traditional methods of storing data involve using directly attached storage, where each server stores its associated data to hard disk drives (HDDs) directly attached to itself. This method has many limitations in today's environment, where end users are demanding ever-greater storage capacity and performance. Directly attached storage systems still exist today, but they are largely giving way to SAN systems, which boast higher capacity, faster access, greater availability, and stronger security at less cost. The different types of SANs in use today include fiber channel (FC) SANs and network attached storage (NAS) devices.

At a basic level, data are stored on a HDD and can be written or read. To ensure that the data will be available in the event the hard disk fails, hard drives can be placed into a redundant array of independent drives (RAID) configuration, with the data copied across multiple drives. A RAID controller is a computing peripheral that keeps the disks in the array in synchronization and manages all the write and read (input/output [I/O]) operations to and from the disks. Four RAID configurations widely used today are RAID 1, RAID 5, RAID 5 with a spare, and RAID 10.

- RAID 1 configurations, also called mirrored disks, use two HDDs: one as the primary HDD and the other as the secondary HDD. This configuration provides redundancy if a HDD fails and boasts fast read performance, as the data can be read from either disk. Unfortunately, it has slow write speeds to the HDD and is more expensive because two HDDs are required.
- RAID 5 distributes the common or redundant information (called parity) to all HHDs in the configuration. If a block or HDD fails, the parity information ensures that the lost information can be restored when a replacement HDD is inserted into the array. RAID 5 requires a minimum of three HDDs, and has the advantage of performing fast HDD reads.
- RAID 5 with a spare configuration contains an additional HDD, called a hot spare; it remains unused until a HDD in configuration fails, at which time the array automatically rebuilds the failed HDD to the spare HDD. This scheme has the advantage of providing an additional layer of redundancy should a HDD fail.
- RAID 10 is a combination of RAID 1 and RAID 5, giving it the fastest performance and highest availability, albeit with the highest cost, because only half of the HHD capacity is used for the actual storage of data.

In healthcare server systems today, RAID 1 is often used to configure stand-alone server operating system drives, while RAID 5 is used as a cost-effective and acceptably performing configuration for both directly attached and SAN data storage environments. RAID 10 is used for SANs that require very high performance and availability. Most mission critical databases are stored on RAID 10, as it provides higher levels of availability and write access. However, it costs almost twice as much as RAID5 because it has almost twice the number of disks.

SANs can be used to support very large amounts of data. To do so efficiently, they allow for the creation of disk pools that vary in size, speed, and cost by using different RAID configurations, HDD sizes, and HDD access times. When a server needs new or additional storage, based on what is needed and how expensive the storage needs to be, logical volumes (LUNs) can be provisioned and presented to the server as a local HDD. SANs communicate with each other using either the Ethernet (also referred to as IP), FC, Fiber Channel over Ethernet (FCoE), or Internet Small Computer System Interface (iSCSI) protocol; they also use high-speed fiber-optic cabling and network switches that support the IP, FCoE, or iSCSI protocols. Modern SAN deployments typically use either 10 Gbps FCoE Ethernet or 16 Gbps FC. With the application of aggregation technology, both Ethernet and FC SAN connections can be increased to higher speeds to support increased traffic loads and higher data transfer requirements.

SANs that may have medium to high storage capacity requirements but do not have high performance requirements, such as file servers, can be configured as NAS devices. NAS systems use the Ethernet (IP) protocol over standard LAN switches to present storage to servers and other devices on the network. This approach has the benefit of being less expensive than FC-based SANs because it uses less costly LAN switches and cabling, and cheaper and larger HDDs. SAN and NAS vendors are continuing to develop easier-to-use management consoles for SAN administrators, reducing the learning curve and skill set needed to troubleshoot and maintain the various SAN technologies.

Voice and Communications

Voice over Internet Protocol (VoIP) and **unified communications (UC)** are emerging technologies that healthcare organizations are beginning to leverage and implement at their facilities. VoIP comprises a family of technologies that enable IP networks to be used for voice applications such as telephony, messaging, and collaboration. With greater reliance on robust data networks, traditional analog-based PBX office phone systems that operate over public switched telephone networks (PSTNs) telecommunication circuits are now being replaced with more cost-effective VoIP solutions that run over existing IP networks. With high-speed, robust LAN and WAN connections in place, and with the Internet being capable of supporting voice traffic over data circuits, voice calls no longer need dedicated analog circuits and can leverage the existing data network. This approach requires a VoIP-enabled phone or a computer and headset. Analog voice calls are converted to packets of data, which are then sent over the data network, and converted back to analog signals. The addition of voice to a data network allows organizations to reduce costs, improve productivity, and enhance collaboration.

Voice over wireless local area network (VoWLAN) is a technology designed to integrate mobile devices using the WLAN. It is proving particularly advantageous as more clinical applications are developed for use with smart phones, tablets, and portable computers. Use of VoWLAN offers the following benefits:

- Improves workflow and productivity by delivering ubiquitous, robust coverage
- Enables roaming of voice clients and high-quality voice communications by using real-time radio-frequency scanning and monitoring to minimize interference
- Minimizes roam time and client connectivity issues
- Provides advanced quality of service (QoS), extended talk-time, and call security

UC is another evolving technology that involves the integration of real-time communication services, such as instant messaging and presence, VoIP and VoWLAN, video conferencing, and web conferencing. Digital signage and wayfinding, and IP television (IPTV), are also considered part of the UC family of services. UC is designed to use a single, consistent user interface to provide one or more of these services, along with transferring data over the IP network. An example of UC in an HIS setting can be seen when virtual

meetings are conducted with products such as Cisco WebEx, Citrix Go-To-Meeting, or Microsoft Lync web conferencing software. Although healthcare workers and partners might be located around the world, they can meet via an online session, sharing voice, video, presentations, chat, and other forms of collaboration—all while using only a web browser and computer or mobile device.

Instant messaging or chat is used often in healthcare environments as the real-time communication needs of clinicians and IT personnel expand. Instant messaging allows users to send messages or files to each other. In a healthcare setting, a *secured* instant messaging application is required to avoid issues with electronic protected health information (ePHI) or other sensitive information traveling over unsecured networks, such as the Internet. Instant messaging has the additional benefit of giving others notice of an individual's presence or status, such as whether he or she is online, offline, busy, or in a meeting.

Figure 4.4 illustrates the multiple components in the WLAN protocol that securely support data and voice traffic.

Video conferencing enables two or more individuals to talk and see each other by transmitting audio and video signals. Although this technology has existed for many years, it has not been widely adopted due to the complexity and high costs involved in using analog circuits and deploying proprietary video conferencing equipment. UC, however, enables video conferencing to be performed over IP data networks with significantly reduced costs and complexity. Popular applications of this technology in healthcare environments include video conferencing over desktop computers and mobile devices, video conferencing in conference rooms using large-screen monitors (which eliminates the need for

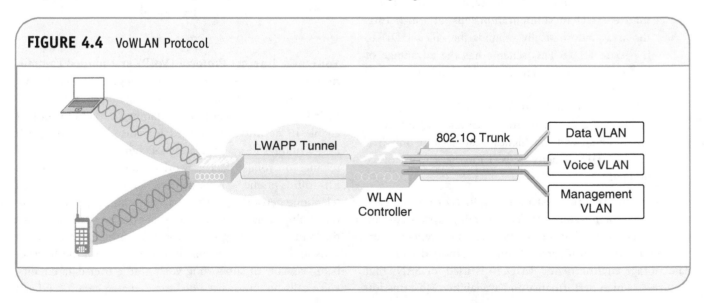

FIGURE 4.4 VoWLAN Protocol

travel and other expenses involved in face-to-face meetings), and cloud-based video conferencing services (which eliminate the need to buy and maintain expensive equipment).

Web conferencing is used frequently in healthcare organizations because of its simplicity, convenience, and low cost. It enables users at multiple locations to hold audio meetings and share desktop computer applications or applications from their mobile devices over the IP network. Given the never-ending quest to reduce costs, web conferencing is being widely embraced as a solution that enables organizations to reduce employee travel requirements while increasing collaboration between all stakeholders. Web conferencing solutions can be cloud based or deployed using an on-premises architecture.

Digital signage and digital wayfinding are other UC technologies that are being deployed in healthcare organizations. Digital signage uses server technology and IP networks to electronically display information, such as organizational training or news, advertising, or other healthcare-related messages, using liquid crystal displays (LCDs) or plasma displays that are placed in various public or internal locations within hospitals and work areas. Digital wayfinding uses digital signage technology, but adds touch-screen technology to allow users to interact with the LCD-presented information.[10] Examples of digital wayfinding technology commonly found in hospitals include interactive touch-screen LCDs that allow patients to obtain directions to various departments, find information about their physician, see cafeteria information, and look up healthcare education information.

Data Centers and Cloud Computing

Ensuring that HIS applications and data are protected, secured, and always accessible to the end users who need to use them is a very important aspect to HIS. **Data centers** are the facilities where HIS are located and are vital to the successful implementation and ongoing support of providing healthcare applications. With the ever-growing reliance on electronic information, healthcare organizations must ensure that their data centers can provide high availability for their computer systems, are secure and modernized to remain cost-effective, and have ample capacity for growth and expansion. One of the first decisions facing healthcare organizations is whether they will maintain their own data center facilities, lease one or more commercially owned co-location data center facilities, or outsource (remote host) both their data center facility and computing equipment to a third party. Due to the high costs and complexities involved in an organization maintaining its own data center facility, contracting with a co-location facility and remote hosting are increasingly popular options with many healthcare organizations.

Another important decision organizations need to address involves data center consolidation. Newer servers, networking devices, and other equipment located inside data centers are increasing in capacity and performance (referred to as computer density) while requiring less cabinet, rack, and floor space. Organizations are discovering that they no longer need multiple data centers but rather can consolidate their IT infrastructure into a single facility. At the same time, to ensure high availability and disaster recovery capability, healthcare organizations need a secondary data center. This is typically a smaller facility that can support running the mission-critical applications (at a minimum) and is often remotely hosted by a third-party data center vendor.

A third important question is how the organization will position itself with the evolving technology of cloud computing. Cloud computing, a recent emergent technology, followed in the footsteps of mainframe, client–server, web, and service-oriented architecture (SOA), all of which were popular at some point in the past. *Cloud computing* is a general term associated with delivering hosted services, with the goal of providing easy, scalable access to computing resources and IT services. As depicted in **Figure 4.5**, these services are organized into three categories: **infrastructure-as-a-service (IaaS)**, **platform-as-a-service (PaaS)**, and **software-as-a-service (SaaS)**, with some healthcare proponents now discussing EMR-as-a-service (EaaS) as a future possibility.[11] An IaaS-hosted solution involves a vendor supplying a data center with all the server hardware and network connectivity needed to support HIS applications. The HIS customer then needs to install and manage its server operating systems, applications, and databases itself. A PaaS-hosted solution is similar to an IaaS-hosted solution, except that the cloud vendor also supplies the server operating systems. With a SaaS-hosted solution, the cloud vendor installs and manages all previously mentioned components. With an EaaS-hosted solution, the cloud vendor fully hosts the EMR solution. In all four scenarios, the HIS customer still manages the processes of entering and extracting data from the service.

A cloud can also be categorized as private or public. Public clouds, such as Amazon Web Services, sell services to anyone on the Internet, typically consumers. Private clouds are proprietary networks and data centers that supply secure, hosted services for use within a particular organization; these are being increasingly adopted among healthcare organizations.

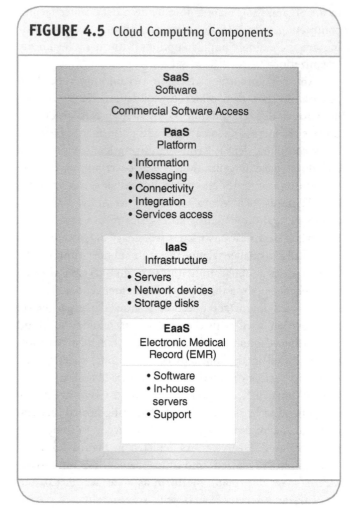

FIGURE 4.5 Cloud Computing Components

SaaS
Software

Commercial Software Access

PaaS
Platform

- Information
- Messaging
- Connectivity
- Integration
- Services access

IaaS
Infrastructure

- Servers
- Network devices
- Storage disks

EaaS
Electronic Medical
Record (EMR)

- Software
- In-house
  servers
- Support

Data center facilities have a number of critical components that must be managed appropriately. The most costly operational expense related to a data center, other than the high capital costs required for building or upgrading the facility itself, is electrical power consumption. The green data center concept is an initiative designed to improve the environment by reducing power usage. In a data center, this goal can be accomplished by using energy-efficient equipment and reducing the amount of physical equipment inside the data center by leveraging technologies such as virtualization and consolidation.

Data centers receive their primary power, called utility power, from commercial utility companies. Ideally, this should be supplied by two separate physical paths (or feeds) into the building's main distribution unit to provide redundancy. The typical power path is 1–10 megawatts (MW) or greater. Through a series of electrical transformers, high-voltage electricity is reduced or "stepped down" so that facilities and computing equipment can be supplied with appropriate voltages. Utility power is routed to power distribution units (PDUs), which are distributed throughout the

data center. In large data centers, remote power panels (RPPs) route power to one or more data center cabinets. Power is then distributed to each cabinet, which can directly connect to computing equipment or a set of smaller cabinet power strips. Most servers and data center equipment will plug into these data center cabinet PDUs, which can be remotely monitored over the network using a branch circuit monitoring system (BCMS) application. Larger facility equipment uses 480- or 220-volt capacities, while computing equipment uses 220- or 110-volt capacities.

In the event that the utility power feeds fail, data centers should be configured to automatically fail over to use backup power, in a battery-supported form. The typical power path is an **uninterruptable power supply (UPS)**, a flywheel-driven **continuous power source (CPS)**, or a combination of the two. Backup power is important to ensure that HIS applications remain available and accessible, as inevitably electrical components suffer outages from time to time. Any disruption in power will translate into these critical HIS applications going offline, in turn negatively impacting patient care. UPS backup systems use batteries to provide electricity and have the advantages of being less expensive and starting up faster than non-battery backup systems, such as CPS systems. However, UPS systems are not considered environmentally friendly and the batteries require regular maintenance and replacement. CPS systems use a continuously spinning flywheel driven by high-speed turbines to generate electricity. They are robust and considered environmentally friendly, but are more expensive and slower to assume the primary load than UPS systems. Generators, using diesel or gasoline fuel, are needed to provide power to both UPS and CPS systems. Due to the high levels of noise generated by CPS equipment, data center personnel must use earplugs to minimize ear damage.

Data centers should have service level agreements (SLAs) with fuel companies to deliver fuel until the utility power is restored, and they often are equipped with local storage tanks capable of holding tens of thousands of gallons of fuel. In many data centers that are large enough to use CPS backup systems, UPS systems are also installed to ensure the primary load is assumed quickly.

In addition to a continuous power supply, cooling is essential to reliably support HIS. Many computer systems are located in densely configured data centers, where a tremendous amount of heat is produced within a confined space. To provide ambient or room cooling, heating, ventilating, and air-conditioning (HVAC) systems are used. HVAC systems utilize water to absorb excess heat: Computer room air handlers (CRAH) draw in the hot air, and then cold water traveling through large pipes absorbs the heat. Subsequently, roof or wall condensers release the heat outside the data center and large, heavy-duty water chillers cool and recirculate the water. As a contingency in case commercial or utility water sources become unavailable, many data centers have wells that can hold tens of thousands of gallons of water.

To protect a data center from damage by fire, fire suppression systems, such as water-based dry-pipe preaction sprinklers or gas-based FM200 fire suppression systems, are used. Dry-pipe systems fill the pipes with water if a fire occurs. They are less expensive than the gas-based FM200 systems but have the disadvantage of potentially damaging computer systems in the event of a fire. However, because individual sprinkler heads open only after a temperature fuse breaks—normally at a temperature of approximately 175°F—water damage will be limited to just the computer equipment directly below the specific sprinkler head where the fire is occurring. FM200 systems contain a fire retardant that will not damage computer equipment, but tend to cost more and require data center personnel to evacuate the area being treated. To help provide early warning detection of a potential fire, very early smoke detection apparatus (VESDA) systems monitor for smoke particles and sound alerts when they are detected.

If a catastrophic and life-threatening event does occur within a data center, in which terminating all electricity is the only option to resolve the situation, an emergency power off (EPO) switch should be available. Once this button is pressed, all electricity to the data center is shut off.

BCMS can be deployed in data centers to monitor and manage electrical circuits, and provide data center staff with the ability to ensure that data center equipment has sufficient electrical capacity. Data center management systems (DCMSs) are hardware and software systems that allow data center personnel to design and proactively manage these and additional data center technologies; they can help reduce unplanned system downtime caused by poor planning or a lack of standardized and documented processes and procedures. A DCMS may include power protection and distribution management, air-conditioning and environmental controls, intelligent cable management, cabinet space management, server and network device remote access, and asset management and tracking (**Figure 4.6**).

Business Continuity and Disaster Recovery

Another area associated with data centers is business continuity and disaster recovery. "Business continuity" describes the processes and steps a healthcare organization puts in place to ensure that its essential business functions will continue during and after a disaster.[12] One of the most important areas of business continuity planning is disaster recovery planning, which comprises the planning, process, policy, and procedures undertaken to prevent interruption of mission-critical IT services, and to reestablish full IT functioning as swiftly and smoothly as possible.

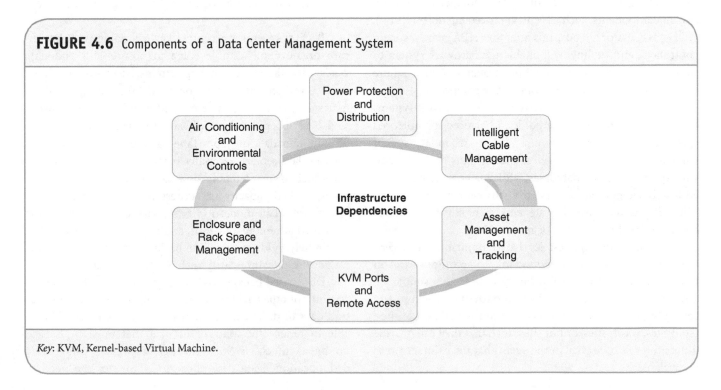

FIGURE 4.6 Components of a Data Center Management System

Power Protection and Distribution

Air Conditioning and Environmental Controls

Intelligent Cable Management

Infrastructure Dependencies

Enclosure and Rack Space Management

Asset Management and Tracking

KVM Ports and Remote Access

Key: KVM, Kernel-based Virtual Machine.

As EHRs and other HIS technologies become more commonplace in healthcare environments, it is critical that the risk of a system outage or data center disaster be mitigated. Many health organizations today have not fully developed their business continuity plan (BCP) or disaster recovery plan (DRP); these organizations should consider performing a BCP or DRP assessment to determine the level of risk that is acceptable. In preparing a BCP, the organization should first identify and prioritize the criticality of the various HIS components and then determine the appropriate recovery time objective (RTO) and recovery point objective (RPO) for each HIS in the event of a disaster or unplanned system outage. RTO refers to the total time (in minutes, hours, or days) during which a server or service can remain unavailable before it is restored to full functionality, while RPO refers to the total time (in minutes, hours, or days) for which data might be lost. Keeping BCP and DRP at the same level of priority as other projects within HIS is often challenging for healthcare organizations to accomplish, but it is critical to do so. The increasing dependence on HIS and technology throughout health care necessitates investment of time and effort to establish and maintain these protective capabilities.

An examination of important DRP concepts will demonstrate the various steps that organizations can take to reduce this risk. Redundancy is one of the simplest concepts that should be implemented at all levels of DRP. Where possible, having two instances of server, storage, or network system components, such as central processing units (CPUs), HDDs, NICs, storage host bus adaptor (HBA) cards, system controllers, and cabling, will enable the hardware system to support the HIS and remain operational should a failure occur that is restricted to any one of the components.

At the next level, servers, storage, and network systems themselves should be clustered, load balanced, or mirrored such that if the primary system fails, the secondary system will continue to provide service. Clustering is typically used with applications and databases, while load balancing is used with web servers, file servers, and various network devices. Mirroring is used to replicate and maintain synchronous copies of data between two or more SANs.

Moving to the highest level of redundancy, data centers themselves should be redundant. To accomplish this in today's environment, each primary data center should be associated with a corresponding secondary or backup data center. Secondary data centers can be configured as cold sites, tepid sites, warm sites, or hot sites, such that they can provide different levels of service in the event that the primary site is unavailable.

- *Cold sites* are facilities that have hardware and software available for use, but are shared with other organizations and contain no data from the primary data center. Should a disaster occur, the cold site systems would need to be configured and the backup data restored to the cold site location. This is the least costly DRP option and has no distance limitation between data centers, but it can take several days to bring an organization's critical systems back online.
- *Tepid sites* are similar to cold sites, but have the data from the organization's critical systems copied over using basic SAN replication. This is the third most costly DRP option, has a distance limitation of 1000 miles or less, and takes only 2 to 3 hours to bring an organization's critical systems back online.
- *Warm sites* improve on the tepid site capability, with the difference being that all systems and data from the primary site are copied over, although noncritical systems will operate in a degraded mode. This is a very costly DRP option, has the same distance limitation of 1000 miles or less as tepid sites, and requires only 1 hour or less to bring an organization's systems back online.
- *Hot sites* can provide rapid, automated and full system and data recovery in less than a minute, but are the most expensive option. They have a distance limitation of either 200 miles or a data transfer round-trip time of 10 milliseconds.

Backup systems are another key technology that healthcare organizations can leverage to ensure HIS and data availability. Tape-based backup systems, such as digital linear tape (DTL) and linear tape-open (LTO) models, use magnetic tape, tape drive systems, and stand-alone or centralized backup application software to make backup copies of computer data on tape. Tape backup systems have been used in data centers for many years but suffer from limitations such as unacceptably slow backup and restore transfer times, limited capacity to address the exponential storage growth found in modern HIS, the risk of losing tapes that are stored at remote locations, and the inability to store data indefinitely. Additionally, tape backup systems lack support for advanced features such as encryption-at-rest capabilities.

Disk-based backup systems address many of the shortcomings of tape backups by backing up system and application data to disk. These systems have the benefits of being able to reduce the amount of data that must be backed up by as much as 90% through a process called data deduplication. Data deduplication eliminates the need to back up redundant or already backed-up data. As a result, disk-based backup systems have higher backup storage capacities and faster backup and restore times. They more easily move and store data to disparate locations using network and cloud-based technologies and are designed to use advanced security features and both encryption-at-rest and encryption-in-transit.

Virtual tape libraries (VTLs) are backup systems that use disk-based arrays to emulate tape libraries. With these systems, the storage medium can be switched from tapes to disks while continuing to use the existing tape backup software. VTLs lack the advanced features of disk-based backup systems.

Server Computing

Servers are specialized computers that are designed to process or "serve" computing requests, such as requests for database information, application processing, or file transfers and storage. Although they have the basic components found in client or desktop computers, they are architected differently. Servers are designed with multiple high-speed CPUs, large amounts of random access memory (RAM), redundant and high-capacity I/O, internal bus systems, and access to high-speed storage, network, and backup systems. These computers are inserted or "racked" in computer cabinets to allow for high density, and they do not require the individual directly connected monitors, keyboards, mice, or other devices that are common with client or desktop computers. As many as 10 to 12 rack-mounted servers may be stored in a single computer cabinet (**Figure 4.7**). A high-capacity server is so large that it requires an entire computer cabinet on its own.

Keyboard, video, and mouse over IP (KVMoIP) devices are centralized systems that give system administrators keyboard, monitor, and mouse access over the network, eliminating the requirement and additional cost to provide these peripheral devices for each server.

Blade server technology represents an advancement in increasing server density and reducing server costs. Blade servers are stored in a compact enclosure called a blade chassis, which has a reduced size and uses less energy. These types of servers boast higher availabilities achieved by sharing common components, such as network, storage, cabling, and power infrastructure. Three to four times more blade servers can fit in the same cabinet space as rack-mounted servers. Unified computing system (UCS) technology is a next-generation data center platform that increases server density, performance, availability, management, and efficiency beyond blade server technology by uniting multiple

FIGURE 4.7 Data Center Class Servers

blade server chassis, networks, and storage infrastructures into a single cohesive system.

Virtualization is another technology advance that has significantly reduced the amount of server infrastructure needed to support today's healthcare environments, thereby greatly smoothing the way for healthcare organization server consolidation initiatives. Physical servers or hosts generally use only 10% or less of their processing ability. The virtualization feature takes advantage of a server's unused processing power by creating multiple virtual server instances, which typically increases server density by a factor of 10 to 15. A hypervisor or virtual machine monitor (VMM) is a piece of computer software, firmware, or hardware that creates and runs virtual machines. These virtual server instances, called virtual machines (VMs), run on servers running Windows, Linux, and Solaris operating systems, and on logical partition arrays (LPARs) in UNIX-based servers, such as the Advanced Interactive eXecutive (AIX) operating system.

Servers that run one or more VMs are called hypervisors, and are defined as host machines. Individual VMs are called guest machines. Hypervisors present and manage the operation of the guest operating systems within the virtual operating platform. By combining or clustering multiple host computers into redundant and highly available server farms so that VMs and LPARs can automatically move between physical hosts, server virtualization significantly reduces server downtime due to hardware failure or planned maintenance. **Figure 4.8** illustrates how virtualization is designed to maximize server hardware and software resources.

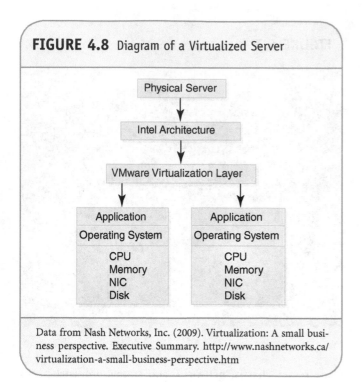

FIGURE 4.8 Diagram of a Virtualized Server

Data from Nash Networks, Inc. (2009). Virtualization: A small business perspective. Executive Summary. http://www.nashnetworks.ca/virtualization-a-small-business-perspective.htm

Despite the many advantages of server virtualization, including the ability to rapidly and easily deploy servers, reduced costs per server, and simplified server management, several challenges need to be addressed when moving forward with this technology. Server sprawl or large numbers of servers may occur due to the relative ease with which systems can be deployed. New charge-back models and processes must be put in place when this approach is used, as most of the server infrastructure must be procured and deployed prior to identifying the need for a new server. Additional care must be given to server architecture and change management because there is increased risk that multiple systems might be negatively affected by any design flaw or problematic configuration change or upgrade.

Servers can be classified in additional ways. Servers that are fully supported and managed by a vendor (usually installed with a proprietary operating system and software) are called appliances. Appliances are typically self-contained, requiring only a network connection; are easy and fast to deploy; and can be a preferred method for delivering a server application, as healthcare organizations or customers do not have to address all the complications and delays involved in setting up the server themselves. Servers are also classified as production, development, or test types, with all three types being stored in secured, highly available data centers.

Infrastructure Servers

Infrastructure servers provide core services that support server system functionality and that need to be implemented properly if a healthcare organization expects to rely on its business and clinical applications. A poorly implemented underlying server infrastructure environment will cause significant issues with HIS application deployments. Understanding the following infrastructure servers and applications will provide insight needed to establish a robust and stable environment that reliably supports HIS applications.

Dynamic Host Configuration Protocol (DHCP) servers assign a unique address to each computer on the network. A misconfigured or inaccessible DHCP server can cause both servers and end users' computers to receive duplicate or incorrect addresses, making them unable to function. Domain Name System (DNS) servers enable users and servers to contact websites and other servers by maintaining a directory listing of server and website names. It is important for organizations to ensure that their DNS servers are properly configured, and if an update or modification is required, thorough testing must be performed. Should the DNS service be disrupted, end-user web browsing via the Internet and server-to-server communications can be inhibited. Active directory (AD) servers maintain lists of users, computers, and printers, along with any associated passwords and security settings. A misconfigured or inaccessible AD server can cause users and computers to have access, connectivity, and password issues. Identity and access management (IAM) servers automate and streamline the management of user, computer, and application accounts and passwords; their use can significantly reduce the number of help desk or IT staff needed for these tasks.

Additional infrastructure servers include enterprise monitoring servers, which are used to monitor servers, applications, storage, and network services. Such servers can send alerts or resolve failed services, thereby greatly increasing system uptime. Systems management servers provide comprehensive management of applications, services, physical resources, hypervisors, and networks. They also provide centralized services such as desktop imaging and software deployment, antivirus and antimalware protection, application security patching and upgrades, and computer configuration and asset management. Endpoint encryption servers are systems that install and manage encryption on client computers.

Database servers maintain a healthcare organization's database instances; they are frequently clustered or configured with multiple servers to support large database sizes. Most HIS and administrative/clinical applications use transactional databases, such as Oracle 11G, IBM DB2, or Microsoft SQL, whereas EHRs may use high-speed object databases, such as Intersystems Cache.

Enterprise web content management (EWCM) servers enable departments to easily update and manage web-based content on the corporate intranet and, in some cases, on the organization's externally facing website. Finally, application virtualization servers enable users to run applications that are installed on centrally located servers, eliminating the need to install the application locally and, in most cases, improving the performance of the application and overall end-user experience. Application virtualization is being widely adopted in healthcare settings due to its tangible benefits.

Client Computing

Client computing describes the computers and devices used by end users. These can be categorized as either stationary or mobile devices, with mobile computing needs on the rise. Nevertheless, the standard client computer issued today is a PC directly connected to the organization's network using a wired or copper cable network connection. Recent advances in technology have significantly reduced the size and cost of PCs, but additional improvements in wireless technology are needed to transition to a fully wireless environment.

Other stationary computers found in a healthcare setting include all-in-one (AIO) computers, wall-mounted computers, thin- and zero-client computers, and electronic tracking board systems. AIOs are often needed in clinical areas with space constraints, such as in operating room (OR) or emergency room (ER) locations, and are designed with all the computer system components (except for the keyboard and mouse) integrated with the monitor, which is typically a 24- to 27-inch LCD plasma screen. Wall-mounted computers are frequently deployed in patient rooms and other locations where space constraints exist. In patient rooms, care must be taken to ensure that these computers are optimally situated to enhance the caregiver–patient experience, as maintaining eye contact between both parties is vital for the proper delivery of care. In some cases, special construction must be undertaken to create stationary workstation areas in the center of rooms that support multiple patients.

Thin-client computers are increasing in use in healthcare settings. These small machines rely on a server to perform and store all data processing, and can be likened to client dumb terminals from the mainframe era. Thin-client computers typically have a small amount of RAM, a reduced-size CPU, a small hard drive that runs a modified version of the Windows operating system (called Windows Embedded), and a NIC. The benefits of thin-client computing include improved maintenance and security due to central administration of the hardware and software in the data center, and reduced client hardware and energy costs.

Zero-client computers are similar to thin-client computers, but offer the additional advantage of having no local hard drive or operating system to secure or maintain.[13] Like thin clients, zero clients are gaining in popularity in healthcare settings, as they are well suited to furthering desktop virtualization and integrating with WOWs due to their light weight, small form factor, and ease of management.

Electronic tracking board systems support the real-time tracking of critical information pertinent to the flow of care for individual patients. Tracking board systems consist of room-sized LCD or plasma computer monitors connected to an EHR or another clinical application. They are often used in ERs.

Mobile computers frequently used in healthcare settings include WOWs, laptops, tablets, and smartphones. WOWs, which are also referred to as computers-on-wheels (COWs) or mobile workstations, are mobile carts that integrate with client computers and peripherals. They can function as either a mobile system or, by locking the wheels at the base of the cart, a stationary system. WOWs are often used in clinical areas such as nursing stations, patient rooms, hallways, and other rooms; due to their larger size, however, it is not always possible to deploy them in smaller or crowded areas. WOWs vary in cost, with the more expensive carts having advanced battery power capabilities, lockable drawers or bins for medication administration and other supplies, power assistance, and advanced cart software. Specialized medical-grade keyboards and mice are often deployed with WOWs to improve infection control. WOWs are often deployed using thin-client computers, zero-client computers, or AIOs.

In some cases, healthcare organizations elect to use laptops and medical-grade tablets with docking stations when deploying WOWs. Laptops and tablets can be readily disconnected from WOWs for easy portability because they have their own battery and operating systems; once disconnected, they can be used as stand-alone devices, and later reconnected to WOWs. Tablets are easier to carry than laptops when making rounds but are not as well suited for clinical documentation as laptops and standard PCs. As a result, iPad and medical-grade tablet usage in clinical settings has seen mixed adoption rates. In a healthcare setting, smartphones are used primarily for communication-related activities such as email, alerting, scheduling, texting, web-based searches, and viewing clinical application data.

Other important client devices and peripherals needed to provide patient care include bar-code scanners, signature pads, printers, document scanners, and identification (ID) badge and access control systems. Bar-code scanners are used to automate the input of patient and medical information, including patient identification from bar-coded wristbands or identification tags, and medication administration that uses pharmacy bar-coded labels. Bar-code scanners are manufactured in wired or wireless configurations, with the wireless modality being both more popular and more expensive. Signature pads are designed to electronically accept patient and clinician signatures, and are frequently deployed at hospital admission and patient accounting areas. Both bar-code scanners and signature pads are among the peripherals often found on a WOW.

Printing and **electronic document management (EDM)** are two final client computing areas that are critical to a healthcare organization. For large healthcare organizations, centralized print servers can be deployed in the organization's data center; these computers typically support as many as 500 printers. EDM is seeing more adoption in health care due to the transition from paper records to electronic records. It involves scanning paper documents and using intelligent optical character recognition (OCR) technology to convert the image into editable text. Low-speed, medium-speed, and high-speed scanners—listed here in order of increasing costs but also better scanning speeds and capacities—are essential EDM devices in today's healthcare environment, particularly in **health information management (HIM)** departments. Portable scanners are commonly used in various clinical areas, such as admissions and nursing stations.

ID badge and access control systems are increasingly widespread in healthcare environments. The important components of badge and access control systems include the ID badge media, radio frequency identification (RFID) badge readers, badge printers and cameras, and badge access control hardware and software. Smart-card ID badges uniquely identify individuals who work in a healthcare setting and are now frequently used to log in and out of computers, gain access to restricted areas within a hospital or healthcare facility, and record start and end times of work shifts. Proximity, iClass, and multi-Class smart-card ID badge technologies are pervasive in healthcare environments, with the latter two having the advantage of not requiring any physical contact between the badge media and the reader. In addition to displaying the user's photo and work information, smart-card ID badges can be configured to hold embedded information,

such as an employee number or medication administration identifier. Use of smart-card ID badges by clinicians to dispense medications reduces the risk of medical errors. RFID badge readers are often deployed on WOWs or other client computers to allow users to quickly log in and out of their computer session. Specialized badge printers and camera equipment are needed to take individual user photos and print the smart-card ID badges. Badge access control hardware and software is required to maintain the list of users who have been assigned a smart-card ID badge, along with their user and access-level information. Such hardware and software are usually deployed with the server system and database installed in the organization's primary data center, with individual servers or appliances installed in a distributed fashion at each facility that has a geographically disparate location.

Virtual desktop infrastructure (VDI) technology is gaining increased acceptance in healthcare settings, largely due to its direct impact in improving patient care delivery. Desktop virtualization is defined as a client's desktop operating system that is hosted within a VM running on a centralized server in the data center. Thin- or zero-client computers are the most prevalent desktop computers running in VDI environments. However, because VDI desktop client hardware requirements are minimal, legacy PCs can be repurposed with a VDI desktop and used for several additional years. It is also common for organizations to deploy VDI software to mobile devices, such as laptops and tablets, which gives them the ability to operate their local desktop or a VDI desktop. Another strategy used in healthcare organizations is to deploy VDI desktops to PC workstations, thereby giving the users of these computers the option to run either both the local desktop and the VDI desktop, or only the VDI desktop. Server computers hosting VDI desktop VMs require a different configuration than host systems running server- and application-based VMs. VDI VMs demand large amounts of RAM, CPUs, and high-speed SAN storage to provide an acceptable end-user experience. In contrast, VDI desktops generally use a standard desktop image that has all the applications and programs preinstalled. A user's personal settings, such as wallpaper and browser shortcuts, along with information on which desktop applications the user has permission to access, can be maintained centrally. Files and documents used during a VDI desktop session can be stored centrally on a file server.

VDI desktops are categorized as either persistent desktops or nonpersistent desktops. When a user logs in to a persistent desktop, he or she receives a new desktop installation each time, along with the user's current personal settings and file sharing information copied to the desktop. If the user then experiences a difficulty with a desktop application or the desktop freezes or crashes, he or she simply needs to log off and then log back in, as doing so will create a new or "fresh" desktop. In healthcare settings, this setup can greatly reduce queries to the help desk. Also, because all users receive the same standard desktop image, significantly less server storage and ongoing maintenance are needed. A downside to persistent desktops is that when the desktop image is upgraded with new applications, care must be taken to ensure that the upgrade will work correctly with the existing applications installed to the desktop.

Nonpersistent desktops function much like a non-VDI experience, except that dedicated server storage for each VDI desktop and the user's VDI desktop is not recreated or refreshed when logging in. This approach is not as effective when addressing end-user help desk requests regarding problematic VDI desktop issues, but does more closely simulate the traditional user desktop experience.

Single sign-on (SSO) and tap 'n go technologies can provide significant benefits to healthcare organizations that are deploying VDI desktops. SSO has the benefit that users have to remember just one username and password for their desktop session and all applications. It works by requiring users to log in to their desktop session with their username and password. Once in the desktop session, the SSO technology automatically logs the user in to each of the various applications without requiring the user to remember or enter application-specific passwords. In a healthcare setting where many different applications are used, each requiring the use of a separate password, this is a significant time saver and user satisfier.

Tap 'n go technology enables users to quickly log in and out of computers with just the "tap" of their ID badge. When moving from computer to computer, the user's desktop session is transferred seamlessly based on proximity of the ID badge to a work station, bringing it over to the next computer exactly as it was left in the previous computer. If an application was opened on one computer, the same application remains open when the user moves to the next computer.

In short, VDI desktops have the potential to improve the desktop experience, reduce desktop support costs, simplify desktop management, increase desktop standardization, and strengthen remote access and data security. Drawbacks to VDI technology are the relatively high up-front capital costs, the more advanced system administrator skill sets needed, the limitations encountered when working offline, and the challenges associated with supporting video and other bandwidth-intensive applications.

Mobile Computing

Mobile computing in health care has emerged as a leading driver for improving the quality, accessibility, and safety of care, as well as increasing the cost-effectiveness of care. For many years, technology adoption in health care has lagged behind that in other industries such as the financial, manufacturing, and retail industries. With the recent development of mHealth (i.e., mobile health), there are now significant opportunities to improve how healthcare professionals deliver care. An important benefit of mobile computing can be seen with how it improves the real-time delivery of care. In addition, with the rapid adoption of smart phones and tablets among clinicians, consumers, and employees, the BYOD phenomenon is gaining acceptance within healthcare settings. Providers of care, who traditionally have been slow to respond to technology innovation, are now taking steps to transform how they deliver health care through the use of mobile computing.

To ensure that mobile computing is successfully deployed in an HIS environment, it is vital that healthcare managers understand how an effective mobile computing strategy can be developed. The steps should be considered when developing a mobile computing strategy.[14]

1. Identify the Key Stakeholders

Four key groups of stakeholders who have unique mobile computing requirements are end users, clinicians, management, and IT staff. To appropriately determine each of these stakeholders' requirements, their input is needed prior to selecting and deploying the mobile solution. End-user concerns typically center on if and how they can use their device, how to obtain assistance or training, what their password requirements will be, what they should do if they lose their device, what the rules are for personal versus company data on the device, and what, if any, reimbursement policy exists.

Physicians and nurses need secure point-of-care mobile technology that will allow them to communicate with each other rapidly and in real time to efficiently do their jobs. Secure text messaging functionality and the ability to integrate with Wi-Fi to provide coverage in areas where cellular signals are weak are two critical areas gaining traction in healthcare settings. Recent research indicates that clinician involvement in technology decision making and use of a single mobile device (instead of multiple mobile devices) improve the quality of care they can provide and increase physician and nurse efficiency.

Management will be concerned about the liabilities, costs, insurance, and changing legal and vendor landscape that are associated with mobile computing. In addition, the ownership and protection of corporate data and assets, along with the ability to measure user patterns, will be an area of management interest. Finally, the focus of the IT staff will be on mobile computing device and application deployment, support, and management; application and data configuration and standardization; and ways to address mobile computing incidents and lost/stolen device issues.

2. Create Policies, Procedures, and an End-User Acceptance Agreement

It is vital that healthcare organizations develop a comprehensive mobile computing policy, including language clearly defining their BYOD strategy. An acceptable use agreement detailing the terms and conditions of mobile computing expectations for end users should be developed by the healthcare organization and signed by each end user prior to that person being given access to organizational resources via his or her mobile device. Typically, this can be implemented by including the user acceptance agreement when deploying the mobile computing software to the end-user mobile devices. Incorporating mobile computing into security awareness training is also an important step toward ensuring ongoing compliance.

3. Understand Regulatory, Legal, and Compliance Requirements

A successful healthcare mobile computing strategy must include all pertinent local, state, and federal regulatory, privacy and security, legal, and compliance requirements. Important legislation such as HIPAA and the HITECH Act at the national level, as well as state-level regulations, such as California Senate Bill (SB) 13863, which includes notification rules that outline requirements for disclosure of breaches, are important regulations that need to be considered before and monitored after implementing mobile computing in HIS environments.

4. Develop Mobile Management Strategies

A number of mobile management strategies have emerged, with mobile device management (MDM) being the most mature in its development. MDM encompasses managing mobility at the mobile device level, with secure email, calendaring, contacts, web browsing, and application store management being standard areas that are typically covered. Enrollment and automatic profile/application capabilities; remote administration; screen passcode settings, remote wipe for lost or stolen devices, and encryption at rest and in transit; secure web browser capability; persistent push email delivery; and compliance/auditing, asset, device, location, and network tracking are additional features that are found in MDM products.

Another mobile computing area that is critical in healthcare environments is mobile content management (MCM), which provides encryption for files and attachments, content expiration, screen capture controls, and online/offline access to secure content. Some MCM products have advanced functionality that restricts data from being physically stored on a mobile device, yet provides full access and functionality to the content. Mobile application management (MAM) gives organizations control over mobile application delivery and app store management, blacklist/whitelist functionality, application tracking, and application security. In addition, it provides a framework for managing a healthcare organization's internal customized mobile applications.

5. Define the Technical Architecture

Four important technical areas must be considered as part of the mobile computing strategy: (1) what the mobile platform will be; (2) whether enterprise directory integration will be needed; (3) which devices and native applications will be supported; and (4) which telecommunications management capabilities and restrictions will be applied. The benefits of cloud computing, including more robust security and reduced costs, have made hosted or SaaS solutions attractive alternatives to on-premises virtual or appliance mobile computing solutions. Other areas to review are perpetual versus monthly licensing, single- versus multi-tenancy architecture, role-based access control (RBAC) support, web-based administrative features, and self-service capabilities.

Medium to large healthcare providers typically require AD, Certificate Authority (CA), and Secure Socket Layer (SSL) virtual private network (VPN) and WLAN integration. The ability to support a wide range of mobile devices using their native applications, particularly for email, calendaring, and contact management, is a necessity, especially for users participating in a BYOD program. It is not uncommon for employers to limit company-issued mobile devices to one or two vendor device lines, with the Apple IOS iPad and iPhone tablets and smart phones having a notably large market share among physicians.

As BYOD gains in popularity, telecommunications management functionality is becoming of increasing importance. This includes controlling and tracking voice and data roaming, cellular and Wi-Fi network data usage and signal strength, and phone call history. Finally, it is important to ensure an optimal and successful end-user experience, avoiding scenarios such as requiring an end user to change his or her existing carrier data plan to a more costly plan to participate in a BYOD program.

Information Security

Ensuring and maintaining the security of HIS data, applications, and supporting technical infrastructure is vital to the long-term viability of healthcare organizations. Without appropriate security program, policies, and corresponding controls in place to (1) define how users and computer systems should behave and (2) protect valuable assets such as computers, applications, databases, networks, and data centers, organizations will be vulnerable to data, financial, and reputational loss. Such losses can be the result of unintentional occurrences, such as unplanned system outages due to poor configuration or a lack of change management. They can also result from intentional acts, such as cybercrime, computer hacking, or malware, which target systems that are not updated or lack appropriate security controls. When designing or implementing HIS, security should be considered at the outset—not just after the systems have been developed and deployed in a production environment. Of course, security controls need to be incorporated in all aspects of technology, including mobile devices, client computers, servers and applications, network devices, and data center infrastructure. In addition to taking security considerations into account in the system planning stages, security needs to be reviewed and adjusted on an ongoing basis to properly protect the ever-evolving technology environment.

Many information security-related systems and technologies can be deployed to protect modern healthcare environments. Firewalls are network devices that limit access and protect an organization's internal network from unauthorized users and external systems. Traditional firewalls use "stateful" network packet inspection to determine whether a network packet should be allowed through the firewall. A network packet's "state" is related to its source and destination address, but does not indicate whether the data inside the network packet are good or bad. Stateful firewalls are becoming obsolete for this reason, as they are unable to determine the kind of traffic or the data inside the network packet. Next-generation (NG) firewalls address the traffic inspection and application awareness drawbacks of stateful inspection firewalls and are now replacing those traditional firewalls. Two of the most important features of NG firewalls are deep network packet inspection and application awareness. Deep packet inspection examines the network packet

payload for anomalies and known malware, while application awareness is a feature that enables NG firewalls to better identify and manage web application traffic. Enterprise class firewalls include other advanced network security features.

VPNs allow remote users to connect to applications or services that are accessible only from computers on the internal or corporate network. VPN connections are secure, encrypted remote-access sessions that use either the Internet Protocol Security (IPSEC) or SSL VPN tunnels to encrypt all data traffic that travels between the remote computer and the internal network. Intrusion detection systems (IDSs) and intrusion prevention systems (IPSs) are intelligent monitoring and analysis systems that detect irregular or inappropriate data traffic occurring on the corporate network; they generate alerts to network and system administrators describing the offending system or device.

Despite the many benefits provided by network firewalls, additional security technologies are needed to thoroughly protect healthcare organization networks, servers, applications, databases, desktops, and other devices. Web security systems are designed to monitor end-user Internet activity; they block or greatly reduce users' ability to access inappropriate and malicious websites, and restrict usage of unauthorized web services, such as unsecured document/file sharing and music/video streaming services. Web security systems can use the Web Cache Communication Protocol to ensure that no end users can bypass the web security system. In addition, most web security systems have data loss prevention (DLP) capability, which is designed to restrict confidential or unauthorized data from leaving the internal network. A current limitation with DLP technology is that it is unable to inspect encrypted traffic traveling about the Internet.

Encryption-in-transit is an important control that ensures the security of all data traffic containing confidential or ePHI information, such as network traffic, web activity, email messaging, file transfers, text messaging, and instant messaging. Encryption-at-rest is a similar security control that protects data stored in databases, applications, storage and backup systems, and laptops and mobile devices. One of the most often cited reasons that healthcare organizations receive fines for HIPAA violations is lost or stolen laptops containing ePHI that was not encrypted. As such, healthcare organizations need to give attention to encrypting all of their laptops.

Two-factor authentication is an easy-to-deploy technology that can be used to provide secure access to remote systems as well as to critical servers or network devices. It works by requiring two forms of identification. The most common form of single-factor authentication in use today is a username and password; this falls under the category of something a user *knows*. Two-factor authentication commonly includes a username and password, plus something a user *has* in his or her possession, such as a smart card or a randomly generated personal identification number (PIN) that is sent to a small device or mobile phone. Two-factor authentication can also include something a user *is*. Although not widespread in healthcare organizations, this technology is found in biometric devices, such retinal or fingerprint readers.

Security information event management (SIEM) is a critical technology that is designed to automate and intelligently analyze system logs for anomalies and inappropriate activity. With increasing reliance on EHRs and other HIS applications, and hundreds of thousands of

system log entries to review for inappropriate user activity, thereby ensuring that access to confidential or sensitive data is restricted to only those who have a need to know, SIEM technology is often the only practical method by which a healthcare organization can detect these types of violations.

System hardening, vulnerability assessments, and penetration testing are three ongoing security activities that are designed to ensure that network, server, application, and database systems are configured in a highly secure manner, fully up-to-date with security patches, and free from vulnerabilities that can exploited to negatively impact the confidentiality, integrity, and availability of production systems.

As seen in **Figure 4.9**, managed security services are cost-effective information security services provided to healthcare

FIGURE 4.9 Managed Security Services

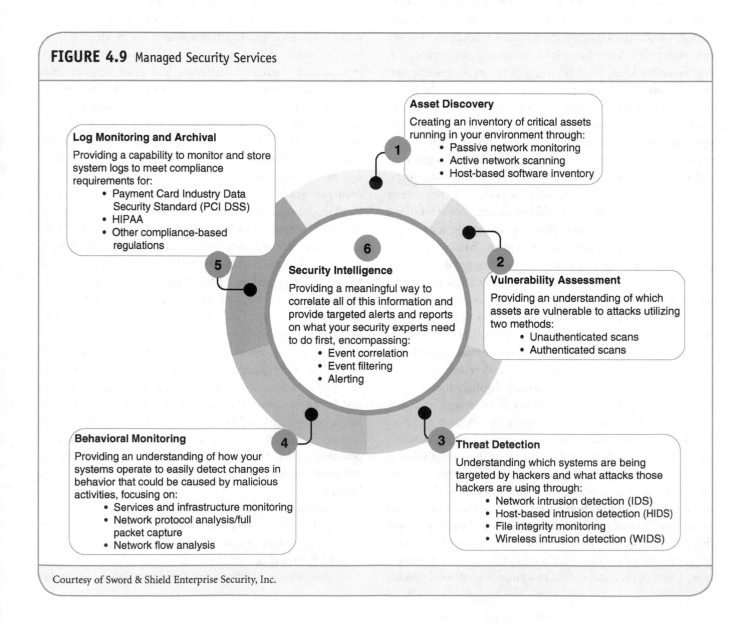

Courtesy of Sword & Shield Enterprise Security, Inc.

organizations by consulting or vendor companies. These services typically manage many of the healthcare organization's information security technologies, such as IDS/IPS, SIEM, vulnerability assessments, and security incident response. Such services provide value by reducing the number of information security personnel needed by the healthcare organization, thereby allowing the organization to spend more time and resources concentrating on its core mission of delivering quality health care.

SUMMARY

HIS applications and their supporting underlying technology infrastructure are complex, yet easily understood when examined through the lens of their smaller, core components (or building blocks). HIS applications are developed using programming languages to define how data will be processed. HIS data are stored in databases that provide advanced processing and reporting functionality. Application integration has been found to be a more superior process for connecting HIS applications than developing and maintaining application interfaces. To develop such applications, the software development life cycle (SDLC) methodology is typically used as the programming development framework. Healthcare organizations are relying increasingly on vendors to develop HIS applications, thereby allowing them to focus on their core competency—that of delivering quality patient care.

HIS applications are categorized as delivering clinical care (e.g., EHRs), clinical support processes (e.g., lab testing, pharmacy, radiology), clinicians (e.g., computerized physician order entry, clinical decision support), and patient flow (e.g., registration, scheduling). Clinical information system (CIS) applications can be either inpatient or outpatient systems. Examples of outpatient CIS applications include ambulatory care systems, personal health records, long-term care systems, and CPOE systems. HIS applications also encompass administrative applications, such as enterprise resources planning, customer relationship management, supply chain management, and home health care. Critical to the success of HIS applications is a smoothly running, properly configured underlying technical infrastructure. This includes technologies such as networks, data centers, server/client computers, and other devices.

Understanding how computer networks operate is essential to ensuring a high level of performance and efficiency for HIS environments. The most important types of computer networks are local area networks (LANs), wireless LANs (WLANs), wide area networks (WANs), wireless WANs (WWANs), and storage area networks (SANs). The Internet is a well-known WAN that is being increasing leveraged by HIS applications due to its robust, highly available platform and pervasiveness. For example, many healthcare organizations are now leveraging the Internet as they strive to improve their communication with patients, develop new marketing strategies, and educate their health plan members. Emerging technologies, such as Voice over Internet Protocol, unified communications, video/web conferencing, and mobile computing are providing new ways for clinicians to collaborate with each other and patients.

The sizes of healthcare data centers are decreasing due to advances in server and storage consolidation, virtualization, and cloud computing. Remote-hosting EHR applications are now more commonplace, with many healthcare organizations becoming increasingly reliant on co-location or vendor-supported data centers to host their HIS infrastructure. As organizations struggle to develop acceptable business continuity and disaster recovery plans, they are discovering that remote-hosted data centers and cloud computing boast high service level agreements and lower costs. But no matter where the systems are housed, they must be protected by viable business continuity and disaster recovery plans. Virtualization and single sign-on advances in client computing have benefited HIS application usability, greatly increasing end-user satisfaction. Wireless workstations on wheels and other peripheral devices are continuing to expand their footprints in hospitals as demands for mobility by clinicians increase. The consumerization of IT and bring-your-own-device models are steadily gaining acceptance in healthcare environments. Finally, challenges with privacy and security remain, but advances in technology are positioning healthcare organizations to mitigate many of these vulnerabilities, with the promise of successfully delivering and maintaining efficient, secure, and high-performing HIS applications.

KEY TERMS

Circuit　62

Client　62

Clinical information system (CIS)　60

Commercial off-the-shelf (COTS)　58

Continuous power source (CPS)　70

Customer resource management (CRM) system　61

Data centers　69

Distributed antennae system (DAS)　66

Electronic data interchange (EDI)　59

Electronic document management (EDM)　76

Discussion Questions

1. Describe the seven stages of the software development life cycle (SDLC) methodology and explain which functions are performed in each phase.

2. Discuss the pros and cons of using application integration versus application interfaces.

3. Identify the various clinical applications (Quadrant I) that support clinical care, clinical support processes, clinicians, and patient flow, and describe how they differ from one another.

4. List three major inpatient clinical information systems and explain how technology enables these systems to deliver improved care.

5. Identify two outpatient clinical information systems, and explain how these systems differ from inpatient clinical information systems.

6. What are the benefits of a computerized physician/provider order entry (CPOE) system?

7. Explain the differences between the various computer networks supporting HIS applications today (e.g., LANs, WLANs, WANs, WWANs, and SANs).

8. Identify some of the emerging technologies being used to support HIS, and describe how they are benefiting the delivery of care.

9. Which technologies are being utilized today in computer networks, data centers, servers, and applications to provide increased availability and allow HIS to remain accessible, even in the event of a hardware or component failure?

10. Discuss the benefits of server virtualization, and describe how it is affecting HIS applications.

11. Identify the various types of client computing devices that are being deployed in hospitals today, and explain which types of advantages they bring.

12. How can ID badge and virtual desktop infrastructure technology improve the delivery of care?

13. What are the important steps a healthcare organization should consider before implementing a mobile computing strategy such as bring-your-own-device technology?

14. Why is security information event management an important technology for managing the security of EHRs and other HIS applications?

REFERENCES

1. StudyMode.com. (2008–2009). The seven phases of the systems development life cycle. http://www.studymode.com/essays/Seven-Phases-Systems-Development-Life-Cycle-163461.html

2. Institute of Medicine. (1991). *The computer-based patient record: An essential technology for health care.* Edited by R. S. Dick & E. B. Steen. Washington, DC: National Academies Press.

3. Institute of Medicine. (1997). *The computer-based patient record: An essential technology for health care.* Edited by R. S. Dick, E. B. Steen, & D. E. Detmer. Washington, DC: National Academies Press.

4. Hanover, J. (2010). Building the right foundation for long term meaningful use. *IDC Health Insights*, p. 21. http://download.microsoft.com/download/D/5/A/D5A9EBCA-3856-4386-B79D-EA497964B9D2/BuildingTheRightFoundationforLongTermMeaningfulUse.pdf

5. Stalley, S., & DesRoches, C. M. (2013). Progress on adoption of electronic health records. In Robert Wood Johnson Foundation, *Health information technology in the United States: Better information systems for better care.* Princeton NJ: Author.

6. Information processing systems—Open Systems Interconnection—Basic Reference Model, Addendum 1: Connectionless-mode transmission, Ref. No. ISO 7498: Add.1: 1987(E). (1984).

7. Outcome 1: IP addressing. The TCP/IP Protocol Suite. HN Computing http://www.sqa.org.uk/e-learning/NetInf101CD/page_15.htm

8. Internet Engineering Task Force. (n.d.). Multiprotocol label switching. Charter for working group. http://datatracker.ietf.org/wg/mpls/charter/

9. Bent, K. (2012, October 19). How the BYOD phenomenon is shaping the next era in managed print services. *CRN*. http://www.mpsconnect.com/articles/437690/how-the-byod-phenomenon-is-shaping-the-next-era-in/

10. Dern, D. P. (2013, December 9). The benefits of integrating wayfinding with digital signage and who's using it now. *Campus Safety Magazine*. http:/www.campussafetymagazine.com/article/The-Benefits-of-Integrating-Wayfinding-with-Digital-Signage-and-Who-s-Using

11. Ontario MD, Inc. (2013). EMR as a service. https://www.ontariomd.ca/idc/groups/public/documents/omd_file_content_item/omd012523.pdf

12. Barnes, J. C. (2004). *Business continuity planning and HIPAA: Business continuity management in the health care environment.* Brookfield, CT: Rothstein Associates, pp. 13–24.

13. Kleyman, B. (2013, October 11). The zero-client: The next-generation in client computing. *Data Center Knowledge.* http://www.datacenterknowledge.com/archives/2013/10/11/the-zero-client-the-next-generation-in-client-computing/

14. Mobile Security Work Group. (2013). 20 questions to ask about bring your own device (BYOD). HIMSS. http://www.himss.org/ResourceLibrary/ContentTabsDetail.aspx?ItemNumber=21437

CHAPTER **5**

Managing HIS and Technology Services: Delivering the Goods

INTRODUCTION

There is little doubt that managing a healthcare organization's information systems is a complex undertaking requiring many highly qualified healthcare professionals working closely together to achieve their goals. Surprisingly, many healthcare leaders do not fully understand the numerous factors involved in planning, developing, implementing, and supporting a comprehensive health information systems (HIS) environment. The *HIS Application Systems and Technology* chapter reviews the importance of developing and maintaining a robust and highly available technology infrastructure. Given the complexities involved with HIS applications, it is imperative that the underlying technology be both stable and consistently available. These characteristics will provide HIS implementation and operational support personnel with the much-needed capacity to focus on managing HIS deployments in order to achieve successful outcomes. To ensure that the technology areas are acceptable and ready to support HIS implementations, it is common for organizations to complete a technology assessment or gap analysis well before the HIS implementation begins. Areas in need of improvement that are found in the assessment (i.e., "gaps") can then be addressed or remediated, allowing the HIS deployment to proceed without being hampered by technology issues.

A key indicator of the effectiveness of an HIS program is the amount of unplanned work needed to mitigate major system "crashes" or other adverse events that cause systems to become unstable, unresponsive, or unavailable compared to the amount of planned work. An effective HIS initiative will have minimal system issues compared to the day-to-day activities of managing HIS activities. Nevertheless, installing hardware and software itself is not enough to ensure success. If HIS are to achieve all of their intended purposes, organizations need to look at the people who manage HIS and the HIS organization's processes from three vantage points: from an operational perspective, from a project view, and in light of how the technology and other IT services are delivered.

For many years, the work of the HIS department in healthcare organizations was seen as filling a purely technical role, with the IT staff often assigned to work in the basement, a data center, or another remote area that left them at a distance from the organization's business and clinical workers. With the advent of healthcare reform and the proliferation of electronic health records (EHRs), the HIS department now must establish a proactive and tightly integrated "hand-in-glove" working relationship with business and clinical staff. In addition to introducing innovative and transformational technology, HIS departments are discovering that partnering and collaborating with other departments within the organizations is key to long-term HIS success. Having covered the technology areas in the *HIS Application Systems and Technology* chapter, it is the goal of this chapter to delve into the remaining two areas in the "people, process, and technology" paradigm—people and process. **Figure 5.1** provides a simple description capturing this concept. This following discussion will provide the reader with a comprehensive understanding of how HIS can not only be deployed successfully, but also experience high staff and end-user adoption and satisfaction ratings.

MANAGING PROCESS

To achieve the successful implementation and ongoing support of HIS, well-defined processes are required. Without structured and formal processes, HIS deployments suffer increased risk of failure, and it is unlikely that high user satisfaction ratings will be achieved once the systems are in place. **Information technology governance (ITG)** is a term used to define this requirement. It comprises the processes that ensure the effective and efficient use of IT in enabling an organization to achieve its goals. ITG can be divided into two additional areas:

- IT demand governance (ITDG) is a business investment decision-making and oversight process by which healthcare organizations effectively evaluate, select, prioritize, and fund their HIS investment, including overseeing their implementations and tangibly measuring the organizational benefits achieved. In other words, it is what IT should be working on.
- IT supply-side governance (ITSG) makes sure the IT organization operates in an efficient and organized fashion. Essentially, it defines who in IT should be doing what.

To implement IT governance in healthcare environments, an ITG framework must be used. Trying to implement governance without a formal and structured framework, or attempting to deploy HIS applications without any ITG at all, will most certainly cause the organization and its HIS initiatives to fail. Several mature ITG frameworks exist today that healthcare organizations can use to develop structured processes for the delivery of HIS. The ITG frameworks that we will discuss here are **Information Technology Infrastructure Library (ITIL)**, **Control Objectives for Information and Related Technology (COBIT)**, and frameworks developed by the **International Organization for Standardization (ISO)** and the **International Electrotechnical Commission (IEC)**.

ITIL is perhaps the ITG framework most widely adopted by healthcare organizations today. It was first developed in the early 1990s by the British government and is made up of a library of books that describe an integrated set of seven process-oriented "best practices" for managing IT services. As seen in **Figure 5.2**, ITIL is well suited for organizations that have a **chief information officer (CIO)** or HIS leader championing HIS-process improvements. Unlike some of the other process improvement models, ITIL provides high-level "how to" guidance via its many generic process flow diagrams and descriptions. IT service management (ITSM) is a term that describes the two primary best practices or core areas of ITIL: IT service support and IT service delivery (**Figure 5.3**).

IT service support is an important process area that an HIS department should consider addressing when

FIGURE 5.1 The People–Process–Technology Paradigm

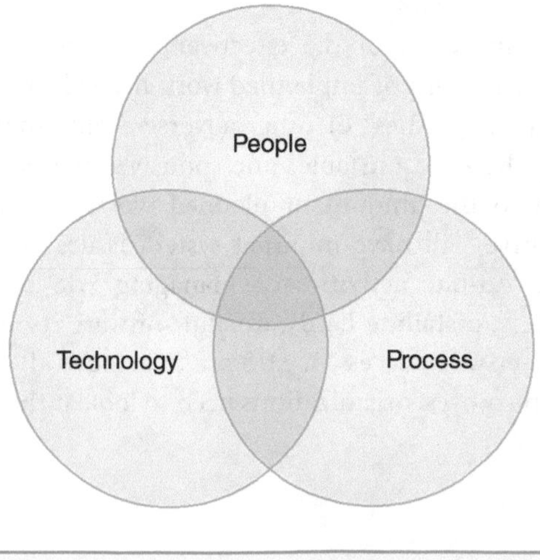

People

Technology

Process

FIGURE 5.2 ITIL Model

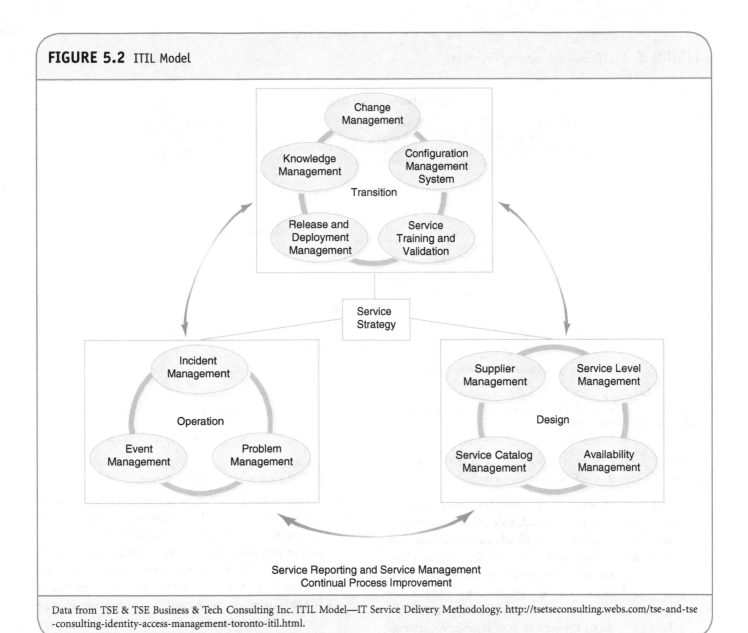

Data from TSE & TSE Business & Tech Consulting Inc. ITIL Model—IT Service Delivery Methodology. http://tsetseconsulting.webs.com/tse-and-tse-consulting-identity-access-management-toronto-itil.html.

FIGURE 5.3 IT Service Management

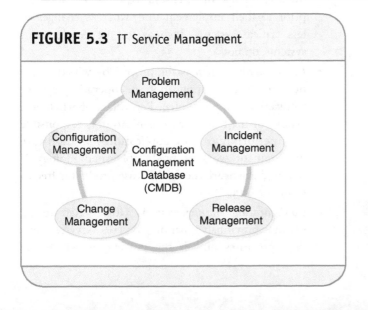

deploying or supporting existing HIS applications. As depicted in **Figure 5.4**, IT service support encompasses the support processes needed to ensure acceptable service. This area is more process oriented than technical, and its activities are accomplished by managing problems and changes in the IT infrastructure. IT service support can be seen most clearly when organizations need to (1) quickly solve issues encountered by staff when using HIS, (2) train staff on how to best use the software, or (3) manage requests for modifications or upgrades in a non-impactful way that does not negate the many benefits of the HIS applications.

FIGURE 5.4 ITIL Service Support Processes

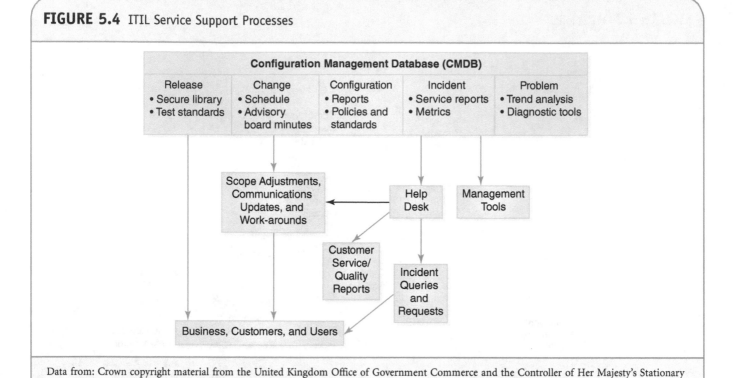

Data from: Crown copyright material from the United Kingdom Office of Government Commerce and the Controller of Her Majesty's Stationary Office (HMSO); titSMF®, 2001.

The IT service support process areas in the context for HIS support include the following elements:

- The *service desk* is the single point of contact for users to report incidents and seek troubleshooting resolution. This component is typically called the help desk in healthcare organizations. In addition to handling calls or online/email support requests for issues, the service desk can manage requests for many other types of purchases or services. A request that has been received by the service desk is generally referred to as a "ticket." An example service desk workflow is presented in **Figure 5.5**.

- *Incident management* is the process by which "trouble calls" or system-related incidents are brought to resolution. Trouble calls are usually directed to the healthcare organization's help or service desk staff, who will resolve the issue or route it to higher-level IT support personnel for more assistance if they cannot resolve the issue themselves.

- *Problem management* is the process by which recurring incidents are analyzed to determine their root causes and provide permanent solutions for the problem at hand. Root-cause analyses (RCAs) are performed and documented after HIS application outages or other unplanned server downtimes; they describe the problem and identify possible solutions to avoid the problem in the future.

- *Change management* is the process by which changes are introduced into the computing environment of an organization. Typically, organizations establish a formal process that describes the HIS modifications or updates. The appropriate managers authorize the change request, and a **change management board (CMB)** convenes to formally approve the change request. Changes to systems that are considered "production" or live most always require CMB approval prior to their implementation, whereas changes to less critical systems, such as test or development systems, do not.

- *Release management* is the process by which major new releases of application or operating system software are implemented. Regardless of whether a vendor or the healthcare organization is responsible for performing the application or software development work, a predictable methodology is required to ensure the final release product is free of errors or "bugs."

- *Configuration management* is closely tied to all of the previously mentioned HIS service support processes and is the process by which the

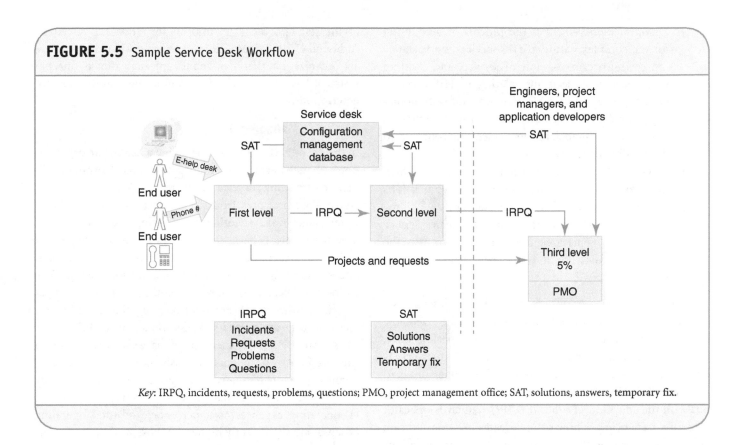

FIGURE 5.5 Sample Service Desk Workflow

Key: IRPQ, incidents, requests, problems, questions; PMO, project management office; SAT, solutions, answers, temporary fix.

computing environment is documented, typically in a configuration management database (CMDB). A CMDB is a valuable resource for resolving issues and maintaining inventory, as it can be used to trace the root causes of problems. For example, if the HIS experiences a problem, the CMDB can be used as a reference to determine if the issue is with the client computer, the application, the database, the server, or the network.

IT service delivery is the second core process area that is important for the proper implementation and support of HIS applications. This area defines the services; describes the roles and responsibilities of those who pay for services (i.e., the customers), those who use the services (i.e., the users), and those who provide the services (i.e., the service providers); and defines the service quality, availability, and timeliness expectations. The IT service delivery process areas in the context of HIS services include the following elements:

- *Service level management* is the process by which **service level agreements (SLAs)** are negotiated with end users and tracked for performance adherence. For example, in a typical healthcare environment, SLAs regarding HIS outages can be categorized as critical, high, medium, or low regarding how much time

can transpire before the system must return to an operational state. This time span often ranges from less than 1 hour for the highest SLA (e.g., a mission-critical production HIS) to 7 days or longer for test or development systems.

- *Availability management* focuses on ensuring that the HIS infrastructure and support services are available to the business functions. Frequent auditing and system checks are useful in making sure that HIS remain available and functioning. For example, database administrators must either manually check or put an automated process in place to ensure that database logs do not grow to a point that all available hard drive space is consumed and the system shuts down.

- *Capacity management* seeks to ensure that the HIS infrastructure has the processing capacity needed by the business functions. Like many other healthcare environments, HIS are often added iteratively without first developing a comprehensive, long-term plan that will factor in future growth requirements. In some instances, the organization may change direction, merge with another healthcare organization, or add a new initiative—all of which will need to be supported by proper capacity management.

- *Financial management* is the process of accounting for the complex nature of HIS services, understanding costs in terms of unit of service, and assisting in management decisions relating to HIS services. Ongoing support and maintenance, software licensing, application upgrades, and hardware refreshes require agile financial management to continue to deliver the needed services.
- *Service continuity management* is the process by which organizations identify their most critical applications and design, test, and maintain alternatives for providing HIS services in the event of a major service interruption. This area is otherwise known as the "disaster recover" or "business continuity planning" function.

ISO/IEC 38500 is an ITG framework that describes six guiding principles for the effective, efficient, and acceptable use of IT: responsibility, strategy, acquisition, performance, conformance, and human behavior. This framework is organized into three major sections: scope, framework, and guidance. ISO/IEC 38500 was first used in manufacturing, but with the adoption of other ISO/IEC standards in health care, this framework is now seeing greater use in healthcare environments. For example, many healthcare organizations are now using the ISO/IEC 27001 Information Security Standard to comply with HIPAA requirements, successfully attest to the meaningful use of EHRs, and build their organizational information security policies and ongoing compliance programs. ISO/IEC 38500 allows organizations to become accredited or registered, thereby assuring customers that the organization adheres to the ISO quality assurance standards. One criticism leveled at the family of ISO/IEC standards is that they require a great deal of administrative overhead to deploy them and there is a cost to becoming registered.

COBIT is an international open ITG standard that was first developed in the 1990s by the IT Governance Institute. Its reference framework is useful for HIS governance, oversight, and process audit, and includes requirements for the control and security of sensitive data. At a high level, COBIT consists of an executive summary, management guidelines, framework, control objectives, implementation toolset and audit guidelines, and a list of critical success factors (CSFs) for measuring ITG effectiveness. The control objectives are made up of four main areas: planning and organization, acquisition and implementation, delivery and support, and monitoring. Relative to HIS, two important supporting areas

of the standard focus on information and HIT resources. Although COBIT does well in describing what characterizes an organization that has robust internal control mechanisms, it has been criticized for falling short in its "how to" descriptions.

Financial Management

In the age of EHR adoption, managing a healthcare organization's financial areas is as important as ever. Hospital profit margins are being subjected to increasing Medicare rate cuts and pricing pressures from commercial payers. Healthcare system chief financial officers are facing the challenges of mounting patient "bad debt" loads as patients struggle with higher copayments and other charges that uninsured and under-insured individuals are having trouble paying. The entire healthcare ecosystem is adapting to major changes associated with healthcare reform, struggling to shift to a focus on a health versus sickness model. In addition, HIS costs from EHR implementations, as well as the costs to support EHRs on an ongoing basis, have put tremendous financial pressure on many healthcare organizations. A study in 2011 demonstrated that actual versus projected hospital IT operating expenses as a percentage of total operating expenses are significantly higher for those healthcare organizations that are just beginning to implement EHRs compared to those at a high EHR maturity level.[1]

When it comes to HIS budgeting, CIOs should take a key lesson from their pioneering CIO colleagues in other vertical industries when developing HIS budgets: The amount spent on support, maintenance, and labor increases by a factor of 4 compared to the average implementation time frame. Meanwhile, technology (both hardware and software) constitutes the easier-to-forecast hard costs in the HIS implementation equation. Another area in which unexpected costs may arise in HIS and EHR implementations is related to project duration: EHR implementations often take longer and cost more than HIS application planners expected. For example, during their transition to EHRs, hospitals saw an 80% increase in their IT operating expenses, which directly impacted the hospitals' overall operating budget—specifically, increasing this budget by more than 200%. Some evidence suggests that those increases could be permanent over the longer term[2] (more on this in the *Implementation* chapter).

The 2011 study also identified the existence of health IT staffing challenges—specifically, the need to attract and retain the skilled talent required to make HIS implementations happen, and to stay on track to meet Meaningful Use requirements. In addition, the cost to maintain operations was found to be high due to, among other things, training requirements. For example, productivity dips occurred when nursing personnel were taken off of their regular assignments to receive training, despite attempts to provide adequate coverage using back-filled personnel. Without a doubt, the pool of highly skilled IT professionals is shallow. Furthermore, healthcare providers are competing for this talent with other vertical industries such as financial services, telecommunications, automotive, and technology companies. This supply and demand gap has driven up the cost to hire an HIS professional, negatively impacting operating costs for providers who are already constrained by limited operating budgets. Skilled talent for HIS is in a shortage situation. According to Accenture (2011), "The war for health IT talent is on."[2] For organizations to qualify for the incentive payments doled out for meaningful use of EHRs, transitioning to a "culture for adoption" is key: 75% of hospital clinicians must consistently use advanced electronic medical record (EMR) components, such as computerized physician order entry, if the hospital is to receive the incentive payments. To achieve this goal, healthcare systems must foster employee engagement, which will in turn lead to effective change management in the organization.

According to Kim (2006), a key indicator of effective ITG is the ratio of unplanned work to planned work. Unplanned work is any activity in the IT organization that cannot be mapped to an authorized project, procedure, or change request.[3] Organizations that spend less than 10% of their time on urgent and unplanned work have been found to have very high levels of operational excellence, compliance, and security. In other words, better governance and planning will lead to fewer "surprises." Examples of unplanned work at low-performing HIS departments can include failed or unauthorized changes, a lack of preventive work, configuration inconsistency, poor security-related patching and updating, improper access, product failures, release failures, human or user errors, and project failures. Failed changes can occur when the production environment is used as a test environment and the customer serves as the quality assurance team. Unauthorized changes often happen when engineers do not follow the established change management process and make mistakes that are difficult to track and fix. A lack of preventive or root-cause analysis will cause repeated failures, as the same problems will most likely continue to reoccur. Configuration inconsistencies in user applications, platforms, and configurations make appropriate training and configuration mastery difficult. Applying

security-related patches and performing system updates will become dangerous if there is inadequate understanding and a lack of consistent configurations. When too many people have user and system access that is not required to perform their job roles, preventable issues and incidents can occur. Product failures often occur when associated software, hardware, and other infrastructure underperform. And, of course, end users' mistakes, whether intentional or unintentional, can be among the largest contributors to unplanned work.

To address financial and budget risks, HIS management should be knowledgeable in the following areas: (1) budgeting and planning; (2) purchasing options such as capitalized and depreciated assets; (3) operating expenses, basic accounting principles, and standards; (4) financial models and methods; and (5) compliance regulations. **Table 5.1** outlines four steps developed by Bogacz (2012) that can be taken to reduce financial risk in a healthcare setting.[4] In addition, **Table 5.2** presents four steps developed by Owens (2012) to consider when managing healthcare budgets.[5]

Vendor Management

HIS departments are increasingly looking to vendors to implement and manage the many complex HIS initiatives that they must undertake. Although large healthcare organizations may employ full-time application developers

TABLE 5.1 Managing Financial Risk

Risk Domain	Steps to Address Financial Risk
Identification	Involves identifying financial risks that can occur as a result of negative factors, or as a result of favorable events (e.g., when unexpected success leads to exponentially increased demand for services)
Quantification	Assesses the likelihood or probability of these risks and their magnitude of impact
Risk response	Involves the organization determining and implementing a response to address the risk, such as acceptance, transference, mitigation, or avoidance
Monitoring	Involves a continuous review of existing and future risks

Reprinted from the Winter 2010 issue of *Strategic Financial Planning*. Copyright 2010 by Healthcare Financial Management Association, Three Westbrook Corporate Center, Suite 600, Westchester, Ill., 60154. For more information, call 800-252-HFMA or visit hfma.org.

TABLE 5.2 Managing Budget Risk

Plan budgets using best estimates carefully at outset of project	• Account for capital expenses • Account for operating expenses • Refine initial budget once specific costs and pricing are negotiated with vendors • Use a milestone-driven, pay-for-performance method in constructing vendor contracts
Include contingency funds in project budgets	• 10% is commonly used, but the percentage amount can be below or above that depending on the preferences of your organization • These funds anticipate and protect the project and organization from unplanned costs
Collaborate with other departments in annual budget processes	• This ensures each department understands and budgets for HIS-related project expenses • Understand project charges and allocations between departments for HIS services
Manage budgets closely!	• Track and report to management the actual versus expected weekly expenses • Communicate quickly when there are budget overages • Be proactive: If you anticipate budget problems or issues, escalate the issue to management right away
Understand the significant components of the budget	• Pay closest attention to the large line items in the budget • Communicate regularly to keep awareness focused on budget adherence • Keep communications about budget awareness and adherence positive: Avoid negative messages and warning tones; instead, build in encouragement, incentives, and rewards when feasible

Data from Owen, J. (2012). *The leadership skills handbook.* (2nd ed.). San Francisco, CA: Jossey-Bass; pp. 189–190.

and programmers to support their in-house systems, most organizations simply do not have sufficient resources to invest in large and ongoing system development projects, or in customized software application development. An increasing number of healthcare organizations are focusing on developing their core competency—delivering quality

health care—and leaving the majority of HIS development and deployment to vendors and consultants, who work in concert with in-house personnel to implement these systems and develop new workflows and processes that fit that organization. In such circumstances, the customer–vendor relationship is critical to the success of HIS initiatives. It must be a collaborative, formal, and mutually agreeable relationship that benefits both parties. In this type of outsourcing partnership, vendors will have the necessary core competency in the area of software or application development and support, consultants may be engaged to provide additional development or implementation services, and in-house HIS departments will importantly need to provide direction and guidance, along with staffing resources to collaborate with end users and support future HIS deployments.

Given the many vendor and consulting companies that populate the HIS landscape, it is vital that healthcare organizations establish truly strategic vendor relationships. Whether the HIS and technology environment is large (several hundred applications) or small to medium (fewer than 100 systems), having too many vendors delivering HIS products and services can be inefficient, costly, and overly complicated. Having too many vendors also results in too many siloed systems and burdens the organization with trying to cobble together disparate systems and varying sources of data and information. Identifying a narrower set of key vendors that will partner with the organization to deliver projects and important initiatives will strengthen the viability of the healthcare organization and is likely to result in better integration of systems. Typically, these strategically aligned vendor companies will have a large portfolio of products and services that can offer value in tandem with standardization and consistency across the organization. For example, having multiple EHR vendors is not recommended, although some large healthcare organizations now face that predicament. Often these strategic vendors will also have a strong portfolio in other HIS areas, such as laboratory services, pharmacy, business intelligence, and data analytics, furthering an integrated systems portfolio. In the supporting technology areas, many of the core hardware and software infrastructure areas (e.g., desktop computers, servers, networking, and databases) can be delivered and maintained by a few companies (e.g., Cisco, Microsoft, IBM, Oracle, Dell). Reducing the number of these vendors will allow both the healthcare customer and the supplier of these systems and technologies to craft competitive and long-lasting contractual relationships.

The vendor management process begins with the vendor selection process. Vendors are needed in healthcare organizations to assist with delivery of a variety of products and services—applications, hardware, networks and infrastructure, and services such as implementation, programming, consulting, temporary staffing, and specialized HIS resources. Healthcare organizations should follow four steps to select the right vendor (**Figure 5.6**):

1. *Formally submit a project request.* This step involves submitting a new project request. HIS planners will create the initial project and business plan and will involve all needed parties.

2. *Analyze their business requirements.* Activities at this level include defining the system scope, feature, and functions; reviewing integration and technical requirements; defining the reporting features needed; and finally issuing a **request for proposal (RFP)** to the appropriate vendors.

3. *Conduct a three-layer HIS vendor evaluation search.* In the first layer (the *functional layer*), features and functions, the upgrade path, the ease of training, the integration benefit, and the workflow supported are evaluated. Here, usability, features, and functions; workflows; and test scenarios are the three elements that need to be reviewed. At the second layer

(the *technology layer*), the technical architecture and specifications of the network, databases, and other infrastructure are considered. In addition, the integration benefits and adherence to IT standards are reviewed. In the third layer (the *business relationship and contract layer*), the company characteristics, survivability, contracting guidelines adherence, business relationships, trust, integrity, and commitment to the project and to the industry are examined.

4. *Select the winning candidate and successfully negotiate a contract.* In this step, the potential vendors are often narrowed down to two candidates. The CIO and legal counsel then collaborate to successfully finalize an agreement with the finalist in adherence with contracting guidelines; the business plan is updated, and the funding source is identified.

A deeper examination of the three layers involved in an HIS product vendor evaluation search can provide additional insight into the vendor selection process. At the functional layer, the product's end-user functionality and usability are addressed. This layer requires the direct involvement of all clinical and business disciplines who will be using the system,

---

FIGURE 5.6 Structured Vendor Selection Flow

Submit Project	Define Requirements	Conduct Structured Evaluation	Negotiate Agreement
• Follow consistent process for all new HIS project requests • HIS planners create initial project/business plan • Involve all necessary parties • Create project charter • Establish project team and steering committee	• Include system scope and feature and functions • Include integration and technical requirements • Include reporting/ analytical requirements • Issue RFI/RFP to appropriate vendors • Include contracting guidelines in RFP	• Usability: Features and functions, workflows, test scenarios • Technology: Technical architecture and specifications • Business relationship and contract: Company characteristics, business relationship, trust, adherence to contract guidelines	• Narrow vendors to two finalists • CIO and legal counsel collaborate • Follow contracting guidelines • Update project business plan with actual plan • Seek funding, including both capital costs and ongoing operating expenses • Select vendor *after* negotiation of key points so terms and conditions are known

along with the HIS experts. Without this involvement, the most appropriate vendor may not be identified. Some of the questions that are asked at this level are the following:

- Does the product have the generally available features and functions?
- What are the development pipeline and timeline dates?
- Does the product perform the tasks required by the end users?
- Does it integrate well into the existing workflow and improve it?
- Are the modules or applications integrated or interfaced?
- Is the end-user interface easy to understand?
- Is training easily and adequately accomplished?
- Does the product support an efficient workflow for the users?
- Will the workflow need to change with the product's implementation? If so, how?
- Does it permit efficiencies and savings in time/money or both?
- Can the system support specialty departments, such as Cardiology, Nuclear Medicine, Dietary, and Oncology?

At the technology layer, it is imperative that all technical aspects of the systems are clearly identified. These include the various *technical components*, such as the hardware platform, operating system, device requirements, network, and security; the *technical architecture*, such as the use of industry-standard technologies and coding/development techniques, modularity design, ease of updates, and disaster recovery; and the *technology standards* and life cycle, along with the availability of resources and expertise necessary to support and maintain technical platform.

In the business relationship and contract layer, all issues with the vendor company should be addressed, including the details of the contractual agreement. In HIS business relationships, issues reviewed during the negotiation include the following:

- The percentage of vendor company resources devoted to this product
- How the company responds to issues that develop over the course of a multiyear relationship, including specific processes for problem resolution and escalation of issues on a timely basis
- The vendor's conformance with HIS contracting guidelines

- The vendor organization's stability and longevity
- The vendor's reputation for completing obligations and conduct according to contract terms and conditions
- The implementation plan
- The training plan
- The support services
- The maintenance agreement and scheduled upgrades and enhancements
- The milestones and payment schedules
- The product life-cycle support

According to *eWeek* (2012), several common pitfalls need to be avoided to achieve successful vendor management.[6] First, it is important to not confuse vendor selection with vendor management; just because you have chosen a vendor, it does not mean you can "check out." Equal importance should be given to managing the vendor relationship both during and after the selection and contracting phase. Second, healthcare customer organizations should not necessarily select the vendor that offers its products or services for the lowest price. Typically a weighting scale should be used in the vendor evaluation process, with price being only one of several factors that are considered. This will promote a strong and mutually beneficial long-term relationship between the customer and the vendor. Third, not measuring the vendor relationship can produce less than desired outcomes. In addition to measuring the SLAs in the contract, the business value of the vendor relationship should be based on business metrics, including whether the vendor relationship is providing value to the organization.

Horine (2009) identifies 10 vendor-management principles that can enable healthcare organizations to develop and maintain strong vendor relationships[7]:

1. Adopt a structured project management methodology that will support proper planning, project sponsorship, clear roles and responsibilities, and formal change and issue management.
2. Understand the different components of vendor management, some of which include evaluation and selection, contracting, and relationship and delivery management.
3. Pay very close attention to the contract details—specifically roles and responsibilities and the use of incentives and penalties—following the contract requirements.
4. Formalize all the important requirements in the contract, such as project changes and communication modifications.

5. Ensure that the contractual details are equal to the level of project risk. Expect a large complex project to have a very detailed contract.
6. If it is important, put it in the contract: Deliverable specifications, methodology used to create the deliverable, specific resources, roles and responsibilities, planned communications, deliverable acceptance criteria, and project success criteria should all be included in the contract.
7. Obtain senior management commitment and buy-in from both the customer and the vendor at the beginning of the project. This will go a long way toward ensuring vendor management success.
8. Look for ways to benefit both the customer and the vendor. This will help the partners build mutually beneficial resolutions should issues and tensions arise.
9. All terms and processes should be clarified, reviewed, and explained to avoid conflicts and misunderstandings.
10. Clarify internal roles and responsibilities, particularly between key functional and project personnel who must work collaboratively to manage the project and perform team-oriented tasks such as redesigning processes and workflows. Examples include the procurement administrators and project team, the contract manager and the project manager, and the vendor project manager with the internal sales, accounting, and legal teams.

Contract Management

One of the key factors in successful vendor management is contract management. Contract management in the context of HIS can be explained as the execution and monitoring of a contract to maximize financial and operational HIS performance and minimize HIS risks. The HIS contract comprises a written agreement between a healthcare organization and a vendor in which the responsibilities of both parties are outlined to ensure the terms of the contract are clearly explained and followed. Contract management brings a number of benefits to both healthcare organizations and vendors:

- Standardized processes and procedures, which decrease uncontrolled spending and supply risk while increasing purchasing leverage, allowing for less cost to be incurred
- Expenditure visibility, which lets an organization see if it is purchasing at the right times, quantities, and prices, and if those purchases are standardized with consistent contract terms and conditions

- Improved compliance management, which, based on the Aberdeen contract management methodology, can increase 55% when a contract management system is put in place
- Enhanced spending and performance analysis, which allows actual delivery to be compared with contracted purchases and helps identify policy or regulation violations
- Reduced uncontrolled spending, stemming from all the important contractual details having been clearly identified, thereby eliminating scenarios where either party might say, "I didn't know we had a contract" or "I didn't know I wasn't supposed to do that"
- Evergreen contract elimination, where proactive alerts are generated notifying the healthcare organization when it is time to renew the contract, reducing the chance it will be unknowingly locked into the contract for another term

Understanding contract management guidelines provides a framework for accountability to both the customer and the vendor, with the end result being a successful engagement for both parties. This set of guidelines and list of terms and conditions serves as the basis of contract negotiation and establishes a level playing field between the HIS customer and the vendor. Promises made during the sales cycle are defined in exact specificity and committed to in writing. In other words, if the requirement is not written down and signed as part of the contract, it does not exist. All mutual responsibilities are to be defined and documented. Escalation procedures when problems occur must be agreed to, ending with the chief executive officer (CEO) of each organization if necessary. The implementation plan, RFP, and other requirements and commitments are also attached to the agreement.

Contract milestones are key areas that both parties must carefully review and agree upon to assure contract success. In HIS terminology, milestones can be likened to pay-for-performance expectations: They are significant accomplishments that signify phases within an HIS implementation, and they reassure both parties that the implementation schedule is on course. Many contracts are written so that vendors receive payment when they complete each implementation phase. Once a particular phase is successfully accomplished, the CIO signs off on the invoice and payment for that phase is issued. Hardware specifications and system performance metrics are also defined within a contract. For example, system response time ranges in terms of milliseconds (ms) will often be quantified in the contract.

This commitment prevents vendors from selling a system for a very low price by under-configuring the hardware and system specifications. The vendor must guarantee that the system will perform as configured according to performance specifications (e.g., the response time during normal usage as well as during a period of peak or maximum user activity).

HIS contracts also typically specify requirements regarding the ownership of data, change control, and maintenance costs. The *ownership of data* will identify if the data in the system belong to the healthcare organization; if the vendor has a need to use the data for a specific purpose, this point is agreed to in writing by the CIO (for one-time use, in most cases). It is very important for the contract to outline clear ownership of the data by the healthcare organization. If not, the organization may end up having to pay the vendor to obtain its own data for analytics or other uses. It is also important that the vendor not be allowed to use the data from the system they are supporting (and thus have access to the data housed in the system) for any purpose outside providing service to the healthcare organization, such as remarketing of the data or use in another product for benchmarking, without express written permission from the CIO for use of the data for a specific purpose. Additionally, healthcare organizations need to spell out what the mechanism is for accessing data housed in a vendor-hosted system and whether there is a charge for this activity. For example, a hospital may need to generate custom reports from its HIS applications. If those applications are hosted by the vendor but the data belong to the hospital or physician practice, services and fees will often be incurred by the healthcare organization when it asks the vendor to dedicate the time and effort necessary to produce the custom reports.

Change of control is useful to manage all changes that occur in HIS implementation. If a vendor acquisition occurs, the contract might specify that the new owner must obtain the customer's permission before transferring responsibility over to the new vendor organization. This constraint ensures that the healthcare organization maintains the right to self-support the system; if there is source code involved, the healthcare organization is given the right to use the source code.

Maintenance costs, which typically average between 20% and 35% of the original purchase price for each additional year following the initial procurement, must be carefully reviewed. In many cases, these costs outstrip the license fee after 3 to 5 years and continue for the life of the system. Because maintenance costs can escalate over time, such expenses must be carefully spelled out in the contract and budgeted for by the healthcare organization.

HIS contracts often specify terms and conditions in additional areas, such as interface requirements, regulatory compliance, upgrade path expectations, cooperation with other vendors, and escalation processes. Finally, a healthcare organization rarely signs a vendor's standard agreement (and it never should); in most cases, it is required that the standard terms and conditions be mutually revised to satisfy the requirements of both parties.

For its HIS initiative to deliver the maximum value with the desired outcomes, the healthcare organization must ensure that four core areas are emphasized. First, achieving strategic alignment is critical. This includes developing a strategic plan, along with a yearly project and support agenda that aligns with the needs of the organization. Second, architectural excellence and balance are critical. They ensure that the HIS is designed and built by following proper HIS architectural principles and practices. In addition, the HIS architecture must be balanced and in line with the organization's priorities and issues. Third, value and benefits are goals that, if attained, will demonstrate that the organization is able to achieve the desired and anticipated benefits associated with the HIS implementation. Questions such as "Is aggressive process redesign intended to be a part of this HIS implementation?" will need to be asked and considered on a case-by-case basis. Finally, service delivery needs to be emphasized. HIS departments should understand that it is imperative that they deliver quality support and services to their users.

Project Management

One of the most important disciplines that plays a major supporting role in HIS implementations is **project management (PM)**. Each HIS implementation can and should be categorized as a project: It is critical that organizations have viable and robust project management methodologies in place. Project management is defined as the discipline of planning, organizing, securing, managing, leading, and controlling resources to achieve specific goals. From a practical perspective, a project is a temporary endeavor with a defined beginning and end. The temporary nature of projects demonstrates how they differ from operational or functional initiatives, which consist of repetitive, permanent, or semi-permanent functional activities. Hospital staff members who are dedicated to day-to-day operational or departmental duties (such as lab, pharmacy, and other services) are called functional staff, and their sponsoring group is referred to as a functional organization. Staff brought onboard as a dedicated resource for one or more projects are called project staff, and their sponsoring group is referred to as a project-based organization. In most cases, healthcare organizations need both functional and project staff. In a matrixed organization, both departmental staff and project staff, although they may have direct reporting relationships with their respective departmental and project management, also have dotted-line or indirect reporting relationships with each other.

How HIS projects start and wend their way to completion can be understood by reviewing the five project management phases identified by the Project Management Institute (PMI)[8]:

1. *Initiating Phase.* In this phase, the project leadership identifies project stakeholders, develops the project charter and the preliminary project scope statement, and obtains approval of the project charter from the appropriate governance bodies.

2. *Planning Phase.* This phase involves planning the project scope, quality and risk management, and the project schedule. The project scope is defined through creating the project management plan, developing the project scope management plan, and creating the work breakdown structure (WBS). Quality and risk management planning involves identifying and analyzing risks, along with planning the risk response. The project schedule is developed by defining and sequencing activities, estimating activity resources and duration, determining the project schedule, and planning for the commitment of human resources to the project.

3. *Executing Phase.* This phase involves directing and managing project execution; acquiring, developing, and managing the project team; performing quality assurance; problem-solving; and procuring project resources.

4. *Monitoring and Controlling Phase.* This phase involves managing the integrated change control process; controlling quality; controlling changes in cost, schedule, and scope; measuring performance; and monitoring and controlling risks. An effective change control methodology will address both reactive and requested changes; will include a process for categorizing changes; and will include a process for determining how changes are requested, reviewed, and implemented.

5. *Closing Phase.* This phase involves performing project closure and contract closure.

PMI has also defined 10 knowledge management areas.[6] These project management knowledge areas include all the aspects of project management that are required for the successful completion of a project on time, on schedule, and with the best output. These nine areas of activity complement the five phases of project management, in that they can occur during more than one phase. For example, all of the knowledge management areas may be addressed during the planning phase, whereas only two of these areas play roles during the initiating and closing phases. Successfully run HIS projects will require a good working knowledge of how to apply these knowledge areas. The following explanations summarize each knowledge area:

- *Project Scope Management.* The primary purpose of project scope management is to ensure that all the required work is performed to complete the project successfully. This is accomplished by defining and controlling what is included in the project and what is not. Project scope management activities include the scope plan, scope definition, WBS, scope control, and scope verification.

- *Project Time Management.* The main goal of project time management is to develop and control the project schedule. Project time management components include activity definition, activity sequencing, activity resource scheduling, activity duration, schedule development, and schedule control.

- *Project Cost Management.* The purpose of project cost management is to complete the project within the approved budget. Accordingly, cost management includes cost estimates, cost budgeting, and cost control.

- *Project Human Resources Management.* The focus of project human resources management is obtaining, developing, and managing the project team who will perform the project work. This area includes planning for commitment of human resources, acquiring the project team members, developing the project team's capabilities, and managing the project team.

- *Project Procurement Management.* Procurement management seeks to manage the acquisition of products and services from outside the project team needed to complete the project. Project procurement management components include planning acquisitions, planning and negotiating contracts with sellers, selecting sellers, administering contracts with sellers, and closing contracts.

- *Project Risk Management.* The intended purpose of project risk management is to identify potential risks and respond to them should those risks become realities. An example of a risk is a shortage of vendor resources necessary to execute the project. This risk can be mitigated by identifying qualified consulting resources familiar with the vendor's software product that could then supplement the resources available from the vendor for the project, allowing it to stay on schedule and within the budget. Project risk management includes planning the risk management, identifying risks, performing a risk analysis, developing a risk response plan, and monitoring and controlling risks.

- *Project Quality Management.* The principal objective of project quality management is to ensure that the project satisfies its objectives and requirements. Project quality management components include performing quality planning, performing quality assurance, and performing quality control. When managing projects, three critical areas that require attention are project scope, time (or schedule), and cost. A change in one of these three areas will require one or both of the other two areas to change as well. As seen in **Figure 5.7**, these three areas—scope, time, and cost—have a direct relationship to project quality. For example, if the project scope increases, either the project cost or the project schedule will need to increase to achieve the desired project quality.
- *Project Integration Management.* The main goal of this area is to manage the integration of the various project activities. Project integration management includes developing the project management plan, directing and managing project execution, monitoring and controlling the project work, and closing the project.
- *Project Communications Management.* Project communications management focuses on ensuring that

project information is generated and distributed promptly. It includes planning communication, reporting the project performance and the project status, and communicating to resolve issues among the stakeholders.

- *Project Stakeholder Management.* A new knowledge area on the PMI list, project stakeholder management defines all stakeholder activity that occurs within a project. Much of this new knowledge area is derived from the project communications management knowledge area, with the principal difference being that stakeholder management seeks not only to identify the project stakeholders, manage their concerns and issues, and communicate with them, but also to keep them engaged throughout the life of the project.

Figure 5.8 depicts the relationship between the PMI project phases and knowledge areas.

An HIS implementation project, whether it be a complex, multiyear EHR deployment or a much shorter-term, narrower-scoped laboratory information system upgrade, requires the addition of key project-based personnel. These individuals can be full-time employees (FTEs) of a healthcare organization who will work on the HIS project, either as part-time or dedicated, full-time project resources. Alternatively, outside services—such as consultants, contractors, or vendors—may be hired to perform the required project tasks. In either case, it is important to understand the roles and responsibilities of the various project-based positions that most HIS projects demand. A failure to properly assess the area of human resources management can cause an HIS project to become severely hampered or come to a halt partway through the schedule due to resource constraints.

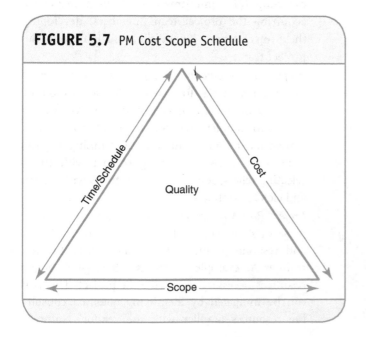

FIGURE 5.7 PM Cost Scope Schedule

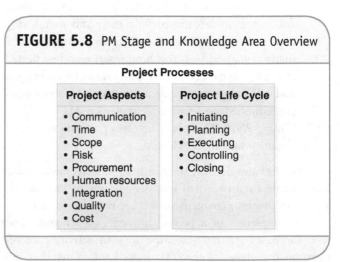

FIGURE 5.8 PM Stage and Knowledge Area Overview

Of the many roles that are observed in projects today, the project manager has the most critical role related to bringing the project to successful completion. The project manager has the following responsibilities:

- Working with project sponsors, the project team, and others involved in the project to meet project goals
- Delivering specific project objectives within budget and on schedule
- Controlling the assigned project resources to best meet the project objectives
- Managing project scope, schedule, and cost
- Reporting on project progress
- Facilitating and resolving issues, conflict, risks, and other items detrimental to a project

Figure 5.9 depicts the internal project coordination relationships of the project manager.

In any HIS project, numerous *customer roles* are likely to exist—for example, executive sponsor, project board member, information systems director, project manager, change manager, application analyst, operational analyst, design analyst, workflow analyst, system administrator, network administrator, operations/systems manager, business analyst, security administrator, testing coordinator, training coordinator, core trainer, go-live coordinator, physician advocate, clinical advocate, user liaison, and project coordinator. Depending on how the project is being staffed, it is possible for consultants or contractors to fill some or many of these roles.

Typical *vendor roles* in HIS projects are the executive sponsor, project manager, financial engagement leader (FEL), revenue-cycle consultant, implementation consultant, analytics and/or decision support systems backload consultant, technology team lead, technology consultant, application or technology delivery consultant, device integration consultant, database administrator, conversions consultant, integration consultant, interface consultant, and project team member. It is important for project teams to understand that successful project completion and accomplishment of the project objectives require that all project team members work together—whether they are HIS department employees, consultants, contractors, or vendors.

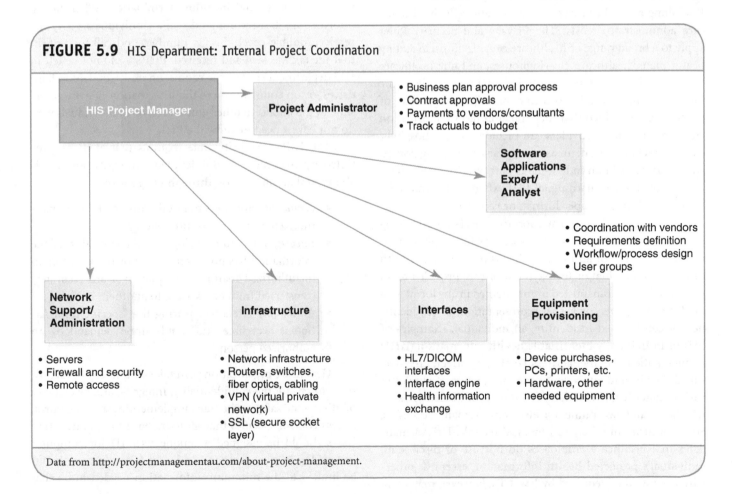

FIGURE 5.9 HIS Department: Internal Project Coordination

Data from http://projectmanagementau.com/about-project-management.

Compliance Management

The Health Insurance Portability and Accountability Act (HIPAA) of 2003 and the Health Information Technology for Economic and Clinical Health (HITECH) Act of 2009 are significant federal laws regulating how healthcare organizations manage the protected health information (PHI) and electronic protected health information (ePHI) of their patients (access control). The HIPAA Security Rule specifies that administrative, physical, and technical safeguards be developed to ensure the confidentiality, integrity, and security of ePHI. HITECH was established with the primary purpose of requiring HIPAA covered entities (CEs) and their business associates to provide notification following a breach of unsecured protected health information. A *breach* is defined as an acquisition, access, use, or disclosure that is not permitted by the HIPAA Privacy Rule and that compromises the security or privacy of PHI. The Breach Notification Rule requires healthcare providers and other HIPAA CEs, to promptly notify affected individuals of such a breach.

In addition to protecting the privacy and security of PHI, HIPAA prevents healthcare fraud and abuse and simplifies billing and other transactions, thereby reducing healthcare administrative costs. The Privacy and Security Rules apply to a broad range of healthcare organizations, including health plans, healthcare clearinghouses, and any healthcare provider who transmits health information in electronic form. CEs include all healthcare providers, regardless of practice size, provided that they transmit health information electronically. Such providers can include doctors, hospitals, clinics, psychologists, dentists, chiropractors, nursing homes, and pharmacies. If an individual is part of a CE, he or she is responsible for safeguarding all PHI, whether it is transmitted electronically, in paper format, or verbally.

PHI is defined as information that meets the following criteria: (1) relates to the past, present, or future physical or mental condition of an individual, and provisions of health care to an individual or for payment of care provided to an individual; (2) is transmitted or maintained in any form, such as electronic, paper, or verbal representation; or (3) identifies, or can be used to identify, an individual. Examples of PHI or **individually identifiable health information (IIHI)** include patient's name, address (including street, city, parish, ZIP code, and equivalent geocodes), name of employer, various dates (e.g., birth date, admit date, or discharge date), telephone and fax numbers, electronic (email) addresses, Social Security number, and medical records. HIPAA mandates that healthcare employees do not use or disclose an individual's protected health information, except as otherwise permitted or required by law. CEs, however, may share PHI for certain purposes, such as treatment, payment, and healthcare operations; disclosures required by law; and public health and other governmental reporting. When doing so, CEs must use or share only the minimum amount of PHI necessary. Exceptions to this rule can be made, but only for requests made by the patient or as requested by the patient to others, by the Secretary of the Department of Health and Human Services (DHHS), as required by law, or to complete standardized electronic transactions, as required by HIPAA. Prior to releasing PHI, CEs must obtain a signed authorization from the patient.

When employees of a healthcare organization are interacting with PHI, they should follow several guidelines. First, individuals should look at or use a patient's PHI only if they need it to perform their job. A patient's PHI should be given to others or discussed only during occasions when it is necessary for those persons to perform their jobs. If it is necessary to discuss PHI, it is recommended that individuals speak in soft tones and do not discuss PHI in public hallways or in elevators. Employees who breach their organization's HIPAA policies and procedures can be subjected to disciplinary action, up to and including termination. When faxing information, it is recommended that individuals verify the receiver, double-check the fax number, and call to confirm that the fax was sent and received. PHI should not be left in HIS department conference rooms, on desks, on laptop hard drives, or on counters where the information may be accessible to the public, to other employees, or to individuals who do not have a need to know the PHI.

The HIPAA Security Rule requires that ePHI be protected by ensuring the confidentiality, integrity, and availability of that information through safeguards:

- *Confidentiality* refers to not disclosing ePHI to unauthorized individuals or processes.
- *Integrity* refers to ensuring that the condition of the information has not been altered or destroyed in an unauthorized manner, and that data are accurately transferred from one system to another.
- *Availability* refers to ensuring that specific information is accessible and usable upon demand by an authorized person.

Healthcare organizations can take a number of practical steps to ensure the confidentiality, integrity, and availability of ePHI. One safeguard entails implementing access control. Access control specifies that all users have unique user IDs. Users should be assigned a unique user ID for computer system log-in purposes, and individual user access should be limited to the minimum information needed to do that person's job. A user's ID should never be shared with or used by another person. Once employees are terminated, their access should be immediately removed.

A second safeguard is password protection. Passwords should not be shared with or used by others and should be changed periodically. Passwords should not be written down, but rather committed to memory.

A third safeguard is workstation security. Workstations include electronic computing devices, laptop and desktop computers, and other devices that perform similar functions; they may also contain electronic media stored in or nearby the device. Physical security measures that can be taken to protect workstations include disaster controls (e.g., surge protectors), physical access controls (e.g., screen savers, locks, or ID badge readers), device and media controls (e.g., backups), and **malware** controls (e.g., software that protects the workstation from viruses, worms, spyware, Trojans, and suspicious emails).

Although a compromised user account or workstation can potentially disrupt one or more HIS user or application, malware has the potential to significantly impact a healthcare organization's network and mission-critical systems. As a result, it is important to understand the various types of malware present today. **Viruses** are programs that attempt to spread themselves throughout workstations, servers, and the entire network; their proliferation can be prevented by installing client **antivirus software**. **Worms** are malicious programs similar to viruses that spread without any user action. Worms take advantage of security weaknesses in the workstation or server operating system or software package; thus their spread can be prevented by ensuring that each computer system has all required security updates installed. **Spyware** is a class of programs that monitor a user's computer usage habits and report this information back to an external computer for storage in a marketing database. Spyware is typically installed unknowingly when end users are installing programs or browsing the Internet. This form of malware often opens advertising windows and slows the computer's performance down; its acquisition can be prevented by installing and running an updated spyware scanner. Remote access **Trojans** are malicious software programs that allow remote users to connect to a client computer without the user's permission. These programs can take screenshots of the user's desktop, assume control of a user's mouse and keyboard, and access client programs at will. Most antivirus software programs can detect and remove Trojans. Suspicious emails, often blocked or "picked up on" by protection software, may include any email that is received with an attachment, any email from someone whose name the email recipient does not recognize, and phishing emails. **Phishing emails** contain web links that appear to be legitimate but, when clicked on, redirect the user to a malicious website where the user's username, passwords, and credit card details can be compromised.

In summary, malware includes a variety of dangerous programs that can significantly diminish the productivity of healthcare workers. Malware can cause client workstations to have reduced performance (e.g., the computer slows down or "freezes"), windows opening by themselves, missing data, slow network performance, and unusual toolbars added to client web browsers. When these symptoms are noticed, the affected end user should contact his or her organization's help desk. To properly protect workstation computers and HIS data, recommended best practices include the following measures:

1. Use client firewalls.
2. Use end-point protection software (e.g., antivirus, anti-spam, antimalware software) and keep it up-to-date.
3. Install computer software updates, such as Microsoft Windows and third-party patches.
4. Encrypt and password-protect portable and mobile devices, including smartphones, tablets, and laptops.
5. Enable automatic disconnect or log-off features.
6. Use password-protected screen savers.
7. Keep computing equipment locked up and in secured locations.
8. Do not store sensitive or confidential information on portal devices.
9. Back up critical data and software programs.
10. Sanitize and safely dispose of old or unneeded hard drives and portable media such as compact discs (CDs), and Universal Serial Bus (USB) sticks (or "thumb drives").
11. Use encryption when transmitting emails, files, text messages, or other information that contains sensitive or confidential information.
12. Report any suspicious activity to HIS management immediately.

In addition to addressing HIPAA privacy and security requirements, data breach regulations, as specified by the HITECH Act, must be carefully considered by CEs. One of the most significant changes to HIPAA that is found in the HITECH Act is the inclusion of the Federal Breach Notification Law for health information. The Federal Breach Notification Law, which applies to all ePHI, mandates that CEs immediately notify the federal government in the event of a data breach if more than 500 individuals are affected, or annually provide notification if fewer than 500 individuals are affected. Such notifications must be also made to a major media outlet and listed on a public website once reported. In addition, CEs are responsible for providing notice to all individuals affected by the breach, to all their business associates, and to the Secretary of Health and Human Services. HITECH requires that all CEs be trained to ensure that they are aware of the importance of timely reporting of privacy and security incidents, and of the consequences of failing to do so. Recent estimated costs from fines and other penalties for data breaches have averaged more have $200 per patient affected, or approximately $3 million per data breach.

MANAGING PEOPLE

The increased adoption of technology in HIS has expanded the role of IT. In addition to traditional or general IT functions, the field of HIS has created new roles and responsibilities. These can include, but are not limited to, roles involved in electronic coding, accounting, and billing systems; EMRs or EHRs; networks for digital imaging such as picture archiving computing systems (PACS); and informatics. Informatics roles include medical informatics, nursing informatics, clinical informatics, and biomedical informatics. Managing these diverse roles is at least as complex and delicate a matter as managing the organization's hardware and software.

HIS-related careers can be found in many different types of organizations—for example, hospitals and healthcare provider systems, healthcare payer organizations, regional extension centers, health information exchanges, community health centers and long-term care facilities, ambulatory centers and small physician practices, education institutions and academic medical centers, government agencies and the military, vendor organizations, and consulting companies. Both IT and HIS roles exist in these organizations. Individuals with a clinical background who are interested in a career in HIS will find excellent opportunities in most of the previously mentioned organization types. Those from IT transitioning to HIS without prior medical or clinical experience may find job opportunities difficult to attain, largely due to the intense competition and large numbers of applicants for some positions.[9]

Senior Management Roles

Board of directors, executive management, and medical executive committee support are essential for the success of HIS initiatives. The CIO is generally the most senior-level IT executive. In many health systems, this role also carries the vice president or senior vice president designation.

Additional IT-related leadership roles can include the chief medical information officer (CMIO), the chief nursing information officer (CNIO), the chief technology officer (CTO), the chief information security officer (CISO), HIS department directors and chairs, and physician and nurse champions. Recently, health systems have developed new roles, such as the chief innovation officer and chief applications officer positions, to meet the needs of the evolving technology environment.

Information Technology Roles

HIS departments are staffed with internal FTEs or outsourced personnel who support traditional IT-related roles. Job descriptions for these roles are categorized as senior level, mid-level, and junior level, and typically include titles such as director, manager, architect, analyst, engineer, technician, administrator, programmer, and developer. Common areas that these roles cover include applications, business intelligence, data warehouses, databases, data centers, directory services, help desks, IT security, mobile applications, servers, networks, telecommunications, storage, systems integration, backup systems, messaging, collaboration, technical documentation, virtualization, and websites.

HIS Roles

To meet the evolving technology demands of healthcare organizations, particularly in light of the increased usage of EHRs, many clinical, business, and project-related roles now require HIS knowledge and expertise. Some of the more in-demand clinical and business positions are analyst roles. These include specialty roles covering systems, administrative support, applications, clinical systems, reports, financial services, the supply chain, human resources and payroll, the revenue cycle, decision support, interfaces, and business intelligence. Two critical roles required to support EHR implementation projects are application analysts and operational analysts. Application analysts translate the healthcare organization's business requirements into a complete and fully tested system that successfully integrates automation with workflow. Application analysts tend to have more technical or IT backgrounds, and are responsible for performing system configuration for one or more of the EHR modules. Operational analysts are the focal point for communication of functional departmental/unit needs, requirements, specifications, decisions, and issues between the user departments, users, and implementation project team. These analysts perform less technical functions, but understand the clinical or business workflow from an operational perspective.

Other important healthcare IT roles include positions in informatics, clinical engineering, go-live events, implementation consulting, integration, project management, quality assurance, and usability. **Exhibit 5.1** presents a comprehensive list of the types of IT and HIS department roles commonly found in large healthcare organizations.

Career Opportunities

To assist those individuals looking to transition into HIS careers, the **Office of the National Coordinator for Health Information Technology (ONC)** developed a program designed to educate and train potential HIS workers. The ONC program has identified six healthcare IT workforce

EXHIBIT 5.1 HIS Job Titles

Active Directory Engineer	HIS Principal Trainer
Application and Technology Specialist	HIS Project Engineer
Cable Technician	HIS QA Engineer
Clinical Content Analyst	HIS Report Analyst
Clinical Systems Engineer	HIS Report Specialist
Data Technician	HIS Security Specialist
Data Technician Per Diem	HIS Sys Test/Document Specialist
Data/Cable Technician	HIS Systems Administrator
Database Administrator	HIS Systems Manager
Database Analyst	HIS Technologist Team Leader
Department Computer Technician	Interface Analyst/Developer
Departmental Financial Coordinator	Interface Testing Coordinator
Deskside Services Tech Team Lead	Knowledge Engineer
Deskside Services Technician I	Lead Active Directory Engineer
Deskside Services Technician II	Lead Desktop Specialist
Deskside Services Technician III	Lead HIS Application Specialist
Desktop Engineer	Lead Project Coordinator
Desktop Specialist	Lead Project Engineer
EHR Security Analyst	Management Assistant I
Electronic Mail Administrator	Management Assistant II
ERP Programmer/Analyst I	Medical Domain Expert
ERP Programmer/Analyst II	Network Engineer/Data Networks
ERP Programmer/Analyst III	Network Operating Systems Engineer
ERP Specialist I	Network/Systems Engineer
ERP Specialist II	PBX Technician
ERP Specialist III	PeopleSoft System Administrator
Executive Assistant	Programmer/Analyst
Field Operations Supervisor	Project Coordinator
Health System Director	Project Support Technician
Health System Manager	Senior Active Directory Engineer
HIS Application Coordinator	Senior Applications and Technology Specialist
HIS Application Specialist I	Senior Business Systems Coordinator
HIS Application Specialist II	Senior Database Administrator
HIS Business Systems Analyst	Senior Database Analyst
HIS Equipment/Stock Coordinator	Senior Desktop Engineer
HIS Financial Team Lead	Senior HIS Application Coordinator
HIS Liaison Analyst	Senior HIS Application Specialist

(Continued)

EXHIBIT 5.1 HIS Job Titles (*Continued*)

Senior HIS Liaison Analyst	Systems Access Coordinator
Senior HIS Project Engineer	Systems Analyst
Senior HIS QA Engineer	Systems Integrator
Senior HIS Sys Test/Doc Specialist	Systems Support Specialist
Senior HIS Systems Administrator	Telecomm Analyst
Senior Electronic Mail Administrator	Telecomm Customer Service Rep
Senior EHR Security Analyst	Telecomm Operator II
Senior Interface Analyst/Developer	Telecomm Operator Per Diem
Senior Network Engineer/Data Networks	Telecomm Project Engineer
Senior Network/Systems Engineer	Telecomm Supervisor
Senior Server Engineer	Telecomm Systems Engineer
Senior Programmer/Analyst	Telecomm Team Leader
Senior Project Coordinator	Time and Effort Report Analyst
Senior Systems Analyst	Time and Effort Systems Coordinator
Senior Telecomm Project Engineer	Video Conferencing Technician
Senior Telecomm Supervisor	Web Technology Specialist
Senior Web Technology Specialist	

roles that healthcare providers will need as they transition to EHRs.[10,11] These roles, which provide a good understanding of the types of duties needed in HIS, include the following:

- *Practice Workflow/Information Management Redesign Specialist.* Workers in this role assist in reorganizing the work of a provider to take full advantage of the features of health IT to improve health and care.
- *Implementation Manager.* Workers in this role provide on-site management of mobile adoption support teams for the period of time before and during implementation of health IT systems in clinical and public health settings.
- *Implementation Support Specialist.* Workers in this role provide on-site user support for the period of time before and during implementation of health IT systems in clinical, administrative, and public health settings. These individuals provide support services above and beyond what is provided by the vendor, ensuring that the technology functions properly and is configured to meet the needs of the redesigned practice workflow.
- *Clinician/Practitioner Consultant.* This role is similar to the practice workflow and information management redesign specialist, but brings to bear the

background and experience of a licensed clinical and professional or public health professional.
- *Technical Software Support.* Workers in this role support the technology deployed in clinical and public health settings. They maintain systems in clinical and public health settings, including patching and upgrading of software. They also provide one-on-one support in a traditional "help desk" model to individual users with questions or problems.
- *Trainers.* Workers in this role design and deliver training programs to employees in clinical, administrative, and public health settings.

Staff Development

Staff development is a key component in assuring that HIS employees attain competency in information and management system tools and skills. Staff improvement programs provide employees with the proficiencies and qualifications needed for advancement within the organization, and they help staff form the necessary attitudes and interpersonal skills to work effectively. Organizations can provide employee development through training and in-service programs, certification classes, community college or university educational courses, conferences and workshops, and professional association involvement. HIS management teams can also promote self-study in HIS employees through books, industry magazines, videos, and online resources.

Training and *in-service programs* are two types of development activities that many healthcare organizations provide for their employees. These can originate from several sources:

- The organization's *human resources department* typically has responsibility for organization-wide training requirements (e.g., HIPAA, security and safety regulations, nondiscriminatory practices, and quality improvements).
- Supervisory, management, and leadership development may be designed and offered by a *leadership department* within the organization or through the human resources department.
- The *department or group in which the employee works* may provide programs such as in-service or line training.
- *Specific HIS projects* for information and management systems usually include a budget for training for system developers, administrators, and end users who will be supporting and using the product.

HIS certifications are another area of interest for both healthcare providers (who are implementing HIS products) and healthcare professionals (who are looking either to transition to an organization that has a specific HIS product or simply to increase their HIS product skills set and knowledge). IT-based certifications have long been a mainstay of IT education and professional credentials. Certification has two main advantages. First, it provides a framework by which technical staff can learn and gain a level of proficiency in a specific HIS-related topic. Second, certification provides the recipient with a credential showing that he or she has a defined body of knowledge in a specific area. Although certification by itself will not qualify a person for a new job or promotion, it does demonstrate that the individual has mastered the basic level of a specific knowledge area and has the desire to increase his or her skills set. Certifications are most often viewed as a positive contributing factor when organizations are making decisions about who to hire. It is recommended that clinicians keep their clinical licensure and certifications active and up to date, even if they are no longer in a clinical role. HIS professionals should also consider keeping their IT certifications active, particularly those certifications that are in high demand in HIS.

Many of today's highly sought-after HIS certifications can be obtained only by employees of organizations that are engaged in a specific vendor-product deployment, such as an EHR or other HIS project. However, healthcare systems also prefer generally available certifications that develop the employee's overall competency and value, particularly if a company is in the process of deploying a certain methodology throughout its organization. These include certifications such as **Certified Professional in Healthcare Information and Management Systems (CPHIMS)**, **Project Management Professional (PMP)**, ITIL, and Lean Six Sigma.

Other avenues that exist for HIS professionals' advancement are *professional development* and *education*. The expenses for these activities are typically borne by the employee, but in many cases are reimbursed by healthcare provider organizations as a benefit to employment. Several of the more often used avenues are the following:

- Healthcare IT conferences and workshops
- National and regional professional association program events
- University bachelor, master, or doctoral degree programs, as well as community college certificate programs, in HIS, informatics, information management, or information systems
- Self-study using books, industry magazines, videos, and online resources

Steering Committees

When it comes to moving HIS initiatives forward, bringing closure to projects, selecting systems, and addressing ongoing system needs, steering committees are an essential tool. In today's healthcare environment, strategic priorities and key stakeholder collaboration are required to ensure that the right decisions are being made and that HIS projects and goals stay on course. According to the Computer Economics IT Management Best Practices 2011/2012 study, nearly 80% of all HIS organizations have steering committees and 69% of those organizations make full use of their committees.[12] Of the 15 practices covered in the study, the use of HIS steering committees ranked as the single most important HIS management practice. Regardless of whether an organization is looking to go forward with a large-scale HIS project or just better manage the existing HIS operational environment, steering committees are useful in driving these areas forward.

A **steering committee** is an advisory committee that is usually made up of high-level stakeholders and experts who provide guidance on key issues such as company policy and objectives, budgetary control, marketing strategy, resource allocation, and decisions involving large expenditures.[13] HIS steering committees are a best practice approach in healthcare organizations for aligning strategic business and HIS priorities. These committees, which usually include executives and departmental heads, focus on three main tasks: HIS strategic planning, project prioritization, and project approval. Clear mandates and a real ability to influence decision making through executive participation increase the value of IT steering committees.

To ensure success in this important area of ITG in HIS, healthcare CIOs should consider adopting a number of recommended strategies.[14] First, it is important to select another name for the committee. For example, rather than calling it the "IT Steering Committee," this group might be named the "HIS Information Management Planning Council"—a name that reflects the organization's work culture and the committee's specific purpose. A committee charter should be developed that includes the desired outcomes. Such a document will help everyone understand the role and purpose of the group, which includes promoting improved communications and recognizing the partnership required for a successful HIS deployment and success. The steering committee should also ensure that its scope reflects a corporate-wide perspective. This broader focus will be helpful when mediating conflicts in priorities or departmental perspectives that may not be in the best interest of the entire organization. The role of the steering committee in ensuring optimal decision making should be identified up front. For example, the committee might be designated as a coordinating body that will resolve priorities, endorse proposals prior to approvals, and monitor progress of major HIS initiatives in lieu of exercising budgetary approval or other departmental expenditure decision making.

Someone other than the CIO may be selected to chair the HIS steering committee. In some organizations, depending on the role of the CIO or IT leaders, assigning a non-IT person, such as the chief operating officer (COO), CMIO, or chief financial officer (CFO), to chair the group communicates the message that HIS is accepted as a critical resource and recognized as such by the entire organization. Best practices regarding how to conduct meetings should be put in place, including scheduling the meetings in advance, sending out meeting agendas, recording meeting minutes, and following up on issues, risks, and action items.

To form an effective HIS steering committee, three essential steps should be considered[15]:

1. Build a case for HIS steering by aligning strategic business and HIS priorities. Focus on core HIS *steering objectives* (strategic in nature), rather than HIS *resource allocation responsibilities* (operational spending decisions). In addition, include shared decision making and fostering a culture of communications between business units.

2. Establish a steering committee charter. This document should outline the key tasks and responsibilities for the committee along with important roles and responsibilities.

3. Keep the HIS steering committee small and meet on a monthly basis. Make sure that the membership communicates regularly and is engaged to address important issues. Also ensure that it includes executive decision-making authority, which is critical to the success of the HIS steering committee.

HIS steering committees are a valuable tool to drive HIS initiatives and align HIS direction with the organization's business objectives. This is especially true in the area of ITG, strategic planning, and project management. By forming HIS steering committees with clear goals, strong senior management participation, and consistent interaction, HIS leadership can accomplish its goals in an enhanced fashion.

SUMMARY

Managing HIS implementations and providing ongoing support for HIS is a complex undertaking. Paramount to this endeavor is clear understanding that HIS applications require a robust and highly performing underlying technical infrastructure. When the technology supporting HIS areas is flawed, system disruptions (e.g., system crashes) and end-user difficulties result. Before all large system deployments, technology assessments should be performed, with sufficient time allotted to remediate any significant gaps or deficiencies. To achieve a highly performing HIS environment, however, additional areas will need attention to ensure they are operating at required levels; these involve process and people.

IT governance frameworks, such as the Information Technology Infrastructure Library, Control Objectives for Information and Related Technology, and standards established by the International Organization for Standardization and the International Electrotechnical Commission are important process improvement methodologies that enable organizations to formally manage their HIS assets. ITIL is an ITG framework that many healthcare organizations have adopted; it offers the benefits of IT service support and service delivery. One key area within IT service support is the service desk (also known as the help desk), which is critical for the proper support of HIS applications. A key area within IT service delivery is service level agreements, which are important for defining the performance of HIS applications and tracking end-user satisfaction.

Financial management, including proper budgeting and maintaining adequate staffing, is critical for HIS deployments to be successful. Adherence to best practices with vendors and contract management are important areas and management needs for healthcare organizations and vendor employees alike. All HIS contracts should specify requirements regarding milestones, the ownership of data, change control, and maintenance costs.

Project management is another key process area that must be formally addressed for HIS implementations to be successful. As both healthcare customers and vendors work together to complete HIS projects, it is vital that they follow the five project management phases and understand the 10 project management knowledge areas as defined by the Project Management Institute.

Nevertheless, technology and process are not enough to deliver and sustain effective HIS initiatives. Equally important is the requirement for new roles and responsibilities in the field of HIS. HIS implementations require appropriate clinical, administrative, and IT resources and expertise, with healthcare experience, advanced skills sets, certifications, training, and professional development opportunities noted as important areas of need. Whether the emphasis is on the individual, or individuals collaborate together through vehicles such as HIS steering committees, it is evident that HIS success relies on "people, process, and technology" to achieve the healthcare organization's goals.

KEY TERMS

Antivirus software 101
Certified Professional in Healthcare Information and Management Systems (CPHIMS) 105
Change management board (CMB) 88
Chief information officer (CIO) 86
Control Objectives for Information and Related Technology (COBIT) 86
Individually identifiable health information (IIHI) 100
Information technology governance (ITG) 86

Information Technology Infrastructure Library (ITIL) 86
International Electrotechnical Commission (IEC) 86
International Organization for Standardization (ISO) 86
IT service delivery 89
IT service support 86
Malware 101
Office of the National Coordinator for Health Information Technology (ONC) 103
Phishing email 101
Project management (PM) 96

Project Management Professional (PMP) 105
Request for proposal (RFP) 93
Service level agreement (SLA) 89
Spyware 101
Steering committee 105
Trojan 101
Virus 101
Worm 101

Discussion Questions

1. Why is performing a technology assessment or gap analysis before deploying an HIS application important, and how can this mitigate future system problems or crashes?

2. What are the benefits of information technology governance?

3. Discuss the differences between IT service support and IT service delivery as defined by Information Technology Infrastructure Library.

4. Why is it important to have a change management board?

5. Which financial challenges related to budgeting and staffing should hospital CIOs be aware of, and why?

6. Describe the process that healthcare organizations should undertake when selecting a vendor to deliver a product or service.

7. Discuss the important principles and areas to avoid when managing vendors.

8. Explain the benefits to both the customer and the vendor from using formal contract management.

9. Elaborate on why HIS contracts should specify milestones, ownership of data, change control, and maintenance costs.

10. Why is project management important in delivering HIS implementations?

11. Describe the five project management phases, and explain how they relate to the nine knowledge management areas.

12. For individuals looking to pursue a career in HIS, which differences in opportunities exist between candidates with clinical backgrounds versus candidates with IT backgrounds?

13. How valuable are certifications in the HIS field, and what are some additional avenues that HIS professionals can utilize to advance their career options?

14. Discuss several strategies that can be used to ensure that HIS steering committees are successful.

REFERENCES

1. HealthPopuli. (2011, January 24). Don't underestimate the costs of adopting health IT. http://healthpopuli.com/2011/01/24/dont-underestimate-the-costs-of-adopting-health-it/

2. Accenture. (2011, January). *Secrets of success on the EMR journey to meaningful use: Leading hospital CIOs reveal key lessons learned.* http://www.accenture.com/SiteCollectionDocuments/PDF/Secrets_to_Success_on_the_Journey_to_Meaningful_Use.pdf

3. Kim, G. (2006, April 10). Unplanned work is silently killing IT departments. http://www.computerworld.com/s/article/110242/Unplanned_Work_Is_Silently_Killing_IT_Departments

4. Bogacz, P. A. (2012). Four-step process for identifying and managing financial risk. http://www.hfma.org/Templates/Print.aspx?id=24400

5. Owen J. (2012). *The leadership skills handbook* (2nd ed.). San Francisco, CA: Jossey-Bass.

6. Perelman D. (2012). Six steps to successful vendor management. http://www.eweek.com/c/a/IT-Infrastructure/Six-Steps-to-Successful-Vendor-Management/

7. Horine G. (2009). *Absolute beginner's guide to project management* (2nd ed.). Indianapolis, IN: Que Publishing.

8. PMBOK. (2008). *PMBOK guide: A guide to the Project Management Body of Knowledge* (4th ed., p. 12). Newton Square, PA: Project Management Institute.

9. Santiago, A. (2013). How to break into a career in healthcare IT. http://healthcareers.about.com/od/administrativeandsupport/p/HealthITjobs.htm

10. HealthIT.gov. (n.d.). Preparing skilled professionals for a career in health IT. http://healthit.hhs.gov/portal/server.pt/community/healthit_hhs_gov__community_college_program/1804

11. HealthIT.gov. (n.d.). Get the facts about Health IT Workforce Development Program. http://healthit.hhs.gov/portal/server.pt?open=512&objID=1432&mode=2

12. Trembly, A. (2012). IT steering committees: Do they have any power? http://www.insurancenetworking.com/blogs/it_steering_committee_ce_it_management_best_practices-28649-1.html

13. Business Dictionary. (n.d.). Steering committee. http://www.businessdictionary.com/definition/steering-committee.html

14. CTG. (2005, April). IT steering committee: Advocate or adversary? http://www.ctg.com/industries/healthcare-providers/thought-leadership/insights-columns/april-2005-it-steering-committee/

15. InfoTech Research Group. (n.d.). Establishing an effective IT steering committee. http://www.slideshare.net/Info-Tech/establish-an-effective-it-steering-committee

CHAPTER 6

Implementation

"If the planning has been thorough, and the team is qualified and committed, the only thing between the starting line and a successful outcome to the project is a lot of hard work."

—J. Balgrosky

LEARNING OBJECTIVES

By the end of this chapter, the student will be able to:

- Describe the planning steps leading up to and included in the implementation of new health information systems (HIS) and technology.
- Explain key steps in HIS and technology implementation planning, and explore the reasons for their importance to the implementation process.
- Define the main steps of system selection and be attuned to success factors and potential pitfalls.
- Discuss reasons for documenting and streamlining workflow and redesigning processes as part of HIS implementation.
- Identify key differences between integrated versus interfaced systems, and explain how these differences play out in HIS and technology implementations.
- Discuss change management and the range of attitudes toward change: opportunities to improve versus resistance to change.
- Describe various roles on interdisciplinary design and implementation support teams and their importance.
- Explain the key steps in selecting a new HIS.

INTRODUCTION

As discussed in the *Health Information System Strategic Planning* chapter, the health information systems (HIS) planning process should yield an approved, funded HIS and technology plan for your organization. Now it is time to face down the monumental challenge of actually *doing* what everyone in the organization has been *talking about* for quite some time. It is time to **implement** the systems conceived in the HIS plan, which means putting new HIS into actual use (**Figure 6.1**). This is a significant shift in focus for the organization, yet every bit of work that went into the organization's disciplined and thorough planning process will pay off as detailed implementation planning commences. While systems are being implemented, everyone participating will use everything they ever learned in their life to get them through the trials and tribulations of HIS and technology implementation. This work is not for the faint of heart—nor is it to be avoided, because it is what really matters in any discussion about HIS and information technology (IT) today. If systems are not implemented and implemented well, all of the talk about the promise of HIS and technology is for naught and a waste of time and energy. Implementation is the opportunity to truly do something that can make health care better both for individuals receiving and delivering care and overall for people and our health system by producing a better quality of care and service and offering improved value and cost outcomes over those available today.

Implementing systems is tough work, even for the HIS and technology devotees among us. To spur HIS implementation, the American Reinvestment and Recovery Act of 2009 (ARRA)

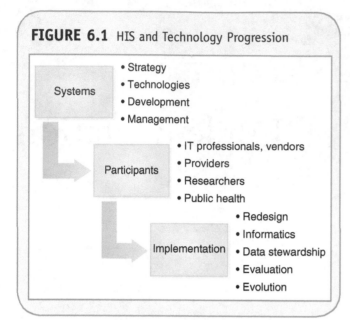

FIGURE 6.1 HIS and Technology Progression

Systems
- Strategy
- Technologies
- Development
- Management

Participants
- IT professionals, vendors
- Providers
- Researchers
- Public health

Implementation
- Redesign
- Informatics
- Data stewardship
- Evaluation
- Evolution

and the Health Information Technology and Clinical Health (HITECH) Act of 2009 stimulus funding provide incentives for physician practices and hospitals to implement electronic health records (EHRs). While these incentives are making a difference in moving up stubbornly low EHR implementation rates in healthcare settings and in health information exchanges (HIEs) in the United States, the road to ubiquitous availability of secure healthcare data continues to be a long and hard one.[1]

To understand what is involved, we should address some important definitions regarding how EHR adoption is currently measured. A **basic EHR system** is a system that uses EHR functionality on at least one clinical unit and includes patient demographics, physician notes, nursing assessments, patient problem lists, laboratory and radiology reports, and diagnostic test results, as well as computerized ordering for medications. By comparison, a **comprehensive EHR system** includes the basic functionality described previously plus 14 other clinical functionalities (**Table 6.1**) and is used throughout the entire hospital.[2] Basic EHR adoption requires each function to be implemented in at least one clinical unit, and comprehensive EHR adoption requires each function to be implemented in all clinical units. More advanced functionalities such as computerized provider order entry, electronic generation of quality measures, and patient electronic access to their records are more challenging to implement for all hospitals.[3] The HITECH stimulus incentives call for these functionalities to be implemented in stages called Meaningful Use Stages 1, 2, and 3 (discussed in more detail later in the chapter).

Recent research shows progress in EHR adoption, although comprehensive adoption continues to elude most healthcare organizations. Jha et al. concluded that only 44%

of hospitals use a "basic" (versus a "comprehensive") EHR system.[3] This is progress considering that the percentage of U.S. hospitals using basic *or* comprehensive EHRs was only 8.7% in 2008 and 11.9% in 2009. **Figure 6.2** shows EHR adoption rates from 2008 to 2012 among U.S. hospitals.[1] Additionally, physician office EHR adoption rates have also increased substantially with implementation of the federal government's stimulus program, with 40% of all physician practices now using the "basic" functionalities of an EHR system.[4]

Participation in HIEs has also been increasing, with 30% of hospitals and 10% of ambulatory practices now active in 1 of 119 HIEs found across the United States. Unfortunately, more than 70% of these exchanges are struggling to find a sustainable business model and are at risk of failing once the governmental stimulus funds are no longer available to help sustain them.[5]

These data show that the HITECH Act has had the desired effect of stimulating the adoption of EHRs and data exchanges among healthcare providers, yet also give some indication of the difficulty associated with these implementations. This scenario provides us with the backdrop for discussing HIS and technology implementations.

Implementation consists of several progressive steps leading up to the profound moment of "go-live" or activation of a new system (**Figure 6.3**):

1. **Implementation planning** (including system selection, elements of contract negotiation, system specification, and documentation of the setting in which the system will be implemented)
2. **System design** (including creation of computer functionality that accomplishes redesigned workflow and processes in user-friendly ways)
3. System or application programming (including the technical aspects of systems engineering and writing computer programs that reflect the system design)
4. Development or "build" (including the creation of applications, interfaces, and interaction between those applications so that the resulting overall system performs desired functions in a smooth and integrated fashion)
5. Testing (including system and integration testing challenging and perfecting the system programs and interfaces to weed out and correct any errors in the development phase)
6. Roll-out or deployment (including detailed implementation and go-live system activation planning and execution)
7. Evaluation (including measurement of system functioning against performance and user satisfaction metrics)

TABLE 6.1 Basic and Comprehensive EHR Functionalities

EHR Functions Required	Basic EHR Without Clinician Notes	Basic EHR with Clinician Notes	Comprehensive EHR
Electronic Clinical Information			
Patient demographics	✓	✓	✓
Physician notes		✓	✓
Nursing assessments		✓	✓
Problem lists	✓	✓	✓
Medication lists	✓	✓	✓
Discharge summaries	✓	✓	✓
Advance directives			✓
Computerized Provider Order Entry			
Lab reports			✓
Radiology tests			✓
Medications	✓	✓	✓
Consultation requests			✓
Nursing orders			✓
Results Management			
View lab reports	✓	✓	✓
View radiology reports	✓	✓	✓
View radiology images			✓
View diagnostic test results	✓	✓	✓
View diagnostic test images			✓
View consultant report			✓
Decision Support			
Clinical guidelines			✓
Clinical reminders			✓
Drug allergy results			✓
Drug–drug interactions			✓
Drug–lab interactions			✓
Drug dosing support			✓

Basic EHR adoption requires each function to be implemented in at least one clinical unit, and comprehensive EHR adoption requires each function to be implemented in all clinical units.

Reproduced from Charles et al. (2012, February). ONC Data Brief No. 1: Electronic health record systems and intent to attest to meaningful use among non-federal acute care hospitals in the United States: 2008–2011. http://www.healthit.gov/media/pdf/ONC_Data_Brief_AHA_2011.pdf

This progression of steps is continually repeated in a feedback loop as enhancements and functionalities are added to the system being implemented. Implementation is a lively, active process that never ends once a system is "live" and being used in the support of real work in an organization (otherwise referred to as the system being in "production"). Once a system is in use, there begins the iterative process of continually making improvements, fixing issues, adding new functionalities or capabilities to the existing platform, adding new end users and new reports, updating and upgrading the system, and so on. Once a system is "live" and stabilized, the addition of more users, more functionality, and additional process redesign becomes the journey that use of a system truly is. The system becomes a part of the daily work and life of the organization and the people who work there and, as such, needs continual care, attention, energy, and resources to sustain it and move down the path of growth and evolution for the organization. Conversely, if a system is not given the attention, resources, and nurturance it requires, the consequences can be dire for the organization, its providers, and patients: Faulty systems or data may result in faulty processes and inaccurate information, which in health care can be disastrous, potentially leading to medical errors. Take heed of this and be courageous, be diligent, and read on about HIS and technology implementation—where the rubber does, indeed, meet the road.

We can think about the scope of HIS and technology implementation in several different ways. In particular, this scope may be envisioned as the implementation of the strategic HIS and technology plan or, alternatively, as the implementation of a new health information and technology system in the organization for use in performing its daily clinical or administrative activities. The focus of this chapter is on the latter interpretation—that is, implementation of a new system for use in a healthcare organization. The process of implementation is similar whether the system is an enterprise system or a standalone system, and whether it is deployed in a hospital system, physician practice, clinic, home health organization, hospice, community health center, public health clinic or organization, research organization, or any other type of healthcare organization. The steps of an implementation effort are consistent—it is only the content, scope, technology, and participants of the implementation that will vary based on the organizational setting and type of system being implemented. These steps and lessons are generalizable and can be tailored to any system implementation scenario.

STAGES IN IMPLEMENTATION

The steps in implementation can be elaborated as follows:

1. *Kick-off and Project Planning.* Create the project planning team and task forces.
2. *System Selection.* Select the system to be implemented using a disciplined process.
3. *Contract Negotiation.* Negotiate agreements for all necessary system components and services, such as software, hardware, devices, consulting services, infrastructure, and others as needed.
4. *Design.* Perform system design in concert with process redesign, including interfaces required for sharing data between systems feeding data to those receiving data.
5. *Development.* Develop the system and "build," including creation of all system files reflecting the organizational specifics, such as numbering systems, providers, sites, and elements.
6. *Testing.* Perform system-wide testing for each module and connections between modules and applications.
7. *Training.* Train IT staff and project participants initially while the system is being developed and built and then train end users closer to time of the system's go-live or deployment point.

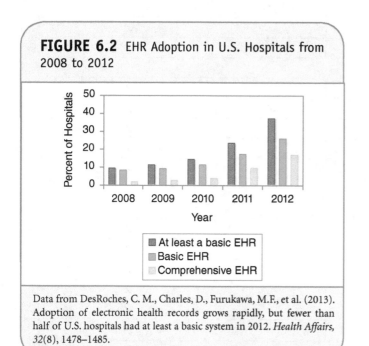

FIGURE 6.2 EHR Adoption in U.S. Hospitals from 2008 to 2012

Data from DesRoches, C. M., Charles, D., Furukawa, M.F., et al. (2013). Adoption of electronic health records grows rapidly, but fewer than half of U.S. hospitals had at least a basic system in 2012. *Health Affairs*, 32(8), 1478–1485.

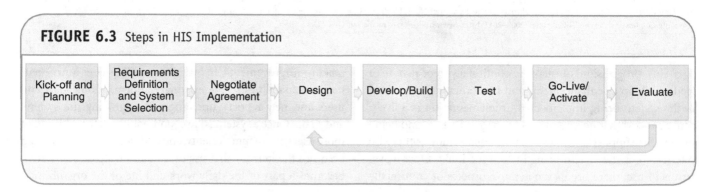

FIGURE 6.3 Steps in HIS Implementation

8. *Deployment*. Prepare the system site, go live, and roll out the system into the production environment for end users to utilize in their work.

9. *Evaluation*. Test and validate systems after going live to make sure everything is working the way it should. Feed the results of the evaluation, and issues identified, back in an organized manner through the steps in the process until the system is working perfectly and any issues are resolved.

Let's look at these steps one at a time. Recall that all of this activity takes place *after* the HIS and technology plan is created, discussed, and approved by as many groups—from senior management to staff nurses to the board of trustees—as possible. Once the HIS plan is in place, the initial projects that get the plan launched need to be defined in detail, approved in the form of business plans, and initiated. In most cases, a rolling list of **strategic initiatives** can be used for this purpose; it provides a useful format for not only organizing and initiating systems projects, but also communicating as necessary to keep the organization up to date on how the HIS plan will be implemented in phases (which typically consist of several projects each), worked on as strategic initiatives comprising the HIS plan.

Multiyear Stages of HIS Strategic Plan

Given that it takes years for most organizations to implement an HIS strategic plan, a good approach to breaking this mammoth effort into recognizable, executable portions is to create stages. Each stage contains phases further broken down into several strategic initiatives and key steps that comprise early foundational work, upon which the basic components of the plan and the more advanced types of systems and functionality that the organization eventually reaches on its implementation "journey."

Phase I begins with the foundational infrastructure, including the data center and other computing environments, the medical intranet for sharing data from existing systems while projects to replace them are pending or under way, the systems that are in greatest need, the oldest systems, and the systems that help sustain the effort by delivering information in the meantime. Phase I also includes thorough analysis and documentation of the current state of how all key processes are performed before designing any new workflow to be built into a new system. The current state is the beginning of the migration path and will be the roadmap from today to tomorrow—a new future state, the goal of the new systems implementations. Another key component of Phase I is the development of the **master patient index (MPI)**, a unique patient identifier or corporate

medical record number that allows data on the same patient from disparate systems to be correctly identified and pulled together. All three phases need the MPI for full functionality of the medical intranet, for instance, although it may not be feasible to implement the MPI until Phase II and the implementation of the EHR.

Phase II can include implementing the basic elements of the EHR. A critical success factor is helping stakeholders see the migration path—that is, understanding the realities of where they are starting from (current state) and where they are going (future state) with this goal of implementing a new computer system to support their work. Everyone needs to understand these two points.

Phase III includes more advanced initiatives, typically involving quality management, outcomes analysis and reporting, business intelligence, clinical intelligence, computerized provider order entry, and other more advanced EHR capabilities such as clinical documentation. These more advanced initiatives build upon the foundation of infrastructure and basic EHR and other software capabilities implemented in Phases I and II.

Implementation of such a multiphase plan means starting at the beginning and growing from there. Any attempts to skip steps or rush the process are usually exercises in futility, and more time and money are wasted with missteps in such a case than if the organization follows the steps in order and stays in touch with the reality of what it takes to revamp an entire HIS architecture and automate new workflows for its employees and processes. Implementing an HIS plan takes years. That is why the future state is a 5- to 10-year view of what the organization would like to look like. It takes that long to implement such massive change. In the following sections we look at each of the three phases in more detail.

Stage 1: Planning

Phase I

Phase I of the HIS plan would most likely consist of a **network infrastructure project**, which would provide the strong foundation and an "electronic highway" for the other new systems to be implemented as part of the HIS plan. In the *Health Information System Strategic Planning* chapter, we compare building a strong house to creating a balanced HIS architecture placed upon the sturdy foundation of robust network infrastructure: All the other systems in the HIS and technology plan rely on this foundation. Other projects that need to be included in Phase I are determined by the organization's priorities for clinical and business systems, as identified in the **current systems review**. The current systems review documents all existing systems in the organization as the baseline for creating an HIS migration plan that will take the organization from its **current state** to its desired **future state** in HIS. The future state comprises a 5- to 10-year view of which systems will be in place after the HIS plan is implemented and a new computing environment has been achieved in accordance with the organization's vision. It should reflect the organization's business plan strategies and the goals that form the basis of the HIS strategies and plans, as described in the *Health Information System Strategic Planning* chapter. As the organization's strategies evolve, so should the HIS plan. The two should always be in sync, keeping the planning process continuous and active.

Once the HIS plan's Phase I projects are identified, each project needs to be defined in the form of a business plan, approved, and initiated. The kick-off is just what the name implies—the formal initiation of the implementation project. During this process, a number of decisions must be made. For example, who is the project manager and which personnel will be included in each project team? For each project, the team membership should possess the necessary skills sets for that project as well as provide for representation from key disciplines that will be using the new system. This facilitates an even exchange of inputs from the various perspectives and enables everyone on the team to learn from one another.

For a network infrastructure implementation project, for example, the project team might consist of three subgroups, led by a project manager. The first subgroup includes technical experts in the areas of networks, technical infrastructure, network monitoring technology, and devices that need to be connected to the infrastructure. The second subgroup includes representatives from the organization's facilities management department, who are essential to the construction aspects of this project: The implementation may require opening up walls and ceilings of the physical plant to allow cabling and other infrastructure components to be built out. The third subgroup comprises representatives from the clinical and administrative areas that will need to be entered and involved to install the infrastructure cabling, routers, and switches into the ceilings, walls, patient rooms, and office areas. Such is the nature of infrastructure projects; they are complex and closely akin to capital construction projects. This type of implementation project moves the technology infrastructure into the patient care and administrative areas so that the network foundation and electronic highway for the other systems are in place; once established, this highway will move increasing amounts of data at subsecond speed so that new clinical and administrative systems can be implemented and workers have ready access to the systems and data they need to do their jobs. Other projects that might be included in Phase I are establishing a medical intranet

for sharing data between existing systems while new, more advanced, integrated systems are implemented, and other important priorities that the organization is ready to implement, such as an upgraded financial system or beginning decision support system such as a case mix system.

Phase II

Phase II of the HIS plan implementation will include systems and technology that are more advanced and require the base systems and infrastructure to be in place. Therefore, the kick-off for the EHR project will occur in Phase II, because it requires the presence of a robust and high-speed network infrastructure and very involved planning phase to initiate these steps. When an EHR project kicks off, it must include a multidisciplinary project team with representation from IT; clinical departments such as laboratory, radiology, pharmacy, and therapies; physicians; nursing; finance; human resources; inpatient and outpatient settings; and other involved functions or clinics. When a financial system project kicks off, it will include members of IT, finance, and additional departments using the new system, such as clinical departments, human resources, strategic planning, and others. The point is to include not only those who will directly use the system, but also those who will be affected by the information produced and used from the system, as a means of transparency in information usage, disclosure, and collaboration (**Exhibit 6.1**).

Key Points

Things to remember in implementing the HIS plan and its strategic initiatives include the following:

- *"Development begins where you are."* This quote (whose source is unknown) is one of my favorites. It seems so obvious, but often when launching a plan or project, we can become so focused on where we are going that we forget that we must begin where we are. We also forget where the people who we are expecting to adapt to such a new system are in their work methods and knowledge base. As much as we might want to change this fact, we cannot. The current HIS state is the place from which we must venture out to make our way to the desired future HIS state; we cannot just take a leap and land in the new place. We must acknowledge the starting point of people, processes, and technologies, and build the path to the new place *from there*. We cannot expect the starting point skills, ideas, comfort zones, processes, or perspectives to be something other than what they are. But if we get on point with them, acknowledge

EXHIBIT 6.1 A Note to CIOs

The key to being a good CIO or leader of HIS and technology in an organization is to engage and involve many people with appropriate representation around you as you lead the charge. Once the vision (the 5-year "future state") for the organization's HIS and technology is agreed upon and established, then the strategic HIS planning process commences.

The first step is to document the "current state" of systems. In one comprehensive electronic health record (EHR) system project I was in charge of overseeing, to document the current state baseline for the HIS planning process, we engaged nine full-time management engineers for 6 months to walk the corridors and doorways of our hospitals and scores of clinics to document—through interviews, flow charts, and narrative descriptions—the current ways we took care of patients. Every key clinical process that would be supported by the new EHR—registration, scheduling, orders management, results reporting, laboratory, pharmacy, radiology, and therapies such as occupational therapy and respiratory therapy—was documented, flow charted, and discussed so that actual steps in the workflows were clear. Front-line workers were interviewed—registration clerks, schedulers, nurses, physicians, therapists, laboratory technicians, and so on—and asked for insights regarding strengths, weaknesses, opportunities, and threats they were aware of in the current ways of providing care and doing their work. The resulting work, which was printed and published in very large fold-outs housed in large three-ring binders, became our roadmap and source of the truth for developing the streamlined and improved processes in the design phase of the EHR system project. This information served as the baseline for the migration from "where we are" (current state) to "where we want to go" (future state). This documentation was very interesting because, in many cases, it reflected people's concern for changing things. Often the workers interviewed would ask to remain anonymous, concerned that their ideas for change might upset others.

Bottom line: It was very important to get stakeholders to participate in the process. Every minute and dollar invested in this planning phase was well worth it. So much truth and intelligence lies in the voices of the grass-roots workers. Never forget that they are just as intelligent as the people in the C-suite—they just have different jobs. Take the time to listen to them, and they will provide some of the best information you can get about a better way to do things.

Go to the ambulatory settings that will be integrated with the inpatient setting. Find out what is important to them and which issues they experience and would like to correct. Make sure these ambulatory processes are documented and understood as well as those of the more powerful departments in the hospital. Make the effort to determine how clinics and ambulatory settings will be integrated into the integrated enterprise system and workflow of the EHR. Remember to follow the flow of the patient, not just the departments providing various services.

Once the HIS plan is in place, break down the total effort into strategic initiatives, each of which then can be broken down into phases; the phases, in turn, should include individual projects that take the organization along its migration path from current state to future state. This migration should include the entire HIS portfolio—infrastructure, financial systems, clinical systems, EHR systems, human resources systems, business intelligence, and decision support systems. *Everything* gets updated, rebuilt, replaced, and revamped as needed. Many older, decrepit systems, left to languish and drag along the workers who rely upon them, will finally be managed and dealt with according to a unified, integrated, updated HIS plan. People will be happy to get updated technology to support their work, and they will work very hard to help bring these systems into reality.

Start with the infrastructure component, including the data center. Develop a project plan, get funding, define the network bandwidth capacity requirements for all the new systems and the data that will be transmitted over that electronic highway, and ensure that everyone and everything get what they need. It is essential to focus on stakeholder engagement and inclusion in the process.

After performing a requirements analysis, the next step is the software product selection process. This is where the importance of detailed plans will be magnified, just as a blueprint is important to the construction of a new house. Each strategic initiative included in the HIS plan needs to be assessed for the level of effort required so that appropriate staffing can be added. Limit the strategic initiatives to three to five that are under way at any given time, but keep three to five in the pipeline at all times. This makes things manageable for the organization as it moves forward with change, while simultaneously supporting existing systems.

the current state, and then present a path to the goal, others will likely be much more amenable to joining the effort.

- *Do not turn over one shovel of dirt unless you know the whole plan*. The best way to run out of budget money, or flub up a design, is to start work on one part of a big plan without having thought the whole plan through from beginning to end. "Thinking it through" includes writing the entire plan down and discussing it with others to obtain their reaction and input (the fodder of the strategic HIS plan). It also means breaking the plan down into its composite project parts and making an honest budget estimate and projection for each of those projects for approval so that the organization can live within its means. An HIS strategy and plan, then, must be thought through from beginning (meaning the current state) to end (meaning the desired future state) before launching into the first project of a multiyear effort. Enough will be changing around you as it is—everything you *can* understand about this whole plan, you *should*.

- *Break strategic initiatives into recognizable, organizable projects.* Strategic initiatives would read something like this: "Build a robust network infrastructure," "Create business intelligence/clinical intelligence capabilities," or "Implement electronic health records." In reality, accomplishing each of these strategic initiatives (termed "strategic" because they enable the organization to achieve its mission, strategies, and goals) usually requires several critical and often large HIS projects.

  For instance, continuing with the Phase I example, building a robust network infrastructure involves at least six subprojects, all related and all part of creating this infrastructure: (1) establishing a relationship with a carrier providing network infrastructure buried in the streets and sidewalks connecting buildings to one another as a utility; (2) placing routers, cables, switches, and other infrastructure components in each building or node on the network; (3) procuring and running cable in the walls and ceilings and corridors of the organization's buildings; (4) installing wireless antennae and infrastructure throughout the buildings; (5) creating a network console and monitoring capability in the organization's data center; and (6) rolling out new workstations and devices to all end users in the organization. Can you imagine trying to tackle all of these activities at once, as part of a single project? It would be a tangled mess and difficult to keep straight. Of course, all of these infrastructure-related projects must be overseen by one overarching coordination point. They are organized as separate projects within the same initiative because each requires a project manager, a separate

team, particular types of expertise, and different types of equipment from different manufacturers and suppliers. Additionally, they need to occur in a specific time sequences. In other words, you cannot implement the personal computer rollout until the cabling and other network infrastructure is in place. This is just one example of how a strategic initiative comprises many projects, which must be organized, budgeted, staffed, and accomplished as separate but coordinated efforts, all of which are necessary to accomplish the strategic initiative "Build a robust network infrastructure."

- *Do not underestimate the importance of training.* The entire process of creating and implementing an HIS plan will be an educational opportunity for everyone involved. Find the right balance between bringing in external expertise to help with these projects (someone who has done it before) and investing in the training and education of the organization's current staff members who have responsibilities in the affected clinical or administrative areas. Do not fall into the trap of thinking that everything has to come from the outside to get these jobs done. Accentuate the knowledge transfer aspects of bringing in consultants so that your staff can learn and grow and be ready to support these new capabilities over the long haul once they are installed. Some personnel will easily rise to the occasion and take on many new responsibilities, even if they are newcomers to the field. Others will need a lot of support and retraining. At the end of the day, the in-house personnel are part of the organization, and they are the people who will carry the day for you in the long run. Invest in their training and development and everyone wins. Help existing staff understand that staying in the same place is not a viable option.

- *Carefully identify and document the "current state."* One implementation method that worked in a large, multihospital system was to engage management engineers (in this case, nine full-time operations experts who were trained in understanding and documenting workflow) to document the current state, processes, and workflows for all key processes involved in clinical care. This work was a predecessor step to the design and implementation of the EHR. It included scores of interviews and a **strengths, weaknesses, opportunities, and threats (SWOT)** analysis with people working at the grass-roots level, those working at the process level, and the process owners and departmental managers for all key processes. These key processes were documented as they were performed *at that time* (thus the name "current state"), rather than how they should or could be performed ("future state"). SWOT ideas were discussed as part of the interviews and results derived from the interview data. These ideas provided a reality check for those working on the project teams as the new EHR system design work was being conducted. It is one thing to have a team of interdisciplinary experts and workers design a new system's functionality based on a desired workflow; it is quite another to have input from literally hundreds of people who do that work every day to ground that design work in reality. Remember—development begins where you are.

- *Do not choose a software vendor or deliver a system without a full current state and SWOT analysis.* The documentation developed by walking the hallways and exam rooms of a clinical environment (all with privacy and confidentiality provisions and safeguards along the way) and talking to the people doing the real work with real patients cannot be assumed, ignored, or made up. This documentation of the current state must be real, as it not only tells system and process designers where opportunities for improvement exist, but also informs them how things are done currently so that implementation plans account for this.

Implementation of new computer systems and thus new ways to do things requires highly specific, detailed work plans that identify changes at very basic levels. Work plans must account for the starting point (current state) and the ending point (new system workflow) for each step taken. This relationship needs to be developed with and explained to the users of the new system, as they are responsible for those workflows now. End users are likely to feel sheer panic if they do not have confidence that the people designing and implementing the new system appreciate and understand all the steps that must be accounted for in performing those clinical or administrative work duties. Otherwise, major confusion may occur, and the implementation is likely to be at best a very unpleasant experience and at worst a complete failure. Always remember that the workers in a clinical setting are taking care of sick and injured people, and they cannot be unduly

disrupted in that work for the sake of a new system implementation. They must know that those staff who are designing and supporting the implementation of the new system "get it" as far as what they do and what is involved. These projects must be carefully and thoroughly planned and communicated to end users—and end users must be told clearly what is expected of them to get the new system implemented.

- *The current state documentation reveals the topography or layout of the new system.* The physical layout of the workflows is a key element of what is discovered during the current state analysis. It shows all of the nooks and crannies of the organization's physical layout to which the system must extend. For example, this gives valuable insight into the size, shape, and configuration of the MPI, which is an essential piece of any EHR implementation. Without a unique patient identifier, or MPI, connecting each patient's information from disparate systems with the various numbering and identification schema located throughout the organization into one consolidated electronic chart (the EHR), the EHR cannot be built to be patient-centric. The MPI is fundamental to receiving and feeding data belonging to the same patient to and from these many different system connections and organizations sharing data.

- *Software systems "out of the box" are raw conglomerations of thousands of capabilities, none of which have yet been shaped to conform to a cohesive whole or to the specific organization's characteristics and desired workflows for key processes.* When viewing a vendor demonstration, it is not apparent that software packages from vendors consist of raw and unshaped features and functions that need to be programmed around and tailored to the needs identified by the project team responsible for designing the workflow to support each key process. Many questions need to be answered and ideas tested to define these requirements and shape the workflow designs for each organization implementing a new system using this software. This applies to any type of system, whether clinical or administrative. During this process, it becomes starkly evident that the people participating in system design "own" the system and the processes, not the vendor. It is a mistake to allow the vendor to design the workflow for the organization—which is not to say that vendor personnel do not have good ideas, cannot suggest workflow innovations, or should not share what has worked at other organizations. To the contrary, great gains can be realized through collaboration with other organizations using the same vendor's software package, especially via user groups. Nevertheless, the system ownership must reside with those inside the organization implementing the system: Design of the system and workflow must be driven internally by people who are accountable for quality patient care and functional business processes. When systems are activated, the end users should recognize what they are being asked to use to care for patients or perform their administrative responsibilities.

- *The new system should be implemented in a basic way first, with more advanced functionality being added only after everyone has some experience with the basics.* For instance, once the foundational functionality of the EHR is up and running (meaning it has the functionality required to support patient care, such as registration, admitting, emergency care processes, orders management, results reporting, clinical data repository, pharmacy, radiology laboratory, and basic documentation), it is important to gradually lay out some new targets to see how much the organization might realistically achieve over the next realistic time frame. Ideally, people will have plenty of time to become *very* comfortable with the base system, to the point where they begin to have new ideas for improved functionality based on their own use of the technology. Those ideas can then be combined into a set of new functions that can be put through the system development process and designed, built, tested, trained, and implemented into the production environment (meaning "going live" with the additional new functionality in the patient care setting).

- *Throughout, take the opportunity to standardize the computing and data environment.* During implementation of a new system, it will become vividly clear where numerous areas' processes have not been updated or standardized, such as in the vast and complex area of supplies and inventory management. These gaps represent opportunities to fine-tune the operational environment in an organization, and such operational "tuning up"

is where many of the efficiency and effectiveness gains attributed to the new system actually occur. The new system brings these opportunities for standardization and improvement to the surface. The needed changes can then be built into the computer-supported workflow. It may be difficult to obtain consensus from everyone, particularly when transitioning from paper to electronic records. Nevertheless, standardization is needed in any organization in the right places, for both quality and cost reasons, and systems implementations will help move this process along. Standardization-oriented work is not about implementing whole new systems, but instead focuses on refining and taking further advantage of the systems implemented in initial phases to redesign and standardize workflows, processes, and numbering schema beyond what was able to be tackled in the early phases. The number of one-off methods and silo systems discovered sprinkled throughout the organization is always mind-boggling, and this refining work is a tremendous opportunity for clean-up, consolidation, standardization, and process improvement.

- *Every project that is part of the HIS plan implementation must be initiated and approved through the organization's formal governance structure: the board of trustees, the HIS steering committee, and the business planning process.* HIS projects must be treated with the same planning discipline as any other project. If your organization does not have a formal business plan template and process, or capital approval process, create your own. Make sure the proper communication takes place with those responsible for finance, operations, and strategy as the projects are being formulated. Regular communication throughout the organization will improve awareness, trust, and cooperation among those who will be working together and whose active participation is needed for any HIS project to be successful. Be aware that HIS projects are likely to be capital and expense intensive: Budgets including 5-year cost projections should accompany each HIS business plan (**Figure 6.4**). Each project must be manageable and assigned to a project manager who has primary responsibility for seeing the project through once it is approved.

FIGURE 6.4 Estimated HIS Project Cost: Categories of Capital and Operating Expenses

	Capital Costs		Operating Expenses						Assumptions
	Year 1	Year 2	Year 1	Year 2	Year 3	Year 4	Year 5	Subtotal	
Software									
Licenses									
Maintenance									
Third-Party Software									
Interfaces									
Subtotal Software									
Hardware and Devices									
Network Infrastructure									
Cabling									
Wireless									
New Hardware									
PCs and Other Devices									
Disaster Recovery									
Data Center Upgrades									
Other									
Subtotal Hardware and Devices									
Implementation									
Project Management									
System Installation									
Data Conversion									
Training and Conferences									
Contracted Resources and Temporary Staff									
Additional Staff Resources									
Travel and Lodging									
Other									
Subtotal Implementation									
Total Capital									
Total Operating									
Contingency (10%)									
Grand Total									

Stage 2: HIS System Selection

The HIS selection process is one that has been tried and tested for many years, and it has become known and accepted industry-wide. Numerous healthcare information systems professional organizations, such as the **Health Information Management Systems Society (HIMSS)**, have published methodologies for this process. Most HIS and technology consulting firms have a consistent methodology that their consultants follow for this type of work.[6] The steps are generalizable to various types of HIS projects and healthcare settings—hospitals, clinics, physician practices, long-term healthcare facilities, community clinics, public health organizations, and others. Moreover, regardless of the type of HIS and technology product the organization might be seeking, with certain modifications in the content or emphasis of the methodology, the HIS system selection process can be used by any organization for software, hardware, services, or other HIS and technology products.

The system selection process should follow an agreed-upon methodology that is used by the healthcare organization consistently for all of its HIS and technology projects. This way, the organization can create familiarity with the process throughout the organization, consistency in the application of criteria, and equity among the various groups seeking systems for the organization. Importantly, this process involves input from all stakeholders in the system and its eventual implementation.

As an example, consider the selection process for a new software system such as an enterprise resource planning (ERP) system (an ERP system is a suite of software applications that support financial, human resources, and supply chain/inventory management). The example scenario will address the work of selecting a software product from the choices available from various vendors in the HIS software marketplace. For clinical HIS, these vendors operate in the healthcare software marketplace exclusively. For business application software systems, such as ERP or business intelligence and analytics tools, sometimes healthcare organizations consider products from outside the healthcare systems and technology marketplace as well as from within that arena. In addition, many vendors of non-healthcare-specific software companies have divisions that specialize in healthcare implementations because the processes being automated that are ubiquitous to all types of industries—for example, finance systems such as the general ledger, accounts payable, and supply chain management—have specific ways of being used in different industries. Such software is applicable to any industry.

The software selection process follows a series of essential steps, outlined in **Figure 6.5** and **Exhibit 6.2**.

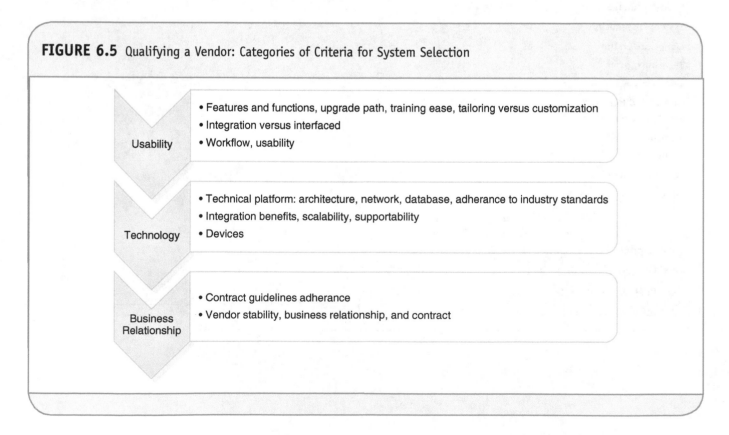

FIGURE 6.5 Qualifying a Vendor: Categories of Criteria for System Selection

Usability
- Features and functions, upgrade path, training ease, tailoring versus customization
- Integration versus interfaced
- Workflow, usability

Technology
- Technical platform: architecture, network, database, adherance to industry standards
- Integration benefits, scalability, supportability
- Devices

Business Relationship
- Contract guidelines adherence
- Vendor stability, business relationship, and contract

1. *Develop the HIS project plan and communicate it to the organization.* This step involves taking much of the work that was accomplished in the HIS planning process and using it to document why the new system is needed, where it fits into the overall HIS plan for the organization, and what the goals are for implementation of the new system. A detailed project plan with a timetable and work plan can be a very useful tool for informing managers and employees about the new system selection process and setting expectations for when the new system might be implemented (in general terms). This communication step marks the beginning of an ongoing communication process that should accompany every step of the selection process and continue through the implementation and go-live point for the new system.

2. *Establish the selection committee.* The selection committee should consist of experts in software and systems (IT personnel with software, hardware, and implementation expertise) along with **subject-matter experts (SMEs)**—in this case, business analysts who are experts in the systems as they are used in the functional areas for which the new system will be selected. In the ERP system selection example, the SMEs include people with finance, human resources, payroll, and materials management expertise and roles in the organization.

3. *Define the system requirements.* This task involves the documentation of all system requirements and forms the basis of the evaluation process. These requirements fall into three categories: software features and functions, technology requirements, and business relationship requirements. These three areas represent very important categories of requirements that deserve discussion with the selection committee and others throughout the organization, as well as with the vendors competing for the business as part of the communication process. Often individuals who have a particular interest in the new system quite naturally tend to believe the selection criteria should be more heavily weighted in the direction of their focus. End users tend to assign a higher value to software features and functions (usability); IT professionals tend to love the technology; and chief information officers (CIOs) and contract negotiators tend to value a solid business relationship.[7] The education process, therefore, needs to explain how each category of selection criteria (usability, technology, and business relationship) is equally important. While different people in the organization may value one category over the others, criteria in all three areas (software functionality, technology, and business relationship) must be successfully satisfied by the vendor for the vendor to be

considered a finalist for selection. It is up to the CIO to make sure a balanced decision is made.

4. *Develop selection criteria.* Selection criteria are the specific requirements within each category that reflect what is important to the selection process for the organization. *Usability* includes desired features and functions and ease of use. *Technology* includes the criteria for specific technical capabilities, supportability, and scalability. *Business relationship* includes the levels of trust between the organization and the vendor, and the contractual negotiation, reflecting the ongoing condition of the working relationship between the vendor and the organization as well as legally binding terms and conditions that will guide the rights, relationship, and interaction between vendor and organization for many years to come. Selection criteria spell out what exactly is important in each of these categories.

5. *Identify potential vendors.* With each HIS project, a host of potential vendors must be considered as candidates during the software selection process. The organization can identify a full list of potential contenders through industry connections and research, which will be narrowed through the request for information process.

6. *Develop a request for information, including the desired rules of engagement, and send it to potential vendors, including the desired rules of engagement.* The **request for information (RFI)** is a concise description of the

---

EXHIBIT 6.2 Steps in the System Selection Process

1. Approve business plan
2. Establish planning assessment and communication with organization
3. Document requirements, technical parameters, business requirements, and constraints
4. Determine selection criteria
5. Identify qualified eligible vendors
6. Create and send request for information (RFI)
7. Narrow field; send detailed request for proposal (RFP)
8. Evaluate responses, hold scripted demonstrations, and conduct site visits
9. Identify two to three finalists
10. Negotiate agreement
11. Finalize project plan and final budget
12. Launch project

healthcare organization, the system requirements, timing, scope, and expectations. It is sent to the full list of possible software vendors, with this list then being narrowed through the RFI evaluation process. The RFI process is intended to gather enough information about each potential vendor to make an initial assessment regarding their viability as a candidate for the in-depth selection analysis without putting both the organization and the vendor through an exhaustive evaluation process. The goal of this step is to narrow the field to seven or so vendors who will be sent the request for proposal (RFP) and earn the opportunity to propose their system to the healthcare organization for possible selection.

7. *Develop an RFP, including contracting guidelines, and send it to the narrowed field of vendors.* The RFP is a more thorough document that outlines, in great specificity, the requirements of the system from usability, technology, and contractual standpoints. The proposal from the vendor in response to the RFP represents a greater commitment than the more cursory response to the RFI. The HIS project team within the organization digs into the details of the RFP responses to validate each specific response. The vendors are held to their representations not only in the evaluation against the criteria and comparisons to other vendors, but also contractually. RFP responses are attached to the agreement with the vendor as part of the contractual obligations. This keeps the vendor honest about what is represented during the proposal and sales cycle; both parties sign on the dotted line and commit to these terms contractually and legally.

8. *Evaluate the RFP responses, narrow the field of vendors, hold scripted demonstrations, and conduct site visits.* This step includes the exhaustive process of evaluating the RFP responses from the various vendors, comparing the responses, and beginning to size up how vendors compare to one another. Ultimately, a field of 7 to 10 vendors that responded to the RFP should be narrowed to 2 or 3 finalists. These are the only vendors that proceed to the next step. The other vendors should be sent a concise, diplomatic, and clear one-paragraph letter notifying them that they have been eliminated from the competition and that the decision is final.

9. *Conduct detailed due diligence on the finalist vendors.* In this step, the organization's internal project team conducts detailed due diligence on each finalist vendor in all three categories: usability, technology, and business relationships. As part of this process, a high-level implementation plan is developed with each finalist vendor as part of the comparisons, and their responses

to the contract terms and conditions initiate the beginning of negotiations with the top contenders.

10. *Negotiate agreement(s).* Initiate contract negotiations with the top two vendors, to see how the negotiations proceed and what the yield is from a contractual perspective. If only one vendor is involved, then the organization and vendor are not really negotiating; the vendor knows it is just having its way with the process and the healthcare organization because it is the only choice. Negotiating with a single vendor is a grave mistake on the part of the healthcare organization: The healthcare organization should *always* have two viable vendors emerge from the first nine steps of the system selection process. Generally a favorite will emerge, but always ask the selection committee to pick two vendors they can accept. When the first-choice vendor knows there is another competitor waiting in the wings, hoping to win the contract, the organization will have greater leverage and the vendor is more likely to compromise and cooperate where needed for a deal.

Send the contractual guidelines to the finalist vendors as part of their finalist packet of information (**Exhibit 6.3**). Few things are as important as these contractual guidelines for increasing the probability of a successful systems implementation. Including these guidelines in the negotiation of the agreement with the vendor forces both parties to discuss responsibilities for the implementation and sign on the dotted line, legally committing them to perform those responsibilities.

The healthcare organization should *never* sign the *standard* agreement of the software vendor. Doing so most assuredly commits the healthcare organization to paying for the entire system based on the passage of time instead of based on the system working or the accomplishment of milestones toward achievement of that goal (a **milestone payment structure**); a standard agreement also likely includes many other terms and conditions that put the vendor company at an advantage and ignore important rights of the healthcare organization. Payment for vendor software based on the passage of time means that the healthcare organization will likely pay for as much as 50% of the system upon signing the contract, with the remainder due typically within 1 year of that date, or by the end of the vendor's fiscal year, so the vendor company can book the revenue. Payment for software based on accomplishment of milestones that leads to a successful implementation protects the organization from paying for a system that is never implemented, thus never gaining the benefit of the bargain with the vendor.

EXHIBIT 6.3 HIS Examples of Contractual Guidelines

1. Percentage of company resources devoted to research and development
2. The vendor's stability and longevity; change of control—what happens if the vendor is sold to another company? Retain the right to change if possible.
3. How the company responds to issues that develop over the long term
4. The vendor's reputation for meeting its obligations and conducting business according to contract terms and conditions
5. RFP response attached to the contract
6. Detailed implementation plan attached to the contract, including a milestone-driven payment schedule
7. Training plan developed and resources available to support training from the vendor
8. Support service: 25% or less, appropriate increases only
9. Conformance to overall contracting guidelines
10. Product life-cycle support: for new releases and versions for 10 to 15 years
11. Clear and acceptable expectations for maintenance: time-to-response based on severity of problem
12. Hardware specifications and system performance metrics well defined, including system performance criteria: The system must operate a subsecond response time with all interfaces, other data feeds, for peak volumes, and so on, with proposed configuration.
13. Mutual responsibilities defined and spelled out
14. Ownership of data: The provider organization owns all its own data and the vendor may not use those data unless expressly approved in writing by the organization's CIO or CEO.
15. Interface requirements spelled out in detail and attached to the contract
16. Regulatory compliance: The vendor must commit to maintaining compliance with all relevant regulations (e.g., HITECH Meaningful Use criteria and other requirements, HIPAA, The Joint Commission).
17. Upgrade path expectations must be shared, and minimum upgrade expectations set in the contract.
18. Cooperation with other vendors: Vendors will cooperate to connect system interfaces and will make other cooperative efforts.
19. Escalation processes: Define specific processes and time thresholds for solving problems when they occur—up to CIOs and CEOs.

If you do not feel comfortable negotiating the contract with the vendor, find a lawyer and a consultant qualified in HIS contract negotiations, and pay those specially qualified professionals to do it either for you or with you. Hiring an expert in contract negotiations is money well spent, and it is far less expensive than buying software that never works—an outcome that will result in a reimplementation project or the purchase of more software to replace the failed implementation.

11. *Finalize the project plan and budget based on the negotiated prices, cost estimate spreadsheet, and specifics of the implementation plan.* This step puts the project plan into complete form and allows roles, responsibilities, timing, and tasks to be identified and assigned to the people who will be participating in the project. Once the project plan is complete, it should be clearly and thoroughly communicated throughout the organization so that all departments and people working on the project can plan accordingly. The time period when a new system is being implemented should be preserved for that activity predominantly—during go-live stages, no other major activities should be attempted in the organization. Systems touch every nook and cranny of the organization, so other projects must go into "freeze" mode as the activation of the new system nears.

12. *Launch the project, including the organizational communication plan.* Now that the system selection and planning phase is complete, it is time to launch the project. Typically this is an exciting and somewhat harrowing time for those close to the project, because they are responsible for a very disruptive, potentially high-risk, high-reward endeavor for the entire organization. But if the planning has been thorough, the team is qualified and committed, and the budget for the project is adequate, the only thing between the starting line and a successful outcome for the project is a lot of hard work.

Final Thoughts on System Selection

The importance of following a disciplined process, with multidisciplinary participation from IT personnel, business people, clinicians, those managing the areas that will be implementing the systems, and process owners or SMEs within affected departments or functions, cannot be overemphasized. Choosing software has the tendency to become a very difficult decision within organizations, depending upon the area for which the software is being selected. The most important thing the CIO or other IT leader of the selection process can do is to set expectations very early in the process regarding the scope of the project, how the selection process will be organized, how the decision will be made, and what the selection criteria will cover. As part of the orientation for those participating in the software selection process, make sure everyone understands what the steps in this process are, why each step is important, who will be responsible for and needed for each step, and how each one contributes to the completion of the task. This information can truly be eye-opening. Each minute spent educating the group and the organization about how software selection takes place can save months of time at the back end of the process and build a common learning base upon which the implementation can continue to grow.

It is also very important to carefully follow the rules on these system selection processes, as vendor salespeople will try to find any opening they can to make inroads into the organization or influence those people who have a role in the software decision-making process. The "rules of engagement" spelled out to software vendors must be strictly enforced, by all parties involved. If a software vendor goes around the rules and thus tries to circumvent the process, that vendor should be warned in writing, and if it happens again, eliminated from the competition. Do this once, and your healthcare organization will not have to do it again: Word will travel quickly among the members of the vendor community that if a vendor goes against the organization's software selection rules, they are out. Think about it: If the vendor is uncooperative during the easier selection phase of the project (when it is trying to win the business), how likely is it that the vendor will be a cooperative partner or prove difficult when the tougher implementation phase is under way? Following the rules of engagement and behaving in a trustworthy manner at the beginning of the relationship throughout the selection process are major points in the vendor's favor in the business relationship category.

REASONS FOR HIS AND TECHNOLOGY PROJECT SUCCESSES AND FAILURES

HIS and technology implementations are multifaceted projects, requiring very careful and smart strategic and tactical planning. Success begins with a carefully thought-out, well-documented, and effectively communicated strategic HIS plan that lays out the sequencing and timing of projects, subprojects, and work tasks within projects (down to the minute for activation "go-live" plans). All of these steps and tasks must systematically fit together, and as discussed at the beginning of this chapter, the foundational components are done first on mission-critical systems (Phase I).

While the focus here has been selection of a new system, it is also essential to think through and plan for building all the interfaces to and from other systems that feed or will receive data from the new one—these interfaces are essential to ensure the new system's functionality—that it is properly working and that its database is populated with data from other sources on which it relies for key data elements. Interfaces must be preplanned for all feeder or upstream sources of data connected to the new system. Necessary changes within downstream and upstream systems must be made in anticipation of the go-live date so that the new system can receive the data it needs from those systems and, in turn, feed its data into other connected systems upon its implementation.

Watch out for silos. Failed implementations or major problems in the completeness or integrity of data can occur if plans for systems projects are too general or do not "fit" together properly. Poor implementations are often planned with a "silo mentality," in which synchronization between other projects and the implementation project is lacking. Imagine making changes to two interconnected computer systems at the same time without informing both parties and then expecting them to work perfectly afterward: It is highly unlikely that the systems would both work properly or that the integrity of the data would be intact afterward. Unfortunately, unless the people who are responsible for supporting each of those systems are communicating actively and are exceedingly careful about planning and synchronizing necessary changes, changes might be made to individual systems independently, resulting in un-integrated systems and out-of-sync data.

HIS and technology projects require motivated, qualified IT personnel and interdisciplinary SME staff representing the functional disciplines whose areas will be touched by the new system. The types of IT staff needed include HIS planners, project managers, trainers, communication specialists, systems analysts, programmers, network engineers, hardware experts (such as for workstation or mobile device roll-outs and other "projects within the project")—and the list goes on. The organization depends on the IT department to provide qualified, well-trained resources who are familiar with the systems and technologies being introduced into the organization. IT staff must be encouraged to not fall into their own silos and always be directed to serve the needs of the organization, rather than simply embracing the technology with which they are comfortable or in which they have become experts during their years in the organization's HIS department. When managing the HIS department, it is important to keep these very specialized staff continuously learning new technologies and systems, working on a variety of projects, using new programming languages, and adapting to new ideas and ways of doing their work. Likewise, it is essential to keep discussing the organizational vision with these professionals so that even as particular individuals specialize in a particular area of HIS and technology, they retain a clear picture of the entire HIS architecture and remember their work touches all systems that support the well-being of patients, as well as support the clinicians and administrative knowledge workers of the organization—not for the sake of the information technology itself.

Almost every HIS professional is a "healthcare person" at heart. If IT staff become stressed with long hours laboring over a large project or problem, a good practice is to have them take a break and walk to the patient care areas, talk with a few caregivers, and see their systems in use. Doing so immediately regrounds them in the purpose of their work and can be amazingly effective at bringing new energy and perspective to their highly technical jobs. Conversely, when nurses and other clinicians have a chance to see and learn what the HIS staff do each and every day, they gain an incredible respect for the intricacy and depth of the work done by HIS professionals on the systems in daily use by clinicians and other members of the healthcare organization. A true epiphany can occur when IT and clinical professionals learn about one another's work, thereby helping to build cooperative relationships that will come in very handy during the trying times of an implementation.

Good contracts are keys to success. Solid, well-negotiated agreements that hold vendors and suppliers accountable to milestones and clarify responsibilities are worth every minute invested in their creation. When negotiating contracts, do not be intimidated by anyone: Do what you know is right for the organization and, most importantly, for the patients and clinicians by locking in favorable, risk-mitigating terms and conditions into the contracts signed with software vendors. Software salespeople can be very convincing—but they are not your friends, even though they definitely want you to think so during the sales cycle. One lesson I was taught as a young, budding CIO by my first boss, then CFO of Holy Cross Health System (now Trinity Health), Sr. Geraldine Hoyler, CSC, was this: "If you go to dinner or lunch and a vendor is present, you pay." It was her way of making sure I was empowered and motivated to keep the power and independence on my side of my business relationships with vendors, and never feel even the slightest bit beholden to anyone.

Good business practices and compliance rules restrict members of organizations from accepting any sort of gifts from vendors. Remember—"There's no such thing as a free lunch." If someone buys something for you, that person always will expect something in return. Do not allow yourself to be compromised by accepting gifts or favors from someone who wants something from you (in this case, a software salesperson wanting a contract). Doing so might just soften your resolve on a difficult contract term negotiation, or make you feel as if you need to give something back. Keep your objectivity and fight hard for a favorable contract for your organization.

Following contract guidelines is paramount when negotiating with vendors. Address the following points at a minimum, and make sure you end up within an allowable range for each:

- Percentage of the vendor company's resources devoted to research and development for the product under consideration.
- How the company will respond to issues that develop over the course of a multiyear relationship (escalation procedures).
- Conformance with HIS contracting guidelines.
- The vendor organization's stability and longevity, including change of control if they are acquired.
- The vendor's reputation with other customers for completing obligations and conduct according to contract terms and conditions. Has the vendor ever fired or sued a client? (Yes, it has happened.)
- Implementation plan: a detailed implementation plan attached to the agreement identifying major milestones that then serve as the threshold for portions of payment to vendor. Never pay the vendor based on the passage of time; always use defined performance milestones as the thresholds to sign off prior to paying a portion of the payment to the vendor.
- Training plan. Devote generous resources to training (remember this comes out of operating expenses, not the capital budget).
- Support services. The norm for support and maintenance fees is 20% to 30% of the license fees. These ongoing costs typically surpass the cost of the license fees after about 3 to 4 years, yet most of the attention in the negotiation is often focused on the license fees. Do not make the mistake of spending all your energy on negotiating the license fee and ignore the maintenance fee. Be sure to negotiate and spell out in the contract the details associated with the vendor's ongoing support and maintenance of the software, such as support fees, expectations for those fees in terms of number of hours and time to response when an issue occurs based on the severity of that issue, escalation and conflict resolution processes, frequency of updates and enhancements to the software, and other support requirements. These costs can add up quickly, and if any expected services are

not included in the maintenance fee, they will have to be paid for separately, causing a potential budget over-run and dashed expectations.

- Maintenance agreements. Although these support and maintenance issues are often relegated to the back burner during the software selection process, nothing is more important than the responsibilities negotiated with the vendor for system support and maintenance (break and fix) once the system is implemented. These terms define the service relationship for what is often a 20-year relationship between a software vendor and healthcare organization. Spell out the expectations of the vendor's time limits for speed of response to issues based on the severity of the problem. Document the escalation process in detail—name names and give titles. After all, if a software problem is serious enough to get the attention of the CEO of the healthcare organization, it is serious enough to deserve the attention and action of the CEO of the vendor organization.

- Milestone and payment schedules. Always use defined performance milestones in your contract: No progress, no payment. Pay-for-performance criteria should structure the payment schedule, not dates. If dates are embedded in the contract for making payments, all too often the healthcare organization winds up paying the vendor for nothing, even if no progress on the project is being made. Structure the payment delivery based on the successful accomplishment of key project milestones.

- **Product life-cycle support.** Negotiate an agreement that includes, as part of the software license, new releases and versions of the software for at least 10 to 15 years. Include all of these updates/upgrades in your license and support fees. If the license and support fees do not include *versions* as well as releases and "bug fixes," the vendor can call a new release of software a "version" and charge the organization an entirely new license fee. Of course, no organization budgets for double the cost of the license to use the system, expecting that a vendor will charge it twice due to the new version. Unless the agreement explicitly states that the software license covers all releases and versions for a specified period of time, however, the organization could face a big unplanned expenditure for which there is no definition or threshold.

- Scope of license. Include all applications and modules that the vendor offers in one site license; think in terms of an enterprise license, even if the organization has no plans to implement all those modules at the time of negotiating the agreement with the vendor. Your leverage will never be greater than it is before the agreement is signed. The contract negotiation is the ideal time to obtain favorable pricing on additional software applications and modules, even if your organization does not plan to use that software in the near term. Also include in the agreement a statement that the healthcare organization will not pay support and maintenance fees on an application or module until that portion of the software is designed and implemented, thus ensuring vendor support.

These types of contract guidelines form the core terms and conditions agenda, or issues list, for the contract negotiation. They can be communicated in general terms to the vendors as part of the RFP. This move is intended to establish a level playing field with the vendor, regardless of whose attorneys are drafting the agreement or whose document is used as a starting point. Additional rules of the road for contract negotiations with software vendors are outlined next.

Promises made during the sales cycle must be written down and defined in exact specificity, attached, and committed to in writing as part of the agreement. Only those items attached to the contract as an appendix and listed in its Table of Contents or List of Exhibits are subject to the terms and conditions of the agreement. If a verbal commitment or implied promise is not specified and written down in the contract that is signed by both parties, no matter what was represented in the sales cycle, how much it was discussed, or how convincing the story is, it does not exist from a legal standpoint and the vendor cannot be held accountable for keeping that promise or representation. For this reason, it is essential to attach the following items to the agreement: the RFP response from the vendor to the contract as an appendix that is referenced in the body of the agreement (someone in the sales division of the vendor organization filled out the RFP, representing what the system can and cannot do); along with the implementation plan, performance expectations (such as **subsecond response time** with the configuration proposed by the vendor); and all other product descriptions and representations made by the vendor during the sales cycle. The language of the contract should confirm that those appendices are within the scope of the agreement and thus are commitments and obligations of the vendor. The vendor will have to review those terms in detail—and you will learn very quickly what the vendor is actually willing to commit to and what it is not.

Although the agreement defines mutual responsibilities, it is mostly about the vendor's commitments for service and support, coupled with terms describing the organization's obligation to pay for the software and services provided by the vendor. The provider organization is the one paying—betting the farm, in many cases—on the system promised by the vendor and the delivery of a software product that works as specified in the sales cycle. Do not be confused about who is at risk here: It is not the vendor.

Link payments of the software license fee (the primary component of payment for use of the software) to successful accomplishment of key milestones in the project that are not payable until both parties' senior project executives sign off on them. In the healthcare organization's case, that person is the CIO or CEO; for the vendor, it is the senior account executive. Spell out in the contract the mechanism that attaches portions of the total license fee to key steps in the system development and implementation. This milestone-based payment process ties each payment to the accomplishment of real progress in the project; it is also the best way to keep the attention of the vendor throughout the course of the implementation and make sure the vendor is incentivized to perform as promised. If the agreement does not specify a milestone-based payment structure, it will likely oblige the healthcare organization to pay for the software license based on dates, which is a very dangerous approach from the customer's point of view. If the payments are due based on the passage of time (meaning a certain percentage of the license fee is paid on specified dates), the vendor simply has to watch the days of the calendar tick off until it receives payment—it does not have to perform and accomplish project work to get paid. In such a case, there is no incentive for the vendor to push forward on the hard work of working with the organization in building and implementing the system and solving the problems that always occur along the way. Thus the risk of project failure and cost over-runs increases dramatically if the payment schedule is not pay-for-performance driven and milestone based. Make absolutely sure that the vendor understands from the beginning of the RFP process that the milestone method is the only one that the healthcare organization will accept in its software agreement.

Key milestones in this "pay-for-performance" approach might include touchpoints such as contract signing (10%); hardware installation and software installation (on the hardware for development, testing, and training; 10%); project plan development and staff training and orientation to the new system (10%); system design and build, which includes *all* modules, applications, and reports that constitute the total system as outlined in the RFP and requirements definition

(15%); interfaces development, system testing, and correction of issues (10%); system activation/go-live (20%); and system final testing to make sure everything is working correctly (25%) (**Figure 6.6**). These percentages can vary slightly depending on the negotiation, but notice that the majority of the payments (at least 50%) come in the latter portion of the project. The healthcare organization is well advised to reserve as large a payment percentage as can be negotiated for the final "system testing," which means that the entire system (all modules, applications, components, and reports) works together correctly as a total system, at least 45 days following the activation of the entire system in the healthcare organization's production environment (meaning it is being actively used in a live work environment by the organization's workers to support patient care, or administrative functions, or whatever the scope and purpose of the software are). Waiting for some period of time to make the final payment is important after the actual go-live date, as it allows the project team to make sure that all the month-end reports work properly and

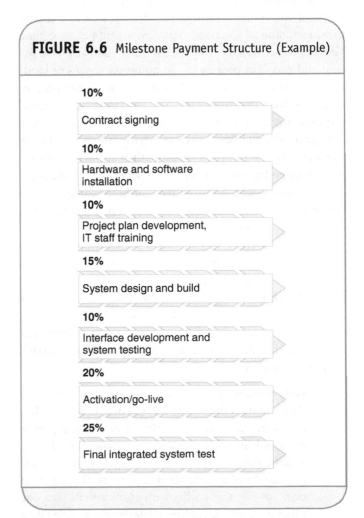

FIGURE 6.6 Milestone Payment Structure (Example)

10%

Contract signing

10%

Hardware and software installation

10%

Project plan development, IT staff training

15%

System design and build

10%

Interface development and system testing

20%

Activation/go-live

25%

Final integrated system test

the system integration and validation tests can be performed and checked off. At least 25% of the license fee payment must be reserved for this last milestone.

If the vendor will not agree to these milestone-based terms in the negotiation, it is time to shift discussions to the second acceptable vendor. This is one reason why it is important to select two finalist vendors: As noted earlier, if the organization does not have a choice, it is not really negotiating. Milestones last as long as is necessary to get the job done correctly and are not based on specific dates. Milestones are defined and committed to, creating a pay-for-performance structure for the project and payments to the vendor.

Document system performance metrics. Hardware specifications and system performance metrics are essential components to the project plan, contract, and milestone-driven project. System performance criteria should be detailed out in the contract and used as a key portion of the system test milestones and criteria. For instance, one critical system performance metric is that the system, as proposed for the number of concurrent end users of the organization and total scope of the system, will operate at a subsecond response time, including all interfaces, data feeds, and peak volumes. Vendors sometimes try to underbid other competitors in the RFP and proposal process by skimping on expensive hardware and its greater capacity. Making the candidates commit in the contract that the system will operate at a subsecond response time on the configuration that the vendor proposes (or pay for the additional necessary hardware to accomplish this goal) is a good way to make sure their configurations are realistic given the size and volumes associated with the organization and system. All too often, hardware configurations are re-estimated and increase significantly in both sizing and cost once a vendor realizes it will be held to meeting a response time metric. Also, the organization must not gauge or measure this system/hardware capacity requirement based on current size and volumes, but rather on the requirements and **peak volumes** projected into the future at least 5 years until a normal hardware upgrade is required.

Additional terms and conditions for the agreement between the healthcare organization and the software vendor include the following:

- **Data ownership**: The organization owns all its own data and the vendor may not use data to which it has access in the system, or otherwise, unless expressly approved in writing by the organization's CIO for a specific purpose (not general usage). Vendors often include in their standard contracts the right to own or use the healthcare organization's data for other purposes, including reselling de-identified data to other organizations for benchmarking purposes and marketing. For example, one hospital had a long-standing contract with a third-party billing service that provided off-site software and billing services for a major payer (Blue Cross). The hospital needed to get its own billing data for another purpose but was told it could not have the data unless the organization paid for it. The hospital's contract with this third-party billing system service gave the vendor the data-ownership rights, so ultimately the hospital had to pay $50,000 to the third party (that was already profiting from the relationship) to get a copy of its own billing data. This example makes a key point: Contracts with software vendors and any third parties that process data for the healthcare organization as a service must spell out that the healthcare organization owns its data and the software vendors and third-party data processors do not. This consideration is becoming increasingly important as the popularity of cloud-based software-as-a-service for processing organizations' data grows.

- Change of control: What happens to the contract and the organization's software implementation when the vendor is sold to, merges with, or otherwise becomes subsumed within another company? This can be a particularly difficult issue, but it is one that must be negotiated. The healthcare organization wants to have a choice about whether it becomes a customer of a completely different company with different people, products, and methods; the software vendor wants to be able to assign the contract of the healthcare organization so that it can include the value of that contract in its own valuation (which is how the price for the vendor company is calculated and established for potential sale to any suitor). Ideally, the healthcare organization can decide whether it wants to remain a customer of the new owner. Short of this, it wants access to source code and other support services to maximize its options if this event occurs. Vendors will typically fight this provision tooth-and-nail because it essentially reduces the value of their company if they cannot count the healthcare organization's contract in the valuation calculation. Of course, acquisition and merger plans are kept highly secret by vendor companies, so the healthcare organization has little way to know if a vendor is about to be sold.

At a minimum, change-of-control provisions in a software agreement should state that all the same contractual provisions will apply regardless of who owns the software company; in other words, the contract should state that all terms and conditions of the negotiated agreement apply to the new vendor. Consider the following example from the author's experience: A vendor had just initiated a contract and project for new patient accounting and billing software for a healthcare organization. Six months into the project, however, the vendor announced that an entirely new company now owned it and its headquarters was being moved to another state. Imagine the fallout from that move—the people who knew and programmed the software that the healthcare organization was about to implement were leaving. The vendor also eventually told the healthcare organization that it planned to "sunset" the software package (meaning it no longer would be a product or available or supported) that the organization had contracted for just months earlier. Additionally, the new vendor decided it wanted to develop its own patient accounting and billing software product. Thus, the healthcare organization was faced with a dilemma: It was contractually tied to a vendor that had no legal obligation to pursue the product the organization bought. Luckily, the healthcare organization had its own in-house–developed and –supported patient accounting and billing system and was able to continue with that system until the dust settled and it could establish a new direction. Eventually, the vendor's new parent company decided to get out of health care altogether. While the healthcare organization lost time and money during this saga, at least it was able to move forward (approximately 2 years after these events took place) and start over again on this project to replace its patient accounting system.

- Interface requirements: All systems require data from other systems, and all systems send data to other systems—hence the need for interfaces. The more comprehensive a system is (e.g., an enterprise EHR or ERP system), the more crucial these interfaces are to the systems' smooth functioning. The name of the game in systems today is integration—integration of data, integration of systems, and integration of workflow around streamlined, patient-centric processes—so interfaces are more important than ever. In the vendor contract, it is therefore important to define the interfaces (while remembering that interfaces go two ways: in and out of systems) and place the list in the contract (typically as an appendix or attachment). This list requires a lot of detailed planning

and deep thinking about what the new and existing systems will share. Take the time and get the right people in the room to have this discussion, such as interface analysts, project managers, systems analysts, end-user representatives, vendor representatives who understand how the new system works, and others as appropriate to the scope of the new system.

- **Regulatory compliance:** The contract should state that the vendor guarantees that the system complies with, and will be made to continue to comply with, all federal and applicable state laws and regulations. HIPAA, ARRA, and Meaningful Use criteria should also be called out separately so that the vendor is obligated to maintain the system and its functionality in such ways to qualify for federal programs and keep pace with these requirements as they evolve.
- Upgrade path expectations: While exact plans for software system enhancements and development are not always predictable or documented, certain key upgrades and enhancements that have been presented in the sales cycle and due diligence should be outlined and committed to in the contract by the vendor. This consideration is especially important in terms of a minimum number of new releases per year and the vendor's planned for major new versions. Make sure these upgrades/updates are included in the price for this license fee (as mentioned earlier) so that your organization does not get caught in the trap of having to pay for an entirely new license or a huge increase in the license fee because the vendor decides it wants to call the software a new "version" somewhere along the way. The vendor should be obligated to share its development plans with the healthcare organization and commit to inclusion of all software enhancements and additions to this product for the entire term of the license.
- Cooperation with other vendors: When implementing systems and building interfaces, there will be other vendors on the other sides of those interfaces; the new system vendor must work and cooperate with those vendors to construct the two-way interfaces that act as bridges between the new system and the other systems with which it shares data. This collaboration is necessary to accomplish the tasks demanded of this new system. The contract should spell out the behavioral and cooperative elements of this type of work, in addition to listing the interfaces, and the vendor must agree to be held to this level of cooperation. Often vendor personnel balk at the prospect

of cooperating with their competitors; such intransigence merely hurts the customer—the healthcare organization implementing these software systems. Vendors may try to displace other vendors rather than cooperate with them on behalf of the customer, so the expectations for cooperation must be spelled out and agreed to in the contract. Vendors have financial incentives to sell more software, of course, and the software marketplace is highly competitive. Thus it is necessary to obligate the vendor contractually to play nicely with others.

Fund projects with adequate resources to succeed. Properly resourced projects (in terms of both money and time) are the ones most likely to succeed. This is not to say that project budgets should be padded or excessive in funding, but rather that projects should be carefully planned at a very detailed level and realistic cost estimates based on those details. This can be challenging sometimes, because HIS and technology projects require resources for many line items that are not related to software licenses. (Figure 6.4 provides details on the typical line items for a software implementation project.) It can be a startling reality check to see the enormous difference between just the license fees (which is what the vendor emphasizes) and the total cost of an implementation. Take special care to think of every single necessary category of license fees—for example, the license fees required for third-party software packages that may be needed to run the software system on the hardware, or do reporting, or connect devices to the network, or upgrade the interface engine software to handle a new volume of interfaces. The devices connected to a new software system need to be new in most cases, because older devices typically do not have the capabilities necessary to extract all the benefits from the new software. Go through the cost spreadsheet in a step-by-step manner, counting all of the users and the square feet of hard-wire and wireless coverage needed for nomadic clinical workers and business personnel. Do not be wasteful, but plan for ample resources to get the whole job done. User departments should not be expected to have budgeted funds for a new IT system being implemented in their area. Instead, the HIS project budget must contain all funds needed to implement the project throughout the organization. End users expect their new systems to be fully implemented, with proper network coverage and bandwidth for moving massive amounts of data quickly. This is critical for adequate training, support, and end-user enthusiasm as the organization adapts to the new system. Users will work hard with you to make the implementation a success if they know you have planned properly on their behalf.

Freeze or minimize other priorities during the period of the implementation. Other implementations and projects should be frozen while a new system is being implemented, especially the large ones. Minimize the number of changes attempted simultaneously to stabilize the environment so that problems can be quickly isolated and solved. This will reduce the number of variables the implementers are trying to handle at any one time; during a time of change, this sort of narrowed scope is crucial.

Provide strong project management. Obtain project managers for systems implementations who are both skilled and experienced in HIS project management. A firm, calm hand must guide these projects, and experience can pay handsome rewards in these circumstances. For the big, complex implementations, pick a staff project manager who has run other projects many times and has been successful. This is not a role on which the organization wants to take a chance.

Devote time and effort to getting the organization's culture ready for the change. A cooperative, forward-thinking collaborative environment among the various disciplines affected by the new system's implementation is not only effective, but also represents a growth opportunity for everyone involved. A well-functioning team is paramount in these challenging projects, and team building can help get the group prepared for productively and successfully working through the inevitable challenges of a system implementation.

Interdisciplinary coordination is essential for a transforming implementation. The promise of HIS and technology is locked in through willingness to redesign processes and workflows as part of the system implementation project, followed by building the new software to support the new, streamlined workflows and processes. This type of effort requires strong interdisciplinary teams to check their egos at the door and work together for the good of the cause. Do not allow the system implementation project to be hijacked by those stuck in their ways, who seek to muscle the implementation to replicate paper-based processes or traditional processes with the new computer system. Workflows are becoming increasingly more integrated, which requires everyone—including IT, management, clinical and business user communities, vendors, and consultants—to coordinate their efforts and cooperate.

One example of improvement in process through redesign and streamlining can be seen in how a large academic teaching hospital in the Midwest redesigned its medication administration process in preparation for a new clinical information system implementation. The original, legacy process had 20 steps, including decision trees, handoffs, and additional steps; the redesigned process had only 9 steps. The hospital's new workflow resulted in a more efficient and effective process for medication administration, an area in which far too many errors occur. As the *To Err Is Human* report revealed, these errors tend to occur during hand-offs in workflow.[8] The redesign work at the Midwestern hospital resulted in potentially 11 fewer opportunities for an error to occur in the medication administration process. The new process was built into the new computer system programs and workflow, and most probably created a better, safer environment for patients. If the software had merely mimicked the legacy way of doing things, it would not have saved time, reduced error opportunities, or moved the organization forward toward its future state. The lesson is clear: Nurture cooperation and unselfish attitudes in process redesign work, insist on cooperative attitudes, address toxic mindsets, and use the new system to support streamlined workflows.

Cooperation is essential to integration. EHR implementations provide a vivid example. The key modules of an EHR reflect the fundamental processes of clinical care. Traditionally, these processes have been performed separately in different departments of the hospital or other healthcare organization—for example, having patients reregister every time they go to a new department, even though those departments are within the same four walls of the same organization. The implementation of a new EHR offers a golden opportunity to integrate processes between departments (becoming patient-centric rather than department-centric). Moreover, the healthcare organization can connect these patient care processes through the integration of the key steps in patient intake processes that are supported by EHR functionality: the MPI, registration/admitting, scheduling, and emergency department. Other EHR modules can then be integrated to deliver a more streamlined patient care experience: orders management and results reporting, CPOE, pharmacy and medication administration, clinical documentation, clinical decision support system (with guidelines, rules, and alerts), and patient-centric data access by clinicians. By working cooperatively using multidisciplinary teams, these processes can be integrated across departments and a more patient-centric experience becomes possible. Charges for populating claims to send to payers can be readily captured via EHR-supported processes and used to populate the billing system with timely clinical data submitted electronically. When these integrated processes are supported by EHR systems,

streamlined, improved care is within the organization's reach. Through cooperation come advancement and improvement.

HIS management can make or break HIS and technology implementations. HIS management professionals with appropriate qualifications and backgrounds are essential to HIS implementation success. When the HIS plan identifies many projects to be carried out simultaneously, HIS management must be able and willing to run consistent, formal processes for system selection and implementation. Important characteristics of HIS managers include steady HIS governance, independence from vendors, nonfavoritism, and egalitarian leadership in selecting systems, determining how they are made available to users, and prioritizing projects. Also important is the ability to minimize risk to the organization by picking reliable HIS software and hardware products and services, and keeping vendors at arm's length. The best interests of patient care and the organization must always remain uppermost in HIS leaders' minds.

SUMMARY

Implementing new HIS and technology systems is challenging and rewarding work. In these transforming projects that are linked together through an HIS plan, opportunities are abundant to enable the organization to achieve its strategic aims and improve its clinical and business processes. The HIS plan is multiyear in its perspective and execution, and multiphase due to its complexity. Thus architectural principles of creating first a strong foundation upon which to build the structures of the system plan are quite analogous to HIS planning and implementation. Sound management and multidisciplinary governance of these initiatives is essential to the HIS plan. Detailed, collaborative planning and thoughtful, well-managed execution will result in a balanced HIS architecture and systems portfolio. The system selection process is a well-defined procedure for systematically defining the organization's requirements for a system and evaluating available products in the market to meet those specifications. Many lessons can be learned—in vendor product surveillance, sharing with organizations, and preparation before and along the way—to improve the probability of success in these implementations. In the end, few things are more satisfying in the world of HIS and technology than achieving the hard fought goal of implementing a new system and witnessing the improvements to clinical and business efficiency and effectiveness that result from a successful implementation.

KEY TERMS

© Johan Swanepoel/
Shutterstock, Inc.

Discussion Questions

1. What is the relationship of the HIS plan to the goals and strategies of the healthcare organization?

2. Which types of HIS initiatives comprise different stages activating the HIS plan?

3. What are the main steps in a system selection process? Describe the three categories of systems evaluation criteria and explain why each is important.

4. In what ways is a good contract with the software vendor important to a system implementation?

5. Why is interdisciplinary coordination and cooperation important in systems implementation projects?

6. What are reasons why some systems implementations succeed while others might struggle or even fail?

7. In what ways do new systems help healthcare organizations adapt to their changing business and clinical environments? How might a healthcare organization be able to innovate using HIS and technology?

REFERENCES

1. DesRoches, C. M., Charles, D., Furukawa, M. F., et al. (2013). Adoption of electronic health records grows rapidly, but fewer than half of U.S. hospitals had at least a basic system in 2012. *Health Affairs*. http://content.healthaffairs.org/content/early/2013/06/27/hlthaff.2013.0308.abstract

2. Jha, A. K., Burke, M. F., DesRoches, C. M., et al. (2011). Progress toward meaningful use: Hospitals' adoption of electronic health records. Harvard School of Public Health, Department of Health Policy and Management. http://www.ncbi.nlm.nih.gov/pubmed/2221677

3. Jha, A. K., DesRoches, C. M., Kralovec, P. D., & Joshi, M. S. (2010). A progress report on electronic health records in U.S. hospitals. *Health Affairs*. http://www.ncbi.nlm.nih.gov/pubmed/20798168

4. Hsiao, C. J., Jha, A. K., King, J., et al. (2013). Office-based physicians are responding to incentives and assistance by adopting and using electronic health records. *Health Affairs*. http://content.healthaffairs.org/content/early/2013/06/27/hlthaff.2013.0323

5. Adler-Milstein, J., Bates, D. W., & Jha, A. K. (2013). Operational health information exchanges show substantial growth, but long-term funding remains a concern. *Health Affairs*. http://content.healthaffairs.org/content/early/2013/06/27/hlthaff.2013.0124

6. Ammenwerth, E., Graber, S., Herrmann, G., et al. (2003). Evaluation of health information systems: Problems and challenges. Research Group Assessment of Health Information Systems, University for Health Informatics and Technology Tyrol. http://www.ncbi.nlm.nih.gov/pubmed/14519405

7. HIMSS Usability Task Force. (2011). Promoting usability in health organizations: Initial steps and progress toward a healthcare usability maturity model. http://www.himss.org/files/HIMSSorg/content/files/HIMSS_Promoting_Usability_in_Health_Org.pdf

8. Institute of Medicine. (1999). To err is human. http://www.iom.edu/~/media/Files/Report%20Files/1999/To-Err-is-Human/To%20Err%20is%20Human%201999%20%20report%20brief.pdf

CHAPTER **7**

Leadership and Adoption of HIS and Technology

INTRODUCTION

Leadership and adoption of health information systems (HIS) and technology are multifaceted. That is, HIS leadership involves more than just one type of role, one type of health-care venue, one method of management, or one vendor's HIS product. HIS leadership occurs throughout the wide variety of healthcare organizations, at all levels, among all disciplines within those organizations, using myriad evolving technologies. In addition to the obvious contributions made by information technology experts, crucial leadership roles are summoned from health care's knowledge workers of today: clinicians, managers, suppliers, vendors and consultants, government workers, researchers, informatics experts, and public health personnel.

In this chapter, we use the HIS conceptual model to describe the layers and levels of HIS and technology leadership. In the HIS model, beginning from the core and working outward, the four spheres are health information systems and management; health informatics; data and analytics; and research, policy, and public health (**Figure 7.1**).

The entirety of HIS and technology is represented by the HIS sphere at the base of the model. This HIS symbol represents everything envisioned through the use of HIS and

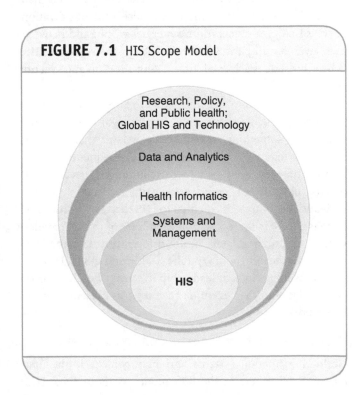

FIGURE 7.1 HIS Scope Model

Research, Policy, and Public Health; Global HIS and Technology

Data and Analytics

Health Informatics

Systems and Management

HIS

technology in a comprehensive way—in other words, the total scope of HIS. But this "total picture" of all the possibilities can be so large that it is difficult to communicate in ways that are understandable by various disciplines, let alone create and document plans, implement those plans, and meaningfully adopt all of the different types of HIS and technology. By definition, the total scope of HIS encompasses many types of systems used for different purposes in different organizational settings; thus, to "see" the complete vision of HIS, multiple perspectives must be taken into consideration. The model depicted in Figure 7.1 presents the total HIS picture in categories that are layered in a particular sequence—specifically, the sequence necessary to successfully implement and use these systems in an integrated fashion. This sequential, integrated view contrasts with what is often the norm in health care: piecemeal implementations of niche systems resulting in "silos" of information and disparate data definitions. Although common practice, this siloed approach precludes the ability to provide seamless, integrated services and accurately tie data from various systems together to create streamlined workflows as well as breed knowledge and insight about ways to improve the quality and cost of healthcare activities.

Truly effective HIS leadership comes from a variety of arenas that we will discuss in this chapter: organizational, governmental/presidential, and clinical/business. Effective HIS leadership requires not only expertise in its own arena, but also an understanding of the various HIS layers and the relationships between them. That arena expertise can then take each of the layers of the HIS model into consideration in ways that create maximum synergies within and between each layer, for all parties involved and for the whole of HIS. When this state is achieved, true HIS integration and synergy become possible.

It is important to remember that in HIS and technology, "everything touches everything." In other words, it is impossible to do something in one arena or layer that does not affect another area, for better or worse. Consequently, leadership within each arena (whether organizations, government, or clinical/business), coordinated with leadership of each layer and the "whole," is essential to HIS success. Additionally, there is a leadership role within each layer of the HIS model: systems and management, health informatics, data and analytics, and research, policy, public health, and global HIS.

We will first look at leadership in terms of each arena or perspective, and then examine each layer as presented in the HIS model.

Health Information Systems and Management

Health information systems and management is the first, foundational sphere in the HIS model. Without these HIS,

the other layers would not exist. However, there is no argument about "either/or" for systems and management; rather, the relationship between these layers is "both/and." In other words, one is not more important or relevant than the other—they are interdependent layers within the totality of HIS. Yet without well-managed, comprehensive systems in place—without the foundation—informatics (the use of these systems in workflow and processes); data and analytics (the availability of effectively stewarded data for analytics); and research, policy, public health, and global HIS would not have the foothold and data sources that they need for their conduct.

The health information systems and management layer consists of the core transaction systems supporting healthcare organizations' clinical and business processes. These systems, which support the daily activities of a healthcare organization, are the "workshop" for **informaticists** and their expertise and passion to improve healthcare processes through enabling information and evidence. *Informatics* is, at its core, the refinement and redesign of process and workflow using insights from scientific literature and information gathered from an organization's computer systems, including automating support of new ways to provide healthcare services or for other healthcare purposes. The automation of workflow and healthcare processes (also known as "implementing new systems") creates the requirement and opportunity for reshaping how work is done. This, in turn, generates the need for informatics—the discipline of understanding the complex relationship between workflow, workers, and the computers. Through their use, the core, transactional HIS create and capture *data* that can then be used for secondary, additional purposes, such as *analytics*, business/clinical intelligence and decision support, and further applied to *research*, *policy* formulation, and connection to *global* networks.

In summary, HIS and their management form the base for the other HIS model layers, which are described in greater depth next.

Informatics

Informatics is a diverse, dynamic discipline that includes clinical and business domains and expertise regarding the interaction between knowledge workers and computers, the development of new workflows, and improvement in processes and outcomes through use of the computers. Informaticists can be clinicians or business experts who also have expertise in the use of computer systems in their domains. In health care, the work of informatics can apply to either clinical or business processes, including medicine, nursing, public health, billing, supply chain, scheduling, and other disciplines' workflows. At a practical level, the idea behind informatics includes the concept that if a computer system is being designed, built, and implemented, the clinical and business process owners and other organizational knowledge workers who will use the system (and can imagine streamlined and improved ways of doing work using computers) should be engaged in the development of the redesigned workflows and processes that the new computer system employs.[1] Those information technology (IT) professionals who are building and implementing the HIS, working in concert with knowledge workers and informaticists, can create important advances in how work is done, thereby providing a key link in the relationship between computers and improving process, service, and outcomes.

Of course, informaticists also participate fully in the analytics, research, and other aspects of the use and interpretation of information that not only inform opportunities for workflow improvement, but also support quality and performance improvement using data created and captured in the new workflows and processes. Underlying these improvements, those data and outcomes are determined by the work of the informaticists through their influence on workflow and processes supported by HIS.

Data and Analytics

The data and analytics layer of the HIS model includes activities directed toward managing data and harvesting the value from the secondary use of data created and captured in HIS as a by-product of patient care and business processes; this layer includes analysis of data stored in databases and data warehouses and made available through analytics platforms. Business intelligence and clinical intelligence (BI/CI) are names that have been coined to describe these many secondary uses of data—data that can be used to develop new knowledge and insights through outcomes analysis, predictive analytics, management reporting, and decision support. BI/CI may also use algorithms to evaluate data for the purpose of anticipating risk. BI/CI activities occur within healthcare organizations of all types as well as within healthcare research organizations and other third parties focused on measuring and evaluating quality, cost, organizational improvement, and the public's health. While there are many different names for these types of analyses, they all provide additional value from the secondary use of data harvested from HIS transaction systems.

Research, Public Health, and Policy

Government organizations, universities, and global organizations such as the World Health Organization (WHO), Commonwealth Fund, Institute for Health Care Improvement (IHI), Institute of Medicine (IOM), and many other esteemed organizations are devoted to the development of new knowledge, methods, insights, and information related to healthcare quality, cost, population health, and other relevant topics that can be put into action to influence the ways health care is delivered. The reach of these organizations' impact is far and wide and, in some cases, ubiquitous. These organizations perform research—that is, inquiries, studies, and reporting on all manner of healthcare topics. Of course, they need data to conduct these activities effectively. Thus the research, policy, and public health impact of HIS depends on the availability of high-quality data from healthcare organizations. The source systems of these data are the core HIS described in the health information systems and management layer of the HIS model. Without these HIS data sources, research, policy, and public health organizations would be forced to conduct primary data collection or find data through other means, which is infeasible. It behooves the entire cause of advancement of learning in health care to connect consistent, comprehensive data sources from the primary sites of healthcare delivery (that is, healthcare and public health organizations) to these secondary users of data for research, policy, and public health purposes.

As this discussion has shown, the four layers of the HIS model interconnect and build upon each other. All of these layers depend on the foundational HIS and their proper management. Each layer informs the overall understanding of the delivery of health care and its improvement. Next, we discuss the variety of perspectives from which the scope of HIS can be considered and the leadership roles that influence them.

HIS LEADERSHIP FROM AN ORGANIZATIONAL PERSPECTIVE

Leadership in HIS and technology emanates from several perspectives, including organizational, governmental, and professional views, initiatives, and interests. Leadership in HIS and technology for organizations includes management responsibilities, policy, and governance programs needed to properly oversee, manage, and steward HIS, technology, data, and projects.

Role of the Chief Information Officer

The most typical lead role of the management positions dealing with HIS and technology in a healthcare organization is the role of the chief information officer (CIO) or its equivalent, regardless of the name (in a smaller organization, it might be director of IT, IT lead, or HIS manager, or something similar). For the purposes of this chapter, this position will be referred to as CIO. No matter what the title given to this position, the requirements of the role are similar, just scaled appropriately to the organization's size.

The role of CIO is multifaceted, complex, challenging, and highly interesting. An organization's CIO performs a broad range of responsibilities, including HIS governance; communicating effectively with those who understand HIS and those who do not; assuring strategic and business alignment with HIS plans and strategies; reaping value from HIS investments (more on this later, but remember the terms *transformation renewal*, *process redesign*, and *change management*); managing HIS department services and performance including decisions related to centralization of services and ways to cost-effectively "source" the myriad HIS functions; creating strong and synergistic relationships with the chief executive officer (CEO) and clinical and business stakeholders; implementing HIS and technology successfully; and building a knowledge-based organization.

The CIO is a member of the senior management team of the organization, and participates in the organization's strategic business discussions and decisions as well as operational and tactical activities. The CIO should always be part of the senior circle of leaders because HIS and technology are strategic to the organization—and the CIO needs to be part of those strategic discussions to inform and communicate HIS perspectives and opportunities on key issues. Also, HIS touches and is critical to each and every function in the organization, so placing the CIO under one of the leaders of a department or division—for example, finance or operations—results in the HIS and technology decisions being biased in the direction of that particular function. It is infeasible for the CIO to support all functions in the organization in a balanced fashion working from within one of those functions, just as it is infeasible for other functions or disciplines to have adequate input into the HIS agenda if the CIO reports to only one of those departments or functions. The CEO is responsible for guiding and seeing the organization from the most comprehensive perspective possible, and HIS is essential to that overarching organizational perspective—so the CIO should report to the CEO. As discussed earlier in conjunction with HIS strategic planning, alignment of HIS with the organization's overall strategy is critical—otherwise, the HIS and technology investment could take the organization off course or be wasted (time, money, and effort). Also, the expenditures associated with HIS and technology are so significant that they need to be fully considered and prioritized from the inner core leadership group of the organization.

The CIO is responsible for HIS strategic planning, department management, staffing and sourcing, budgeting, projects, and services delivery. Steering committees form an integral part of HIS management, given that HIS projects are almost always interdisciplinary efforts. Committees provide the organizational forums for collaboration from multiple disciplines to take place outside the normal "hierarchical" organizational structure and reporting relationships. As HIS projects are initiated, conducted, and closed, the CIO is responsible for setting up, running, and retiring steering committees, project-specific task forces, interdepartmental work teams, and the like.

CIO leadership involves engaging others in the organization in dialogue and structured discussions to establish the all-important HIS principles and standards that the organization agrees to in its disciplined approach to HIS management and stewardship. While it is everyone's responsibility to work according to these principles and standards, one executive—the CIO—must have primary responsibility and authority for systems projects and adherence to these important principles (e.g., integration versus interfacing of HIS). The CIO is also responsible for three main functions or branches of the HIS department or function: planning, development and implementation of new systems, and operational support of existing systems and end users. He or she plans, leads, and manages HIS people, projects, services and services quality, budgets, and support over the long term. The CIO makes sure that HIS investments and projects take the organization in *one* concerted direction—and the introduction of electronic health records (EHRs) into healthcare organizations requires this directional integrity more than ever.

Ultimately, the CIO is responsible for guiding HIS and technology systematically in the direction desired by the organization and advising the CEO and others of the types of support the organization will need and can expect from HIS to accomplish its goals and objectives. Significant emphasis in the CIO's work is placed on the following elements: (1) HIS vision and plans; (2) HIS budget and costs, because the HIS plans and budgets must be affordable over the long haul; (3) assured security of information not only from HIPAA compliance and operational perspectives, but also for purposes of business continuity and disaster recovery in the event of a catastrophic occurrence; and (4) engaging externally with others in the community regarding local or regional HIS initiatives, in addition to meeting internal organizational needs.

CIO leadership is a highly collaborative process, especially since many key stakeholders in projects typically are not HIS professionals but rather are subject matter experts (SMEs); thus a balance must always be struck between HIS, clinical and business requirements, budgets, and priorities. The nuances involved in this balance are very interesting—namely, holding responsibility for a balanced agenda, while also holding responsibility for guiding the organization in its intended direction (recall the enabling capabilities of HIS and technology). Open communication, active listening, education and sharing by the CIO about the important elements of a system for each stakeholder, and a structured requirements definition process guided by overarching principles are all necessary elements of a successful, balanced HIS agenda. The elements of the HIS strategy come in handy here: engaging in multidisciplinary leadership, communicating the vision, running a disciplined process, documenting a migration path from the current state to the desired future state, redesigning processes as part of the HIS implementation, and keeping people all pulling in the same direction through the challenging but rewarding change and implementation process.[2]

When it comes to implementing an EHR system, nothing is more important than active participation of physician, nursing, and other clinical leadership. These people are the stewards of clinical care in the organization, and their expertise, insights, commitment to the process, and plain old hard work are essential to successful EHR implementation. This brings us to the next types of organizational leadership essential to HIS and technology—namely, the chief medical information officer and chief nursing officer.

Role of the Chief Medical Information Officer

Rule number one in initiating an EHR project or other clinical system implementation is to fully engage physicians and nurses. Physicians need to hear the purpose, rationale, and story behind these projects from a respected peer—that is, another physician who is held in high esteem by his or her physician colleagues. They need to be able to ask their questions and get straight answers from someone who knows medicine and what it means to be a practicing physician—someone who sees things from their perspective. The physician who fills this physician leadership role and becomes a member of the HIS department is typically called the **chief medical informatics officer (CMIO)**; he or she should also have an affinity for—and perhaps some training in—informatics. In the case of EHR implementations in large, complex organizations, the CMIO position or role may be filled by one of a few physicians who join up formally with the EHR effort on a part-time or full-time basis. The CMIO works as a part of the HIS organization, typically reporting to the CIO, but also may continue to practice medicine on a roughly part-time basis. A physician who still cares for patients while becoming a member of the HIS team for clinical system implementations keeps a peer relationship with other practicing physicians, enhancing his or her credibility with this important group. Additionally, a CMIO who still practices medicine stays in touch with the reality of using the new systems and technologies, such as an EHR, and keeps his or her medical skills honed. This is all very helpful in providing guidance to the HIS group as well as the physicians and other clinicians in the design, development, and implementation of new HIS.

The CMIO is a key player in the presentation of new ideas and HIS initiatives to other clinicians. The person who fills this role listens to and addresses concerns about changing the ways things are done clinically. Key CMIO functions include the following:

- Help translate the process of using computers for those who did not learn to practice medicine with automated support
- Run physician discussions, question-and-answer sessions, and workshops for workflow redesign as part of the design of a new system
- Lead physician **advisory groups** for clinical HIS projects, such as the multiyear process of implementing and refining an EHR
- Research external sources such as other organizations, conferences, and published materials about new ways of using systems to support clinical care, while participating in EHR system selections and implementations
- Engage other physicians in these projects who can bring their energies, ideas, and areas of specialty into the process and encourage adoption of the new system
- Aid in detecting and resolving clinical issues in the EHR implementation

Nursing Informatics and Role of the Chief Nurse Executive

Nursing leadership is especially important in leading collaboration among nurses for HIS implementations; this role is often filled by the **chief nursing officer (CNO)**. Nurses possess clinical workflow knowledge because of their close relationship to the specifics of daily and hourly patient care processes. Their collaboration and leadership are essential to defining key elements of EHR design and implementation from nursing and patient care perspectives, such as medication administration records and standardized clinical documentation methods. Add to this the fact that a significant percentage of clinicians who will be interacting with the EHR system will be nursing professionals and it becomes clear that nursing will drive the EHR implementation in many important aspects. Nursing leadership is required for confirmation of patient-care workflow and documentation methods developed for use within the EHR, as well as for engaging with a broad spectrum of nursing perspectives and disciplines, all which need to be supported by and addressed by EHR functionality. Bottom line: If the nurses do not support the EHR implementation, it will not develop beyond the basic functions of registration, scheduling, orders communication, and results reporting, and much of the content of the EHR will not reach the development goals of the EHR vision, as much of that documentation and population of the EHR with data is accomplished by nursing processes. Graduate degrees in **nursing informatics**—the use of computers to support and enhance nursing workflow, documentation, and care processes, as well as the use of information for analysis of clinical quality and effectiveness properties of clinical care—are becoming increasingly available in university-based graduate nursing programs.

Role of the Chief Executive Officer

The CEO and the CIO have a key connection in preparing the organization and its resources for HIS plans to be implemented. The CEO must engage in HIS planning as part of the overall strategic planning and management process. It can sometimes be tempting for busy CEOs to avoid the topic of HIS and technology because chances are they did not receive much if any training in this discipline, especially in comparison to their training in other areas such as operations, finance, human resources, and other more traditional management functions. Eventually, this lack of familiarity of CEOs with HIS and technology will become less of an issue. The most important thing a CEO can do for the HIS and technology agenda is to actively participate in the HIS planning process and place HIS on the executive management team's agenda on a regular basis, just as that team regularly discusses financial issues, human resources and operations topics, strategic planning, clinical quality, and marketing strategies and tactics. Then the CEO and other senior management team members can engage in meaningful ways with others in the organization regarding HIS plans and implementations. The CEO–CIO working partnership is key to the success of HIS and technology investments, plans, and implementations, all of which are significant to the future of the organization, as well as key to its ability to perform efficiently and effectively from quality and cost perspectives.

Role of Department Managers

Managers of departments and key functions within healthcare organizations are vital to the successful definition and accomplishment of HIS plans. The departments for which these managers are responsible exist for a reason: They are essential parts in the healthcare processes that support patients and the communities served by these organizations. Managers and directors are key participants on steering committees, task forces, process redesign initiatives, and implementations of new HIS. Their leadership and encouragement of those staff members who are asked to work and participate in HIS implementations can make a major difference in how those staff members feel about the changes they are being asked to help define and implement. Change is not easy for anyone, and in busy healthcare organizations managing change, even if desired, is often the toughest challenge. Supporting and leading staff members "into the fray" of an HIS implementation is truly a leadership role that cannot be provided by anyone other than those people already managing those departments within the organization. No external consultant or HIS vendor can meet this leadership requirement for a successful HIS implementation.

Clinical Leadership and Medical Staff Leadership

One category of leadership in HIS and technology that deserves special mention is leadership by clinical and medical staff. The clinical and medical staff departments that make up healthcare organizations are the groups necessary to provide care processes provided by the organization. Especially significant in HIS projects is medical staff leadership as a means of reaching the majority of the physicians providing care in the organization. Also essential is the need to reach each and every physician who treats patients in a clinical setting. A story about an HIS implementation that went awry due to lack of connection with the majority of staff physicians at a large, highly regarded healthcare organization (**Exhibit 7.1**) emphasizes the importance of this principle.[3]

To avoid disastrous outcomes, EHR project teams must avoid *only* working through the medical staff *leadership*: The project team must always infiltrate the ranks of the *total medical staff* through their communications, orientation, and engagement in the EHR project. In the Cedars-Sinai example (see Exhibit 7.1), only approximately 15% of the total medical staff knew much at all about the project or felt as if they had a voice in the system's design. Even though medical staff leaders were involved, receiving word about the project on a secondhand basis was insufficient for the remaining 85% of the medical staff. What was needed was direct, individual interaction with all members of the medical staff. The example in Exhibit 7.1 paints a poignant picture of a team doing the right thing by working with medical staff leadership, but missing the fact that this engagement was not enough; that is, each and every medical staff member needed to be reached by the project team and system trainers, which did not happen.

EXHIBIT 7.1 Lessons Learned from an Early EHR Implementation

In 2005, after $34 million and several years were invested in developing a new electronic medical record, physicians at Cedars-Sinai Medical Center in Los Angeles revolted after 3 months of using the new EHR system, demanding that it be abandoned.[1] Of course, in a dire situation like this, it becomes painfully clear that the physicians who admit patients to a hospital have the power to get their voices heard, especially in regard to new ways of taking care of patients. If most members of the medical staff had decided to admit their patients to a different hospital, Cedars-Sinai would have been in dire straits clinically, financially, and from the standpoint of reputation in the community. Cedars-Sinai found itself in this very predicament and made the decision to abandon the HIS project at great financial, operational, and cultural cost.

At the time, many other healthcare organizations across the United States were also in the midst of EHR implementations, or considering the investment in these expensive, transformative systems. Fear loomed in the hearts of these people who watched the Cedars-Sinai situation unfold, who were undoubtedly saying something like, "There but for the grace of god go I." The Cedars-Sinai EHR failure attracted national and international attention, and those who were in process of EHR implementations learned from this story. Many hospitals most assuredly took on additional efforts and special care in engaging and involving their medical staff members and other clinicians in the process of introducing a new computer system into a patient care environment.

Connolly, C. (2005, March 21). Cedars-Sinai doctors cling to pen and paper. *Washington Post*, p. A01. http://www.washingtonpost.com/wp-dyn/articles/A52384-2005Mar20_2.html

After the unfortunate public and organizational situation at Cedars-Sinai, other healthcare organizations throughout the United States that were planning their implementations or go-live activities took clear note, and decided to invest the time, money, and energy needed to reach as many of their own medical staff members as possible regarding their EHR implementations. These organizations did their best to involve physicians in the design of their new EHR systems, and then sought to orient and train the clinicians on the new system before it went "live." They now recognized that these key users—the physicians, clinicians, and other healthcare professionals essential to the minute-to-minute functioning of the hospital—had a choice whether to use the new system, and they accepted that each and every one of these professionals must be given the opportunity to learn about and participate in the design and development of the new system. At the minimum, these essential participants need to be trained on how to use the new system to take care of their patients.

Everyone in an organization implementing a comprehensive system such as an EHR must feel that she or he has a role and investment in the successful implementation of the new system. The days of making assumptions about the acceptance of a new system without thorough communication and involvement of medical and clinical staff are clearly over, especially after the extreme trial at Cedar-Sinai. As a happy footnote, since this trying experience at the renowned institution, the Cedars-Sinai Medical Center and Cedars-Sinai Medical Group have implemented a new comprehensive, integrated EHR, serving well their patients and their families.

Quality and Safety Leadership

Quality and safety officers in healthcare organizations are also key players in the design and implementation of new computer systems, especially in the clinical arena. Certainly, those who are responsible for measuring and assuring quality of care should take part in the definition of data elements needed to populate those measures, and should make sure those data elements are built into the new systems. Thinking about the outcomes of care, as the workflows and processes supported by the new computer system are designed and developed, assures that the programs written for the new computer system will support the measurement and tracking of those outcomes of care. This is one of the most exciting areas of implementing new computer systems—the ability to think about the desired end state of the work and processes of the functions being automated, so that the quality and effectiveness measures are seamlessly woven into the fabric of the workflows and processes they support.

Change Management Leadership

The term **change management** is often used in other industries, but was not part of the training of many people working in healthcare organizations. Nevertheless, this concept determines the ability of healthcare workers and organizations to successfully meet their goals and for such organizations to successfully adapt to forces in their environment.

Change management is the carefully planned move from a current way of doing work or caring for patients, to new ways; it requires involvement of the involved disciplines in the planning of these new methods, followed by the systematic introduction of these methods supported by HIS and technology.[2] Lessons in change management include that successful HIS and technology implementation must have strong leadership, commitment to addressing the details ensconced in healthcare workflow and processes, involvement of knowledge workers from clinical and business domains, and the will to pursue the implementation of new systems while the organization continues its busy work of caring for people at a particularly vulnerable time in their lives.

REALIZING THE VALUE FROM HIS AND TECHNOLOGY INVESTMENTS

Realizing the expected benefits from an HIS implementation can be an elusive goal that requires strong and persistent leadership. Historically, while the benefits to be achieved from HIS and technology have been debated, the "promise" of health information systems and technology has certainly been widely touted. The Meaningful Use criteria of the Health Information Technology and Clinical Health (HITECH) Act of 2009 for EHR implementations and incentive payments have been set up to spawn the achievement of HIS benefits that fall into three categories: (1) improving the accuracy, timeliness, and availability of health information to care providers; (2) improving access to information, thereby allowing providers to better anticipate the diagnostic and health needs of their patients and share this information among other providers as appropriate; and (3) empowering patients to more actively participate in their health care and wellness, and have access and input to their health data.[4] Reality has proved that achieving these benefits requires a longer journey than most imagined at the outset. For instance, while recent statistics point to the fact that approximately half of all physician practices have implemented EHRs, a much lower percentage have achieved Meaningful Use Stage 1 and 2 criteria. This demonstrates the difference between real and desired use of EHRs to care for patients and influence workflow and HIS adoption.[4] The discrepancy between reality and plans also paints a picture of what is meant by the challenge of "achieving the value or promise" of HIS, EHRs, and technology in health care.

Value in HIS and technology aligns around four areas: strategic alignment, architectural excellence and balance, realization of intended system benefits, and HIS services delivery. Here, we look at these areas one at a time, thinking about how they connect with other concepts presented.

First, strategic alignment means that the HIS and technology plan directly supports the intended direction of the organization and, likewise, that it does not take the organization's momentum in any direction different than that. This harkens back to the earlier concept of creating a balanced HIS portfolio so that the various needs of the organization are addressed more or less equivalently by the components of the HIS architecture. HIS and technology are expensive, strategic investments, and misalignment of these resources and "hard-wired" clinical and business processes would be disastrous for the healthcare organization. Clearly, then, strategic alignment of HIS plans and organizational strategy is essential to the short- and long-term well-being of the organization and, by extension, the community it serves.

Second, architectural excellence and balance means that the HIS and technology are designed and built according to proper HIS architectural principles and practices. This builds on the notion of strategic alignment, and emphasizes proper construction of the HIS and technology architecture. It means building systems according to open systems standards, not proprietary technologies that do not integrate or interface easily. Also, systems must be designed to meet the HITECH Act's Meaningful Use criteria, data and security requirements, and technical standards.

The third element of HIS value realization involves verifying that the implementation's intended objectives are actually being achieved. Post-implementation evaluation helps make the connection between newly automated workflows and processes with the benefits to be achieved. Disciplined metrics associated with desired yet realistic objectives and measurement of their accomplishment or failure is the only way to measure, manage, and know the progression of HIS and technology. In this way, the organization can realize the hoped for value and benefits from the investment of time, money, and talent in that implementation.

Lastly, high-quality HIS and technology services delivery must never be overlooked. It is wonderful to talk about, plan for, and invest in the implementation of new HIS and technology for healthcare organizations, but new systems do not work by magic. At the end of the day, having properly trained HIS staff plentifully available to support the new system and end users through their struggle to adapt to a new HIS is crucial to ongoing clinical and business activities. Remember, we are not talking about building widgets here—we are talking about taking care of people in their most vulnerable state, as patients needing lifesaving healthcare services and support.

The HIS Value Proposition

The U.S. Department of Veterans Affairs (VA) has implemented a very successful EHR and established a track record of leadership in EHR adoption over the last several decades. In a comparison of the IT investment and value derived at the VA versus private-sector healthcare systems based on estimated costs and benefits, it was shown that the VA spent proportionately more than private-sector health systems but achieved higher adoption and quality of care, with the value of the VA's IT investment estimated at $3.09 billion net of cumulative costs.[5] This methodology provides a framework for estimating the benefits and costs of HIS resulting from the federal health IT stimulus efforts as well. The VA estimates it costs approximately $68 per patient per day to build, support, and maintain the department's system. This amount is roughly the cost of a lab test; thus, if the system saves the organization from performing just one duplicated lab test per patient per day, the system pays for itself and the cost is justified in the organization's eye.[6]

Realizing the benefits of HIS and technology depends on creating a deliberate, organized system implementation that focuses on defining the benefits the organization hopes to achieve through the adoption of the new system, broken down into measurable, realistic objectives for each benefit or goal. These objectives (steps toward each major goal) must be set in ways that recognize the organization's starting point in pursuit of its desired outcomes and must be achievable within the established time frames; once accomplished, the objectives must then be reset to new levels. If the targeted benefits are too lofty, nonspecific, or unrealistic to accomplish in the designated time frame, they will be ignored or avoided and progress will be thwarted. An important, ever true working principle is to keep targeted objectives realistic and within reach. Otherwise busy workers, facing the prospect of trying to implement a new HIS and change their work processes while still performing their normal duties, can easily become discouraged or overwhelmed. It is better to go a little more slowly and make steady progress in the changeover and implementation process than risk such overload of employees. Benefits can be identified and measured in numerous areas, such as patient, provider, or employee satisfaction, clinical quality, efficiency and patient safety, sharing and reporting of electronic information and data, patient education and prevention, and cost savings.[7]

Historical HIS Leadership by Organizations

Many innovations and documented advancements in the use of HIS and technology over the course of the past 25 or so years have occurred at a few noteworthy healthcare organizations: Intermountain Health Care (IHC), U.S. Department of Veterans Affairs, Regenstrief Institute (Indianapolis, Indiana), Partners Health (Boston, Massachusetts), El Camino Hospital (Mountain View, California), and University of Pittsburgh Medical Center (UPMC). In fact, in a comprehensive review of the high-quality literature in HIS and technology from 1995 through 2007, the first four of these organizations published a full 25% of all studies of HIS, most of which addressed the use of clinical decision support HIS capabilities and computerized provider order entry (CPOE).[8,9] These pioneers blazed the trail, publishing research results for other healthcare organizations to learn from—other organizations that might not have the appetite for risk or innovation, or the HIS expertise, needed to accomplish this type of advancement. Many healthcare organizations continually struggle to maintain even the slimmest of positive financial margins, so the innovation process and investment in pilot projects in HIS and technology or inventing new ways of doing work are often left to a handful of organizations whose cultures and bottom lines are better suited to tackle these types of high-risk research and development efforts.

Community-based hospital systems and religion-based healthcare systems have also provided HIS and technology leadership, particularly in the area of quality measurement and reporting. For example, Trinity Health, a Catholic healthcare organization headquartered in Michigan, has been a leader for decades in the use of business and clinical intelligence systems to track and report across its member hospitals on system-wide quality measures. It publishes these results on its website as a source of information not only for the organization, but also for patients who seek care at its member institutions.[10] This type of organizational leadership sets standards of excellence, transparency, and respect by providing this information publicly.

The measures reported by Trinity Health on its website for heart attack, heart failure, pneumonia, and surgical care improvement/surgical infection prevention are consistent with measures in the Hospital Compare program of the Centers for Medicare & Medicaid Services (CMS) and the Hospital Quality Alliance (HQA).[11] The Hospital Compare program has published a comprehensive list of measures organized into the following categories[12]:

- Structural measures, such as "participation in a systematic database for cardiac surgery" and "participation in a systematic database for stroke care"
- Timely and effective care measures in key areas such as acute myocardial infarction and emergency department throughput, such as "median time from emergency department arrival to emergency department departure for admitted emergency department patients"

- Readmissions, complications, and deaths, which include measures such as 30-day death and readmission rates, and surgical complications rates
- Medical imaging measures, such as outpatient imaging efficiency in areas like magnetic resonance imaging of the lumbar spine for low back pain and mammography follow-up
- Survey of patients' experience measures, as found in the Hospital Consumer Assessment of Healthcare Providers and Systems Survey (HCAHPS), including communication with nurses and communication with doctors
- Number of Medicare patients treated
- Medicare payments

These measures can be used internally and may also be reported by hospitals to outside organizations: The more hospitals participating across the country, the greater the availability of comparative data for participating hospitals for the public and for potential patients to use to assess their options and make informed choices. This type of organizational leadership elevates awareness about quality of care within the organization and generally across the public. The quality crisis in health care in the United States will be solved only when organizations and providers are willing to be transparent—internally and externally—and key performance indicators are measured, tracked, and reported on a continual basis.

PRESIDENTIAL/POLITICAL/NATIONAL LEADERSHIP PERSPECTIVE IN HIS AND TECHNOLOGY

The role of leadership in health care can also be described from the perspective of the highest office in the land—that of the president of the United States—and the national political system where policy is put into action in the form of federal legislation and regulations. As many have witnessed in the past decade, presidential involvement in the healthcare debate and stimulus legislation has had far-reaching effects on regulations and spending in health care. This is not just a political debate around different philosophical viewpoints regarding a person's "right to care" versus "privilege of coverage"; it is an economic and strategic discussion of great importance to the budgets and expenditures for health care in the United States. To the degree that HIS and technology can improve the quality and efficiency of health care in the country, there is much to be gained by reducing the estimated $750 billion to $765 billion in unnecessary spending owing to

inefficiencies and, ideally, improving health outcomes as we decrease this level of waste.[13]

In recent years, U.S. presidents and their offices have been actively engaged in addressing questions not only about health care and healthcare spending, but also about HIS and technology and whether such advances might improve the quality and cost of care as well as keep the United States competitive with other nations. President George W. Bush and the 109th U.S. Congress debated these issues, resulting in President Bush's declaration of support for HIS and technology, including seed-grant funding to encourage pilot trials in the implementation of HIS innovations. This presidential support stimulated much new dialogue and energy among healthcare providers (physician practices and hospitals alike), developers of new health IT products and services, health services researchers, and the HIS and technology community in general. As part of this presidential support, the Office of the National Coordinator for Health Information Technology (ONC) was established and David Brailer, MD, PhD, was named its director in 2004.[14]

These actions set the stage for the major initiatives that are under way today under the Obama administration and built momentum that culminated in President Barack Obama's inclusion of HIS and technology in sweeping economic legislation of 2009. Recognizing the growing trend that saw many of the nation's healthcare organizations begin implementing electronic health records, President Obama and the 111th U.S. Congress included major incentives for EHR implementations in HITECH as part of the overall stimulus legislation known as the American Reinvestment and Recovery Act (ARRA) in 2009.[15] This effort launched the development of major policy and spending changes directly tied to the implementation of HIS and technology in accordance with Meaningful Use criteria—measurable targets to which monetary incentives are tied for types of functionality and connectivity to be implemented over a series of staged thresholds.[16] This policy intervention and the commitment of $25 billion stimulated the adoption of HIS and technology and created a nationwide IT infrastructure; it has fueled sharp changes in how healthcare institutions work since that time. While HIS, technology, and EHRs have been "under construction" in many U.S. healthcare organizations since the 1970s, the pace of development has quickened significantly due to HITECH incentive payments that are available for a period of time to hospitals, clinics, and physician practices implementing EHRs. After 2016, the incentives become penalties for those physician practices and hospitals not achieving Meaningful Use (**Table 7.1**).[17]

TABLE 7.1 Summary of Meaningful Use Criteria Stages 1, 2, and 3

The Meaningful Use criteria, objectives, and measures will evolve in three stages over the next 5 years:

1. Stage 1 (2011–2012): Data capture and sharing
2. Stage 2 (2014): Advance clinical processes
3. Stage 3 (2016): Improved outcomes

Stage 1: Meaningful Use criteria focus on:	Stage 2: Meaningful Use criteria focus on:	Stage 3: Meaningful Use criteria focus on:
Electronically capturing health information in a standardized format	More rigorous health information exchange (HIE)	Improving quality, safety, and efficiency, leading to improved health outcomes
Using that information to track key clinical conditions	Increased requirements for e-prescribing and incorporating lab results	Decision support for national high-priority conditions
Communicating that information for care coordination processes	Electronic transmission of patient care summaries across multiple settings	Patient access to self-management tools
Initiating the reporting of clinical quality measures and public health information	More patient-controlled data	Access to comprehensive patient data through patient-centered HIE
Using information to engage patients and their families in their care		Improving population health

Reproduced from healthit.gov. (n.d.). EHR incentives and certification: How to attain Meaningful Use. http://www.healthit.gov/ providers -professionals/how-attain-meaningful-use

LEADERSHIP FROM PUBLIC HEALTH RESEARCHERS AND SCIENTISTS IN HIS AND TECHNOLOGY

The aforementioned presidential and political actions were fueled by a series of essential research reports, particularly from the IOM, describing the overall context for HIS within the U.S. health system. First, *To Err Is Human: Building a Safer Health System* (1999) sounded the clarion call for increased quality of care in U.S. hospitals, citing avoidable medical errors as being responsible for the unnecessary deaths of 44,000 to 98,000 patients in U.S. hospitals each year.[18] Evidence of unacceptable levels of avoidable errors and preventable deaths stared members of healthcare organizations in the face and could no longer be denied. Second, *Crossing the Quality Chasm* (2001) was the IOM's report and call to action detailing reasons for the quality problems in U.S. hospitals that should be systematically addressed to turn the tide from unacceptable levels of quality to a safer health system.[19] One reason cited for the occurrence of avoidable medical errors was insufficient use of health information systems and technology.

Taken together, these two IOM reports clearly placed the focus on increasing the use of HIS and technology, especially EHR systems, to improve the quality and safety of health care. The IOM called out the need for specific capabilities within those EHR systems, such as CPOE and clinical decision support with rules and alerts to aid clinicians in the medication ordering process, as important elements of the solution for medical errors. The IOM's reports also motivated the inclusion of health IT in the presidential and political legislative and policy agendas. Sadly, a new study published in 2013 estimated annual deaths in U.S. hospitals now range between 210,000 and 400,000.[20]

The IOM has also published another report in this topic area: *Health IT and Patient Safety: Building Safer Systems for Better Care* (2011). It summarizes the existing evidence regarding the impact of HIS and technology on patient safety and recommends to Department of Health and Human Services actions to take in conjunction with two key themes: using health IT to make patient care safer and continually improving the safety of health IT.[21] This report and its recommendations, which are consistent with the earlier IOM reports' calls to maximize the safety of care via health IT, are discussed more fully in a later section of this chapter on unintended consequences of health IT.

LEADERSHIP OF PROFESSIONAL ORGANIZATIONS IN HIS AND TECHNOLOGY

The world of health care includes several organizations that provide professional development for key leadership roles in HIS and technology, clinicians and informatics, vendor and services companies, and healthcare management and administration. These leadership functions cover a wide range of activities, such as designing, provisioning, implementing, using, and improving HIS and technology.

Health Information Management Systems Society

The roots of the Health Information Management Systems Society (HIMSS) lie in an organization originally established in 1962 for management engineering professionals in health care called Hospital Management Systems Society (HMSS). HMSS morphed into HIMSS in 1986 as the organization modified its "systems" purpose from a focus on process alone to a focus on information systems. The new focus on information systems represented an opportunistic shift from the more general "systems" and processes that management engineers in health care historically sought to improve by applying their industrial engineering techniques and expertise.[22] Thus Health *Information* Management and Systems Society was born. It has since evolved into the primary HIS and technology professional organization in the United States, with a growing international reach.

HIMSS's mission statement expresses a not-for-profit philosophy aimed at developing and advocating for HIS professionals and their roles, in an industry full of highly profitable vendor products. The mission statement implies a commitment to objectivity and the needs of healthcare organizations striving to successfully adopt HIS and technology systems. This stance is necessary given that HIS and technology vendor selections in provider organizations should be made without bias or undue influence. HIMSS seeks to improve health care and patient safety: "HIMSS is a cause-based, not-for-profit organization exclusively focused on providing global leadership for the optimal use of information technology (IT) and management systems for the betterment of healthcare."[23]

Worldwide, HIMSS has more than 50,000 individual members; more than two-thirds of those members work in healthcare provider, governmental, and not-for-profit organizations. HIMSS also has more than 570 corporate members, and 120 not-for-profit associations as members. It holds annual national and regional meetings, which typically include extensive educational sessions. The organization also maintains an analytics database containing data about use of HIS and technology in provider organizations and publishes reports on HIS and technology including the annual statistics on its EMR adoption model. HIMSS operates both regional and international chapters.[24]

American Health Information Management Association

Originally known as the Association of Record Librarians of North America (ARLNA), the **American Health Information Management Association (AHIMA)** aims to "elevate the standards of clinical records in hospitals and other medical institutions."[25] This farsighted recognition of the importance of medical record quality to patient care and research underlies the organization's strength today. The American Medical Records Association (AMRA) was founded in 1928 to improve health record quality and provide a professional organization for medical record librarians. Since then, these roles have gradually evolved through the 1960s to the 1990s, when the accreditation title for health information management professionals was changed to Registered Record Administrator (RRA), and eventually updated to Accredited Health Information Administrator (AHIA). AHIMA provides strict accreditation and certification tests as well as processes for achieving and maintaining Registered Health Information Administrator (RHIA) accreditation for health information professionals and Registered Health Information Technicians (RHIT) certifications for coders. AHIMA has consistently played a leadership role in the effective management of health data and medical records needed to deliver quality health care to the public.[26] The professionals accredited by this organization are the managers (RHIAs) and coding experts (RHITs) of health information departments found in hospitals and clinics (traditionally the "medical records department"). They also provide critical skills regarding medical records and electronic health records to others in the healthcare and HIS industry such as patients, HIS vendors, payers, researchers, and legal entities. Their responsibilities include proper documentation, and diagnostic and procedure coding of data in the medical records using classification systems and medical terminologies and upholding standards related to clinical activities, administrative functions, and the privacy of protected patient information.

As computerization of health records has occurred gradually over the past few decades, AHIMA has evolved as well to provide education, training, certification, and accreditation for its professionals to achieve expertise in EHR systems plus reporting, medicolegal, research, analysis, and business uses of the data in the medical record for healthcare organizations.

American Medical Informatics Association

The **American Medical Informatics Association (AMIA)** promotes and develops the science and practice of informatics in health care. Its focus is the practice of informatics—the clinical application of health IT and data analytics in health care, with the intent to improve healthcare delivery, practices, and outcomes. Formed in 1989, AMIA is the result of the combination of three organizations with complementary missions: the American Association for Medical Systems and Informatics (AAMSI), the American College of Medical Informatics (ACMI), and the Symposium on Computer

Applications in Medical Care (SCAMC).[27] Through conferences, education, meetings, research, and policy, AMIA strives to educate, promote, and support the science of five informatics domains: translational bioinformatics, clinical research informatics, clinical informatics, consumer health informatics, and public health informatics.

Alliance for Nursing Informatics

Supported by both AMIA and HIMSS, the **Alliance for Nursing Informatics (ANI)** represents more than 2000 nurses and brings together 18 independent nursing informatics groups. ANI provides leadership and productive relationships between its various nursing informatics organizations with the aim to transform health and health care through nursing informatics.[28]

The common theme among the organizations described in this section is a devotion to professional development, leadership, and collaboration among those in the HIS and technology-related disciplines. These groups have been in existence for decades and were often formed through a cooperative decision to combine separate, smaller organizations that developed simultaneously during the early years of HIS and technology development. This is analogous to the early development of HIS and technology software, hardware, and services companies—an initial proliferation of products and services with similar purposes eventually merged or were acquired into larger organizations (i.e., big fish eating little fish). Thus, although the development of HIS and technology might seem like a recent, attention-grabbing movement, it is not: It has been under development and in action in healthcare organizations in the United States for the past 50 years.

Medical professional organizations promote the development of HIS and technology and its integration into clinical practice. These organizations include the American Medical Association (AMA), Medical Group Management Association (MGMA), American Hospital and Health Network Association (AHA), Health Care Management Association (HFMA), American College of Health Care Executives (ACHE), and other national, state, and international organizations. They provide professional leadership support, and development for those in the clinical disciplines of medicine, nursing, clinical therapies, radiology, laboratory, pharmacy, and others; they have added HIS and technology to their agendas for education, collaboration, research, conferences, and other activities. Leadership provided by these professional associations develops, promotes, and evolves the productive and safe use of HIS and technology in health care through the integration of HIS into the normal activities and research conducted by these professional development organizations.

ADOPTION OF HIS AND TECHNOLOGY

"I believe we're on a series of 'change curves'—one for adopting the technology and another for actually using it."

—Mike Painter*

"Make a better mousetrap, and the world will beat a path to your door."

—Ralph Waldo Emerson**

For all its virtues, health care has been markedly slower than other industries (industries with simpler processes and fewer complexities) to use IT ubiquitously to accomplish its work. Such use of HIS and technology is called "adoption," meaning that the providers and healthcare industry change the ways that clinical care is provided and the work of health care is done. To adopt disruptive HIS and technology also means that organizations "adapt" to automated work processes—a huge change from the paper-based processes and workflows that typically take much longer than anticipated with even the most conservative of estimates. Adding to the dynamic nature of this change, adoption of HIS and technology occurs amidst the hustle, bustle, and stress of today's dynamic healthcare environments, which are normally fast-moving, unpredictable settings of high priority to the patients and clinicians involved. As far as the drive to develop business intelligence and analytics in health care is concerned, the ability to use information to adapt to changes in the environment quickly is essential—whether responding to changes in the health status of a population, or to shifts in the major regulations governing health care, or to competitive pressures in the healthcare marketplace. The adoption of HIS and technology within a highly dynamic backdrop of complex relationships, clinical advancements, and human realities takes on special meaning and risks. And, of course, there is always the added layer of complex change in the development and evolution of technology itself: New types of hardware, software, wireless devices, telecommunications, and biomedical technologies are being launched every day. It is no wonder, then, that when the question "Why does it

---

* Reproduced from: Michael Painter. Electronic health records: Are we there yet? What's taking so long? Robert Wood Johnson Foundation, June 4, 2013. http://www.rwjf.org/en/blogs/culture-of-health/2013/06/electronic_healthre.html

** Reproduced from: *Borrowings: A compilation of helpful thoughts from great authors.* 1889. http://historiesofecology.blogspot.com/2012/11/build-better-mouse-trap-and-world.html

take so long for health care to change or adapt?" is asked, the answer is often that health care and the adoption of HIS and technology are more complex than the environments found in other industries or lines of work.

Adoption Patterns

Before discussing the history and current status of adoption of HIS and technology in the United States, it is necessary to explore the term "adoption" and the theory behind it. The adoption of HIS and technology is thought to follow the pattern of the diffusion of innovation and adoption of disruptive technologies, as described by Rogers in 1962 in his landmark book, *Diffusion of Innovations*. This book was published when computer systems and other new electronic technologies capable of "disrupting" traditional work processes were being developed and introduced with increasing regularity into our world.[29] Studied by many, Rogers' theory is as much about social structures and communication as it is about technologies. The **adoption curve**[29] (**Figure 7.2**) Rogers describes has five groups or segments that play roles in the adoption of disruptive, new technologies such as HIS into an organization or other setting: Innovators (2.5%), Early Adopters (13.5%), Early Majority (34%), Late Majority (34%), and Laggards (16%).[30]

Innovators are the initiators of the change—the curious, restless, brave types who enjoy being on the cutting edge, who are comfortable with uncertainty and failure, and who always want to try something new, get a new tool, or experiment with new methods to do their work. Innovators are important communicators to others in the organization about the attempted change or modernization.

Early Adopters (a term often used in many venues other than technology adoption) are often respected opinion leaders of the organization, accepting of change and new ideas, who use the experience of the Innovators to inform their decision to attempt the adoption of the innovation. They are often knowledgeable and savvy—people who are interested in trying new technologies and new ways of doing things, but are not reckless in how they approach the innovation. Rather, they make carefully thought-out, well-informed decisions.

The *Early Majority* is the group of careful, cooperative, attentive people who embrace the innovation as part of a move toward a positive change and the desired direction of the leaders. They have strong connections with their compatriots and are satisfied to observe the experience and listen to the communications of the Early Adopters and Innovators, basing their decisions to embrace the change based on others' opinions and input. While they are careful about change, they adapt more quickly than average.

The *Late Majority* consists of people who will eventually adjust to the change or use the new technology, but usually only after most others have already done so, and when it becomes more trouble to not change than to change. Late Majority members can be the skeptics of the organization, with low tolerance for risk and uncertainty.

Laggards are described as traditionalists, resistant to change, who prefer the old ways of doing things. They adapt to the innovation only when it has become the norm and is not seen as complying with anything radical or drastic.[31,32]

The adoption of innovation is led to the point of Early Majority adoption by the actions and communications of opinion leaders, meaning the Early Adopters and Innovators

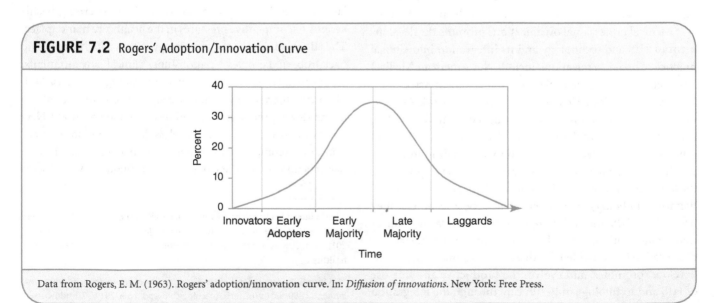

FIGURE 7.2 Rogers' Adoption/Innovation Curve

Data from Rogers, E. M. (1963). Rogers' adoption/innovation curve. In: *Diffusion of innovations*. New York: Free Press.

of the group. This achievement of Early Majority adoption is also popularly referred to as the tipping point, sociologically rooted in the more gradual progression through the phases described by Rogers. Recent further interpretation of Rogers' adoption curve and diffusion theory speaks to the "chasm" between the Early Adopters and the Early Majority, noting that as the progression of change moves through these categories, jumping across this chasm is very difficult, much more so than surviving the Innovator and Early Adopter phases.[33] Getting past this chasm to the point where the change gains critical mass momentum is where many innovations fade or fail, and making it to the Early Majority phase is seen as the true determinate of widespread adoption and recognition of the change as the "new normal."

With the backdrop of Rogers' diffusion of innovation theory in mind, we next review the lengthy evolution and adoption of HIS and technology in health care—a process that has been actively under way since the 1960s. Along the way, we will draw some connections between and insights into the theory of diffusion of innovation, and the adoption of HIS and technology in health care.

The Long History of Adoption of HIS and Technology

Amid the sense of urgency and recent major legislative and regulatory thrusts to stimulate the adoption of HIS and technology in the United States, one might think this was a brand-new idea, an innovation just emerging from the laboratories of Silicon Valley technology firms and Cambridge software development start-ups. Most would be surprised to learn that the development and introduction of new information technologies for use in health care has been vigorously and continuously taking place since the 1960s in hospital data processing departments, clinical computer laboratories, home offices, garages, and other humble, dedicated origination points of innovation.

Early Beginnings

The early beginnings of HIS and technology were in the 1960s, relatively closely following the advent of computerization of U.S. society in general. The few hospitals able to afford expensive mainframe hardware and programmers to write software developed the early healthcare computer application software. These mainframe computers were so large and generated so much heat they had to be water cooled, which required a significant investment in this infrastructure and the data centers that housed them. The early software applications focused primarily on the accounting and financial applications arena, with rare instances of specialty clinical

research applications being developed by these hospitals' data processing departments. Clinical applications, however, were few and far between and predominantly isolated to single research departments or siloed specialty areas.

For several reasons, early HIS largely began as support for hospital finance and accounting departments. Finance departments controlled budgets and accounting information, and their processes followed Generally Accepted Accounting Principles (GAAP) rules. Plus, the "data" of finance and accounting involved dollars and cents, elements long standardized and universally understood. Thus these departments had processes that adhered to well-known accounting standards, which made computerization easier: Accounting functions represented repeatable, consistent functions and tasks that lent themselves to being programmed into a computer system.

In the 1970s, with the advent of air-cooled minicomputers, things began to change. Companies that distributed and supported hospital financial software applications emerged. These were the early HIS and technology vendors. One example of such a vendor was Shared Medical Systems (SMS), an early version of today's application services provider (ASP) or software as a service (SaaS; e.g., "the cloud") provisioning method. SMS, which was acquired by Siemens in the late 1990s, remains a very viable competitor in the financial and patient accounting HIS software market, supporting many hospital systems remotely from its data centers and original headquarters in Malvern, Pennsylvania. This company also provides clinical systems now, but financial accounting systems have always been its specialty and mainstay products.

In the meantime, many hospitals that made the independent decision to invest in hardware, programmers, and data centers developed much of their own software for financial, patient accounting, and order communications systems. This early HIS work gave rise to the first health information systems professional organizations: Hospital Information Systems Sharing Group (HISSG) and Electronic Computing Hospital Organization (ECHO). Each of these professional organizations consisted of hospital members who developed software and collaborated on the development of software for use in their hospitals. In addition to sharing ideas and functionality definitions for these software systems, the members actually "shared" or gave software programs and applications to one another. For example, if one hospital had developed (programmed) a successful patient accounting software system and another had developed (programmed) a successful software system for laboratory, personnel from the two hospitals could meet one another and establish a collaborative relationship through which they would exchange copies of the software programs for use in their respective institutions. ECHO was the organization for the hospitals using IBM hardware, and HISSG served the same purpose for the hospitals using non-IBM hardware. In those days, it was all about which type of "iron" (hardware) was used in the data center of the hospital: "Big Blue" (IBM) mainframes or non-IBM minicomputers (e.g., Digital Equipment Corporation and eventually Hewlett-Packard).

The first HIS were really extensions of charge-capture systems for patient billing system purposes. The first comprehensive medical information system (akin to today's EHR systems) was designed and built through a federal grant to Lockheed Martin; it was eventually commercialized and named Technicon, and it was initially implemented at El Camino Hospital in Mountain View, California, in 1971. The people who developed this software came out of the aerospace industry and worked with those who understood hospitals and health care. Also in the 1970s, Science Applications International Corporation (SAIC)—a large, successful employee-owned company with expertise in information systems work for the defense industry and federal government—developed an early clinical information system for VA hospitals. (This system was replaced in 1982 with a newer version system called Veterans Health Information Systems and Technology Architecture [VistA], an integrated EHR that is currently in use in more than 1400 VA hospitals and ambulatory clinics across the United States.[34])

The 1980s ushered in the era of the minicomputer, which offered fierce competition to the expensive, water-cooled mainframes of the 1960s and 1970s; the "minis" were smaller, generated less heat than the big mainframes, and were less expensive and easier to support because they could be cooled with less expensive air conditioning rather than water systems. Hewlett-Packard, Digital Equipment Corporation, and eventually even IBM developed highly competitive air-cooled minicomputers. Not only were these computers more efficient and less expensive to buy and operate, but fewer and less expensive personnel were needed to operate the computers and keep them up and running compared to the systems engineers and other highly technical professionals required for mainframe support. This trend made automation more affordable for hospitals, large clinics, and even large physician practices, which in turn stimulated the development of clinical applications as well as more widespread adoption of the typical financial accounting systems.

Vendors of software packages also started to emerge from entrepreneurial communities in great numbers in the 1980s. This trend occurred in part because a huge market was emerging: the improved affordability of systems for more hospitals and some large, multispecialty physician practices (think Mayo or Scripps Clinics), and in part because enough good software had been developed in hospitals in the 1970s that vendor companies could be formed to commercialize these software developments as "software packages." During the 1980s, many hospitals and a number of larger physician practices began to buy and implement computer systems to support their financial systems, and increasingly some ancillary clinical (e.g., laboratory, radiology, pharmacy) and practice management (e.g., registration, scheduling, and billing) systems. Numerous entrepreneurs sought to acquire software from hospitals that had developed such programs in-house; these entrepreneurs then relicensed the software to other hospitals—and the hospital information system software industry was born. Occasionally, these entrepreneurs would develop software from scratch within their companies' development teams as well, but did so less frequently than commercializing software that had been developed within healthcare organizations. As a result, the roots of very few vendor software systems today were actually developed by vendor companies; rather, many of the early software systems sold by vendors were originally developed in hospital data processing departments for the sponsoring hospital organization. Notable exceptions to this model include the HIS vendors Technicon, Cerner, Meditech, and Epic, although each of these companies needed a brave hospital or clinic to be willing to step forward for the "alpha" implementation project to get started and establish a toehold in the emerging HIS industry.

Evolution of Clinical Systems and the EHR

The first-generation HIS clinical order entry systems were really extensions of charge-capture systems for patient billing system purposes, rather than systems with functionality truly grounded in clinical care processes. The ethos of the financial underpinnings and motivations of hospital information systems were reflected in the early clinical systems built and implemented primarily to capture charges in the billing and claims processes. As noted earlier, Technicon developed the first comprehensive medical information system—a system focused on clinical care—in the mid-1970s. The requirements document for this system reads very much like the requirements documentation for one of today's modern EHR systems. This was truly an innovation that disrupted the healthcare industry. The VistA system, described earlier, was another early HIS that in a continually more advanced version is still in use today in VA hospitals across the United States. Specialized niche ancillary clinical systems began to emerge especially in the 1980s, seeking to provide automation of profitable hospital departments such as laboratory, radiology, and pharmacy management. These niche systems often competed to be recognized as "best-of-breed" systems. Also blossoming were physician practice management systems for large medical practices.

At this point, hospitals still developed much of their own software in-house and used their IT staff to interface a growing number of vendor-supplied systems with their in-house developed systems. To do so, they would build a data center, buy hardware, hire programmers and analysts, contract with SMEs, and create data processing departments to work with clinicians and administrators to design and develop systems internally. Universities developed some software, usually oriented to specialized clinical departments or siloed functions. Initial clinical information systems included "order entry" systems, early versions of CPOE. In some instances, these software applications were modeled after hotel software; think about the similarities in workflow between checking in and out of a hotel and being admitted, transferred, and discharged from a hospital. In the outpatient arena, only very large medical practices could afford computer systems and data processing departments during this time period.

From then through the 1990s, the number and types of healthcare organizations implementing computer systems expanded vigorously. The advent of the World Wide Web and Internet transformed healthcare computing, just as it transformed computing and telecommunications in all industries. In lockstep with this disruptive innovation, the federal government enacted the Health Insurance Portability and Accountability Act (HIPAA) to protect the security and privacy of citizens' data in anticipation of the significant increase in use of the Internet along with an increasing scope of electronic systems and technology in healthcare processes.[35] While HIPAA was intended to ensure the security and privacy of protected health information (PHI) as that information was transferred from one insurance plan to another (thus the "insurance portability and accountability" language in the title of the legislation), this legislation has had sweeping effects regarding the privacy and security of *all* PHI: (1) for patient care purposes as data are created and captured in EHR systems that share data across multiple organizational settings involved in a patient's care and (2) as

information is created via secondary uses of those data for analytics and data sharing among providers. Since 1999 and 2001, when the IOM published its watershed reports *To Err Is Human: Building a Safer Health Care System* and *Crossing the Quality Chasm*, respectively, healthcare organizations have been building comprehensive HIS and technology architectures in earnest, with the intent of improving quality and efficiency of care as summarized in the **Six Aims of *Crossing the Quality Chasm***. These six aims of high-quality care state that care should be[19]:

1. *Safe*: avoiding injuries to patients from the care that is intended to help them
2. *Effective*: providing services based on scientific knowledge to all who could benefit and refraining from providing services to those not likely to benefit (avoiding underuse and overuse, respectively)
3. *Patient centered*: providing care that is respectful of and responsive to individual patient preferences, needs, and values, and ensuring that patient values guide all clinical decisions
4. *Timely*: reducing waits and sometimes harmful delays for both those who receive and those who give care
5. *Efficient*: avoiding waste, including waste of equipment, supplies, ideas, and energy
6. *Equitable*: providing care that does not vary in quality because of personal characteristics such as gender, ethnicity, geographic locations, and socioeconomic status

The implications of these IOM reports—and the outright shock at their revelations about the preventable problems occurring in healthcare quality in U.S. hospitals—have driven the HIS and technology and regulatory agenda for the decade of the 2000s, as a potential means of improving the dire statistics published by IOM.

As we proceed through the decade of the 2010s, in the aftermath of the IOM reports and the recent update of the *To Err Is Human* study, as well as in the face of unsustainably high levels of healthcare expenditures, we are compelled to improve the quality and efficiency of health care in the United States—and HIS and technology are essential tools in that process. Significant governmental federal legislation on this front has included the American Recovery and Reinvestment Act (ARRA; Public Law 111-5), which includes the HITECH Act of 2009. Under Title XIII of this $787 billion economic stimulus bill, the U.S. Department of Health and Human Services is spending $25 billion to provide incentives for the adoption of EHRs among hospitals and physician practices; in addition, it hopes to generate savings of about $10 billion through the application of Meaningful Use criteria as part of that incentive program, through adoption of technical and data standards to facilitate the secure sharing of data between clinicians through system interoperability.[36] HITECH funding also provides training grants to colleges and universities to prepare the estimated 57,000 health IT workers needed to accomplish widespread EHR adoption. These criteria and standards are being designed to improve patient safety, reduce instances of repeated diagnostic tests and other medical processes, increase timeliness of care by speeding transmission of information to clinicians, and bring greater overall efficiency to the U.S. healthcare system.

As hospitals and physician practices persevere through the challenges of implementing EHR systems and meeting Meaningful Use criteria, the shape and texture of healthcare delivery are beginning to change on a widespread basis. Will this massive effort and investment in HIS and technology bridge the chasm between the Early Adopters and the Early Majority as described earlier in this chapter? Many think so. Next, we look at the facts, trends over time, and current status of the national effort to adopt HIS and technology on a widespread basis.

Challenges in Adoption of HIS and Technology in Health Care

The contrast is stark between the promise of HIS and technology versus the reality of implementing these systems for use in healthcare organizations. This dramatic schism is in part due to the fact that radically changing the ways patients are cared for and work is done is difficult at best and tries the patience and wills of even the most motivated organizations. Healthcare providers have been slow to adopt HIS and technology in their hospitals, clinics, and physician practices, especially those in rural settings and smaller practices that often lack adequate IT staff to manage their implementations and ongoing support of HIS and technology.

In many ways, the difficulties in implementing EHRs are compounded by the fact that the benefits of all that expense and hard work are often ambiguous. These benefits may occur in the long term versus the short term, or they may accrue to others (for example, many benefits of implementing EHR systems accrue to the payer and provider organization and not to the clinician typing in the claims-related data points). Most certainly, EHRs and other HIS implementations are expensive undertakings, and they are very disruptive to busy healthcare practices and settings. Reluctance on the part of physician practices to adopt EHRs due to these misaligned incentives of physician practices paying for the EHR and implementation effort, and the health plans and insurance companies benefiting from those efforts, is something the HITECH incentive payments are intended to ameliorate, at least in part. Physician providers can receive as much as $48,400 per physician for participating in the Medicare EHR incentive program and consistently achieving the Meaningful Use criteria through all three phases prior to 2016, and as much as $65,000 per provider who can demonstrate that at least 30% of his or her patients are covered by Medicaid and meet the criteria in any year through 2016.[36] These HITECH financial incentives are aimed at covering some of the capital and ongoing costs associated with acquiring and implementing "Meaningful Use–certified" EHR HIS and technology products. The funds may also partially offset the dip in physician productivity that occurs with the disruption to workflow associated with the introduction of a new computer system into a busy practice.

Other barriers to adoption include a mismatch between the idea of a computer system making work easier and the actual activities of those who end up doing that work. In fact, a common complaint among physicians is that current EHR systems create additional tasks on the computer for busy clinicians that hamper their productivity, not just during the transition period but permanently.

High up-front capital costs, ongoing costs of maintenance associated with new EHR systems, instability among vendor companies providing EHR software, and concern about whether the new system will meet clinicians' needs combine to create a high-risk situation for physician practices that invest their precious capital and other resources in these HIS products and implementations.[37] The EHR software market for physician offices and clinics is overloaded with more than 365 different products, most of which will not survive the highly competitive phase of initial entry into the early market for EHR products. If a software vendor goes out of business, the physician practice using that product has little choice but to go through the cycle again and replace it with another, ideally more stable EHR software package from a vendor with greater staying power. This uncertainty and steep financial requirements have been major barriers to physician practices taking the leap and investing in EHR systems, especially solo and smaller practices.[38]

This historical account shows that the evolution and adoption of HIS and technology in health care has relied on not only the hard work and ingenuity of the original visionaries of HIS in this country, but also leadership at many levels (i.e., organizational, presidential/governmental, and clinical/business). So what else needs to be understood to improve the adoption and widespread diffusion of EHR systems, HIS, and other technology? This question has many dimensions. What we do know is that we are challenged to understand how to achieve the promised EHR system, HIS, and technology benefits for physician practices, hospitals, and patients.

Where do we stand today in terms of EHR adoption? In 2011, a 21% to 46% difference in specific functionalities implemented was reported among adopters, yielding moderate to large differences in the use of EHR systems. Among smaller medical practices with one or two physicians, fewer than 2% reported adoption of fully functional EHRs and 5% used a more basic EHR functionality (see **Table 7.2** for definitions of functionality[39]); among larger practices with 11 or more physicians in the group, adoption rates reported in 2011 were 13% for fully functional systems and 26% for basic systems. Among the EHR adopters, there are also significant differences in the types and frequencies of use of functionalities in the EHR systems (**Figure 7.3**).[40] As of 2012, 40% of physicians used a basic EHR, but 9.8% of those systems met Meaningful Use criteria (which reveals the depth of use of EHR functionality, both qualitatively and quantitatively); 26% of solo practitioners had at least a basic system, compared to 58% of those in practices of 11 or more physicians.[41]

Among hospitals, adoption of basic EHRs and comprehensive EHRs has increased substantially since the HITECH incentives were put in place, but levels of adoption are not yet meeting the overall goals of widespread adoption. In 2012, 44% of hospitals had a basic EHR system—an increase of 17 percentage points from 2011 and about three times the percentage in 2010. Approximately 16.7% of hospitals had adopted comprehensive EHRs by 2012, about twice the proportion in 2011 (8.7%).[41]

Along with general environmental trends to implement EHRs in healthcare settings, clearly the HITECH incentive program has had an encouraging and accelerating effect on EHR adoption in hospitals as well as physician practices. Even so, a long journey remains before these health provider organizations achieve ubiquitous, interoperable, comprehensive EHR adoption. Many might wonder why it is taking so long to adopt this technology in the United States—but it can be safely said that healthcare organizations are picking up the pace in implementing HIS and technology.

Unintended Consequences of HIS and Technology

Through the efforts of healthcare organizations throughout the United States, HIS and technology are being increasingly used to achieve safer patient care, greater patient and provider satisfaction, improved efficiency of care, better analytics and reporting through the secondary use of data, and streamlined processes supported by automation. But that is not the whole story. The detection of all the effects of automation has, quite naturally, lagged behind its implementation. Thus, while counting the number of organizations that have implemented HIS and technology reveals a greater number of organizations using various types of systems, the depth, breadth, and quality of the actual functionality

TABLE 7.2 Survey Items Defining Minimally Functional, Basic, and Fully Functional Electronic Medical Record Systems

Features of Computerized Systems	Minimally Functional System	Basic System	Fully Functional System
Patient demographics		X	X
Patient problem lists		X	X
Physician clinical notes	X	X	X
Medical history and follow-up notes			X
Guideline-based interventions or screening test reminders			X
Test results (lab or imaging)	X		
Lab results		X	X
Out-of-range values highlighted			X
Imaging results		X	X
Electronic images returned			X
Computerized orders for prescriptions	X	X	X
Drug interaction or contraindication warning provided			X
Prescription sent to pharmacy electronically			X
Computerized orders for tests	X		X
Test orders sent electronically			X
Public health reporting			
Notifiable diseases sent electronically			

Reproduced from Hing, E., & Hsiao, C. J. (2010). Electronic medical record use by office-based physicians and their practices: United States, 2007. National Health Statistics Reports no. 23. Division of Health Care Statistics. http://www.cdc.gov/nchs/data/nhsr/nhsr023.pdf

of those systems is less well understood. Additionally, as more research is being conducted on HIS and technology implementation, evidence is emerging that the consequences of introducing these systems into healthcare organizations

FIGURE 7.3 Office-Based Physicians' Adoption of EHR Systems by Level of Capability

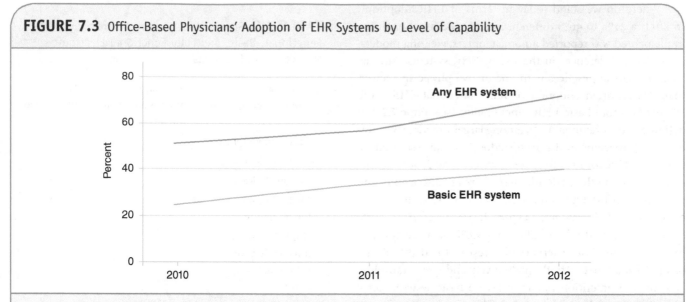

are not always positive or benign—that, in fact, harm can be attributed in some cases to the ways chosen to automate healthcare processes.[42]

In 2011, the IOM published its report *Health IT and Patient Safety: Building Safer Systems for Better Care*, pointing out existing evidence of the known effects of HIS and technology on patient safety and making recommendations to organizations, federal agencies, and suppliers of HIS and technology products and services to improve their impact on safety. The report describes safety as a system property, a consequence of a broader sociotechnical system consisting of technology (hardware and software), process, organization, external environment, and people (**Figure 7.4**).[42] The nature and degree of harm that may be caused by unintended consequences of HIS and technology, including EHRs, is not well known. This is in part due to the fact that health IT products are varied; they have wide-ranging and diverse impacts on healthcare environments, processes, and workflow. Vendor-favoring contracts contain legal language forbidding open disclosure of system problems, thus blocking transparent reporting of software product-related problems, as does "inadequate and limited" evidence for the variance in the literature.[42]

The IOM report describes features of safer HIS and technology in key areas, including features of health IT such as workflow, usability, balanced customization, and interoperability; design and development, including software, user

interfaces, testing deployment, maintenance, and upgrades; and implementation characteristics such as careful planning, benefits realization, system stabilization, and optimization.[42] The report identifies a lack of hazard and risk reporting data on health IT as a factor hindering the construction of safer

FIGURE 7.4 Sociotechnical System Underlying Health IT-Related Adverse Events

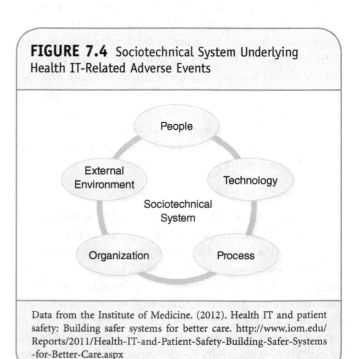

systems; it also warns that current market forces are contributing to the risks that may accompany HIS and technology. The key to addressing these safety risks is to be thorough and careful when planning HIS and technology implementations, use multidisciplinary project teams to design and implement these systems, create a transparent system of reporting system issues and quality problems attributable to the HIS, and develop standards for HIS and technology safety. The next priority of all three layers of leadership driving the adoption of HIS and technology—organizational, presidential/governmental, and clinical/business—must make certain these implementations result in the intended outcomes, without additional risk of harm to patients, their loved ones, and providers.

As sobering as these types of recommendations are, we would be wise to heed the reality that anything as powerful as HIS and technology also has the power to do harm if improperly designed, implemented, used, or maintained. Anyone who works in the arena of HIS and technology will tell you that these cautions are valid—thus those working in healthcare organizations must be realistic and exceedingly careful as systems are implemented. While this does not mean everyone should be paralyzed with fear, it does mean that healthcare organizations must be very disciplined, detail oriented, patient, and systematic in how these systems and technologies are introduced.

An interesting question when considering the risks of introducing new errors as a result of automating healthcare processes is, "How does one determine the cause of the errors?" Are they due to problems within the computers or to problems with the humans who are using those computers? One study reported of the total number of errors studied, 56% were computer system related and 44% were attributable to human error.[43] Of particular note was the finding that workflows that use *both* paper-based and electronic records (a very common practice) seem particularly problematic as more organizations transition between paper-based and electronic systems.

Another word of caution regarding HIS and technology is to be realistic about the cost of adopting HIS and technology. As enthusiastic as organizations typically are about implementing HIS and technology, and as carefully as those projects might be planned, this effort almost always takes longer and costs more than expected. In fact, during the transition, hospitals often see an 80% increase in IT department expenses.[44] Hospital CIO and chief financial officer (CFO) estimates also differ by about 75% regarding the cost of implementations. This significant variance is because CIO estimates include support costs and other operational expenses associated with HIS implementations that CFOs

generally underestimate. The amount spent on labor to support and maintain the new system increases by four times over the average implementation time frame.[44] Thus, the total cost of ownership of HIS and technology usually varies significantly from initial estimates, especially considering that projects typically take much longer to become reality than expected.

SUMMARY

Leadership in HIS and technology takes several forms consistent with the HIS model and can be considered from a variety of perspectives, including the organizational, presidential/political, and professional organization leadership arenas. The adoption of HIS and technology can be seen as rooted in the overall social system theory known as Rogers' diffusion of innovation, and as progressing through five stages of adoption demarcated based on the types of personalities and social systems within the organization, driving and responding to change: Innovator, Early Adopter, Early Majority, Late Majority, and Laggard.

The 50-year history of HIS and technology adoption has taken U.S. health care through a series of developments and technological innovations originating mostly within hospitals and other healthcare delivery organizations. Vendors of software emerged as a result of these hospital software development innovations, a fact that often surprises those individuals with a more recent exposure to the health information technology industry.

Successful HIS and technology adoption faces numerous challenges, including barriers such as high capital and ongoing costs, concerns with vendor stability, ability to select software that will meet the organization's needs, disruption to workflows, and productivity dips during implementation cycles. Trends toward adoption of such systems and technologies are gaining momentum, in part due to HITECH financial incentives to physician practices and hospitals for EHR implementations and achievement of Meaningful Use. Even so, adoption rates are increasing more slowly in the United States than in some other countries. Recent evidence points to unintended negative consequences to patient safety associated with implementing HIS and technology, and cautions are becoming more pronounced as all parties seek to develop safety standards for HIS and technology products, projects, and risk reporting processes. Additional realities of HIS and technology implementations should also be kept in mind, such as the tendency to underestimate the costs associated with these implementations, and the fact that both computer and human errors contribute to these unintended consequences.

KEY TERMS

Discussion Questions

1. In which ways is leadership required for each layer of the HIS model?

2. Discuss organizational, presidential, and professional leadership roles in HIS and technology. Is one type of leadership more important than the others? How have these three arenas of leadership helped the others? Have they hindered the progress of HIS and technology in any ways?

3. In future election cycles, we will again face the question of whether presidential leadership will keep HIS and technology on course as a driver of health reform. What do you imagine will happen?

4. What is HIS and technology adoption?

5. Rogers' theory of diffusion of innovation provides a backdrop to understanding the keys to success, issues, and challenges associated with adoption of HIS and technology in health care. Identify ways in which the concepts of Rogers' theory and adoption curve relate to HIS and technology adoption.

6. How did HIS and technology begin in the United States? What lessons can be learned from these early beginnings that will help us now and in the future as U.S. healthcare organizations strive to create a connected HIS and technology-supported health system?

7. Describe ways that HIS and technology can potentially help the Six Aims of *Crossing the Quality Chasm* be achieved.

8. What is the current status of electronic health record systems adoption in U.S. physician practices and hospitals? Which types of organizations seem to have an easier time adopting EHR systems? Which types struggle the most?

9. Why has adoption of EHR systems proceeded more slowly than anticipated in the United States? Why has adoption of EHR systems been less thorough in the United States than in some other countries? Will the HITECH incentive program change this situation and help close the gap?

10. Explain ways that HIS and technology have resulted in unintended consequences as reported by the IOM in its 2011 report, *Health IT and Patient Safety: Building Safer Systems for Safer Care*. In what ways does this report connect with the IOM's previous reports, *To Err Is Human: Building a Safer System* (1999) and *Crossing the Quality Chasm* (2001)? Is the focus of these reports HIS and technology or safety? Why?

11. What should healthcare organizations implementing new systems do to take the findings in the IOM reports into account?

12. Categorize areas of cost for HIS and technology systems and implementations. Define why these total costs of ownership are often underestimated. Describe ways to avoid underestimating these costs within healthcare organizations that are initiating an HIS and technology project.

13. Explain ways that computer-related errors are associated with the people using those computers. Contrast that with errors made by the computer systems directly.

REFERENCES

1. Brown, G., Patrick, T., & Pasupathy, K. (2013). *Health informatics: A systems perspective.* Chicago, IL: AUPHA Health Administration Press, p. 2.

2. Austin, G. L., Klasko, S., & Leaver, W. B. (2009). The art of health IT transformation. National Center for Healthcare Leadership. http://www.himss.org/files/HIMSSorg/content/files/doccopy4770_uid815201111226322.pdf

3. Connolly, C. (2005, March 21). Cedars-Sinai doctors cling to pen and paper. *Washington Post*, p. A01. http://www.washingtonpost.com/wp-dyn/articles/A52384-2005Mar20_2.html

4. HealthIT.com. (n.d.). Benefits of meaningful use. http://www.healthit.gov/policy-researchers-implementers/meaningful-use

5. Byrne C. M., Mercincavage, L. M., Pan, E. C., Vincent, A. G., Johnston, D. S., & Middleton, B. (2010). The VA experience: The value from investments in health information technology at The U.S. Department of Veterans Affairs. *Health Affairs, 29*, 629–638. doi:10.1377/hlthaff.2010.0119

6. Caroline Lubick Goldzweig, MD, MSHS. HIT and Quality Improvement: Summary of the Evidence and a Case Study. Presentation at UCLA Health Policy and Management 440A Health Information Systems and Technology May 17, 2012.

7. HIMSS. (n.d.). HIMSS health IT value suite. http://www.himss.org/valuesuite?src=sm or http://himss.files.cms-plus.com/HIMSS%20Health%20IT%20Value%20Suite%20Executive%20final.pdf

8. Chaudhry, B., Wang, J., Wu, S., et al. (2006). Systematic review: Impact of heath information technology on quality, efficiency, and costs of medical care. *Annals of Internal Medicine, 144*(10), 742–752.

9. Goldzweig, C. L., Towfigh, A., Maglione, M., & Shekelle, P. (2009). Costs and benefits of health information technology: new trends from the literature. *Health Affairs, 28*(2):282–293. doi: 10.1377/hlthaff.28.2.w282.

10. Trinity Health. (n.d.). Quality report cards. http://www.trinity-health.org/quality-report-cards

11. Medicare.gov. (n.d.). Categories of hospital compare measures. http://www.medicare.gov/hospitalcompare/Data/Measures-Displayed.html

12. Medicare.gov. (n.d.). Measures displayed on Hospital Compare. http://www.medicare.gov/hospitalcompare/Data/Measures-Displayed.html

13. McCullough, J. C., Zimmerman, F. J., Fielding, J. E., & Teutsch, S. M. (2012). A health dividend for America: The opportunity cost of excess medical expenditures. *American Journal of Preventive Medicine, 43*(6), 650–654.

14. Brailer, D. J., personal communication, June 1, 2013. http://www.amia.org/about-amia/leadership/acmi-fellow/david-j-brailer-md-phd-facmi

15. Brailer, D. J. (2009). Presidential leadership and health information technology. *Health Affairs.* http://content.healthaffairs.org/content/28/2/w392.abstract

16. Centers for Disease Control and Prevention. (n.d.). Introduction. http://www.cdc.gov/ehrmeaningfuluse/introduction.html

17. Lowes, R. (2013, April 3). CMS report details incentive program winners and losers. *Medscape Medical News.* http://www.medscape.com/viewarticle/781882

18. Committee on Quality of Health Care in America, Institute of Medicine. (1999). *To err is human.* (L. Kohn, J. Corrigan, & M. Donaldson, Eds.) Washington, DC: National Academy Press.

19. Committee on Quality of Health Care in America, Institute of Medicine. (2001). *Crossing the quality chasm: A new health system for the 21st century.* Washington, DC: National Academy Press.

20. James, J. T. (2013). A new, evidence-based estimate of patient harms associated with hospital care. *Journal of Patient Safety, 9*, 122–128.

21. HealthIT.gov. (n.d.). Health IT and patient safety. http://www.healthit.gov/policy-researchers-implementers/health-it-and-patient-safety

22. HealthTech Wire. (n.d.). HIMSS celebrates 50 years. http://www.healthtechwire.com/himss/himss-celebrates-50-years-2529/

23. HIMSS. (n.d.). About HIMSS. http://www.himss.org/AboutHIMSS/index.aspx?navItemNumber=17402

24. HIMSS. (n.d.). Frequently asked questions about HIMSS and its members. http://www.himss.org/himss-faqs?navItemNumber=18017

25. AHIMA. (n.d.). AHIMA history. http://www.ahima.org/about/history.aspx

26. AHIMA. (n.d.). AHIMA facts. http://www.ahima.org/about/facts.aspx

27. AMIA. (n.d.). AMIA mission. http://www.amia.org/about-amia/mission-and-history

28. Alliance for Nursing Informatics. (n.d.). About ANA. http://www.allianceni.org/about.asp

29. Rogers, E. M. (1963). *Diffusion of innovations.* New York, NY: Free Press.

30. Robinson, L. (2009, January). A summary of diffusion of innovations. *Enabling Change.* http://www.enablingchange.com.au/Summary_Diffusion_Theory.pdf

31. Diffusion of innovation theory. (2012, January). *News-on-Mobile: NEWSLAND.* http://quipuapps.com/wp-content/uploads/2012/01/diffusion_of_innovation_theory_.pdf

32. Stanford discussion of *Diffusion of Innovation* by Everett Rogers. (1995). http://www.stanford.edu/class/symbsys205/Diffusion%20of%20Innovations.htm

33. Chris Spagnulo's EdgeHopper: Approaching technology with mindfulness. (2008, October 14). How to cross the chasm. http://edgehopper.com/%E2%80%A8-what-geoff-recognized-was-that-there-is-more-to-this-curve-he-recognized-that-there-is-a-difference-between-disruptive-innovations-those-that-are-changing-the-game-altogether-and-gard/

34. World VistA. (n.d.). VistaA history. http://worldvista.sourceforge.net/vista/history/

35. U.S. Department of Health and Human Services. (n.d.). Health information privacy. http://www.hhs.gov/ocr/privacy/

36. athenahealth, Inc. (2009). A summary of the HITECH Act: Whitepaper. http://www.athenahealth.com/_doc/pdf/HITECH_Fact_Sheet_Whitepaper.pdf

37. DesRoches, C. M., Campbell, E. G., Rao, S. R., et al. (2008). Electronic health records in ambulatory care: A national survey of physicians. *New England Journal of Medicine.* http://nyehealth.org/wp-content/uploads/2012/07/DesRoches_EHRNational-Survey.pdf

38. Rao, S. R., Desroches, C. M., Donelan, K., et al. (2011). Electronic health records in small physician practices: Availability, use, and perceived benefits. Mongan Institute for Health Policy, Massachusetts General Hospital. Abstract retrieved from http://www.ncbi.nlm.nih.gov/pubmed/21486885

39. Hing, E., & Hsaio, C-J. (2010, March 31). Electronic medical record use by office-based physicians and their practices: United States, 2007. National Health Statistics Reports no. 23. http://www.cdc.gov/nchs/data/nhsr/nhsr023.pdf

40. Hsiao, C., Jha, A. K., King, J., et al. (2013). Office-based physicians are responding to incentives and assistance by adopting and using electronic health records. *Health Affairs, 32*(8), 1470–1477. doi: 10.1377/hlthaff.2013.0323

41. DesRoches, C. M., Charles, D., Furukawa, M. F., et al. (2013). Adoption of electronic health records grows rapidly, but fewer than half of US hospitals had at least a basic system in 2012. *Health Affairs.* http://content.healthaffairs.org/content/early/2013/06/27/hlthaff.2013.0308

42. Institute of Medicine. (2012). Health IT and patient safety: Building safer systems for better care. http://www.iom.edu/Reports/2011/Health-IT-and-Patient-Safety-Building-Safer-Systems-for-Better-Care.aspx

43. Sparnon, E., & Marella, W. M. (2012, December). *Safety implications of HER/HIT.* Pennsylvania. http://www.patientsafetyauthority.org/ADVISORIES/AdvisoryLibrary/2012/Dec;9(4)/Pages/113.aspx

44. Don't underestimate the costs of adopting health IT. (2011). *Health Populi.* http://healthpopuli.com/2011/01/24/dont-underestimate-the-costs-of-adopting-health-it/

SECTION III

Health Informatics

CHAPTER **8**

Health Informatics

By the end of this chapter, the student will be able to:

- Relate health informatics to the other spheres of the health information systems (HIS) model.
- Define informatics.
- Describe health informatics in the context of all of biomedical informatics disciplines.
- Explain interdisciplinary synergy as it applies to health informatics.
- Discuss the relationship of health informatics to electronic health record (EHR) implementation.
- Describe what an informaticist does, from medical, nursing, and public health perspectives.
- Explain clinical decision support systems and the "Five Rights."
- Describe the role of informatics to both workflow design and analytics.
- Define internal and external sources of data for informatics reporting and analytics purposes.
- Identify unintended consequences of HIS and technology and give some reasons why they occur.

INTRODUCTION

As reflected throughout this text and the health information systems (HIS) model, each layer of the HIS model (systems and management; health informatics; data and analytics; and research, policy, and public health) depends on the foundation of the many systems and technologies that are used throughout health-related organizations and activities. Health informatics is the second layer of the HIS model, as it

speaks to the use of those systems; the interactions between people, computer systems, and work; and the ultimate additional uses of all the data derived from those interactions. This chapter aims to provide an explanation of health informatics and its multiple facets. After all, computers are just machines without the humans who figure out the best ways to design and use them to support their clinical, administrative, and analytical work. Such is the work of health informatics.

HEALTH INFORMATICS DEFINITION AND PURPOSE

Health informatics is both art and science: It is aimed at improving, redesigning, and informing health and clinical care, organizations, processes, and research capabilities through the use of HIS and technology. It employs the science of language as it relates to uncovering data and meaning; redesigning workflow and processes; creating a better understanding of the proper interface between humans and computers; studying and providing direction to software development, functionality design, data and information content, and supported workflows; and developing decision support and analytics computing capabilities to inform and enhance knowledge in the areas of health, medicine, clinical, organizational, and population-based outcomes. Health informatics is a broad concept, to be sure, but an important one because it speaks to reshaping how we work in health care using HIS and technology, as well as harvesting insights, gaining knowledge, and improving health outcomes, organizational effectiveness, and the health status of the populations we serve. To get our arms around this broad concept, we will break it down into components that help us recognize "informatics" when we see it and understand its importance in actually getting what we hoped for from all the work and expense involved in implementing the enabling systems and making HIS and technology ubiquitous and purposeful in health care.

Informatics has evolved in concert with automation. Automation has become the norm in every walk of life as we computerize our society, innovating new ways of doing work, managing data, connecting people and organizations worldwide, and creating information and new knowledge. In 2004, the National Institutes of Health (NIH) issued an enhanced perspective on informatics as part of an important report by Freidman et al.,[1] a product of its Biomedical Information Science and Technology Initiative. The phrase used by the NIH to encompass informatics in health and medical science is **biomedical informatics**, which comprises four categories: bioinformatics (including molecular and cellular processes), imaging informatics (including tissues and organs), clinical informatics (involving individual patients), and public health informatics (involving populations and society).[1(p. 7)] While these four categories of biomedical informatics cover vast territory and each contributes to the others, the following two categories are relevant to the scope of health informatics as described in this text: clinical informatics and public health informatics.[2] These two areas relate predominantly to HIS and technology in healthcare organizations and public health; thus they are the focus of this chapter.

As a practical matter in health care, clinical and public health informatics involve the efforts of multidisciplinary groups of knowledge workers and researchers applying expertise in their respective clinical, public health, research, and business disciplines. Informatics involves the structure of data and information *and* HIS and technology, particularly electronic health record (EHR) systems and business intelligence/clinical intelligence (BI/CI) analytic systems. The interdisciplinary nature of health informatics ideally creates synergies by combining expertise from the distinct disciplines of computer science, information science, clinical medicine, nursing, biology, social systems and organizational culture, and health care (**Figure 8.1**).[3] In this case, the definition of synergy certainly applies—the whole is greater than the sum of its parts. Because health and health care are ideally integrated around the person and the patient, the expertise of many disciplines is called upon to understand the essentials of what is happening in any particular situation. Health informatics is no different: A variety of disciplines offer their

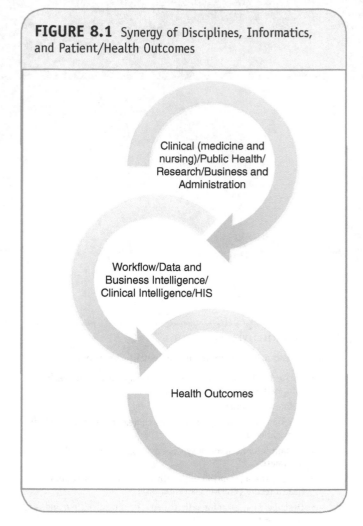

FIGURE 8.1 Synergy of Disciplines, Informatics, and Patient/Health Outcomes

Clinical (medicine and nursing)/Public Health/ Research/Business and Administration

Workflow/Data and Business Intelligence/ Clinical Intelligence/HIS

Health Outcomes

perspectives to the collective to determine new and better ways to work, or create the collective intelligence needed to understand any situation. The different masteries come together in ways that no single discipline could to understand a situation and interpret new information.

Health Care: An Industry in Transition

Health informatics has always been important, ever since the first bits of data handwritten on paper or otherwise recorded were used to communicate and document aspects of medical and clinical reality. Knowing how to interpret a piece of data about a patient (or many bits of data grouped into information about one or multiple patients) is essential to medicine and clinical care. The massive rollout of EHR systems in the United States over recent times, however, has greatly accelerated the need for study of the science associated with understanding clinical data structures and decision making, as well as the relationship of these EHR systems to clinician workflow and documentation.

Figure 8.2 illustrates the primary and secondary uses of EHR systems and the data created and captured in them. The need is now paramount to provide data standards and documentation methodologies that will result in consistent and safe data for patient care purposes, as well as quality data and information for population health management, research, clinical and business intelligence, external reporting, and other secondary uses of the data. The nature of data sources and information has changed radically as we have shifted from manual to automated methods of creating, capturing, gathering, preserving, and analyzing data.

We will refer to the HIS planning framework to consider different types of systems and the informatics activities that apply to each quadrant (**Figure 8.3**). In the framework's Quadrant I (i.e., repeatable day-to-day clinical transactions supported by the computer), informatics involves understanding, designing, and improving clinical and business workflows and processes through automation. Quadrant I informatics also relates to the interface between clinicians and EHR systems. This quadrant's form of informatics extends outside the organizational context to include patient engagement through the use of patient portal information

capabilities; mHealth applications such as the integration of mobile devices in the **quantified self** movement, connections in remote areas using texting, smartphones, and crowdsourcing; the ability to exchange and connect data between systems, organizations, devices, and people; and applications as far-reaching but completely accessible as integrating personalized genomic information into clinical practice.

Informatics activities in Quadrant III (data analytics, **data mining**, algorithm development, and clinical intelligence) have to do with the secondary use of the data that are created and captured in Quadrant I (clinical transactions) and Quadrant II (administrative transactions), and can take in information created in Quadrant IV (institutional information) as well. These data are collected, aggregated, mined, reported, and analyzed in Quadrant III clinical intelligence systems to gain insights into outcomes connected with processes, key clinical performance indicators, and quality of care, population health management, research, and clinical analytics associated with all types of clinical and other relevant data.

Although the term "informatics" in health care is typically thought of in relationship to clinical activities, it is also relevant to increasing business and operational insights

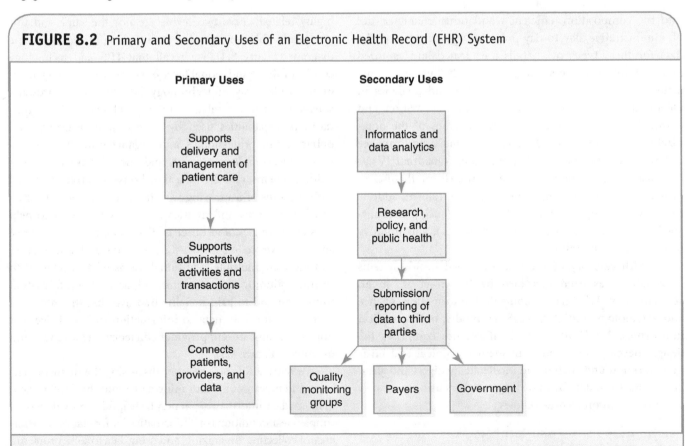

FIGURE 8.2 Primary and Secondary Uses of an Electronic Health Record (EHR) System

Data from The Institute of Medicine. (2003). Key capabilities of an electronic health record system, letter report: Committee on Data Standards for Patient Safety, Board of Health Care Services. http://www.providersedge.com/ehdocs/ehr_articles/key_capabilities_of_an_ehr_system.pdf

FIGURE 8.3 HIS Planning Framework and Informatics Activities

	Transaction/Functional Support Systems	Management/Decision Support Systems (BI/CI)
Clinical	I • Clinical workflow and process design • Clinical decision support systems • Data definition/standardization • Patient engagement • mHealth • Clinical data exchange	III • Data analytics and mining • Algorithm development • Quality analysis and reporting • Outcomes analysis • Clinical intelligence
Administrative	II • Operational workflow and process design • Service and process improvement	IV • Business intelligence, analytics • Data mining, reporting, and analytics

Key: BI, business intelligence; CI, clinical intelligence.

Modified from Jay McCutcheon's Systems Planning Framework.

into the composition, efficiency, and other characteristics of administrative, day-to-day processes and workflows. The data for these types of analysis are created and captured in Quadrant II systems (supporting daily business transactions), as well as business intelligence and analytics in Quadrant IV systems. The creation of information and knowledge regarding these business activities of the organization or health system focuses on financial performance indicators and business-related outcomes (Quadrant IV) as healthcare organizations struggle to transform themselves in light of the need to navigate healthcare reform, address runaway costs, support new models of care (such as accountable care organizations and medical homes), and improve inadequate quality results.

A fifth category of informatics, called health systems informatics, has been identified by Brown et al., in an adaptation of Friedman's biomedical information science and technology initiative (BISTI) model of biomedical informatics.[1(p. 9)] Health system informatics comprises the design, development, and refinement of clinical and business workflow and analytics to intellectually digest and glean knowledge from data by knowledge workers using computer systems and automated workflows.

Relationship of HIS and Technology to Health Informatics

Sometimes the term "health informatics" is used interchangeably with the term "health information technology." While highly related, these two terms are not the same and this interchangeable use is incorrect. Referring to the HIS scope diagram (**Figure 8.4**), we recall that HIS and technology consist of the foundational layer of systems and management of the wide array of technology infrastructure, hardware, software systems, databases, interoperability, and communications capabilities used by clinical, administrative, and public health professionals and organizations. Informatics is the *understanding*, *shaping*, and *use* of these HIS capabilities, systems, and the data they house and transport—all with the aims of improving workflows, processes, outcomes, and health status. Informatics is practiced in ways to help physicians, nurses, and other clinicians be more productive and effective; to enhance access to data and information and integrate multiple, additional forms of data relevant to each situation; to create meaningful, accessible information from data; and to gain insights by traversing the informatics continuum from data to information to knowledge that improve healthcare and provider efficiency, effectiveness, and outcomes (**Figure 8.5**).

Perhaps at this point—after discussing the many dimensions and nuances of health informatics and the development of biomedical informatics—it may be helpful to provide several simple, clear definitions of "informatics." Informatics is the science of collecting, organizing, and using data to solve problems, innovate, and improve. Health and biomedical informatics is informatics applied to healthcare and biomedical research.[4] The NIH offers a definition of biomedical informatics based on the

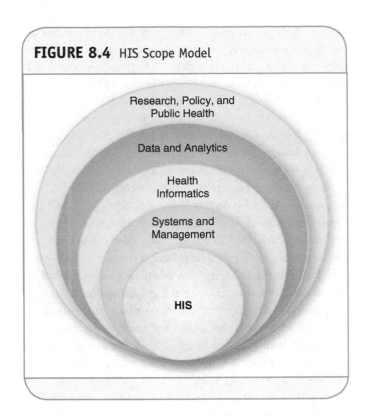

FIGURE 8.4 HIS Scope Model

Research, Policy, and Public Health

Data and Analytics

Health Informatics

Systems and Management

HIS

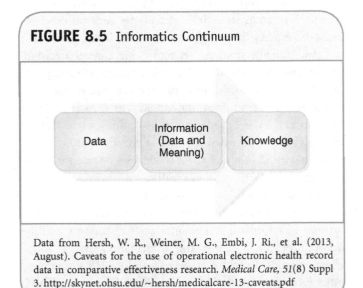

FIGURE 8.5 Informatics Continuum

Data

Information (Data and Meaning)

Knowledge

Data from Hersh, W. R., Weiner, M. G., Embi, J. Ri., et al. (2013, August). Caveats for the use of operational electronic health record data in comparative effectiveness research. *Medical Care,* 51(8) Suppl 3. http://skynet.ohsu.edu/~hersh/medicalcare-13-caveats.pdf

principles of information science, stating simply but profoundly that informatics equates to data plus meaning.[5] These ways of describing informatics begin to build a construct of the many facets that compose the multidisciplinary and multipurpose activities of informatics. Numerous descriptions and definitions provide insight into informatics—some of which may resonate more than others to you—but all of which offer some clarification of health informatics and its many elements.

Informaticists are professionals who devote their careers or at least a portion of their careers to working on improving, redesigning, and transforming health care and the clinical processes that comprise this vast arena. They are paving the road to realizing the promise of HIS and technology, guiding it toward achieving the goals identified in the Institute of Medicine (IOM) reports *To Err Is Human: Building a Safer Health System* and *Crossing the Quality Chasm.* Informaticists in the world of health, health care, and public health are medical, health, and information science professionals with skills and an affinity for their original discipline of medicine, nursing, or other clinical and therapeutic profession, *plus* information technology (IT), analytics, language science, data, workflow, and social and cultural impacts of employing the use of technology. Very interesting work, indeed.

ADDITIONAL MOTIVATION TO PURSUE HEALTH INFORMATICS

Eliminating Avoidable Errors Caused by Health Information Technology

The IOM's third health IT-related landmark report was *Health IT and Patient Safety: Building Safer Systems for Better Care.* The findings of this report and informatics are interconnected; they point to unintended consequences of HIS and technology.[6] The IOM report links the possibility of untoward outcomes of HIS and technology to the way systems are designed and used, and to the interface between systems, processes, and people. The report also emphasizes the sociotechnical aspects of HIS adoption. With its interdisciplinary approach that yields many perspectives on one problem or one process or one measure, health informatics helps us design good systems and better understand the many aspects of the sociotechnical environment in health organizations and population health. Emphasizing the fact that the impacts of EHR systems are not well understood, the IOM report points out that results published in the literature on similar, EHR-related topics are wildly varying and inadequate. Certain errors and risks are not yet detectable in the use of EHRs, and the IOM report brings our sights up to squarely face the problem of unintended consequences. *Health IT and Patient Safety: Building a Safer Health System* identifies risks of HIS and technology systems intended to, and promoted as tools to, enhance patient safety; it also lays out actions to reduce errors caused by EHRs.[6] Many of these actions revolve around informatics activities, including good system design—all too often, medical errors in EHR environments are rooted in poor user-interface design, poor workflow, and complex data interfaces (**Figure 8.6**). If the presentation of data on the EHR screen makes it difficult for clinicians to

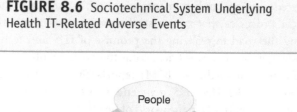

FIGURE 8.6 Sociotechnical System Underlying Health IT-Related Adverse Events

Data from the Institute of Medicine. (2012). *Health IT and patient safety: Building safer systems for better care.* Washington, DC: National Academies Press.

access or see important results, key values could be missed, or the difficulties might at least delay appropriate intervention. Similarly, lack of system interoperability is a barrier to informing clinical decisions and improving patient safety.

Thus the science and art of health informatics means bringing to bear problem-solving skills in the content and structure of data and information; having subject-matter expertise in disciplines and departments being automated; understanding workflows and processes, data content of key performance indicators, and measurements related to achieving desired outcomes; and discovering how HIS and technology can be integrated with clinical workflows to improve efficiency, effectiveness, and performance, and achieve improved processes or results. When we think of the variety of types of specialized work this includes, we immediately see how interesting, challenging, and painstaking informatics work, when done well, can be. The challenge of informatics reflects its importance: Making sure that the data and information presented to clinicians and others are accurate, timely, and appropriate means the difference between streamlined workflows and inefficiencies, between confident decisions and confusion or frustration. As the chapter progresses, we will describe examples of these types of activities to get a feel for what is involved in the dynamic role of informatics.

Increasing Complexity of Information

Informatics evaluates and dissects the process of decision making and explains how information presented at the right

time in the right format can improve the decision maker's ability to move forward in the clinical or business process to help the patient or organization. Intuitively, we know that *more* information is *not* necessarily better. The ways that the quantity and quality of information available to a decision maker can be optimized are the subject of a great deal of work in informatics, with roots in information science and its intersection with clinical medicine. In complex situations, which is increasingly the norm in medicine and healthcare settings, people typically choose a less complex option that they would otherwise decline if fewer options were available. Thus, the greater the complexity of a situation and the more options available to a decision maker, the more likely the decision maker is to gravitate toward a simpler option—and paradoxically, the more options available to contemplate or digest, the more attractive the status quo option becomes.[7] Despite all the development of more sophisticated diagnostic tests and sources of biomedical information supported by automated availability of as much information as possible, under the assumption that "getting all relevant information to a decision maker is wise," it turns out that we may be detracting from that person's ability to process relevant information because of excessive complexity and volume of information. If not properly introduced to the knowledge worker, more information sometimes defeats its very purpose—to assist those using the information to make better decisions.

Additionally, findings reflecting on clinical decision-making nuances indicate a dynamic tension between policy or group-level considerations and the decision making of a physician when treating an individual. The clinician is more likely to exhaust a broader array of options when treating an individual than when looking at the same information across a group.[8] Many of these tendencies or nuances occur in clinical decision making, creating an impetus for informatics researchers to find out how, why, and when people are influenced differently by varying amounts and presentation formats of information. The intricacies of the relationships between people, systems, and information are profound when one considers the massive roll-out of EHR systems and other forms of information availability in health care. This is not to say that the increased availability of information for clinical decision making is necessarily either better or worse, but evidence strongly suggests it will be different.

Increasing Complexity of Medicine, Health Care, and Healthcare Processes

Informatics takes on certain characteristics as it is applied to different types of work done by clinical knowledge workers such as physicians, nurses, therapists, researchers, public health experts, and others. In 1990, David Eddy asserted, "The complexity of modern medicine exceeds the inherent limitations of the unaided human mind."[9] It is commonly lamented that there is too much new information for physicians, nurses, and others working in health to keep up with using traditional methods—that is, by reading professional peer-reviewed journals and other publications. There simply is not enough time in the day or the capacity in the human mind to hold and process all of this information and still perform one's daily work. Thus informaticists become alchemists in their attempts to manage the science and art of informatics: How much information is the right amount?

One principle used by people in information professions regarding the provision of data and information to support clinical decision making is called the **Five Rights of Clinical Decision Support**: right information, to the right person, in the right format, via the right medium or channel, at the right place or time in the workflow.[10]

1. The *right information* means that information is accurate, specific to the situation, relevant to the patient or decision at hand, and based on evidence when possible.
2. To the *right person* means identifying and making sure the information is delivered to the professionals who need the information to effectively perform their duties in patient care or other health-related information usage situation.
3. In the *right format* signifies that the information should be provided in a presentation or structure suitable to the situation, condition, or location of the caregiver and patient.
4. Through the *right medium or channel* means the information should be delivered in a usable, actionable format through secure, appropriate information devices, workstations, or media as is practical and convenient for the clinician.
5. At the *right place* means at the right step in the workflow of the clinician. At the *right time* means not too early, not too late, but at the "just right" time, so that thought and action can take place on a timely basis to positively influence patient outcomes and assist in the efficiency of care processes.

Another principle involving a set of five factors also influences health informatics: The **Five Rights of Health Information Management** are consistent with the Five Rights of Clinical Decision Support. These points should also be taken into consideration in the work of informatics. The Five Rights of Health Information Management include[11]:

1. *Right time*: Information should be available to authorized personnel whenever they need it.
2. *Right route*: End users need access to data regardless of where they are or which device they are using.
3. *Right person*: Ensure only the right people have access to certain information.
4. *Right data*: Prevent unauthorized tampering or accidental corruption of data.
5. *Right use*: Ensure only the "minimum necessary" information is provided.

Although the Five Rights of Health Information Management have a slightly drier, more administrative and security-based flavor to them, they absolutely influence the parameters within which all informatics, including clinical, must operate. It does no good to develop clinical or health informatics practices, workflows, or systems that do not take proper data administration practices into account. If they do not adhere to the proper data safety and security management practices, the hard work to develop automated workflows will be wasted and the systems rendered unusable. Clearly, informatics teams have a lot to think about as they do their work, which is one more reason why interdisciplinary collaboration is essential in health informatics.

The Changing Complexion of Data Sources and Information

Health care is no different than any other walk of life in our society as it relates to **automation**—vast automation of the entire healthcare ecosystem is under way. Some of this is helpful, some not. Some of the automation simply computerizes existing processes, but much of it is transformative, fundamentally changing the ways people work and deliver service. Certainly, all of this activity needs sound discipline according to the basic tenets of implementation (as described previously) plus the necessary informatics expertise to redesign work processes and achieve the desired objectives of introducing new HIS and technologies. A disciplined process will translate HIS and technology into meaningful improvement, leading to an actual transformation of the ways care is delivered, work is done, information is created, and new knowledge is gained.

Inherent in this massive evolutionary period is the transition from predominantly manual and paper-based processes to computer-supported processes and methods for acquiring data for purposes of analysis. The transition from manual to automated processes and aggregation of data for analysis is a particularly disruptive and difficult one: It challenges us to think not only of new ways to do work, but also ways with which we are completely unfamiliar. Unfortunately, it can leave us with a "mixed bag" when tallying up our sources of data, with some sources newly automated and some sources still on paper. Stated another way, the transition from paper to computers is almost always a gradual one because trying to change too much all at once can be overwhelming for an organization. This piecemeal implementation results in the organization relying on part paper and part computer for a good part of the evolution to a "paperless environment" and prevents the work of the organization in a particular department or arena, such as niche areas of patient care or patient record keeping, from being in the correct place and available to those who need it. It is tempting in some areas to hold on to traditional paper-based processes even after the automated support is implemented; however, this simply duplicates the workflow. The transition from existing paper-based to newly computerized workflows is much more difficult than starting with a clean slate when a brand new building is being constructed and opened. In a new facility, the computer system can be designed and implemented as part of the design of that new site. Of course, that happens only rarely, and sometimes even then the opportunity is missed to begin with new HIS and technology from the start; sometimes the systems used in the old building are transferred for use into a brand new facility!

Dealing with these types of decisions and challenges is where informatics earns its keep—by engaging subject matter expertise with process redesign know-how, as well as helping determine whether an implementation of a new computer system should be done using a gradual method versus a "big bang" method. Informatics is essential to getting some real transformational gains out of the implementation of a new computer system: By imagining and developing the improved, streamlined processes, the implementers of the new computer system might enable the organization to achieve true progress. Going through the effort and disruption associated with a computer system implementation only to customize computerized workflows and processes to mirror traditional paper-based methods is a waste of an opportunity, and typically eventually gets reversed again to a new, streamlined process supported through automation.

One is hard-pressed to think of any other field in which the relationship between the knowledge worker and the computer is more crucial to "get right" than in health care: In health care, patient lives are at risk. Health informatics is key to making safe what might otherwise be a very risky transition from manual to computerized processes. For example, EHR systems make clinical content available to the end users, such as providing medication content and decision support to physicians placing medication orders, thereby eliminating the need for those clinicians to access clinical data on a paper chart. The additional content provided within an EHR's process for entering orders for tests and therapies can include drug formulary and cost information for medications, drug–drug interaction and drug-allergy alerts, and disease-specific interaction checking. This type of content in the medication ordering process can be of great assistance to the ordering clinician, and the ways that this content is presented can have a beneficial effect on clinician efficiency and effectiveness. The science and art of informatics includes making sure the EHR presents the right data content in the right layout, format, and timing to best support clinician workflows.[12]

Even in the context of an EHR implementation, and in our zeal to automate or achieve Meaningful Use criteria to qualify for Health Information Technology for Economic and Clinical Health (HITECH) Act incentive payments, it is important to remember that sometimes having all information on the computer is not the answer—that being able to print off and review only critical information on a piece of paper may be the most efficient and effective method for the clinician. In some instances, EHR-driven processes should allow for this practice, as the goal is to improve the healthcare delivery system, not just computerize for the sake of HIS and technology.

The transition from manual to automated aggregation of data for analysis is important to consider when discussing health informatics. It applies just as equally to clinical care of individual patients in healthcare organizations (the domain of clinical informatics) as it does to analysis and reporting across populations, societies, and geographic areas (the domain of public health informatics). As discussed in the previous section, informatics is essential to design new workflows for automating clinical care, such as when implementing EHRs and interoperability between systems and organizations involved in the care process (Quadrant I); informatics is likewise essential to automation of supporting administrative processes and workflows (Quadrant II). Consider the role of informatics in secondary analysis of data aggregated from the variety of data sources (including those in Quadrants I and II), as well as other data sources such as mobile devices, web sources, and third-party data sources of various types. Through multidisciplinary work, informatics is important in assuring data integrity and quality and relevance of data emanating from clinical systems. Informatics gathers, accesses, preserves, and manages data in databases and analytics systems, making these data valuable and enhancing their accessibility, both for primary uses (patient care) and for secondary uses (data analytics). The interdependency of data with informatics and informatics with data lays the groundwork for secondary uses of data, creating information and ultimately knowledge (see Figure 8.5). Informatics is to good data what good data are to informatics.

To elaborate on the diagram portraying BI/CI and secondary uses of data (**Figure 8.7**), there are many sources of data in healthcare organizations: computerized information systems (from all four quadrants of the HIS planning framework detailed earlier in the planning section of this text); registries and logs; direct observations as documented in EHRs; data from external sources such as payers and research organizations; web sources of data; monitors, mobile devices, and sensors; and others. These data sources can be accessed and the data gathered, then cleaned, normalized, and placed into a processing environment that organizes, protects, and allows for data to be carefully managed. *Data integrity* is a term that encompasses the quality, accuracy, and reliability of data elements as they are created, stored, and moved from system to system. Data integrity is as important as any system, software package, or hardware platform that creates, captures, and provides data. Information emanating from those data sources is only as good as the quality and integrity of the data. Stated another way, HIS are only as good as the data used and stored within them. Poor-quality data are potentially dangerous clinically, financially, operationally, managerially, and any other way one can categorize their use. In less extreme terms, information is often imperfect, and the first means to perfect it is to ensure the integrity of each data element used to create that information. We will discuss this topic in more detail later in the chapter.

How does this relate to informatics? We know that informatics includes stewardship of data, pays attention to data definitions during system implementation, and relies on the availability of good data to ensure effectiveness of the knowledge workers using those data in their jobs (primary uses) and the quality of information created using those data elements (secondary uses). So how do we achieve excellence in data through the work of informatics and subsequent use by informaticists? First, a by-product of a good system implementation is good data: Successful system implementation is achieved only through the interdisciplinary work of clinicians, clinical informaticists, business personnel, process owners, subject matter experts in relevant disciplines, IT professionals, departmental staff and employees, and others. The practice of informatics involves perspectives, skills, and methods for assuring the discipline necessary for good data management:

- Developing adequate data definitions that are understood by all users
- Training end users of systems in the importance of careful attention to data quality, because they are the ones who create the data elements that are first

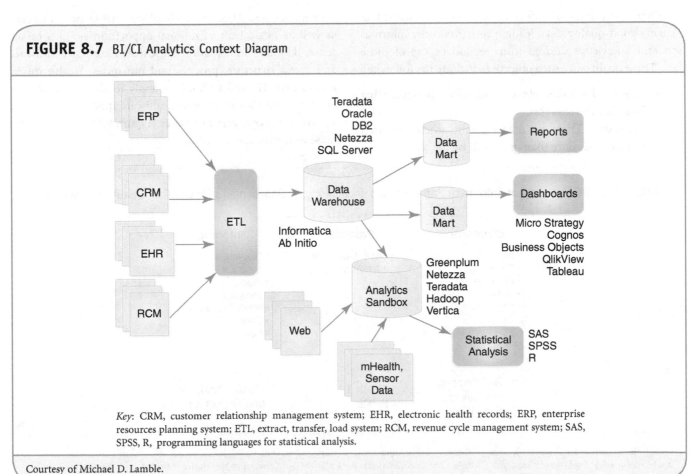

FIGURE 8.7 BI/CI Analytics Context Diagram

Key: CRM, customer relationship management system; EHR, electronic health records; ERP, enterprise resources planning system; ETL, extract, transfer, load system; RCM, revenue cycle management system; SAS, SPSS, R, programming languages for statistical analysis.

Courtesy of Michael D. Lamble.

captured and broadcast into other systems (e.g., registration data), and then migrated to analytics databases for secondary utility

- Establishing roles and relationships pertaining to data ownership by assignment of data owners and stewards, the people responsible for maintaining the quality of a particular type of data

- Identifying sanctioned sources for each type of data and actual data element, as the one recognized and agreed-upon owner and single source of truth for that value or type of data element (e.g., the EHR is the sanctioned source of patient data, not the billing system)

- Dedicating positions to data management and updating existing job descriptions to include data management, duties upon which personnel are evaluated and compensated

- Establishing groups that work together to analyze data for accuracy, consistency, and integrity, as well as reverse-engineering information to ensure the groups understand each data element used to create a report or other information and that the sources used for those data are the correct ones

Other objectives of informatics work are directed at assuring good-quality data, leading to trustworthy information and knowledge derived from secondary use of those data. These quality-oriented objectives include the following:

- Validity: Each data element actually represents what its definition says it is.
- Reliability: The same data element, when measured or recorded more than once, will be the same.

- Standardization and normalization: Common, consistent nomenclature and codes for types of data are used by informaticists, analysts, organizations, vendors, reporting organizations, and others. These standardized nomenclatures and codes (such as ICD-10) are key to appropriately sharing data elements for benchmarking and other evaluative or interorganizational reporting.

- Affordability: Data are economically feasible to create, capture, store, and use.

- Consistent: Data follow standardized definitions, guidelines, Meaningful Use requirements and standards, policies and procedures, payer requirements, and third-party reporting requirements such as those established by The Joint Commission.

- Secure, private, and confidential: Data collection, storage, and use follow HIPAA and other regulations, guidelines, and proper clinical practices.

RELATIONSHIP OF HEALTH INFORMATICS TO DONABEDIAN'S HEALTHCARE QUALITY FRAMEWORK

Informatics and HIS and technology enable new strategic as well as tactical organizational opportunities. In a broad sense, data and information are used to support, measure, and assess structure, process, and outcomes. Health informatics and HIS and technology apply to all three elements of Donabedian's widely used healthcare quality framework: structure, process, and outcomes (**Figure 8.8**). Let's examine these elements one at a time.

FIGURE 8.8 Relationship of Informatics and HIS and Technology to Donabedian's Health Care Quality Framework

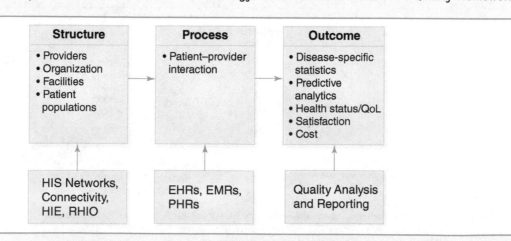

Data from Donabedian's Framework from McDonald, K. M., Sundara, V., Bravata, D. M., et al. (2007, June). *Closing the quality gap: A critical analysis of quality improvement strategies* (Vol. 7: Care Coordination). Rockville (MD): Agency for Healthcare Research and Quality (US); (Technical Reviews, No. 9.7.) 5, Conceptual frameworks and their application to evaluating care coordination interventions. Available from: http://www.ncbi.nlm.nih.gov/books/NBK44008/

Structure

From a structural standpoint, health informatics and HIS influence what is feasible in terms of organizational structure, primarily by taking geography and physical barriers presented by the size and shape of organizations out of the picture. In other words, a new organizational construct can be conceived and implemented not by sticking any shovels into the ground to build a new physical plant, which traditionally was synonymous with "new organization," but rather by reconfiguring relationships and patient workflows via connections through information and technology infrastructure. For example, today's health information exchanges (HIEs), "medical homes," and accountable care organizations (ACOs) are modern versions of the health maintenance organization (HMO) of the 1970s, the prospective payment system of the 1980s, the managed care organization of the 1990s, and the continuum of care in the 2000s. The only fundamental difference is that ACOs have the distinct advantage of having information and technology infrastructure to enable them—for real—this time. With enabling electronic highways, EHRs, outcomes databases, secure email, and HIEs, these organizational constructs are truly implementable, with existing physical structures connected through new relationships, corporate structures, contracts, Internet-enabled connectivity, information aggregation and reporting, and analytical capabilities. **Exhibit 8.1** profiles the data sources available in this context.

Additionally, the ubiquitous use of smartphones, sensors, and other mobile devices is transforming access to healthcare providers for populations in remote, previously inaccessible locations. For example, the Ugandan Ministry of Health and UNICEF have teamed up to create connections and communications between health clinics with malaria medicine using inexpensive mobile phones' SMS (short message systems, or texting) capability to alert Ugandans living in remote locations as to where and when the medicines are available and to disease outbreaks.[13] In the past, these medicines had to be "rerouted" to private clinics or else would be in short supply without proper accounting, thus making them inaccessible to remote citizenry. Often, the medicine's availability would not be communicated in any way to the people, leaving them without any protection against malaria. Moreover, the outbreaks of malaria would go unannounced, leaving people vulnerable to exposure because they did not know about disease-affected areas that could just as easily be avoided. As modest as it seems from the standpoint of a healthcare system in which large organizations seem to be the major focus,

EXHIBIT 8.1 Data Sources

Internal data sources for informatics purposes include clinical databases such as EMR, EHR, and PHR systems; order management systems including CPOE systems; and clinical systems such as laboratory, radiology, pharmacy systems, quality management, and surgery systems. Other data sources include administrative databases such as claims and billing systems; supplies and materials management systems; credentialing and privileging records; documents influencing policies and procedures; surveys from patients, providers, and employees; interviews and direct observations; case-mix systems (including ICD-9 and ICD-10, DRG claims data, and estimated data costs); medical records abstracts; vital statistics data (e.g., births, deaths, disease, and tumor registries); cost information systems; emergency department (ED) logs; other specialized "silos"; and direct measurement and observation.

External data sources include a vast array of source hubs including the following: Improving Chronic Illness Care (ICIC; http://www.improvingchroniccare.org/); Integrated Healthcare Association (IHA) Pay for Performance (http://www.iha.org/); Institute for Health Care Improvement (IHI; http://www.ihi.org/); The Joint Commission (http://www.jointcommission.org/); Leapfrog Group (http://www.leapfroggroup.org/); Robert Wood Johnson Foundation (http://www.rwjf.org); *US News & World Report* (http://health.usnews.com/health/best-hospitals); The Commonwealth Fund (http://www.commonwealthfund.org/); Simpler Health Care (simpler.com/healthcare.html); Center for Health Transformation Agency for Healthcare Research and Quality (AHRQ; http://www.ahrq.gov/); California Health Care Foundation (evaluating pay-for-performance; http://www.chcf.org); California Hospital Assessment and Reporting Taskforce (CHART; http://www.chcf.org/topics/hospitals/index.cfm?itemID=111065); Guideline Clearing House; Hospital Mortality reports on Medicare; National Quality Forum (NQF; http://www.qualityforum.org/); National Quality Measures Clearing House (http://www.qualitymeasures.ahrq.gov/); National Committee for Quality Assurance (NCQA; http://www.ncqa.org); Office of the Patient Advocate Quality Report Card (http://reportcard.opa.ca.gov/rc2013/); VA QUERI (http://www.Queri.research.va.gov); and World Health Organization's (WHO) ranking of health systems (http://www.who.int/whr/2000/media_centre/press_release/en/).

in many parts of the world a simple text message from one person to another makes a massive difference in the ability of populations, one person at a time, to gain access to lifesaving information. Health informatics, HIS, and secure Internet-enabled technology are essential new conduits of communication and information sharing, as well as components of modern healthcare structures, integrating providers, organization, facilities, and populations.

Process

Process in health care is founded in patient–provider interactions and the ancillary clinical and administrative activities to support them. The majority of this chapter speaks to ways that health informatics influences the systems supporting provider–patient interactions through the careful design of EHR systems, patient engagement connectivity, and other HIS and technology-enabled capabilities. The interaction between clinicians and these systems heavily influences the content, timeliness, and quality of patient care. For example, Kaiser Permanente's project called KP HealthConnect has demonstrated new ways of supporting clinicians with an EHR system, engaging patients in their care processes, and connecting patients and clinicians electronically through secure email and other messaging and communication methods.[12]

Outcomes

Secondary use of data for analytics capabilities in the practice of health informatics allows for retrospective analysis of data as well as predictive analytics, based on access to organized data stores of historical data for large patient populations as well as near real-time access to disparate data sources in support of particular topics of interest. These types of uses of "Big Data" are enabling researchers and informaticists to better measure outcomes, understand the effects of new patterns of care, predict the occurrence of diseases across a population and evaluate genomic data's influence on patient outcomes, thus driving a "learning engine" from data to information to new knowledge. This, in turn, can influence care processes in ways that achieve increasingly better outcomes.

For example, the CPRS/VistA system at the Department of Veterans Affairs (VA) has made it possible to monitor the quality and outcomes of diabetes care, as well as follow performance indicators and clinical reminders to help providers, patients, and the system to achieve specific goals (**Exhibit 8.2**).[14] These reports are results derived from analyses of data from the VistA system database, which has been in use at the VA for more than 25 years, from VistA's inception to the present time.[14] A lesson learned during the course of this 25-year journey is that transforming care in the challenging condition of diabetes takes more than technology and data: It requires a culture of academic clinicians and healthcare personnel who value quality and care based on scientific evidence and accountability. These values and findings can demonstrate new methods of care for other organizations to consider and touch every aspect of healthcare delivery, including population health management, and public health.

Additionally, informatics emphasizes the use of key performance indicators (KPIs), measurement benchmarks, and process improvement targets. These can include goals and standards of care, evidence-based practice guidelines built into clinical workflows and analytics, and best practices from studying comparable organizations and other geographic regions. Secondary use of data and analytics allow these metrics and measurements to drive improvements in patient care and services through feedback to those managing care processes and administrative activities. This feedback

---

EXHIBIT 8.2 Examples of Use of Information to Monitor Quality of Care

The VA uses information to evaluate how closely its clinicians adhere to the VA's guidelines for diabetes care. Controlling diabetes is an area that is particularly challenging, because it must take place on an outpatient basis on a continuous basis. The VA uses information aggregated from its VistA EHR system that captures lab and other data, and monitors key outcome indicators for diabetes care, such as HbA_{1c} (a blood test that shows whether blood sugar is under control) among its diabetes patients (**Figure 8.9**). It then compares their performance across all clinicians for adherence to guidelines and progress toward goals for diabetes care, such as performing foot visual, foot sensory, and eye exams, in addition to HbA_{1c} blood glucose tests for all diabetes patients across numerous years (**Figure 8.10**).

EXHIBIT 8.2 Examples of Use of Information to Monitor Quality of Care

FIGURE 8.9 CPRS/VistA Trends in Mean Glycosylated Hemoglobin (HbA$_{1c}$) Levels Among Veterans Health Administration (VHA) Clinic Users, By Age Category, October 1998–September 2000

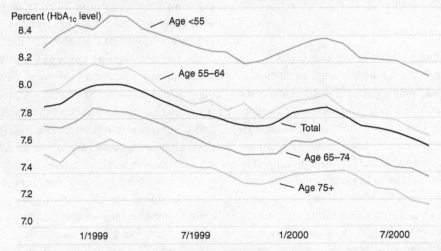

Note: Additionaly, a regression model that adjusts for clustering (patient and facility and seasonal effects) was used to confirm the downward linear trend in monthly HbA$_{1c}$ levels overall (−0.013, $p \leq .0001$) and minimal differences in this trend by each age category ($p = .492$).

Copyrighted and published by Project HOPE/*Health Affairs* as Kupersmith, J., Francis, J., Kerr, E., et al. (2007). Advancing evidence-based care for diabetes: Lessons from the Veterans Health Administration. *Health Aff* (Millwood). *26*(2), 156–168. The published article is archived and available online at www.healthaffairs.org.

FIGURE 8.10 Diabetes Process Quality in the Veterans Health Administration (VHA), Selected Years 1995–2005

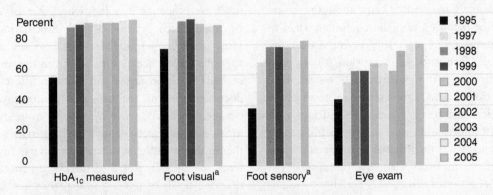

Note: Results are for VHA primary care outpatients with diabetes mellitus.
[a]Data for 2004 and 2005 are not provided.

Copyrighted and published by Project HOPE/*Health Affairs* as Kupersmith, J., Francis, J., Kerr, E., et al. (2007). Advancing evidence-based care for diabetes: Lessons from the Veterans Health Administration. *Health Aff* (Millwood). *26*(2), 156–168. The published article is archived and available online at www.healthaffairs.org.

reveals levels of performance in terms of overuse, underuse, and misuse; variations in performance and outcomes; and comparison of actual outcomes to benchmarks, guidelines, standards of care, and agreed-upon performance metrics.

HEALTH INFORMATICS CAPABILITIES AND DISCIPLINES

Now that we have reviewed the purposes and characteristics of informatics, we next consider characteristics of some of the main informatics roles in healthcare organizations today.

Medical/Clinical Informatics

Medical informatics includes a number of facets, one of the most important of which is the design and implementation of clinical decision support capabilities of EHR systems and other clinical systems. Such support provides end users with prompts and alerts about a specific patient, and other information such as lab results or medication data contained in the EHR system. Clinical decision support systems deliver information support to physicians, nurses, professionals from laboratory and other clinical areas, therapists, and others. Some of the more commonly used capabilities are alerts for allergies, drug–drug interactions, and drug–allergy interactions. Clinical rules and algorithms programmed into the EHR system are used to assess noteworthy conditions or risk factors as a patient's care progresses and more and more data for that patient are entered into the system.

Because clinical decision support system capabilities are driven by the data and information stored in the EHR, and those data and information are sometimes incomplete, caregivers may not know all that might be happening with a specific patient. Consequently, alerts should be reviewed in context, always with the notion that clinicians may also be able to take into account anything else they know about the patient that might not yet be recorded into the computer. Thus, in the term "clinical decision support," *support* is the operative word: The computer is not *making* the decision, it is *supporting* it. Especially with a newly implemented EHR system, there are often inadequacies in data completeness or accuracy—a shortcoming of which clinicians are mindful. Clinicians must take these sources of information into account, adding them to information gleaned from their actual presence and interaction with the patient, and make their determination of the appropriate course of action based their experience as well as the information available to them from the computer. Medical informatics involves the science and skill of working with the IT staff to design such decision support capabilities.

Nursing Informatics

Clinical decision support systems are part of the arsenal of information that nurses can use as they provide care in a continuous, comprehensive, and integrated fashion for patients—more so than other caregivers who have more specialized roles. Nurses, in many ways distinct from other clinicians, are responsible for the care of the "whole" person, through assessments and constant monitoring to keep track of all the elements of that person's care. In turn, the nursing informaticist's aim is to bring to bear all perspectives, including any medical-, pharmacy-, and nursing-related information, such as the social and emotional consideration of the patient. Nursing requires the integration of the available data and information, all to be synthesized by the nursing professional who has direct contact with the patient. It is within that broader context that clinical decision support and other information are considered in the total picture of the patient. In hospitals and other clinical settings, most care is based on the work of nurses. Physicians, therapists, and others may come and go throughout the day and night to do their rounds and check in on patients, perform surgeries, deliver therapies, and so on, but nurses are present 24 hours a day. Nurses are responsible for making sure that all needs—physical, emotional, educational, and logistical—of the patient and the patient's family are met. Consequently, nursing informatics has some overlap with, but differs from, clinical informatics for physicians; the work of physicians is frequently based on the medical interventions and workflow, with a focus on access to results, placing orders, performance of procedures, and other medically oriented objectives.

Simply stated, informatics for each clinical discipline must be based on the key workflows of each discipline. Moreover, each type of clinical informatics—even for the same discipline—must be tuned into the environment or specialty of practice. For nurses, given the continuous nature of their work processes and the significant role of nursing documentation in the care and communication processes between professionals, informatics is quite in-depth and can include more facets relative to informatics for physicians, therapists, or other healthcare providers. To date, EHR systems are typically not as conducive to meeting these multifaceted needs of nursing informatics as they might be for more medically driven processes. Design, development, and implementation of nursing documentation and workflows usually lag behind the implementation of physician-oriented workflows, due to the depth and breadth of functionality required by nursing. For example, nursing documentation includes styles and standards for nursing notes and observations, medication administration, assessments, and care plans. These types of documentation vary significantly from one type of care to another, so reaching agreement on the methods and standards for nursing workflows and documentation methods requires a great deal of collaboration and cooperation among nursing professionals. Nursing workgroups are often used to establish these documentation standards and workflow designs.

Adding to the challenge, informatics or clinical decision support for nursing comprises a comprehensive set of capabilities that relies on numerous other parts of the EHR system being available to integrate into the nursing support features. As a result, nursing documentation (as well as clinical decision support) portions of EHR systems tend to be implemented further down the road in an organization's EHR implementation journey—which means that it is more likely to be delayed or put off altogether. When looking at the statistics for adoption of clinical documentation and nursing informatics capabilities across EHR system implementations, the challenge of accomplishing nursing informatics becomes clear, being reflected in lower adoption rates for nursing functionality than for some of the more straightforward aspects of EHR functionality, such as laboratory results reporting. For example, in U.S. hospitals, adoption of basic EHR systems grew from 9% in 2008, to 15% in 2010, to 27.3% in 2012; by comparison, comprehensive EHR system adoption (which includes extensive EHR system functions such as documentation and clinical decision support capabilities) increased from 8.7% in 2011 to 16.7% in 2012.[15] While these statistics reflect impressive increases in the rates of adoption, they also show that as of 2012, 56% of all hospitals had no EHR system. In addition, the practice of nursing informatics and clinical decision support for nurses were available in a relatively small percentage of hospitals—according to these statistics, only 16.7%.

In ambulatory care settings such as physician offices and clinics, as of 2010 approximately 25.8% of physician practices had basic EHR systems; by 2012, that percentage had risen to approximately 38.2%.[16] Thus some 61.8% of physician practices did not have basic EHR systems—which translates to the majority of practices lacking the comprehensive types of clinical decision support and documentation capabilities necessary for automated support of medical or nursing

informatics. The goal of Meaning Use criteria is to urge these statistics upwards. It will take time, probably years, for EHR system implementations in the United States to mature and for comprehensive clinical decision support and documentation capabilities to become available more broadly. Once again, it is important to remember, "Development begins where you are." For the U.S. health system to advance to providing such informatics capabilities, we have to progress from exactly this point.

Public Health Informatics

Public health informatics includes information capabilities that (1) identify and understand health trends, health status, and the incidence of illnesses across populations or segments of populations locally, regionally, nationally, and globally; (2) monitor and survey disease and conditions across a broad geographic and population scope; (3) detect, prevent, intervene, and monitor in the event of an outbreak of a biologically related condition, the increase in the incidence of a disease, a natural disaster, or bioterrorism; (4) promote health and prevention; and (5) provide for preparedness through means such as biosurveillance, illness notification, and education.[17] Public health informatics employs the analysis of health information to identify threats to or changes in the public's health. The move from paper-based to electronic reporting has been a radical change for public health departments, agencies, and organizations; it has also been a move that expanded opportunities for meeting public health goals.

The government has a strong interest in public health informatics because changes in the public's health can indicate threats to national security. For this reason, the U.S. government is investing in both public and private IT initiatives, such as the American Reinvestment and Recovery Act (ARRA) and HITECH, representing an outlay of $25 billion for EHRs and networks. Investment in this publicly funded program contributes to public health informatics efforts as well as private HIS and technology capabilities. This investment not only advances the private healthcare system, but also benefits the totality of public good: The creation and capture of health data and information within the private sector creates data that can be securely shared for research, policy, and public health purposes as well.

The increased availability of data from hospitals, clinics, and physician practices across the United States is expanding our ability to study and survey these data locally, regionally, and nationally, looking for disease patterns, prevention opportunities, public health preparedness, and other areas of public health interest. Public health informatics, like other branches of informatics disciplines, is an interdisciplinary profession that applies computer science, health and medical sciences, mathematics, engineering, information science, and related social sciences to public health issues, surveillance, analytical, and preventive processes.[18] It provides support to other arms of public health work such as bioinformatics, disease monitoring, medicine, nursing, prevention, health promotion, and public health administration.

Public health informatics identifies threats to public health and the spread of disease processes; aids the development of strategies and tactics that might be effective in ameliorating those threats and diseases; and buoys the implementation and evaluation of those programs. As new technologies are implemented throughout the U.S. health system, public health organizations are adapting to the availability and use of these new electronic data sources. This adaptation opens up tremendous opportunities, but is no less disruptive and difficult in the public health sector than adoption of EHR systems and other HIS and technology is in acute healthcare institutions and clinical settings.

As informatics emerges in the two previously distinct and separate categories of "health" versus "medicine," there seems to be a "graying" of the previously bright lines between the public and private sectors, and healthcare organization centric perspectives versus public health perspectives. As IT envelops both areas, the connections are clear: The keys to health, safety, prevention, and health promotion are also vital to healthcare quality, efficiency, and effectiveness. Thus, both the public and private sectors stand to reap the rewards of developing and using informatics.

UNINTENDED CONSEQUENCES OF CURRENT USES OF HIS AND TECHNOLOGY

In spite of the challenging but optimistic view of the promise of health informatics for improving care, knowledge, and health, the introduction of HIS and technology (including the important role of EHR systems) poses difficulties and threats to the usefulness of the data emanating from these systems for use in both private institutions and public health informatics. For instance, the IOM report *Health IT and Patient Safety: Building a Safer Health System* warns that a growing body of evidence displays the unintended consequences of implementation of EHR systems and other HIS and technology.[6] These warnings lead us to question why some of these unintended consequences occur: reasons such as incomplete data in the EHRs; persistent "silos" of information telling an unfinished story about patients or health issues; data codified first for billing and claims, then for patient care, public health informatics, or research; difficulties capturing data contained within narrative documentation and free-form notes; lack of granularity in EHR data needed for public health informatics and research; and different data needs for patient care versus public health analyses.[19] These issues may be addressed at least in part by the meaningful and comprehensive adoption of EHR systems including data standards, interoperability capabilities, and technical standards.

Ultimately, the potential gain is worth the struggle. Without public health informatics guiding us to preserve, promote, protect, and monitor health, we will continue to waste inconceivable amounts of money on excess medical expenditures. The opportunity cost of this waste dwarfs what it is estimated it would take to feed hungry children, provide primary health care and vaccinations to all citizens, ensure safe routes to school, give proper education, deliver clean water through improvement of waste and storm water treatment, supply career training for the unemployed, advance rural development, and bolster programs already in place such as the Job Corps program, the Supplemental Nutrition Assistance Program (SNAP), and the "Up Front" transportation system.[20] These opportunities could potentially be funded by improved efficiency and effectiveness of the U.S. health system, a large part of which is monitored, supported, and protected through public health informatics capabilities.

SUMMARY

The proper fuel for informatics consists of good data and information, regardless of the discipline. Data and a culture devoted to improving process and quality are required for optimal patient care and organizational management. Such data encourage the art and science of informatics at the clinical level, the organizational level, and the public health level. Evidence-based clinical guidelines drive many informatics functions, resulting in processes and workflows with baked-in knowledge. Informatics aims to achieve excellence and improvements in outcomes through analytics, data mining, and business/clinical intelligence. Data warehousing is one increasingly available technology encouraging and playing a role in data stewardship, protection, and preservation. Clinical intelligence and business intelligence comprise retrospective decision support and management information, analytics, predictive analytics, and other forms of informatics. New ways of accessing real-time disparate "Big Data" sources for predictive and outcomes analytics are emerging and will further change the complexion of informatics and information availability for research, patient care, and public health purposes.

Health informatics is the effort to transform health and clinical care, organizations, processes, and research capabilities through the use of HIS and technology. A number of specialized informatics disciplines exist, and within health informatics are clinical informatics and public health informatics. As a result of the evolution of HIS and technology, and in particular the massive introduction of EHR systems globally, informatics is now going through its own evolutionary phase.

The tasks of health informatics include process improvements, workflow redesign, and outcomes analysis; these elements constitute the discipline and impact of informatics. Analytic methodologies rely on the availability and secondary use of data created and captured during clinical processes and workflows, which are also the subject of health informatics. Health informatics includes both clinical informatics and public health informatics. Clinical informatics includes the subdisciplines of medical informatics, nursing informatics, and informatics for other clinical disciplines such as therapies. Public health informatics deals with detecting, monitoring, analyzing, preventing disease, and promoting health.

As we struggle through the challenges and early stages of adoption of HIS and technology, and in particular EHR systems and analytical capabilities, the work of informatics and informaticists will gradually free us from our current condition of inadequate levels of quality, excessive costs, and waste of resources and lead to a more efficient and effective U.S. health system, thereby improving the health status of each individual and the population overall.

KEY TERMS

Automation 169
Biomedical informatics 164
Data mining 165

Five Rights of Clinical Decision
   Support 169

Five Rights of Health Information
   Management 169
Quantified self 165

Discussion Questions

1. Describe health informatics and identify its place among the other layers of the HIS and technology model.

2. What role does health informatics play in the design, development, and implementation of new HIS and technology, especially EHR systems?

3. Identify and explain synergies between clinical disciplines, informatics, and health outcomes as depicted in Figure 8.1. Which two areas of informatics do you think have the most impact on each other? Defend your answer by providing its rationale.

4. Why is health informatics important in today's health care and public health environment in the United States? In the world? What type of transition is health care going through in the way it handles and processes information, and why is health informatics essential to that transition?

5. Which types of professionals participate in the work of health informatics? What do they do in their health informatics work? What do practicing physicians and nurses contribute and what do they gain from the work of clinical informatics?

6. Explain how the practice of medicine is becoming increasingly complex. What does this mean for the amount of information people working in clinical settings are expected to know, remember, and make use of in their clinical practices? How can computers help this situation?

7. What is the paradox of decision making with "few versus many" alternative choices available? How can informatics help this situation?

8. Give several examples of types of health informatics analytics and uses of secondary data.

9. Describe internal and external sources of data for analytics and outcomes analysis.

10. What are clinical decision support systems? How are they used by physicians? By nurses? In what ways do the clinical decision support needs of physicians and nurses differ? In what ways are they the same?

11. What warnings does the IOM's report *Health IT and Patient Safety: Building Safer Systems for Better Care* provide regarding EHR systems data that are used for secondary uses? Which types of flaws potentially exist in EHR data?

REFERENCES

1. Brown, G. D., Patrick, T. B., & Pasupathy, K. S. (2012). *Health informatics: A systems perspective.* Chicago, IL: Health Administration Press.

2. American Medical Informatics Association (AMIA). (n.d.). The science of informatics. http://www.amia.org/about-amia/science-informatics

3. Gennari, J. (n.d.). Medical informatics definition. http://faculty.washington.edu/gennari/MedicalInformaticsDef.html

4. Northwestern University, Feinberg School of Medicine. (n.d.). Health and Biomedical Informatics. http://www.preventivemedicine.northwestern.edu/divisions/hbmi/

5. Bernstam, E. V., Smith, J. W., & Johnson, T. R. (2009). What is biomedical informatics? *Journal of Biomedical Informatics.* http://www.ncbi.nlm.nih.gov/pmc/articles/PMC2814957/

6. Institute of Medicine (IOM). (2012). *Health IT and patient safety: Building safer systems for better care.* Washington, DC: National Academies Press. http://www.iom.edu/Reports/2011/Health-IT-and-Patient-Safety-Building-Safer-Systems-for-Better-Care.aspx

7. Redelmeier, D. A., & Tversky, A. (1990). Discrepancy between medical decisions for individual patients and for groups. *New England Journal of Medicine.* http://www.nejm.org/doi/full/10.1056/NEJM199004193221620

8. Evidence on the costs and benefits of health information technology. (n.d.). http://www.cbo.gov/sites/default/files/cbofiles/ftpdocs/91xx/doc9168/maintext.3.1.shtml

9. Millenson, M. (1997). Demanding medical excellence: Doctors and accountability in the information age, United States. Chicago, IL: The University of Chicago Press, p. 5.

10. DOQ-IT. (n.d.). The "5 Rights" of CDS. http://www.ddcmultimedia.com/doqit/Care_Management/CM_CDS/L1P4.html#

11. Finn, D. (2011). Protecting patient data: The 5 rights of data administration. *In Defense of Data.* http://www.symantec.com/connect/blogs/protecting-patient-data-5-rights-data-administration-0

12. Chin, H. L. (2004). The reality of implementation: Lessons from the field. *Permanente Journal* (Kaiser Permanente). http://xnet.kp.org/permanentejournal/fall04/reality.html

13. Luscombe, B. (2012, August 27). Disease can't hide: How cheap phones—and quick thumbs—are saving lives in Uganda. *Time,* 50–52.

14. Goldzweig, C. (2012, October). Lecture at UCLA Fielding School of Public Health Department of Health Policy and Management.

15. DesRoches, C. M., Charles, D., Furukawa, M. F., et al. (2013, June 27). Adoption of electronic health records grows rapidly, but fewer than half of US hospitals had at least a basic system in 2012. *Health Affairs.* http://content.healthaffairs.org/content/early/2013/06/27/hlthaff.2013.0308.full

16. Hsiao, C. J., Jha, A. K., King, J., et al. (2013, July). Office-based physicians are responding to incentives and assistance by adopting and using electronic health records. *Health Affairs.* 10.1377/hlthaff.2013.0323. http://content.healthaffairs.org/content/early/2013/06/27/hlthaff.2013.0323.full

17. AMIA. (n.d.). Public health informatics. http://www.amia.org/applications-informatics/public-health-informatics

18. Centers for Disease Control and Prevention. (2012, July 27). The role of public health informatics in enhancing public health surveillance. (2012, July 27). *Morbidity and Mortality Weekly Report, 61*(3 suppl), 20–24. http://www.cdc.gov/mmwr/http://www.cdc.gov/mmwr/preview/mmwrhtml/su6103a5.htm

19. B. H. Johnson (Ed.). The Electronic Data Methods Forum, 2013: Advancing the national dialogue on use of electronic clinical data to improve patient care and outcomes. (2013, August). *Medical Care, 51*(8 suppl 3). http://journals.lww.com/lww-medicalcare/Citation/2013/08001/The_Electronic_Data_Methods_Forum,_2013__.1.aspx

20. McCullough, J. C., Zimmerman, F. J., Fielding, J. E., & Teutsch, S. M. (2012). A health dividend for America: The opportunity cost of excess medical expenditures. *American Journal of Preventive Medicine, 43*(6), 650–654.

SECTION IV

Data, Analytics, and Business Intelligence/ Clinical Intelligence (BI/CI)

CHAPTER **9**

Data

INTRODUCTION

The study of healthcare data has two dimensions. The first dimension is that of technical, pedantic knowledge. This technical dimension is paramount to data organizational bias, security, integrity of data, and system performance. Without highly skilled personnel, a poor infrastructure for data will prevent the true utility of these data from being realized.

The second dimension is the need to imaginatively understand data and its properties for analysis as the foundation for organizational growth. This dimension is less technical and more connective in nature. It is the responsibility of a nontechnical participant in business intelligence (BI)/clinical intelligence (CI) to contribute to the translation of data for technical professionals into the form needed for analytics. Finding ways for data to support their respective needs is a creative and rewarding process.

Health care has a history of reinventing itself to adapt to macroeconomic and political influences. It is now adopting new technologies and care delivery methods that are profoundly increasing the volumes of data to levels heretofore unimagined. The ultimate goal is to leverage these data to provide more affordable and quality care. For the purposes of this chapter, we will define data (with a tweak for health care) as follows:

> Base-level computer information that may consist of numerical or word elements, facts, values, or combinations of stored information that can be either qualitative or quantitative, and from which knowledge is derived and decision making may be made better and more logical.

Implicit in this definition is the message that data can be valuable. If an industry may make better decisions based on data, then it is incumbent upon that industry to capitalize on its use. In the case of health care, data have always had some value, but due to the recent acceleration of development and adoption of technology, massive changes in how data are sourced, assimilated, integrated, stored, and mined as assets are beginning to significantly, and positively, affect the healthcare industry. The landscape and complexity of health care have changed due to national and state economic politics, operational introspection from both clinicians and business leaders, and rapid evolution of technology in medicine.

Health care's data may take varying forms. Simple data such as patient demographics, including date of birth, sex, and so forth, are generally formatted and similarly available across computer software systems. (Note that this is a generalization; later we will discuss issues of data normalization, including varying structures in different systems for the same data element and referential integrity, including incorrect and/or inconsistent spelling and referencing for the same name, code, and other seemingly unambiguous terms that are simply entered improperly.) Conversely, **clinical data**—such as lab results, previous or ongoing conditions, and so on—may be of a confusingly disparate nature requiring **normalization** and, as a result, may be more difficult to access. For example, an older medical office practice management system may have 1000 unique data elements, whereas a contemporary electronic health record solution may have more than 5000 discrete data elements. Trying to merge data from these two disparate data sources would be challenging indeed.

The vast sums of data collected over the years in health care have principally served the internal and operational purposes of separate healthcare organizations; that is, these myriad players have processed the data for their patients and employed administrative functions for their own purposes. With the new political attention and intense focus on consistently lowering costs, however, the healthcare industry is now looking introspectively into how it might use these data to perform better. With better data—and while remaining aware of the political consequences—the healthcare industry can measure quality improvements that were previously only theoretical. In this way, healthcare organizations can make an effort to better analyze both business and clinical metrics.

In comparison to other industries, health care is great at adopting acronyms and buzzwords but often not so great at achieving real movement. The industry is notorious for exceedingly slow adoption of new health information technology (IT) methods. Yet, clinical tools and methods and today's cellular phone technology are to some extent eroding this reluctance to change. In relation to data, healthcare organizations are now talking about **Big Data** and **velocity, volume, and variety** (the "Three V's"—more on that later). Major companies with expertise in working with massive data sets in other industries, such as mobile communications, retail, petroleum, and banking, are circling around to health care and providing previously unavailable data storage and access methods. However, the healthcare environment is complicated by heavy federal and state regulation. Just recently, Amazon—one of the leading vendors in this business—elected to depart from healthcare data storage due to the data security liability issues associated with the Health Insurance Portability and Accountability Act (HIPAA) and the need for high degrees of security, privacy, and confidentiality of protected health information (PHI). Soon after, however, Amazon reentered the healthcare data storage market, but only after performing the technical and organizational work necessary to meet the healthcare data management requirements described earlier.

Compared to other industries, health care has more than its fair share of challenges in leveraging the incredible asset represented by data. The notion that "health care is local" is most assuredly true in many ways; in regard to data, it is profoundly true. By this, we mean that not only are people treated in their neighborhood, but also that their neighborhood healthcare organization approaches and records their data differently than a healthcare organization in another region might. Healthcare organizations "do the same thing differently," including generation, storage, accessing, and mining of data elements. While business-oriented data have significant overlap and commonality, clinical data are siloed and not communicated between the hundreds of commercially dissimilar software systems. In other words, the emergency room on 5th Avenue may collect and catalog its data differently than the surgery center on 8th Avenue, or the clinic on 45th Avenue, and so on. However politically convenient, the expectation of aggregating data for public health purposes or having electronic health records communicate with one another—whether across the nation or just across town—is fairly spurious and remains far from reality.

The current state of data within health care is problematic. Many theories have been advanced regarding data safety matters, data organizing methods, medical lexicon standardization, and the ways in which access and availability should work. Overlay this with arguably the most stringent privacy legislation within any industry, and the result is an area fraught with intense intellectual challenge and opportunity. With improved methods for data generation, capture, storage, analysis, and other competing practical uses, proper data management may produce tremendous clinical value and business process efficiencies to an industry desperately in need of both.

DATA SOURCES

The 2011 U.S. gross domestic product (GDP) was approximately $17.6 trillion: Health care's share was approximately 18% of this amount and growing proportionately faster than the other larger segments of the U.S. economy. It is forecasted that health care may represent 20% of the GDP by 2020.[1] Commensurate with these statistics, the data generated and the data necessary for the operation of the U.S. healthcare industry are proportionately outpacing other industries for a host of reasons.

At a macro level, an estimated 2.5 quintillion bytes of new data is created daily worldwide across all industries and uses.

Further, 90% of all the digital data created worldwide has been created *within the last 2 years.*[2] Mobile technology takes the credit for most of this proliferation of data. Smartphones, tablets, and other mobile devices are growing in exponential popularity within health care and are being used by clinicians, patients, and other industry players. In addition, countries with little traditional infrastructure (e.g., India) have jumped into mobile and wireless computing, skipping the development of many of the more traditional types of system platforms requiring a more significant infrastructure investment that other countries have invested in over the last 25 years.

As a result of several converging trends—the adoption of mobile devices, the government's financial incentives fueling proliferation and expansion of physician adoption of electronic health records (EHRs), imaging technologies, and privacy legislation—data's preeminence is finally an imperative for the entire healthcare industry. Much of this movement has compelled healthcare organizations to adopt a "got to do" something attitude versus the older ambivalence of "want to do" something.

Historically, most of the focus on healthcare data was on information in revenue-cycle (i.e., billing and claims) systems along with bits and pieces of fragmented clinical data (**Exhibit 9.1**). Living within modified managed care and fee-for-service environments without an electronic clinical record allowed providers and payers to principally survive on claims and billing data as means to assess their respective financial status, acumen, and success. Under the provisions of the **Affordable Care Act (ACA)**, however, economic risk is being rebalanced with financial incentives for providers to implement EHR systems and to be measured and compensated for improved, calculable patient outcomes.

Within health care today, hundreds of discrete revenue-cycle and health record operational systems or data sources are used among payers, hospitals, physician groups, clinics, and other provider settings. Some systems may be very small, used in a single department for a specific application that produces small packets of data, creating an information "silo." At the other extreme, enterprise-wide and mission-critical applications are commonly used to accomplish multiple functions, applications that are used constantly all day long by a majority of employees. Enterprise systems produce prolific volumes of data and may communicate these data to third parties such as insurance companies, governmental agencies, and others, as well as retain the information for internal use (**Figure 9.1**). These very different **data sources**—places from which data emanate—may have applications for both clinical or business processes and analyses.

EXHIBIT 9.1 Revenue Cycle Management

In the healthcare industry, financial issues related to **revenue cycle management (RCM)** are often complicated by changes to insurance products and contracting terms with providers. These insurance-related changes are somewhat fluid but mostly involve tactical, daily activities, including claims preparation, billing for services, and accounts receivable. In spite of these changes, the patient–provider visit process has changed little and still generally involves the *how much, who, what, when,* and *where* of the procedural and diagnostic experience. The data packets derived from these visits are relatively static in data size—yet overall volumes of data are increasing due to the growing number of medical visits associated with the growing U.S. population and the aging of the baby boomers.

In many business contexts, the phrase "Follow the money" has relevance. The U.S. healthcare system is capitalistic in nature and, therefore, no exception to this notion. Health care is provided through an extremely complex environment of procedures, codes, diseases, materials, tools, facilities, and human resources. Unaligned contractual relationships between providers, insurers, suppliers, government, and employers are omnipresent at all levels. In turn, healthcare providers at all levels must document and report their services to payers, which then pay them through the contracts they have with employers and individually insured patients. Federal and state entities follow similar processes through insurance claims for the Medicare and Medicaid programs. The unfortunate overabundance of uninsured patients must also be processed. The bureaucracies and administrative requirements for all of these activities are intricate and create an unnecessary inefficiency in the U.S. healthcare system. Notwithstanding this fact, providers must manage this cycle of procedural reporting and spend excessive resources to assure the sufficient collection of revenues so that their practices can survive and grow. Like any other organizations, healthcare organizations must be able to predict streams of revenue accurately to stay financially viable. With the ever-growing complexity described previously, this task is especially challenging for healthcare organizations of all sizes.

FIGURE 9.1 Organizational Chart of the House Democrats' Health Plan

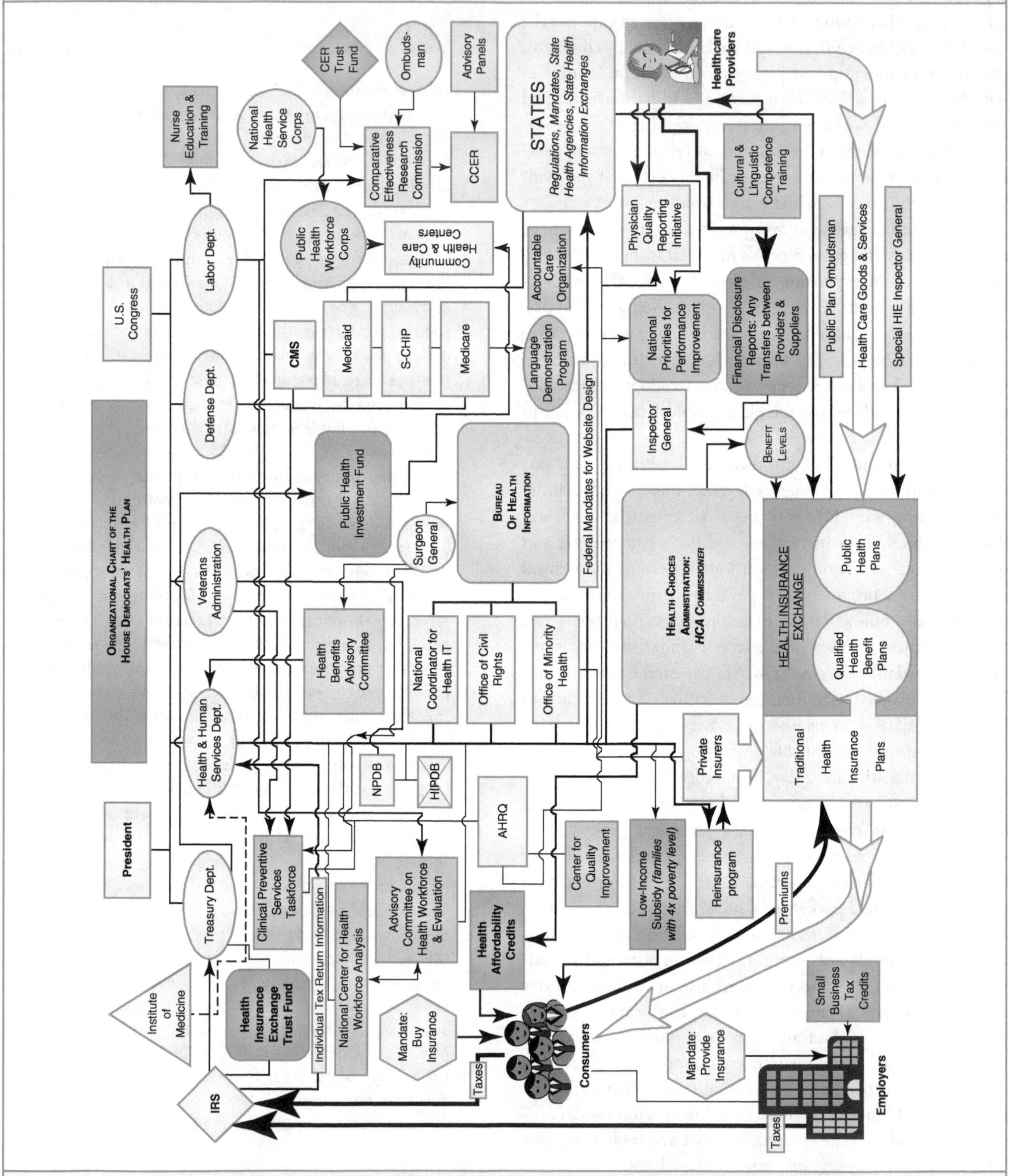

Reproduced from the Joint Economic Committee, Republican Staff. Congressman Kevin Brady, Ranking House Republican Member

Some of the most significant and voluminous sources of healthcare data are profiled here:

Clinical

- Electronic health records/electronic medical records/personal health records (EHRs/EMRs/PHRs)
- Images and image management systems (e.g., picture archiving and communication systems [PACSs], digitized X-rays, CT scans, PET scans)
- Case mix, care management, and disease management systems
- Independent laboratory and other clinical results (e.g., blood, tissue, fluids)
- Monitoring systems (e.g., maternity, cardiology, ICU)

Transactional/Operations

- Hospital information systems (e.g., admissions, emergency department visits)
- Hospital departmental systems (e.g., radiology, laboratory, pharmacy, surgery, emergency department, order entry)
- Materials management, supplies, and cost accounting systems
- Physician practice management systems (e.g., scheduling, billing)
- Revenue-cycle processes (e.g., provider billing, claims, patient accounting)
- Post-acute clinical and billing systems (e.g., skilled nursing, home care)

Payer

- Payer claims and contracting systems (e.g., benefit rules, risk calculations, claims adjudication)
- Care management systems (for coordinating transitions of care and discharges to home or other facilities)

Third Party

- Research systems (e.g., universities, human, animal)
- Clinical trials systems (e.g., pharmaceutical companies, universities)
- Satisfaction surveying systems (e.g., patients, providers, staff)

External

- Internet resources
- Registries, population management, statistics, and risk adjustments
- Industry reporting (e.g., benchmarks, score cards, report cards)
- Cellular devices and applications

Government

- Federal government programs (e.g., Centers for Medicare and Medicaid Services [CMS], State Children's Health Insurance Program [SCHIP], Department of Defense TRICARE and TRICARE for Life programs, Veterans Health Administration [VHA] program, and Indian Health Service [IHS] program)
- State and local government programs (e.g., Medicaid, MediCal, State Health Insurance Assistance Program [SHIP], Children's Health Insurance Program [CHIP], Health Resources and Services Administration Primary Care: The Health Center Program, healthcare marketplace regulatory programs)

Types of Organizations

Listing the principal participants in creating healthcare data will set the stage for understanding the kinds of data sources they require. The following groups all generate and process data in different intervals, including real time, daily, and monthly:

- Providers (e.g., physicians, nurses, and other clinicians)
- Hospitals and hospital systems
- Outpatient care facilities (e.g., imaging, urgent care, physical therapy)
- Payers and third-party administrators
- Government, including military organizations
- Post-acute care facilities (e.g., skilled nursing, hospice)
- Home health
- Pharmaceutical companies and laboratories
- Research centers (e.g., universities, government)
- Public health organizations

With more than 850,000 licensed physicians in the United States,[3] 3.1 million registered nurses, more than 500 healthcare insurance companies (and many more health plans offered by provider groups), nearly 6000 registered hospitals, and a multitude of government programs, one can begin to imagine the interrelated dependencies and the complexities of healthcare data.[4] From each system and in each participant environment, vast sums of information are generated and subsequently stored in the complex practice of medicine and delivery of health services. Examples for discrete data elements include a Current Procedural Terminology (CPT) code (**Exhibit 9.2**), an incremental lab result, an insurance

EXHIBIT 9.2 Complexity in Coding Healthcare Diagnoses and Procedures

The complexity of health care becomes clear when one considers that the kernels for healthcare billing and revenue-cycle management include **International Statistical Classification of Diseases and Related Health Problems** (ICD-9 and ICD-10) codes, **Current Procedural Terminology (CPT)** codes, and **diagnostic-related groups (DRGs)** coding. There are approximately 14,000 ICD-9 and 68,000 ICD-10 unique codes, each three to seven characters in length, along with potential modifiers that must be used by providers to attain contractual reimbursement for their services. Currently, ICD-9 codes are being replaced by ICD-10 codes. This process is leading to tremendous changes in personnel training and software systems—the transition will have a deleterious cash-flow effect on providers, while the greater specificity of ICD-10 codes will allow for more precise matching of codes to complex diagnoses and conditions. There are 7800 CPT codes with even more potential modifiers. DRGs are used in acute care as a bundling method for multiple patient care activities grouped based on similar consumption of resources. All of these codes may be used by employers as methods to compensate providers, project income, plan for facilities and materials, and serve as input for population management evaluation and trending. Tens of thousands of coders must translate what providers do into these diagnostic and procedural codes to properly complete and adjudicate an insurance form. These codes must be retained and available for extensive periods of time for a host of analytical and legal reasons.

payment denial code, the sex identifier or resident ZIP code of a patient, the name of a prescription drug, and a chronic disease code. While these are rather straightforward and simple data elements, a patient might have a single digital image result stored in his or her medical record that takes up 200 megabytes of data; a chronically ill patient may have gigabytes of historical data associated with his or her care.

The magnitude and the growth of types and volume of data in health care are staggering. To quantify some of the issues, consider the following sizing example:

- One digital image approximates 200 (or more) megabytes (about 60 MP3 songs).

- Each image may be redundantly stored at the imaging site, within the patient's EHR, and/or by the PACS vendor site.
- When extended to the maximum scope, this *one type of data—the image*—might be present as more than 50 billion images worldwide, or a total worldwide data requirement of 70 exabytes (18 zeroes) of data (more than 3.3 trillion MP3 songs).

Importantly, in contrast to data in other business environments, good data in health care are essential in making clinical decisions that improve the health of patients and may even save lives. Conversely, untimely or wrong data may contribute to inaccurate decisions with potential implications for patient mortality. Unlike employees in other data-rich industries, healthcare providers make real-time decisions based on laboratory results, images, trends in patient histories and across communities, and other data points. As undesirable as it may be to miscount inventory or overbill someone in the retail environment, it is quite another matter to conclude a course of medical action based upon misinterpreted data that leads to a negative outcome.

VELOCITY, VOLUME, AND VARIETY (THREE V'S) AND BIG DATA

The importance of the velocity, volume, and variety of data is endemic throughout the world and not exclusive to health care.

Velocity

Velocity suggests that data have momentum that is accelerating through increased applications and consumer and business uses. This momentum is virtually exponential. Everyone who has used cellular technology has experienced this velocity of data through their phones' enhanced technology and the Internet's growth. Just a few years ago, consumers could not track their exercise performance, research extensive disease narratives, or communicate with their providers by digital means with ease. Now consumers can perform all these tasks with personal electronic devices, portals, and websites.

Volume

Volume suggests similar exponential growth of accessible and seemingly necessary data. Earlier in this chapter, we discussed a volume example based on imaging; it is extremely relevant for understanding the ramifications of the increasing amounts of data in health care. Data growth in the future will likely be larger in health care than in any sector other than global security.

Variety

Variety suggests that data are associated with, and will continue to take on, seemingly limitless descriptions. The use of new personal electronic devices will make fluid, organ, and almost any other bodily function measurement feasible. Cellular devices will serve up various health data such as blood glucose, blood pressure, cholesterol levels, and other essential measures in an attempt to improve the quality of medicine and disease management. Data reflecting issues of public health concern not only personal data, but also environmental, social, and other systemic data.

In concert with the notion of the Three V's impacting health care, three types of software applications and technologies, along with their associated data sources, hold out the promise of improving health care. At the same time, these three areas present some critical challenges related to data management. When these areas are combined with health care's exacting security and safety requirements regarding data, one can see a whole new operational frontier opening. These three areas are:

1. Imaging
2. EHR/EMR systems
3. Mobile communications and devices

Imaging

Imaging's uses are expanding as it evolves into an enhanced and noninvasive diagnostic utility for continuous care management. In fact, more and more test results are taking the form of digital images in health care; for instance, with biopsy results, a picture may accompany the written pathology report. The use of digital imaging is precise: It better leverages physician time and, compared to radiological films of the past, its portability, storage, and retrieval are more convenient. Moreover, digital imaging is very popular among clinicians. Predictably, there is a direct correlation between enhanced imaging technology and an exponential increase in data requirements. As explained elsewhere in the text, this important medical tool has created a challenging data source for analytics.

As imaging technologies are enhanced such that the granularity and acuity of images increase further, there will be a proportionately greater data volume problem: More detailed images necessarily take up more space. More importantly, images or image readings may be digitized simply as singular data files. Unfortunately, the translation of the image's detail into any sort of a granular bit-mapped data set can currently be stored only as a retrievable location of the image in aggregate. In other words, an X-ray image or scan is stored as a single picture, but you cannot extract any data other than that picture or image stream as a whole. For example, an X-ray of a foot "No.7.24.13.XYZ" is without judgment, bone description, dimension, or any data narrative. The X-ray data storage and retrieval would be made based on the code "No.7.24.13.XYZ." In the near future, an exciting development will make these static data references (images) available with more data analytics based on new technology. In turn, a very large data volume will be required for a single diagnostic element such as a diabetic glucose reading.

EHR/EMR Systems

The second area is of tremendous importance to data storage: the proliferation of EHR or EMR systems. Part of the American Recovery and Reinvestment Act of 2009 (ARRA) includes financial incentives paid to hospitals or physicians or their practices for the various stages of implementation for an EHR. As discussed in other chapters, before ARRA's investment incentives were made available, healthcare organizations' embrace of EHRs was much more tepid. The typical EHR contains an incredible amount of data; easy, fast, and relevant retrieval of a patient's data is a highly desirable result of an EHR, but it comes at the price of extensive clinician data entry and large storage requirements. The addition of personal genomic data to EHRs is an even more momentous undertaking, considering the fact that we as a society are only just learning how to use such data for patient care, predictive purposes, and other analytic purposes.

Mobile Communications and Devices

The third area of challenge for data concerns mobile technology. Excitingly, we are at the early stages of mobile health, more succinctly called **mHealth**. There is a frenzy of development and idea promotion around the propagation of applications that are focused on enhanced communications through cellular devices. This includes personal health management and even diagnostic capabilities. Further, one can now use handheld or small body-attached information-sensing wireless medical devices to measure blood glucose, blood chemistry, heart monitoring, and other "*Star Trek*–like" diagnostic workups.

In contrast to other historically transient technology applications such as universal patient identification cards (e.g., credit card–like items containing a person's medical history), developments in these three areas—imaging, EHR/EMR systems, and mobile communications and devices—will likely be sustainable and are already bringing environmental and cultural changes to healthcare organizations. As in other facets of their lives, consumers are demanding responsiveness and breadth in all forms of electronic communications related to health care. To some extent, these demands are putting strains on the traditional structures of health care. Healthcare providers are now struggling to manage the consequences of making data accessible to consumers via cellular phone technologies. Nevertheless, consumers' demand for access to their own and their family's medical data is here to stay, as is the movement by healthcare organizations and providers to engage patients in their care processes.

DATA CHALLENGES

All healthcare institutions—small and large—have a growing obligation and need to develop, adopt, and manage their data strategy (i.e., their HIS plan). Each institution will face philosophical differences, budgetary constraints, lack of experience, resource limitations, and a multitude of other challenges as it works through its respective needs.

Data Ownership

The importance of the healthcare organization retaining the ownership of its data is discussed in the *Implementation* chapter in the section about contracting with software vendors. Yet, within the organization, who "owns" or is assigned responsibility for the accuracy and quality of the data? The ownership and stewardship of data are critically important, yet these may be contentious issues. Traditionally, one would assume that a CIO or lead IT person would be the logical owner. Those personnel may, in fact, be well suited for this purpose. However, there is a difference between data's technical nature and the real *purpose* of data. A simple analogy is that a person may store a car in a full-service parking garage where it is kept clean, safe, maintained, and always available, but it is the driver who uses the automobile. And so it is with data: IT is responsible for the physical storage and safety of data, while end users are responsible for the quality of data. Each institution should dedicate an individual and/or group to the single responsibility of data management.

Data Delivery and Translation

The data management team will be responsible for **data delivery and translation**, architecting the data environment, cataloging the data, securing data integrity, managing data definitions and normalization, sanctioning data sources, and generally ensuring the reliable availability of data for their constituents (or customers). A critical skill set is necessary to bridge the inherent gap between the data management team's incredibly technical environment and its generally nontechnical customers—not everyone makes a good translator. Another convenient analogy is that of a homeowner

(the data customer) whose attitude about the home's infrastructure is that he or she cares little about the source, dimensions, or material composition of the home's plumbing, but rather just wants clean, reliable water on demand.

An essential part of the data management role is translation. This task is addressed in more detail in the chapter on business and clinical intelligence, but basically it means that the data management team members need to possess the ability to understand what their customers need and work backward to the data architecture to ensure data delivery. Frequency, presentation, modifications, integration, and other data requirements require tremendous listening skills and empathy for whatever purpose the customer has for the data. Ways of connecting with customers—often clinicians providing health care to patients—include daily use of **key performance indicators (KPIs)** that measure anomalies relative to standard performances, dashboard presentations based on the user's skills and role, and appropriate data available for the ambiguity of ad-hoc analytics. Data need to be made available to the customer set in a relatively easy and understandable manner. Moreover, data need to be "packaged" for role-based utility, as different customers need very different manifestations of data to perform their respective roles.

Data Storage

On the Big Data continuum with regard to the three most voluminous healthcare application environments (imaging, EHR/EMR systems, and mobile communications and devices), a disproportionate share—approximately 70%—of the current global data storage is consumed by those three elements alone. Moreover, as imaging is enhanced and EHRs and mHealth mature, these three applications will contribute disproportionately more new data than all the other categories combined, requiring more incremental storage. Imaging data are challenging to analyze, and EHRs and mobile devices are fragmented. These data sources may be valuable in their purpose, but they are difficult to integrate within data storage and retrieval strategies.

Software "Openness"

In the production of data, one can find hundreds of commercial EHR, **practice management system (PMS)**, hospital management, and PACS software packages that are written in myriad programming languages and may be decades old. Because data in one system may be formatted or identified differently than data in another system, the challenge of combining or communicating among similarly purposed computer systems (being "open")—whether nationally or locally—is significant. For systems whose roots are embedded in traditional, less flexible technologies and languages, this integration is more challenging and creates major barriers to the current goal of interoperability between systems from different organizations. There are inherent conflicts for vendors who choose to make their systems truly "open" when others are unable or unwilling to do so. As with any business, one must quantify and assert a motivation to participate in an investment to be open to others. For software vendors to be "open," they must first define with whom and what they are open to, who is willing to financially support or mandate this openness, and whether it is a level playing field for all to make such an investment. Currently, the EHR market is an extraordinarily competitive environment in which software application features are quickly changing, thereby requiring vendors to invest significant development dollars to keep pace with industry changes, much less meet the complex and ever-changing requirements to be open and interoperable. Because data in one system may be formatted or identified differently than in another, the challenge of combining or communicating among similarly purposed but different systems—whether nationally or locally—is significant.

Technical Lexicon and Lack of Universal Terminology

The healthcare industry has a complicated lexicon for everything it does. Providers may use highly technical terminology that is not understandable by patients. For example, one physician may use the term "high blood pressure" while another may use "hypertension" to characterize the same chronic patient disease. Within the healthcare supply chain, a differentiated organizational bias in terminology is apparent: Vendors that build and supply materials used in the industry often use different nomenclatures, while academic reporting and analytical organizations may enforce their own imprimatur for medical terms. Further, with healthcare delivery "being local," differences in terminology may make **data sharing** more complicated.

An important element of data transmission, storage, and retrieval has to do with normalizing information. A data element needs to represent what it says it is. The reliability of data includes the notion that the same data element, when measured or recorded more than once, will always be the same.

Data Sharing

As use of EHR or EMR systems proliferates within a given community, multiple methods for sharing data among those systems may emerge. Individual patients may keep records of their activities, diets, and personal biological

testing by using personal computer or cellular methods to create a personal health record (PHR). Their physicians are likely to have EMRs for their offices' purposes in caring for each patient. The local hospital may have an inpatient EHR that tracks testing ordered by each physician and for hospital-based procedures for each patient. If patients have used community-based physical therapy, psychiatric, dental, or other caregiving modalities, disparate data may be present in those siloed medical record-keeping systems that may have different data management architectures and terminology. One can easily imagine the overlapping and unaligned longitudinal care difficulties, which result in substantial data inconsistencies and coordination challenges.

Attempts at communication standards have offered some help in navigating these often incompatible systems, but universal adoption has not occurred. Health information exchanges (HIEs) are environments for the purpose of sharing data that communicate or aggregate disparate healthcare-related data into a single, universally accessible mechanism or location. These exchanges have been introduced at the state and regional levels and within small and large urban areas. They are relatively new and have experienced mixed reviews and results: Some have already failed, whereas others are demonstrating some efficiency. HIE organizations and initiatives are terrifically ambitious and involve the alignment of often strange bedfellows. The bottom line today, however, is that data remain siloed and the jury is still out on how successful the healthcare industry will be at electronic data exchange, notwithstanding the inclusion of HIE and system interoperability in the government's Meaningful Use criteria.

Another invention of recent healthcare law is the accountable care organization (ACO), which is addressed elsewhere in this text in the context of care providers. ACOs look much like capitated care, managed care, and other models seen in the past. The difference is that health information systems and technology infrastructure are now available to integrate care across the continuum, so this model is now actually feasible to accomplish. Applicant healthcare provider organizations were granted "Pioneer" ACO status by the federal government based on a multitude of qualifying criteria. In relation to their data, these ACOs will be taking on financial risk—in the form of sharing in the rewards or losses—based on performance, cost, quality, appropriateness, efficiency, and other measurements. Risk, in this context, means being responsible for the financial consequences of providing cost-effective and contractually viable health care. This involves a very real operational change for the healthcare organizations that have joined this movement, and many ACOs will be woefully tested in managing their data and operationalizing decisions. Current Pioneer ACOs are achieving a variety of results; some are making their way, and others are leaving the program (**Exhibit 9.3**).

Interfacing Data Within an Organization

Data are resident within any number of disparately purposed software applications. It would not be unusual for a large hospital to have licensed, purchased, or developed 50 to 100 different software applications, all concurrently used to run its business. It is important to understand that between these software applications, data are never fully integrated. True "integration" using interfacing software is almost impossible. Aggregating, normalizing, and applying other methods to combine data from software applications constitute an interfacing process that does not lead to true integration. (Integration and interfacing are discussed in more detail in the *Managing HIS and Technology Services: Delivering the Goods* chapter.) Interfacing these disparate data sources involves internal software and infrastructure requirements for such uses as data warehouses, portals, departmentally used applications, and more. Further, with third-party application updates and software changes, these systems' data interfacing tools must be modified on a regular basis. A whole world of vendor-offered interfacing hubs and networks with tools attempting to enhance these laborious and challenging responsibilities has emerged.

EXHIBIT 9.3 Kaiser Permanente

For decades, the quintessential ACO in the United States has been Kaiser Permanente. It has been successfully taking financial and actuarial risks with a truly integrated healthcare delivery and insurance model. With its often-criticized disciplines surrounding managed care, Kaiser Permanente is also thought to be exacting in its patient relationships and employment and contracting methods: It is now a bastion of what is needed for a successful and well-functioning ACO. One of Kaiser Permanente's greatest accomplishments is that it understands and uses its own data at least as well as any other similar organization.

Even a small physician practice must invest in software that supports sophisticated patient scheduling, claims processing, and patient billing that often involves different formatting for each insurance company covering patients (clearinghouses attempt to simplify this effort), procedure coding validation, authorization and referral authentication, and patient billing functionality. In a medical community of 500 physicians, there may be a dozen or more different PMS software packages being used.

DATA SECURITY AND PROTECTION

Many industries—banking, security, and communications, for example—face challenging **data security** issues. The healthcare industry deals with similar demographic and financial data, yet its environment is also complicated by special circumstances owing to the laws governing the protection and privacy of patients' clinical information. As a consequence, healthcare data are subject to not only the same federal protections as banking (or any other industry), but also a host of additional regulations specific to health care. With so many users of patient information, there is tremendous data protection exposure and risk for the myriad provider, insurance, and supporting healthcare entities. Of course, protecting the security, privacy, and confidentiality of patient data has always been considered a hallmark of good medical record management, even when all records were based on paper. In 1996, however, in recognition of the exponentially increasing automation and data availability and communication in health care, HIPAA was passed by Congress to distinguish PHI as a special category of data warranting extra safeguards. The purpose of this law was to establish methods and safeguards for nondisclosure of clinical and demographic patient data other than for use in care delivery and healthcare processes. HIPAA has not always been carefully enforced in spite of severe mandatory penalties imposed for "willful neglect" (fines between $250,000 and $1.5 million), although this situation is changing (see recent examples and recent upgrades to sharpen HIPAA's "teeth"). These laws have included, or have been expanded to include, both civil and criminal penalties for business associates (e.g., vendors, consultants) that may peripherally have access to the same data.

A singular data element may need to be protected, yet available, within the same employer. For example, a physician may need to see the history of a patient's HIV testing, yet this same clinical finding should not be accessible by all other institutional employees. Thus granular data elements need to be tagged for their appropriate use. This differentiation—based on the reason for the use of the data—makes accomplishing good data management and protection difficult, given the complexities of data structures and disparate systems in healthcare entities. Further, according to HIPAA regulations, an audit capability must be integrated into systems at this granular data level to ensure protection and discovery of attempted inappropriate access. HIPAA requires an electronic audit trail for each and every transaction within a healthcare system—one of the many HIPAA requirements that healthcare software vendors are legally required to meet as a standard part of their products.

Laws also protect patient medical histories by describing the term for retention of medical data. For example, federal law requires a hospital to retain a patient's data for 5 years and 3 years after the patient's death. The American Health Information Management Association suggests retention for a period of 10 years after the patient encounter.[5] Most organizations save medical records forever, a practice that has further implications for data security and storage. It is almost as if keeping records is simultaneously a security measure (protection against litigation) and a risk (more fodder for data breach).

SUMMARY

Data have become an increasingly valuable resource for healthcare organizations and providers. Data support clinical work and business processes, and they provide fuel for information creation and analytical opportunities. Data are created and captured in transaction systems that support the daily activities of health care, both clinically and from a business perspective. Healthcare data continue to exponentially increase in terms of their velocity (usefulness), volume (amount), and variety (types). Ultimately, these combine to form a resource yet to be defined, called Big Data, which creates notions of limitless possibilities for insight, information, imagination, and intelligence. None of these goals will be reached easily, as the challenges and barriers to intelligent information usage are many. Disparate source systems and silo processes continue to plague healthcare organizations, and it will be many years before this fragmentation is overcome. Data must be kept secure, private, and confidential. To not do so defies long-standing principles of health care and respect for the patient, but to do so requires persistent human and technological efforts.

By considering the technical and analytical needs and uses of data, the healthcare industry is attempting to accelerate implementation of the long-standing belief that the economics and efficacy of health care may be enhanced through evidence-based medicine. The exponential growth of data production will be both the foundation to measure this belief and a technological challenge to manage. Systems must be developed to more efficiently collect, normalize, and integrate data to be analyzed on both a real-time and a retrospective basis.

A growing number of healthcare institutions, however nascent, have undertaken the monumental task of providing a solution for the data explosion. In the long run, this discipline will provide an opportunity for growth of organizational cultures into learning organizations, as well as individual employee development and career growth. Technical positions for data architecture and management will proliferate.

KEY TERMS

Affordable Care Act (ACA)   187
Big Data   186
Clinical data   186
Current Procedural Terminology (CPT)   190
Data delivery and translation   192
Data security   194
Data sharing   193
Data source   187
Diagnostic-related group (DRG)   190
International Statistical Classification of Diseases and Related Health Problems   190
Key performance indicator (KPI)   192
mHealth   191
Normalization   186
Practice management system (PMS)   192
Revenue cycle management (RCM)   187
Velocity, volume, and variety (Three V's)   186

Discussion Questions

1. Is this subject too technical for you to fathom? Describe the areas that you do not understand.

2. Can you envision any other new data source that might become part of the healthcare arena?

3. Are there any roles described within this discussion on data that are of interest to you?

4. If sharing of data between healthcare organizations may have a macro industry benefit, how do you think this could happen?

5. Have you worked or are you currently working in a healthcare organization that has emphasized data as being strategic? How has the organization communicated this idea throughout its entire team?

6. Describe how disparate data might be converted into a single vocabulary.

7. Have you personally experienced an encounter with a provider and felt it beneficial that the provider might have access to or use real-time data to help your care?

8. What strikes you as the three biggest data challenges in health care?

9. Do you believe that other industries that have been using data for their own operational efficiencies may help the healthcare industry better navigate the adoption and use of data for both business and clinical benefit? If yes, how so?

10. Is there a single best source of data for health care to start with in terms of managing the inherent responsibilities to collect, aggregate, and store data? Or do all the data sources need to be tapped at once?

REFERENCES

1. *Kaiser Health News.* (2012, June). Health care costs to reach nearly one-fifth of GDP by 2021. http://www.kaiserhealthnews.org/daily-reports/2012/june/13/health-care-costs.aspx

2. IBM. (n.d.) Big data at the speed of business. http://www-01.ibm.com/software/data/bigdata/

3. Young, A., Chaudhry, H. J., Rhyne, J., & Dugan, M. (2011). A census of actively licensed physicians in the U.S. in 2010. *Journal of Medical Regulation.* http://www.nationalahec.org/pdfs/FSMBPhysicianCensus.pdf

4. AFL-CIO, Department for Professional Employees. (2012, April 12). Nursing: A profile of the profession: Fact sheet 2012. http://dpeaflcio.org/wp-content/uploads/Nursing-A-Profile-of-the-Profession-2012.pdf

5. Enterprise content and record management for healthcare. (2008). *Journal of AHIMA, 79*(10), 91–98. http://library.ahima.org/xpedio/groups/public/documents/ahima/bok1_040405.hcsp?dDocName=bok1_040405

CHAPTER 10

Business Intelligence and Clinical Intelligence (BI/CI)

INTRODUCTION

The generic definition of business intelligence (BI) is a set of theories, methodologies, processes, architectures, and technologies that transform raw data into meaningful and useful information for business purposes. This term—and the practice—is applied widely throughout various industries. BI handles large amounts of data and information to help identify and develop new opportunities. Making use of new opportunities and implementing an effective strategy can provide a competitive market advantage and long-term stability. BI technologies provide historical, current, and predictive views of business operations. Common functions of BI technologies include reporting, online analytical processing, analytics, data mining, complex event processing, business performance management benchmarking, text mining, predictive mining, predictive analytics, and prescriptive analytics.[1]

Clinical intelligence (CI) is an emerging adjunct to BI that is focused on the healthcare industry. With the proliferation of various forms of electronic clinical data use, as well as industry and political pressures to obtain and utilize clinical measurements, BI is the obvious technological foundation for CI. The aforementioned BI definition works perfectly as CI's mechanics and functionality underpinning. Thus a generic definition of CI is a set of theories, methodologies, processes, architectures, and technologies that transform raw data into meaningful and useful information for clinical purposes. Specific uses for healthcare BI and CI include statistics, scorecards, quality metrics and reporting, multipurpose presentation dashboards, outcomes-based compensation, longitudinal care management, key performance indicators (KPIs), alerts, supply-chain analysis, experience-based rating engines, and population management.

There is no convenient singular description or collections of words to create a cogent definition for the many meanings and types of healthcare BI and CI. Healthcare BI and CI are very subjective—remember, "Health care is local," and so is data use. The application of an intelligence process may be static and trivial, or it may be dynamic and extremely complicated. Thousands of discrete software applications and tens of thousands of discrete data elements are used daily by providers, payers, and related health organizations, all of which would have their own description for what and how data intelligence is relevant for them.

There are a nearly infinite number of current and imagined healthcare BI and CI content examples. We will review some next.

Business/BI Example

A CEO wants a **dashboard** that is refreshed nightly. A single dashboard screen presentation includes all of the organization's profit and loss data, accounts receivable (A/R) status, insurance payment denials, patient throughput volumes, prospectively booked appointments, and additional KPIs. The CEO will be able to review the insurance payment denials graphic and hover her computer mouse over the bar chart for the Blue Cross/Blue Shield (BCBS) payer indicator, double-click, and open the details for all the claims without outstanding denied payments. She may then tag this detailed report and send it to her CFO with questions and a requested response expectation.

Clinical/CI Example

In the purchasing department conference room, the director of materials management for a mid-sized hospital is listening to a pharmaceutical sales representative propose certain purchases of disposable surgical items and associated pharmaceuticals. From his laptop, the hospital executive selects multiple items within his CI system to display in a count, cost, shelf-life, surgeon preference, and surgical room scheduling pie chart. He compares these metrics with the recommendations from the pharmaceutical representative and places a very focused order.

Integrated BI/CI Example

A clinic administrator is negotiating with an insurance company over an at-risk contract for the insurer's largest business client's employee population. The administrator searches the BI/CI data for the same population (including subscriber family dependents) currently seen in the practice. Then the administrator sorts the list of patients by diagnostic procedural codes, stratifying them by age, weight, ethnicity, comorbidities, charges and payment history, IDC-9 and CPT codes, and prescriptions. The administrator produces the same summary for three other payers and large employer contracts and subsequently produces a comparison to these existing contracts and the proposed compensation by the new insurer.

Assembling and preparing all these data for specific subsequent use is hard, technical work. Adoption of BI/CI has been slow—slower even than electronic health record (EHR)

adoption. Perhaps 20% of U.S. healthcare providers have implemented data warehouses and BI/CI software to support clinical decision making, **pay-for-performance (P4P)** programs, and comparative effectiveness research (CER) and to track clinical outcomes as part of healthcare quality measurement initiatives.[2] Given the government mandates for information from providers, increasing sources of clinical data from EHR systems, greater transparency through public reporting of healthcare outcomes, and for a host of other circumstances, in the future BI/CI will become more pervasive and vendor tools will become easier and more robust to use.

HEALTHCARE BUSINESS INTELLIGENCE AND CLINICAL INTELLIGENCE

Healthcare organizations have had very mixed experiences in regard to BI/CI. With the support of sophisticated internal information technology (IT) departments, the more advanced healthcare providers have created valuable **central data repositories (CDRs)**, or data warehouses, through diligent attention to quality, organization, and maintenance of those new data storehouses. Where nascent BI/CI solutions were designed for accuracy, performance, and breadth of purpose, these organizations have achieved marked successes. Conversely, where data have been contained in silos and where either an IT or finance department has restricted use of those data to a chosen few parties, there have been some black eyes for vendors and for BI/CI initiatives. Expectations often are not met by actual outcomes of those projects: Expectations may be inflated due to the vendor overselling its methods, an organization misunderstanding the level of expertise, investment and commitment necessary, or both parties failing to appreciate the complexity of BI/CI (**Figure 10.1**).

CI is a term that has only recently been coined, in conjunction with the increased adoption and use of the EHR, electronic medical record (EMR), and personal health record (PHR), all of which overlap to some extent in terms of their functionality and usage. Their differences generally reflect who collects the data, the setting where this occurs, and the comprehensiveness of the application.[3] An EHR system comprises the broadest description of a patient's medical and health history, covering a larger collection of clinical data including ambulatory, acute care, and holistic care information. It is used to facilitate clinical care processes on a real-time basis. An EMR is often employed in a singular ambulatory or acute-care setting, such as a free-standing physician's office or hospital, and is not connected to another facility such as an ambulatory or hospital setting. EMRs lack functionality with regard to offering a longitudinal view

FIGURE 10.1 Relationship of Complexity for Content Use and Creation

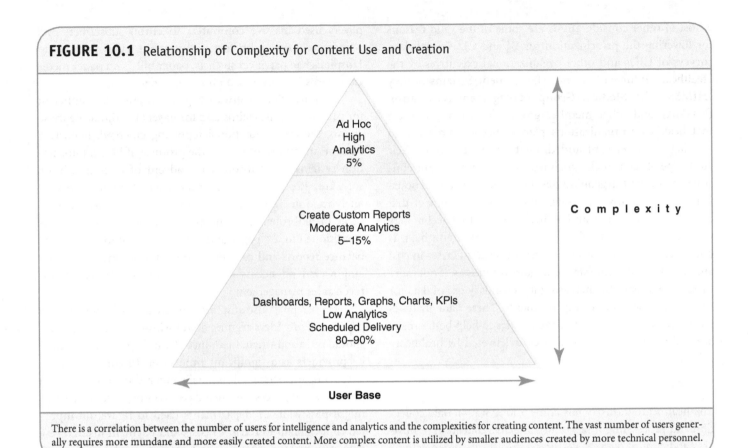

There is a correlation between the number of users for intelligence and analytics and the complexities for creating content. The vast number of users generally requires more mundane and more easily created content. More complex content is utilized by smaller audiences created by more technical personnel.

across multiple settings of care. The PHR is managed by the patient (or a parent or guardian) and populated with personally acquired medical and health-related information. The varying terminology and need to integrate these dissimilar platforms create a significant challenge when attempting to implement analytics using data from these and other systems.

CI, when properly implemented, not only will support more focused clinical analysis than BI, but also should be designed and managed to integrate "business data" for broader analysis, including, for instance, cost accounting data within a clinical analysis. A longitudinal patient medical history combined with the business history (e.g., charges, payments, or disposable medical equipment consumption) for the same patient would provide invaluable insights for outcomes measurement and monitoring as well as process effectiveness. Consider the following example of BI/CI integration to see how this works: Suppose a patient with cardiovascular disease receives a stent in a catheterization procedure. Future and concurrent caregivers might like to know the stent's source, cost, SKU identification, and date of manufacture and installation (as well as by whom and where); provider follow-up observations; patient-reported

experience; related diagnoses and other therapies provided; patient outcome including complications; and other related medical issues. Hypothetically, in the event of the patient's continued complaints or a manufacturer's recall, the organization could search the patient's integrated data and take appropriate action.

In spite of tremendous industry and governmental attention—as well as technology advances—healthcare organizations' adoption of comprehensive BI/CI has been disappointingly slow. Some components of reporting, analytics, and data presentation are being used, but usually in siloed application environments. Siloed application environments such as revenue-cycle or laboratory systems that pull data from separate repositories tell only part of the story of what is going on for the patient or the organization, rather than providing a more holistic or comprehensive viewpoint. These silos can deter progress and syphon off resources that could be devoted toward more integrated BI and CI implementation projects.

Cost, limited experience, restricted implementation resources, numerous mandates and industry requirements (e.g., the proliferation of EHRs and ICD-10 conversions), and a host of other considerations are some of the valid reasons for lowering the prioritization for BI and CI. Nevertheless, surveys of CIOs and other organizational executives by the Healthcare Information and Management Systems Society (HIMSS), the **Medical Group Management Association (MGMA)**, and other member groups consistently indicate that healthcare organizations plan to become proactive in tackling more relevant and dramatic projects within their landscape of data. Such expanded capabilities would be consistent with the burgeoning development of data warehousing and BI initiatives in other industries, a movement that creates greater overall availability of BI and CI technology product and talent. Challenging as this work might be, it is both exciting and rewarding. Given the current crises in cost and quality, health care stands to gain as much as, if not more than, any industry by increasing its secondary use of data for BI and CI insights and improvements. These data analytics platforms will offer essential capabilities to help better manage and improve the quality of care delivered by healthcare organizations.

HISTORY OF BI AND CI

The healthcare industry has come a long way in data collection and processing: It has built a massive collection of business and clinical data. Nevertheless, healthcare organizations have a long way to go in effectively organizing and analyzing these data to realize workplace efficiencies and better medical outcomes.

When computers entered the marketplace in the late 1960s and early 1970s, healthcare-related data were generally focused on processing billing and automating the byzantine world of insurance claims. At that time, the landscape for the dominant fee-for-service model for charges, payments, and adjustments was straightforward. Getting paid as providers and paying as payers according to the appropriate procedure and diagnostic codes worked rather well. The financial environment was characterized by straightforward fee-for-service reimbursement rather than today's complex risk arrangements, with concomitant detailed contracting and productivity measures. Interestingly, the notion of using dormitory refrigerator–sized computers for coding and sending off insurance claims both stressed and fascinated healthcare providers during that era. Principally, the adoption rate for computerization was slow because it required a significant resource investment—too much for many self-employed physicians and investment risk-adverse hospitals. Pharmaceutical companies just needed to count things they sold, laboratories sent out results and bills on paper, and

payers used massive computers to enroll subscribers and adjudicate claims with fewer contracting rules than today. Hospitals had paper census lists, paper bills, and paper medical records (and overused photocopy machines).

As transactional software began to capture data sufficient for providers to file claims and for payers to adjudicate those claims, the art of functional reporting emerged. Reporting became an important part of the promise of health information systems (HIS) through the advent of early healthcare software. Reports were the now ancient predecessors of analytical intelligence. Limited tabular screen shots provided some breakthrough efficiencies in an environment that was conditioned to use paper and pencil. For example, aged trial balance reports and computer-based appointment registries empowered physicians and became the staple reports for receivables management.

These reports also amplified the ensuing friction between payers and providers arguing about whose pocket the money should be in and when. Insurance claims began being printed by providers as a significant time saver. In contrast, insurance company personnel manually entered the claims. When providers and payers conducted contract negotiations, weeks might pass while IT departments tried to figure out inputted (but difficult to retrieve) costs and payment history. Few data processing directors (the forerunners of today's chief information officers) spent any time with "information," but rather treaded water while trying to keep hardware working and prevent software and hardware from crashing. Accessing data was profoundly difficult.

Reports were typically structured or "**canned**." User requests for report changes joined a queue of reporting enhancements to be eventually delivered by IT departments and software vendors. With fewer software offerings available, reports were produced for specific applications for specific operational audiences. If some executive at hospital X wanted to see information across her fiefdom of departments and within her niche computer applications, she would likely call upon someone from her IT or accounting team to populate a basic spreadsheet. Over time, the spreadsheet started to overtake reports as an analytical tool.

During the early days of computing, multitasking software and PCs were not available. Terminal screens were gray, orange, or green. A storage capacity of 10 megabytes might suffice for a busy 10-provider group practice; 200 megabytes would carry the day for a small hospital. Larger institutions often used service bureaus with larger computers along with slow phone line connections to run their businesses. To meet the need for reporting, a programmer who knew COBOL,

FORTRAN, or early MUMPS (early software programming languages still in use in many systems worldwide) would have to manually program each report. Adding an unforeseen data element to the application at a later date meant going back to the programming cubicle and rewriting code. There was no such thing as email or the Internet; likewise, networks (either hard-wired or wireless), now such a familiar part of life, were not broadly available.

As with many innovations in the computer and software world, an evolutionary development occurred in the mid-1990s. The notions of **executive information systems (EISs)** and **decision support systems (DSSs)** were introduced in the healthcare industry. These types of application software brought together data from multiple sources. As their names suggest, EISs and DSSs were designed to help management teams at healthcare organizations make decisions by providing relevant information from data acquired from transaction systems. In spite of the fact that this BI effort was still generally static, it represented a quantum leap forward. Unfortunately, producing these reports took an inordinate amount of time, and they were primarily focused on BI rather than CI. Universities, pharmaceutical companies, and laboratory testing companies started to provide some analysis for limited clinical measures, mostly for internal knowledge. For example, disease management gained some theoretical traction in trying to predict better clinical care and apply early cost-control measures. Managed care had progressed to the point that payers wanted better information principally for the purpose of actuarial and underwriting for risk evaluation—a relatively narrow area of concentration.

All of these efforts were limited by the computer power of the time and constraints associated with the older programming languages. However, this was also a point in history when an uncomfortable political focus on quickly rising healthcare costs began, which helped prepare the way for early EHR systems, increased computing power, use of Internet technologies, and less expensive data storage. Little could these early adopters and innovators possibly imagine the world of healthcare computing today!

CURRENT CHALLENGES FOR ANALYTICS

Most healthcare processes can be described and managed at a very scientific level. Chemistry, biology, radiology, and other macro disciplines in the practice of medicine should be "black and white." By extension, one might assume that science would breed objectivity. However, there is a great deal of subjectivity in the delivery of health care and BI/CI. Reasons for this subjectivity and variability include the constantly growing nature of evidence-based medicine, opinionated and differently trained human practitioners and managers, inherent patient uniqueness, and challenges in communication. This conundrum is reflected in the computer and software systems that attempt to support these divergences.

No single computer hardware or software system has taken the healthcare world by storm, becoming the standard, dominant selection. For almost any application, there is a handful of leading competitive systems that vie for customers in the niche. Available to any healthcare organization are well in excess of 1000 vendors espousing their singular superiority while running on different hardware platforms, relying on different operating systems, and using a host of programming languages, many of them proprietary and all of which are modified, enhanced, and upgraded on a regular basis, thereby affecting the continuity of data, interfaces, and operational use. One could walk through any metropolitan city's hospitals and medical clinics and find disparate vendor software packages, computer configurations, and strategies for IT and business management. These organizations' views of the world and the purpose of HIS are manifested in very different ways. As a result, it might be argued that many of health care's macro inefficiencies are inherent in the confusing landscape of software and derived from the independent methods of delivery utilized by the healthcare industry's participants.

In the retail, manufacturing, and banking industries, for example, the adoption of business intelligence, analytics, modeling, and forecasting has outpaced that in health care. None of these other industries is modest in its complexity, and information system implementation and data use are certainly no small tasks. In defense of the healthcare industry's relatively slow embrace of CI/BI, its amorphous and complex nature brings about a number of profoundly challenging issues when it comes to the subject of analytics. Health care is extremely fragmented. As stated elsewhere in the text, common entities, professionals, and components in this industry more often than not "do the same thing differently." Following are some major reasons why healthcare analytics can be a challenging environment:

- Health care is a nearly $3 trillion industry, fast on its way to accounting for almost 20% of the U.S. gross domestic product, and with lots of moving parts.[4]
- Little financial incentive exists for coordination of medical care among competitors.
- More than 3 million healthcare providers of various types provide services in the United States.

- In the United States, there are more than 6000 hospitals,[5] more than 200 insurance payers,[6] 141 medical schools,[7] and more than 16,000 nursing homes[8]—all "doing the same thing differently."

- Dozens of "legacy" (meaning retired) and contemporary programming languages and operating systems are contemporaneously in use throughout the healthcare industry.

- From single departments to enterprise-wide applications, there are more than 1000 commercially sold and "home-grown" software offerings for healthcare practices, including nearly 200 disparate EHR/EMR/PHR solutions with potentially 10 times more discrete data elements than a revenue-cycle software system.

- Several (but no single, de facto) communications or formatting standards exist.

- Disparate terminologies and entry errors in data entry are commonplace.

- Software systems must adapt to ever-changing healthcare laws and industry operations, which affect data elements, functionality, security and interoperability requirements, interfaces, and operational use.

- Public health and population management's access to nongovernmental health delivery is limited.

Despite these hurdles, healthcare organizations must use their data to help solve and improve all facets of the industry. A plethora of solutions must be adopted or invented, with their varying degrees of success and failure only then becoming clear. Next, we walk through some models for an enterprise architecture and strategy that might lead to better healthcare analytics.

MODELS FOR DATA ARCHITECTURE AND STRATEGY

Figure 10.2 illustrates the critical components necessary to arrive at a usable analytics solution. A few terms and acronyms require definition:

- **Source data.** Operational or transactional software applications may be used as a "point" solution (laboratory, radiology, or materials management) or may serve as a multipurpose, mission-critical solution such as the hospital's admit, discharge, and transfer (ADT) system; revenue cycle management (RCM); or EHR. Data are entered for that application's operational use, with those data then becoming available for subsequent extraction to a CDR (discussed later)

or BI/CI system. Materials management involves purchasing, inventorying, and pricing such materials. "E-Apps" are any of the myriad web-based software applications. These systems acknowledge that the Internet is a source of much valuable, usable data.

- **Extraction, transformation, and load (ETL).** ETL is a generic term used across industries that refers to the process for creating data repositories for analytical purposes. This process starts with a host software application into which data have been entered through use of that application. These data can be formatted for extraction by the developer or a third party. In either case, the data need to be transformed, which may include normalization, organization, redefinition to ensure aligned vocabulary, and assurance of referential integrity. The source data may then be imported or loaded into the target repository, typically a BI/CI solution or other applications software. New extraction methods are being developed, but ETL is the most widely used method at the current time.

- **Metadata.** The literal definition of metadata is data about data. In the study of BI/CI, metadata refers to data identifying where the source data were created, when (time and date), by whom, and for what purpose; where they are located within the computer architecture; and whether standards were used in the data creation process. Metadata may be modified and created by nontechnical personnel and may provide grouping and logical similarities and/or differences among the data.

- *Central data repository (CDR).* In years past, the CDR might have been called a data warehouse. It stores larger amounts of information, provides a replication of data from the source systems, organizes the data for extraction for analytics, and may provide an environment for **disaster recovery (DR)**. The CDR supports a system's ability to replicate and rebuild data if the original hardware is destroyed.

- *Business and/or clinical intelligence (BI/CI).* These terms are synonymous with analytics. BI has been a practice throughout various industries for more than decade and more recently has been embraced in health care. CI is newer and parallels the proliferation of electronic health information, where clinical data are both voluminous and have tremendous mining value.

FIGURE 10.2 Example of an Architectural Map. This illustrates critical components necessary for any usable analytics solution.

Physician Name

Date

Pat Satisfaction

You will receive an individualized Press Ganey patient satisfaction report, if you participate, under separate cover.

	Physician		Department		Work RVUs			Appt Sched (as a % of Total Visits)								Pat Satisfaction	
Fiscal	Billing	Collections	Billing	Collections		YMC Calc	UHC Calc	Benchmark	Arrived	No Show	Arrived	No Show	Bumped	Cancel	Pending	Total	Overall	Likelihood
2012 1	1,190,603	−505,491	2,805,470	−1,238,238	Aug-12	1,581	1,583	3,403	97%	3%	452	2	162	14	0	466	0.00	0.0
2012 2	1,151,452	−578,269	2,597,546	−1,204,422	Sep-12	1,465	1,469	3,151	97%	3%	441	45	210	13	0	454	87.20	89.9
2012 3	1,134,793	−588,372	3,032,861	−1,312,866	Oct-12	1,763	1,767	3,788	98%	2%	447	56	167	9	1	457	88.20	90.9
2012 4	1,446,108	−622,234	3,217,966	−1,440,810	Nov-12	2,029	2,029	4,337	98%	2%	547	29	176	9	0	556	88.60	91.7
2013 1	1,030,034	−545,163	2,402,640	−1,210,946	Dec-12	1,535	1,539	3,269	97%	3%	366	34	142	10	0	376	87.70	90.0
2013 2	1,189,373	−609,869	2,593,554	−1,304,771	Jan-13	1,771	1,774	3,823	97%	3%	444	33	171	13	0	457	87.20	90.0
2013 3	902,794	−488,571	2,628,876	−1,171,230	Feb-13	1,128	1,131	2,434	98%	2%	303	23	117	7	0	310	87.60	91.0
2013 4	1,002,335	−511,740	2,853,424	−1,325,702	Mar-13	1,204	1,206	2,617	96%	4%	266	21	164	12	0	278	87.10	89.1
2014 1	589,427	−294,831	1,819,795	−808,639	Apr-13	1,741	3,487	7,568	99%	1%	398	41	160	3	1	402	88.20	91.7
					May-13	1,666	1,668	3,610	98%	2%	366	20	125	6	0	372	88.60	90.7
					Jun-13	1,089	1,096	2,375	97%	3%	285	10	78	10	0	295	87.40	90.3
					Jul-13	1,201	0	0	98%	2%	297	19	105	5	0	302	88.50	91.3
					Aug-13	1,316	0	0	99%	1%	279	18	102	4	0	283	87.80	90.3

Top 10 Referrals

Physician 1	8,957
Physician 2	6,083
Physician 3	5,331
Physician 4	4,871
Physician 5	4,563
Physician 6	4,305
Physician 7	3,719
Physician 8	3,726
Physician 9	3,209
Physician 10	2,398

Top 10 Payers

ANTHEM BC/BS	65,938
MEDICARE	53,923
HEALTHNET	23,523
CIGNA HEALTHCARE	14,953
AETNA/US HEALTHCARE	12,034
UNITED HEALTHCARE	11,475
SELF PAY	10,391
PHCS	6,052
CONNECTICARE	5,436
OXFORD HEALTH PLAN	2,144

Top 10 CPTs

99212	PROBLEM FOCUSED/STRAIGHTFORWARD	116
17304	CHEMOSURGERY (MOHS):FIRST	84
99242	EXPANDED PROBLEM/STRAIGHTFORWARD	13
17305	CHEMOSURGERY (MOHS):SECOND	42
17003	DESTRUCTION OF LESION, ANY	31
11100	BIOPSY OF SKIN LESION (INC SIMPLE	29
13132	RPR WND/LSN,CMPLX	16
17000	DESTRUCT LESION,ANY METHOD	15
13131	REPAIR WND/LSN,CMPLX	11
17306	CHEMOSURGERY (MOHS):THIRD	11

Top 10 Diags

1733	OTHER MALIGNANT NEOPLASM OF SKIN OF OTH
709.2	SCAR CONDITIONS AND FIBROSIS OF SKIN(709.2)
702.0	ACTINICKERATOSIS(702.0)
239.2	NEOPLASM OF UNSPECIFIED NATURE OF BONE,
173.0	OTHER MALIGNANT NEOPLASM OF SKIN OF LIP
173.1	OTHER MALIGNANT NEOPLASM OF SKIN OF EYE
173.4	OTHER MALIGNANT NEOPLASM OF SCALP AND SKIN OF NECK
173.5	OTHER MALIGNANT NEOPLASM OF SKIN OF TRUNK
873.30	OPEN WOUND OF NOSE, UNSPECIFIED SITE
173.8	OTHER MALIGNANT NEOPLASM OF OTHER

TY E&M Percent   TY E&M FPSC Ratio — Office/OP Visit, New Pt and Est Pt (99201, 99202, 99203, 99204, 99205, 99211, 99212, 99213, 99214, 99215)

TY E&M Percent   TY E&M FPSC Ratio (99241, 99242, 99243, 99244, 99245)

TY E&M Percent   TY E&M FPSC Ratio — Initial Hosp Care and Subsequent Hosp Care (99221, 99222, 99223, 99251, 99252, 99253, 99254, 99255)

Courtesy of Yale University School of Medicine.

- *Utilities and rules.* Within the IT solution, one will find administrative utilities, object management, and rules such as those governing distribution or content scheduling. The functionality for analytics, ad-hoc reporting, dashboard tools, KPIs, score card methods, and other application software capabilities are programmed here.

As healthcare analytics matures and is more broadly adopted, certain outcomes will be accepted as means to measure their value. Following is a list of requirements and functional attributes for a viable BI/CI solution.

Requirements for BI/CI Solutions

- *Secure.* Whether combined within a CDR or in a BI/CI solution, all data must be secure. For PHI and HIPAA compliance, the system's architectural environment must ensure that each data element maintains a secured utility to limit access, use, and improper exposure. Thus each data element is tagged to control its use and to provide an essential audit trail indicating when, how, and by whom the data have been accessed.

- *Extensible/scalable.* Considering the expanding direction of healthcare data, the BI/CI solution must be able to scale up and extend to new areas. Just as the adoption of EHRs has proliferated over the last decade, so newly expanded uses for the Internet and mobile technologies will require more data as they are developed. Additionally, government's role is still rather fluid, but it seems relatively safe to assume that government agencies will demand increased care measurements and reporting in the future. Lastly, like most maturing industries, the healthcare industry is consolidating: Smaller shops are coming together to create mega-organizations that will be combining huge amounts of historical data during their mergers.

- *Integrity.* Health care is a professional industry populated by a highly educated workforce. Science and pragmatism are pervasive throughout the healthcare arena. Nevertheless, there is always a level of subjectivity and variability for the reasons discussed earlier; additionally, there is great emphasis on humanity in sustaining a patient's health. From both of these vantage points, accuracy and integrity are imperative. *Data must have high integrity.* For users to trust the system there must be a high degree of veracity and authenticity across software applications, the resulting data sets, and any analytics and reporting. You do not have to look far to find voluminous anecdotal history of software systems failing to be adopted because providers did not trust the output.

- *Performance.* EHR, laboratory, and other clinical point of care systems must provide real-time information for healthcare providers. Their clinical decision making depends on the timeliness of this information. Conversely, BI/CI is inherently a retrospective analysis of transactional and clinical systems. Different data feeds to the BI/CI system may be real time, daily, monthly, or even quarterly. Well-timed performance is a subjective observation: Each output must be timely (whether the information is needed immediately or periodically). When an output from a BI/CI system is required, it must be readily accessible. Depending on the form of output, the system should provide the information in a few seconds to a few minutes. A responsive solution will have automated utilities for the scheduled delivery of many objects such as KPIs, dashboards, statistics, or other predetermined requirements. Ad-hoc demands will take longer in the first run of an inquiry.

Functional Attributes of BI/CI Solutions

- *Accessibility.* All modern workers are knowledge workers who require information to perform their jobs most effectively, and a properly designed BI/CI system should make access to data relatively easy for those who have been trained in its use. Most internal consumers or users will never create intelligence content, but they or their managers should understand the concept of how the system works if they are to have properly trained personnel develop content to their needs. From a control standpoint and to satisfy general security concerns, a healthcare organization may choose to program utilities that identify improper commands or inordinate demands from the **central processing unit** (**CPU**) to control illogical or improper personnel access. In environments where operational personnel are dependent upon a small IT or analytics group to develop content, there will be an untenable bottleneck.

- *Usability.* One reason for the relatively slow adoption of BI/CI solutions is that many are still rather complex to use. The more content that can be built or modified by nontechnical personnel, the greater the likelihood of success. For example, a clinician doing the hands-on work of health care may appreciate which kind of BI/CI is usable "in the field" better than an IT staff member: If they can drill down into the information themselves, the BI/CI system can provide users with information agility that would not be possible otherwise. In addition to tables and spreadsheets, graphic and visual representations of data are invaluable. Because of its functional value, a BI/CI solution may regularly generate hundreds of unique content displays at any one hospital.

- *Actionable.* If the content from a BI/CI solution is not "actionable"—that is, if it does not improve decision making, enhance day-to-day performance, solve relevant problems, or improve processes—then it will undoubtedly be discarded onto the giant heap of unrealized clever ideas. A BI/CI solution can only provide visibility into an organization's data; by itself, it will not make decisions. The BI/CI solution must provide clear evidence so that appropriate personnel feel comfortable in changing methods, managing their function, doing their work, and making decisions to improve the organization in ways that matter based on those data.

- *Asking from the answers.* This principle is based on the adage, "You don't know what you don't know." Once a BI/CI solution is in the hands of healthcare workers, they may know better which kind of questions to ask. A competent analytics solution will allow an inquiry's "answer" to be queried time and again. In the world of BI/CI, you do not know the next question until you see the answer to the first. In theory, this may occur ad infinitum, especially as the questioning audience grows and multiple thoughts begin to challenge the results. In turn, an analytical result may promote a follow-up question or the addition or deletion of data to better refine the original inquiry. It becomes a circle of better investigation of data based on digging and creatively using stages of analytical output.

- **Roles-based use.** Every employee has one or more work roles. DSS and EIS are antiquated concepts, as every worker—not just executives—needs some level of actionable information to perform his or her job or role. The dissemination of information is imperative and no longer valuable only to management and executives. Such distribution may consist of the presentation of small, daily refreshed tactical data such an insurance denial report or an appointment follow-up list. Also appropriate to her or his role, an executive may want to review more sweeping views of different tactical or strategic business operations, with the ability to drill down into highlighted areas of interest or concern. There may conceivably be as many daily, weekly, and monthly analytical outputs as there are users in the enterprise.

- *Dashboards.* Dashboards allow often used data sets to be graphically presented in one or a few locations on a regular basis, where the user has unlimited access and may toggle between information with just a few keyboard or mouse clicks. The idea is to centrally locate lots of information, according to agreed-upon KPIs. A first glance gives a summary level, which can be clicked on to access supporting detailed data.

- *Retrospective nature of BI and CI.* Real-time clinical decision making is based on a combination of the clinician's experience and the information available within the EHR. While more real-time analytic innovations are under development, with today's technology, the traditional frequency of updating a CDR or pure BI solution is daily. Therefore, analytical reports, dashboards, and other outputs are generally produced for the various users the morning after systems have been updated on the prior evening. This gives end users data to inform decisions going forward in the new day.

EXAMPLES OF BI/CI AT WORK

Example 1

A relatively small obstetrics/gynecology practice had problems tracking compliance in its administration department and inventorying Gardasil. The Gardasil vaccine is used to prevent human papillomavirus infection, which may lead to cervical cancer; for maximum effectiveness, it needs to be administered as a series of doses in the same patient. This drug has a limited shelf life, so an expensive inventory must be destroyed if not used.

Using HIS and technology systems to provide a BI/CI solution, the practice combined data from its purchasing, scheduling, EMR, and provider productivity systems to stratify by provider which patients were receiving Gardasil. To better manage the inventory of this vaccine, it then calculated the drug volumes that would be necessary based on trending appointments and the targeted patient population demographics. The data provided (1) a list of patients for scheduling and (2) an order process for Gardasil. The resulting analytics provided a quality factor to ensure proper patient scheduling and administration of the drug (including a potential recall) while saving the practice hundreds of thousands of dollars in wasted inventory. This example demonstrates the many different disciplines involved in improving a single clinical process, along with the resulting impacts on cost management and clinical quality.

Example 2

A busy, university-based practice combined a dozen data sets relating to provider productivity, comparative patient satisfaction feedback, benchmarked relative value unit (RVU) measures, and other data sets. The ultimate goal was to deliver a month-end summary of each provider's compensation. Heretofore, this exercise necessitated more than eight unique report formats, took many employee hours, and was delivered more than a week after the month-end closing.

The new BI/CI-driven single-page summary included an information dashboard with nine different windows combining all of the former discrete reports. The process was completely automated, was deliverable in the provider's preferred modality (email, fax, or hard copy), and was customized for each department reflecting the specialty nuances of measures.

This combination of data to present timely, actionable information was challenging to create, but once it was in place, it became a valuable management tool, useful to many.

THE FUTURE OF BI/CI

There will undoubtedly be tremendous opportunities for individuals who understand the complexities of health care's BI/CI. Prospective provider organizations and BI/CI application vendor roles will include the following:

- *BI/CI executives and SMEs*: operations, quality, planning, medical staff leadership, nursing leadership, strategy, and management who understand the problems inherent in each discipline and, therefore, what the information solutions might be
- *Systems architects*: personnel who are generally highly technical and create the environment for acquiring, storing, and accessing the data necessary for BI/CI
- *Programmers*: personnel who program or create software applications and then support and enhance these programs once the software is developed and used in production
- *Data analysts*: personnel who work with data and often act as the liaisons between technical and non-technical users of data and information
- *Content creators*: personnel who format and structure data in a desired or logically deliverable design for all roles in the organization
- *Implementation*: trainers and personnel who deal with interface creation, data translations, roll-out to users, updates, and issues resolution
- *Project managers*: managers of BI/CI implementations

The notion of intelligence and analytics is profoundly useful and beneficial at so many levels. Considering the healthcare industry's size and influence on the U.S. economy as well as its dependency on the voluminous amounts of data and types of BI/CI for its operational efficiency and clinical performance, it must and will accelerate the adoption of better methods in leveraging those data. Talented project managers are the key to organizing the detailed tasks into projects, persevering to pull together the many threads inherent in BI/CI solutions, and helping users adopt their use. As in other healthcare IT pursuits, BI/CI work is not without significant challenges, but it is greatly rewarding once accomplished. Despite the structural and logistical limitations that must be overcome to reach this goal, there is now enough political, consumer-based, and industry demand to support its achievement.

SUMMARY

If we all agree that making current, practicable information available to workers will likely improve performance within the healthcare workplace environment, then BI/CI is a viable concept. Health care has an inordinate number of moving parts and an incredible plethora of raw and uncoordinated data. In lay terms, bringing all those data into a single location, harmonizing them, and making the results available to the masses of potential users is a very good thing.

Beyond good, it is necessary. Health care's unsynchronized and unaligned methods of providing care have become untenable and unaffordable as organizations attempt to effectively manage their businesses. As the government, quality watch groups, employers, and patients as consumers of health care prescribe necessary change, the healthcare industry must put into practice proven methods of gathering and distilling information into intelligence. Other industries have already demonstrated the value of BI, and so, in growing ways, has health care.

All healthcare organizations have limited capacity to implement IT investments. Currently, there are mandated priorities, such as with EHRs and ICD-10 conversions; organizations are developing Internet strategies, e-mobile integration, security solutions, and other competing initiatives as well. However, recent surveys of C-level and IT executives, as well as industry member groups such as the Healthcare Information and Management Systems Society and the Medical Group Management Association, consistently espouse the need for better BI.[9] There are no precise data on the use of BI in health care, but best estimates would suggest fewer than 20% of all provider organizations have implemented a true BI/CI solution and even fewer have done so on an enterprise-wide level.

In addition to the pure logic of using analytics, the BI/CI paradigm has a very intellectually rewarding and creative side. The process of identifying what needs better workflow process and obtaining distinct business and clinical answers, plus the ability to dig around and present data solutions, can be deeply fulfilling. With properly designed and implemented data architecture and intelligence mining software, one can discover empirical answers to both mundane and extraordinarily complex healthcare questions.

KEY TERMS

© Johan Swanepoel/Shutterstock, Inc.

Discussion Questions

1. Who might use and benefit from healthcare BI/CI?

2. What do you think might be the preferred way of structuring a BI/CI group within a hospital? For a multispecialty ambulatory group?

3. How might you describe the differences between non-healthcare industries' and the healthcare industry's use of analytics?

4. If applicable, how have you used analytics as part of your work in a healthcare organization? Did you use BI or CI?

5. Do you believe that healthcare organizations might "push" personal analytics out to patients for their own monitoring and improvement of health and quality of life issues?

6. Would you use more personalized health information in your own life? How might you do so? What would be your preferred method of communication?

7. Do any of the roles described in relation to the use of BI/CI interest you, and why?

8. Are the existing HIPAA, PHI, and other security measures sufficient to allow you to trust healthcare organizations in aggregating, mining, and analyzing data?

9. Do you believe that BI/CI should be mandated and controlled by the various government agencies that are involved in health care? Why or why not?

REFERENCES

1. Mulcahy, R. (n.d.). Business intelligence definition and solutions business intelligence topics covering definition, objectives, systems and solutions. *CIO*. http://www.cio.com/article/40296/Business_Intelligence_Definition_and_Solutions

2. Agosta, L. (2010, June 7). Healthcare business intelligence systems: An IT laggard no more? *Search Business Analytics*. http://searchbusinessanalytics.techtarget.com/news/2240019450/Healthcare-business-intelligence-systems-an-IT-laggard-no-more

3. Institute of Medicine. (2003). *Key capabilities of an electronic health record system: Letter report*. http://www.nap.edu/openbook.php?record_id=10781

4. Health costs: How the U.S. compares with other countries. (2012, October 22). *PBS News Hour*.

5. American Hospital Association. (n.d.). Fast facts on U.S. hospitals. http://www.aha.org/research/rc/stat-studies/fast-facts.shtml

6. U.S. News & World Report Health Insurance Top Health Insurance Companies. Evi Heilbrunn. December 16, 2013. http://health.usnews.com/health-news/health-insurance/articles/2013/12/16/top-health-insurance-companies

7. Association of American Medical Colleges. (n.d.). Medical schools. https://www.aamc.org/about/membership/378788/medicalschools.html

8. Centers for Disease Control and Prevention. (n.d.). Nursing home care. http://www.cdc.gov/nchs/fastats/nursingh.htm

9. 2008 HIMSS/HIMSS Analytics Ambulatory Healthcare IT survey final report. (2008, October). http://himss.files.cms-plus.com/HIMSSorg/content/files/2008_HA_HIMSS_ambulatory_Survey.pdf

SECTION V

Research, Policy, and Public Health

HIS and Research, Policy, and Public Health

By the end of this chapter, the student will be able to:

- Describe the relationships between research, policy, public health, and the other spheres of the health information systems (HIS) and technology model.
- Explain uses of HIS-based research in health policy and public health activities.
- Outline various data sources for research in healthcare, policy, and public health organizations.
- Discuss ways that policy, HIS, and technology interrelate.
- Review the practical and analytical uses of HIS and technology in public health.
- Assess the pros and cons of current HIS, including EHR systems, in their ability to support comparative effectiveness and other types of health research.

INTRODUCTION

The health information systems (HIS) model presents types of activities—namely, research, policy, and public health—that, among other important endeavors, make secondary use of data and information collected from systems used in healthcare organizations for health-related activities. Ultimately, data created and captured in systems used in healthcare settings (*primary* uses) provide for these additional or *secondary* uses: materials for the informaticists' workshop; definitions and format to aid in the organization of data; and the clinical and administrative data needed for the work of health-related research, policy work, and public health. In **Figure 11.1**, which depicts interactions between layers of the HIS model, we see that each HIS layer is fed by the previous one, moving progressively outward from the

systems and management center of the model to health informatics, to data and analytics, to research, policy, and public health. But there is more: After supporting and enabling each layer of the model, each sphere is then informed through feedback, insights, and knowledge created by the work of research, policy, and public health, the outermost circle. Research, policy, and public health build the knowledge necessary to better understand healthcare efficiency and costs, effectiveness and quality, how to approach population health management, threats to the public's health, and issues surrounding access to care. These insights can then be used to inform the types, functionalities, and data capture needs of HIS *and* the design of workflows and processes necessary for informaticists to build into those systems. This work helps HIS to produce appropriate, high-quality data and analyses, all of which improve and advance the work of the research, policy, and public health spheres. The continuous feedback from these ultimate secondary uses of HIS and data to create knowledge provides learning loops so that constant progress can be made in HIS primary uses, in an attempt to create harmony and cogency among the many activities related to building and managing HIS, electronic health record (EHR) systems, and other information components related to the HIS model's spheres. In other words, as each progressive use of systems and data occurs, it creates insight and feedback to inform and improve the HIS layers that fed it, as represented in the model.

Take heed: Opportunities for collaboration are limited by the planning and intention of the work of each layer either to include just itself or to take an expanded view to include the interests and needs of the other spheres.

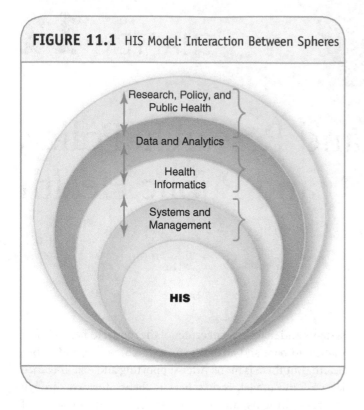

FIGURE 11.1 HIS Model: Interaction Between Spheres

This expanded perspective not only contemplates the needs of the healthcare organization or setting of the HIS under construction, but it also takes into consideration the needs and perspectives of other healthcare entities along the continuum of care (think of a health information exchange or accountable care organization [ACO]). Careful HIS planning at the organizational level feeds into many purposes within each sphere: informatics and the work of informaticists as they strive to create streamlined processes and integrated, patient-centric workflows; the comprehensive ability to create and capture data in any healthcare provider setting for the purpose of combining with data from other settings, thereby enabling comparative effectiveness analyses and research; and ultimately, supporting the data analytics needs of researchers, policy makers, and public health professionals through the availability of high-quality, consistent data from throughout the healthcare system.

Collaboration among multiple parties is more feasible than ever before due to the work of the Health Information Technology and Economics Act (HITECH) standards committees; Institute of Medicine (IOM) standards-setting bodies; interorganizational connections of professional groups such as Health Information Management Systems Society (HIMSS), American Medical Informatics Association (AMIA), American Health Information Management

Association (AHIMA), American Medical Association (AMA), and American Nurse Informatics Association (ANIA); and health information exchange groups and university consortia. These professional organizations and standards committees are working to provide long-needed data and technical standards for HIS and related organizations in the United States. It is not feasible to successfully aggregate data from disparate sources without some semblance of data standards to create consistencies to aid data normalization and to guide correct definitions and structures of these data originating in systems foreign to one another.

This collaborative, cohesive approach that envisions the productive needs of all spheres stands in opposition to the myopic, legacy habits of building HIS in silos. Unfortunately, this practice of building information silos remains rampant among U.S. healthcare organizations. Silos effectively destroy the opportunity to appropriately compile and aggregate data from the hundreds of thousands of HIS implemented in various departments within healthcare organizations across the country. (Exceptions to this lack of standards are the ICD-9/ICD-10 diagnosis and CPT codes used for documenting and codifying clinical care and procedures, providing data for claims and billing processes, for which standards for government payers such as **Medicare** and **Medicaid** exist.) Silo systems exponentially reduce the ultimate "return on investment" of the cost and effort to build and implement HIS, because their usefulness is limited to confined needs within the boundaries of the department or organizational unit they are intended to serve or at best within a system to which the silo system is interfaced. A collaborative, expansive, integrated vision that contemplates all spheres of the HIS model when designing and implementing an HIS—even when the immediate objective is to support the needs of a single organization or department—is not much additional work and creates enormous synergies among all disciplines and purposes represented in the HIS model.

Looking at this model (Figure 11.1) from its center, we can see that HIS provides the platform for the work of informatics, creating data that facilitate analyses (by researchers, policy makers, and public health officials) that directly impact activities, outcomes, and knowledge about organizations, clinical processes, patients, and populations. These many and varied data and information resources are the fuel for today's research, policy, and public health engines. Thus, research, policy, and public health represent major categories of secondary uses of the data created and captured in the HIS (**Figure 11.2**). This theme is consistent with the "secondary use of data" *within* organizations—organizations can

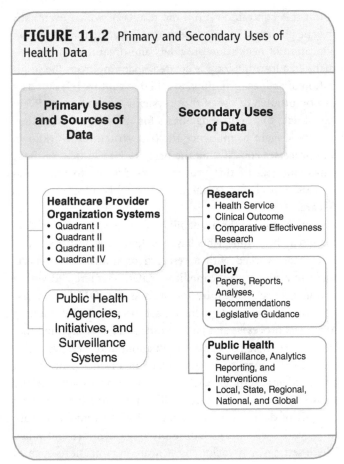

FIGURE 11.2 Primary and Secondary Uses of Health Data

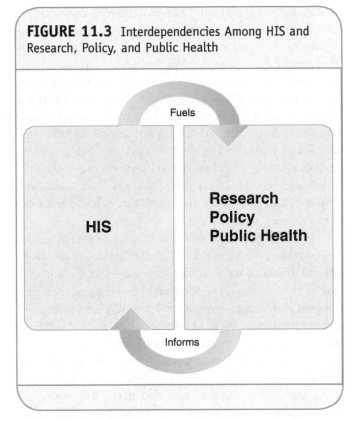

FIGURE 11.3 Interdependencies Among HIS and Research, Policy, and Public Health

use data created and captured in their transaction systems for analyzing and reporting for many purposes within the organization's scope. The only difference between the two (i.e., primary and secondary uses) is the purpose of the data use; in other words, in secondary uses of data, the types of reporting and analytics are geared toward the interests and purpose of the organization or discipline doing the analysis. Each of these uses is entirely appropriate: Hospitals want to report and analyze hospital-related issues; research organizations seek answers to various research questions; policy organizations search for alternatives and trade-offs on policy-related questions; and public health organizations try to find meaning across entire populations on public health issues.

In describing each layer of the HIS model, the relationship between these major disciplines is bidirectional (**Figure 11.3**). HIS and management activities carried out in healthcare and public health organizations provide sources of data for the research conducted and the information used in the domains of research, policy, and public health. The research performed, in turn, provides insights, evidence, and policy recommendations to the originators of the data,

helping define workflow and process improvements, functionality, and data requirements to be implemented into the source HIS. This information and data ecosystem improves the content, capabilities, and roles contained within these systems.

Now that we see the whole scheme of interrelationships between the layers and feedback loops created with an integrated view of the HIS model, we are ready to explore the relationship of the research, policy, and public health domains to HIS and management one at a time.

HIS MODEL: RESEARCH, POLICY, AND PUBLIC HEALTH RELATIONSHIPS TO HIS

In this section, we discuss the role of foundational HIS and their management in the sphere of research, policy, and public health. We examine the relationships of research, policy, and public health to other layers of the HIS model.

Relationship of Research to HIS and Management

HIS create and capture data as a by-product of transactions associated with the daily activities of health care. These data are created and captured in the computer systems that support the workflows of care and patient management such as the data in EHR systems and administrative processes such as patient billing or inventory management. Following the completion of these transactional processes, the data can then be aggregated and combined for researchers to use. (These EHR systems are not without shortcomings in their ability to provide the types of data needed for research, a topic that will be discussed later in this chapter.) Through the use of data originating from core HIS, health services clinical researchers, policy analysts, and public health professionals are able to analyze, evaluate, and identify associations between variables and themes reflected in the data. Thus, new information and ultimately new knowledge are created through secondary use of healthcare transaction data.

Results from research are then communicated to healthcare provider communities through conferences, proceedings, lectures, publications, webinars, newsletters, and reports. As part of their continuing education and honing of their professional knowledge, providers and practitioners are required to stay up to date with the new findings and work of researchers, by reading, presenting, discussing, debating, and otherwise digesting and keeping up with research developments published in peer-reviewed journals, known collectively as "the literature." In this way, new evidence, information, and knowledge are continually shared with other healthcare providers so that they may take these points into consideration as they do their work and help shape the HIS that support care for patients and the business of health care.

How do the development and dissemination of new knowledge relate to HIS and management? In very important ways, as this learning can be further applied to the data systems and sources from whence the analytics originated. This new knowledge can be built into the clinical decision support capabilities of EHR systems, in the form of new alerts, rules, or parameters. It can become the task of informaticists to reevaluate workflows for the purpose of changing them in ways that take this new knowledge into account. For example, an informaticist, based on new research, may design a check-off confirmation within an EHR system for identifying whether a patient's medication has been cross-referenced against a newly understood contraindicated condition or drug therapy. A question to be asked as part of patient assessment about the contraindicating condition/therapy can be added to the intake process. The data elements reflecting the contraindicated condition/drug combination can be added to provider workflow as data then interfaced from the EHR system to the quality reporting database for tracking and reporting purposes. Finally, researchers can begin asking questions regarding further evaluation of the new finding

about this contraindication, the results of which eventually may be published in the professional literature for the further education of healthcare providers and organizations. In this manner, a learning loop is created, spanning from the origination of an idea or finding, to HIS that capture relevant data as a by-product of use of those systems (such as an EHR), to use of data to populate databases for analysis and reporting, and back again to influence the data structures, workflows, and processes constituting the primary HIS sources of those data. The goal of this process is to inform workflow and process/clinical improvements to favorably affect outcomes of care.

In examining the availability of primary sources of data for research, anyone who has ever known a health services researcher, worked with a research or informatics department in a university or medical center, or interacted with a national research organization such as the IOM knows that getting access to good quality data, especially data pertaining to clinical processes and patient outcomes, is something that these researchers constantly think about and seek. Data fuel research. Such research takes place in myriad professional and academic settings, each with a mission to advance the knowledge and practice of health care through the careful analysis of data leading to actionable improvements in care or processes with the goal of improving outcomes and value. These settings may include healthcare organizations such as university medical centers; community hospitals and health systems; medical practices; research organizations such as the Agency for Healthcare and Research Quality, Institute for Healthcare Improvement, and National Institutes of Health; and life sciences companies such as biotechnology and pharmaceutical firms, and other organizations that collaborate with healthcare organizations to perform clinical trials. Many clinicians such as physicians and nurses gear their careers toward research as well as clinical practice.

Research needs data like crops need seeds.

Relationship of Policy to HIS and Management

Governmental policies are far-reaching and intended to address issues that the private sector is not able to address, or issues that are related to civil liberties, national security, and public safety. Policy influences business and clinical activities carried on in healthcare organizations, establishes regulations to protect the public, and preserves and protects the public's health.

The relationship of policy within the research, policy, and public health sphere of the HIS model shows that policy work needs data from HIS just as research does, but for its own special purposes, including policy analysis, program evaluation, white papers, reports, and recommendations.[1] Also, policy influences HIS in a significant fashion. We will examine both of these statements in some depth.

First, the layer of HIS and management automates clinical and business transactions and processes that create and capture data for many secondary uses. Policy analysts and policy makers are able to use data originating from healthcare organizations' HIS to evaluate the quality and efficiency of clinical processes, utilization, and access to care, for various purposes such as program evaluation. For instance, policy analysts might assess healthcare utilization or compare specific services delivered to various groups in different parts of the country to evaluate government-sponsored insurance programs, such as Medicare (for the aged), Medicaid (for low-income and disabled individuals), or **Children's Health Insurance Program** (**CHIP**; for children from low-income families who do not qualify for Medicaid but cannot afford private insurance).[2] Utilization and outcomes of care may also be evaluated to detect whether there are issues with the levels and types of resources and services being delivered to the populations whom the policies are intended to address.

Policy also drives legislation at the national, state, and local levels. Throughout the United States, public programs are tracked and evaluated using data gathered from HIS and other sources as part of program participation to monitor quality and ensure appropriate use of funds. In essence, if the government is paying for care through Medicare, Medicaid, or other programs, it receives data as a result of the claims and reporting requirements that mandate health provider organizations to send in such data to receive reimbursement for care provided to program beneficiaries. By reviewing and analyzing these claims data, policy makers can evaluate the amounts and types of care being delivered to these groups, and ensure compliance with many guidelines, performance metrics, and regulations for those programs. HIS provide data that help policy makers understand where there might be the need for new policy or adjustments to current policies or programs, or closer program audits.

Likewise, policy affects HIS. HIS must meet the requirements dictated by all federal and state regulations, which can significantly impact software functionality needs (e.g., HITECH's Meaningful Use criteria and the Health Insurance Portability and Accountability Act's data interchange, privacy, and security requirements). Recent policy and regulations—including those stemming from the Accountable Care Act (ACA), the American Recovery and Reinvestment Act (ARRA), and HITECH—have set criteria

for the functionality of software, standards for technology, and metrics for measuring and reporting quality of care. These policies and regulations have a tremendous influence on how HIS are implemented and used, and which functionality and technology are provided by software vendors in their HIS products that are sold and used in healthcare organizations throughout the United States.

As can be seen, the policy layer and the systems and management layer of the HIS model are interdependent, with policy makers relying on HIS as key sources of data and analytical capabilities for examining utilization, cost, and quality of healthcare services provided as part of government-sponsored programs. For example, Medicare's Hospital Compare program provides information about all U.S. hospitals participating in the Medicare program and their level of performance, such as measures tracking clinical results between visits or levels of communication with nurses and doctors. Hospital Compare is part of the Hospital Quality Initiative established by the **Centers for Medicare and Medicaid Services** (**CMS**). The Hospital Quality Initiative uses a variety of tools to make benchmarking information available to hospitals to support their efforts related to quality of care.[3] The intent is to help improve hospitals' quality of care by distributing objective, easy-to-understand data on hospital quality from consumer perspectives. Conversely, HIS are influenced by policy when regulations require certain data, functionality, and reporting capabilities in HIS to allow for measurement and evaluation of quality and adherence to governmental programs in healthcare organizations.

Relationship of Public Health to HIS and Management

The third area of the research, policy, and public health sphere of the HIS model is public health. Like the other areas, public health functions such as surveillance, reporting, analysis, and intervention need data emanating from HIS. Like research and policy, the sphere of public health influences HIS, perhaps more now than ever, as healthcare organizations venture into **population health management** as a means of anticipating and trying to better manage costs and outcomes of chronic disease for their covered populations. The prevention aspects of population health management overlap with public health and affect the types of HIS needed to support these organizational initiatives.

Several areas of public health practice need data from HIS and influence the functionality of those systems. HIS provide these data, which are created and captured in transaction systems supporting patient care and administrative

FIGURE 11.4 HIS Planning Framework—Example Systems

	Transaction/Functional Support Systems	Management Information/Decision Support Systems (BI/CI)
Clinical	I • EHR, EMR, PHR, medical intranet • Outpatient systems • Radiology, laboratory, pharmacy • Transcription/dictation • Cardiology, ECG, ECHO • Maternity monitoring • Home health • PACS for imaging • Surgery • ICU systems, monitors, devices	III • Clinical intelligence (CI) • Clinical analytics • Predictive clinical analytics • Case mix analysis • Decision support systems • Cardiac outcomes • Quality analysis & reporting • Outcomes analysis • External reporting: (Joint Commission, Leapfrog, CHART, other)

Administrative	II
	• Enterprise Resource Management (ERP):
	  • General ledger (G/L), accounts payable (AP)
	  • Human resources/payroll
	  • Materials management/supply chain
	• Patient accounting (billing/accounts receivable)
	• Contracts management
		IV
		• Business intelligence (BI)
		• Predictive business analytics
		• Financial, supply chain, HR reporting
		• Cost accounting
		• Data warehouse
		• Financial decision support
		• Enterprise data archive
		• Budgeting, G/L, etc

Key: BI, business intelligence; CI, clinical intelligence; ECHO, echocardiogram; EHR, electronic health record; EMR, electronic medical record; ECG, electrocardiogram; HR, human resources; ICU, intensive care unit; PACS, picture and archiving communication system; PHR, personal health record.

Modified from Jay McCutcheon's Systems Planning Framework.

processes (think Quadrants I and II of the HIS planning framework, as displayed in **Figure 11.4**), as well as offer reporting capabilities that support clinical and business reporting and analyses. The public health realm uses data from a wide variety of sources for surveillance purposes, and aggregates data that can be used for analysis of population health status measures. For example, this surveillance analysis may give early warning detection of increases in diseases such as influenza, or infection rates to detect early signals of possible bioterrorism.[4(p.51)] HIS represent important sources of data for public health surveillance; indeed, as we proceed through this section, we will look at specific sources of data used by public health organizations, including HIS.

As mentioned earlier, goals of public health entities and healthcare organizations are converging due to growing emphasis on population health management. Population health management on a large scale was not feasible until recently, other than in the rarest of instances; notable exceptions included "closed systems" or integrated delivery networks such as Kaiser Permanente in which the health

plan (insurer), provider organizations (hospitals and clinics), and patients (members) were all under the same organizational umbrella and all systems were integrated around that objective. Population health management was not feasible historically primarily due to the lack of information technology connectivity necessary to gather and analyze information from inside *and* outside provider organizations, including from patients in their homes or workplaces. Now, however, the infrastructure often exists in forms that facilitate data collection and analysis to a greater extent than was previously possible. Now we have (1) widespread implementation of EHR in healthcare organizations, (2) increasing ability to exchange health information between organizations and settings, (3) health information exchange (HIE) and mobile health (mHealth) technologies for obtaining personal health data fueled by newly ubiquitous smartphone infrastructure, and (4) powerful analytical capabilities including predictive analytics that allow for earlier anticipation of health issues on an individual basis and that might affect the public's health in aggregate. Capabilities such as

HIE and mHealth allow collection of data from people as they go about their daily lives through use of smartphones, wireless devices, mobile apps, and social media; these same capabilities enable healthcare organizations not only to care for patients when they are sick and need care in the physician's office, the clinic, or the hospital, but also to engage people in wellness activities and self-management of chronic illness risk factors from their homes, offices, or schools. All of this creates the ability to gather data for conducting predictive analysis of a population's risk factors for disease and develop prevention-oriented programs to manage these risk factors, stem the development of chronic illness, and keep people healthy.

These capabilities are not here a moment too soon, as chronic illnesses are reaching crisis proportions in the United States, resulting in rising costs for healthcare insurance, which are becoming unsustainable for individuals, businesses, and federal and state governments alike. In addition, we are finally realizing that the U.S. healthcare system, in its current "medical model," is relatively ineffective in dealing with the problems faced by the majority of Americans: The reimbursement system has been based on fee-for-service methodologies that reward treatment of medical conditions and does not reward prevention. In other words, our health system is focused on sickness, not health and wellness. It has created a population whose members too often passively expect to be cured once they are sick; with chronic illness, this approach does not work. Unfortunately, this is an unsustainable scenario, given the aging population and significant increases in chronic illnesses such as diabetes, heart disease, cancer, and obesity. The IOM estimated recently that $750 billion to $765 billion in health spending is wasted each year in the United States. These expenditures are the excess over what should be spent to achieve our current health outcomes.[5] The fact that many of the illnesses developed by Americans are chronic *and* preventable gives a clue as to why our sickness- and procedure-focused health system is failing to produce the desired health effects, and the cost of this current path is unsustainable to the point that it is harming the United States' competitive position in the world.

Thus prevention and population health management among healthcare organizations and public health's goals and objectives are now converging. Practitioners in these areas have the tremendous and urgent opportunity to work hand-in-hand to achieve better outcomes. The extant population health management/public health need is vastly influencing HIS and technology strategy within healthcare organizations as they strive to right the ship in the stormy seas of the present reality of climbing costs and worsening health status of their covered populations.

Population health management and prevention, delivered through new organizational models such as ACOs and medical homes, require significant information technology infrastructure and capabilities to connect the organization and its providers with patients in their homes or wherever they are. Through the use of mHealth capabilities to gather data that are both actionable and relevant to managing their health, we can engage people in management of their risk factors and chronic conditions. Healthcare organizations are also building databases and tools for predictive analytics, tracking the health status of the populations for which they are responsible, and suggesting preventive measures to engage with patients by exploiting the mHealth capabilities. **Figure 11.5** presents a Venn diagram showing the convergence of healthcare provider organizations and public health. These population health management leverage points portray the convergence between the domains of health provider organizations, research/policy, and public health—planets that previously rotated in mostly separate orbits.

Now that we have outlined the relationships between HIS and research, policy, and public health, we will examine different types of research, policy, and public health, and the specific types of HIS and data sources used to support those activities.

FIGURE 11.5 Convergence of Healthcare Provider Organizations and Public Health—Population Health Management Leverage Points

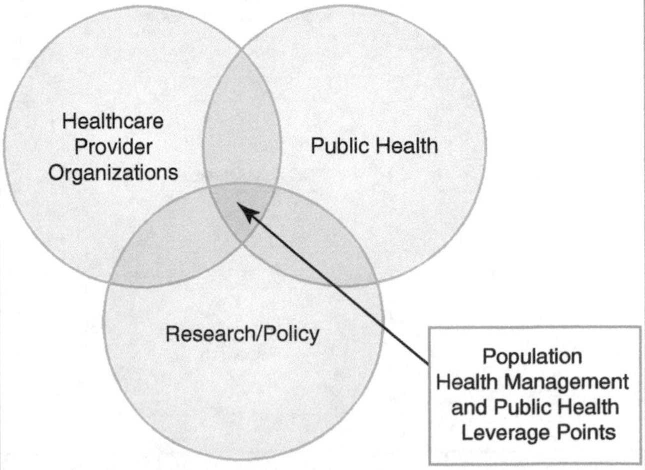

TYPES OF RESEARCH AND SOURCES OF DATA FROM HIS

Research is conducted in a wide variety of organizations, for a multitude of purposes. In this chapter, research is considered a concept that applies to several categories of health care and public health, each of which uses data from a variety of sources. **Figure 11.6** displays different kinds of research and sources of data that can be useful for each category. Types of research activities include **health services research**, clinical outcomes research, clinical trials/technology innovation, policy analysis and research, and public health research.

Health Services Research

A useful and straightforward definition of health services research is provided by the **Agency for Healthcare Research and Quality (AHRQ)**: "Health services research examines how people get access to health care, how much care costs, and what happens to patients as a result of this care. The main goals of health services research are to identify the most effective ways to organize, manage, finance, and deliver high quality care; reduce medical errors; and improve patient safety."[6] The diversity of interests and topics is reflected in the range of disciplines from which health services

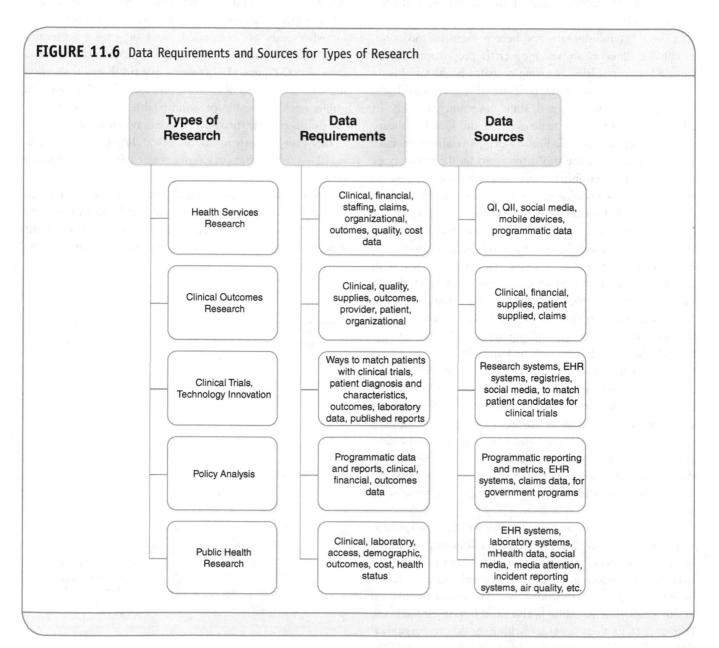

FIGURE 11.6 Data Requirements and Sources for Types of Research

researchers come: medicine, nursing, dentistry, pharmacy, and allied health; social and behavioral sciences; economics and management; epidemiology and biostatistics; information technology and science; and various subdisciplines of engineering. The range of types of data from HIS used to conduct health services research is likewise vast and interdisciplinary—for every niche of clinical care, healthcare setting, clinical specialty, condition, and reimbursement scenario, there is no end to the list of important and interesting topics on which health services research can be conducted. Health services researchers work in universities within schools of public health, medicine, nursing, psychology, sociology, management, and public policy. They work in agencies, organizations, and institutes devoted to the pursuit of new knowledge in all things health care, clinical, process, access, outcomes, public health, and organization related.

Health services researchers provide public and private policy makers, clinicians, healthcare organizations, and others with the latest research findings, methods, and concepts regarding financing, organization, processes, evaluation, systems, and outcomes associated with health services, plus analysis of their relationships to clinical practice, management, and policy. Examples of areas of health services research include the following[7]:

- Issues related to processes and outcomes associated with delivery of care
- Assessments of the impact of or changes in specific policies and interventions on healthcare delivery—for example, Medicare and Medicaid, and other payment policies and programs
- Evaluation of disease prevention, chronic disease management, and community-based efforts to integrate services or promote health
- Impact of adoption of health information technologies in healthcare and public health organizations
- Changes in health services organizations, systems of care, and payment mechanisms, as assessed through local, regional, state, national, and international comparisons
- Study of health care, including social, political, behavioral, and biological factors, as influencers or determinants of health outcomes

Additionally, health services research provides a mechanism for linking various disciplines engaged in such research and disseminating results to those charged with improving the health of individuals and communities as well as setting evidence-based policy. Examples of types of HIS that provide

data for this research include EHR systems, patient billing/claims systems, case mix systems, and quality management systems. Increasingly, data are also being created and captured through the "quantified self" movement—that is, use of personal mobile devices to track individuals' own health conditions and enable them to participate actively in the management of their own health and medical conditions, such as diabetes, obesity, and other chronic conditions. Because these vast research objectives create an enormous demand for data from source HIS, they encourage data stewardship and definition of needed data elements. This guides users of EHRs and other HIS to carefully define, create, and capture the specific data elements needed for research, and to do so by building these data elements directly into clinical and administrative workers' workflows, thereby creating and capturing the necessary data as a by-product of the ongoing care and work processes. This is an example of building systems not just to meet the immediate needs of providing patient care and administrative support functions, but also by thinking through all needs for data. Thoughtful design, implementation, and updating of HIS ensures their roles as excellent data sources for secondary purposes such as research, policy, and public health. In other words, as stated in Stephen Covey's oft-quoted Rule 2 in *The 7 Habits of Highly Effective People*, "Begin with the end in mind."[8] In doing so, HIS and technology can be designed to hardwire the support of necessary clinical and administrative workflows and processes, while simultaneously establishing the ability to create and capture data for many purposes.

Clinical Outcomes Research and Types of Data Requirements/Sources

What is clinical **outcomes research**? Clinical outcomes research studies the end results of medical care—the effect of healthcare processes on the health and well-being of patients and populations.[9] Who is interested? Who conducts outcomes research? Outcomes research is accomplished by clinicians and healthcare provider organizations; universities and teaching institutions with schools of medicine, nursing, dentistry, and public health; health services research organizations such as the Agency for Healthcare Research and Quality, Institute of Medicine, National Cancer Institute, and Institute for Healthcare Improvement; health plans and insurance companies; employers; private companies such as pharmaceutical and life sciences firms; state and federal governments; and consumers. In short, outcomes research evaluates the results of healthcare, therapeutic, and clinical processes in the real-life world of healthcare providers such as hospitals, health systems, physician practices, university teaching hospitals, clinics, long-term care, public health organizations, and other are settings including the home.[7]

Clinical outcomes research requires data that can be provided from HIS, including clinical, quality, supplies, outcomes, provider, patient, and organizational data. The sources of such data include Quadrants I, II, and III systems, including EHR systems, which provide clinical, financial, supplies, patient-supplied, and claims/billing data.

Clinical Trials and Data Requirements/Sources

Clinical trials are early-stage research about new therapies and drugs, with the conduct of these studies following the pure science research phase that includes controlled experiments of potential new drugs and treatments. The results of these trials help determine whether the drug's or therapy's developer will do further studies, pursue FDA approval, and potentially bring that drug or therapy to the healthcare market. The relationship between clinical trials and HIS centers on identifying ways to match patients with the clinical trials, patient diagnoses and characteristics, outcomes, laboratory data, and reports of other studies published in the literature.

Sources of data required for such studies and clinical trials include primary data collected through experiments; HIS data sources such as EHR systems; surveys; claims databases; registries of patients with certain conditions such as cancer or diabetes; social media; websites; and other means to match patient candidates with appropriate clinical research.

The number of new clinical trials and case reports being conducted and published each year has been increasing significantly over the past decades. Since the 1950s, the number of clinical trials has steadily grown, with 27,000 clinical trial reports now published each year; the number of case reports now exceeds 150,000 per year, or 3000 case reports per week (**Figure 11.7**).[10] Keeping up with this volume of new information (published as reports of clinical trials or case reports) relevant to one's area of research is infeasible for any individual practitioner, so systems are needed to help organize, store, search, mine, and access such results and information. HIS in the form of research databases, along with websites focused on certain conditions or organizations, are essential for clinical researchers to glean the needed information and to gain insights into research questions, hypotheses, methods, subject matter, and study design.

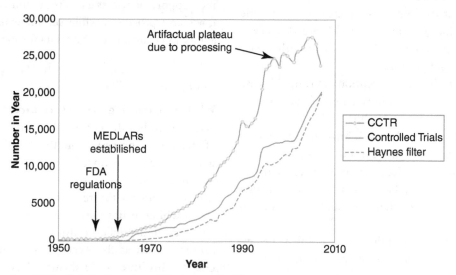

FIGURE 11.7 Clinical Trials (per year, 1950–2007)

Key: CCTR, clinical trials register; MEDLAR, medical literature analysis and retrieval system.

Policy Studies and Types of Data Requirements/Sources

Policy analysis produces reports and recommendations for policy makers at local, state, and national governmental levels. To produce a fully vetted policy recommendation, alternative scenarios and viable possibilities should be addressed. This requires examining the potential alternative approaches to a policy decision and providing evidence-based justification of the recommended alternative. To complete such policy analyses, which are vast in their range of topics, a wide variety of types of data must be available. Each analysis requires the appropriate types of data to support the questions being studied and the alternatives and trade-offs being considered. Because health policy deals with health programs and regulatory issues, many types of data that are useful can come from "workhorse" core HIS in healthcare organizations that support clinical and administrative processes—Quadrant I and II systems, to be exact. Programmatic and quality reporting systems, cost accounting and billing data, and EHR systems all may be viable sources of data for policy studies and analyses, depending on the topics being examined. Study methods must take into account what data are available from a particular source in order to design and perform valid analyses and address research questions in an appropriate manner.

Public Health Inquiry and Research, and Types of Data Requirements/Sources

Public health research covers a vast array of possible subjects and scopes, including all things associated with population health status. Historically, public health has focused on physical health and communicable disease, infectious disease, chronic illness, costs of health care, issues of access, exposure to toxic substances, substance abuse and behavioral problems, traumatic injury, and product and transportation safety. Emerging issues of cosmetic, genetic, and social functioning, as well as global warming, are now drawing attention to concerns such as disasters, climate change, technology and biohazards, and newly emerging infectious diseases.[4(p.9)]

Although the range of issues dealt with at a public health level continually evolves, the common theme is that public health work always has a population's or group's health status, safety, security, reduction of risk, and prevention of disease, injury, or harm in mind. Public health research, therefore, requires a broad range of data types from myriad sources, including clinical, laboratory, access, demographic, environmental, incident, outcomes, cost, health status and other data. These data are available from an increasing number of organizational sources such as EHR systems, laboratory systems, and administrative systems; mHealth data sources such as electronic messaging and social media; sensors from mobile devices; and external sources such as air quality and traffic reports, incident reporting systems, early warning systems, media reports, and environmental alert capabilities. These varied and numerous data sources are evolving along similar lines as public health, to the point now that they, too, converge as shown in Figure 11.5. Leverage points from public health, population health management, *and* healthcare organization perspectives are now better supported by data for research.

Given the increase in numbers and types of HIS serving as sources of data from around the country, it is clear that massive volumes of data are being aggregated in healthcare databases. Web and sensor data from mobile devices used by individuals and person-supplied data are rich new computerized data sources. Soon, genetic data will be even more prominent in healthcare analytics. With emerging evidence-based, patient-reported, customized medicine and health initiatives in addition to widespread adoption of EHR systems, opportunities for public health practitioners to understand and address issues to improve the public's health status, safety, and engagement are plainly in our sights.

Public health and population health management opportunities are also increased by the fact that health information exchanges and interoperability make feasible new scopes of analysis by local, regional, state, national, and global communities. Technical and data standards such as **Logical Observation Identifiers Names and Codes (LOINC)** and **Systematized Nomenclature of Medicine—Clinical Terms (SNOMED)** increase the types of data that may be compared among organizations. Evolving natural language processing capabilities born from LOINC and SNOMED are allowing analysts to mine data formerly "trapped" within narrative documentation contained in EHR systems and other HIS. Tools such as Notifiable Condition Detector mine and conduct predictive analytics on these data, yielding greater value than was previously possible.[11] Through such data-driven analysis, public health can be bolstered and perhaps transformed, just as healthcare organizations can be disrupted through the widespread implementation of EHR systems, data warehouses, and new technologies to mine these data. The greater dimensions of the new data and technical capabilities will increasingly allow for more precise and timely creation of predictive information and research findings.

To further understand the relationship of HIS to public health information and research, we must understand the categories of sources for these additional types of data—the so-called **Six S's of Sources of Public Health Data**.

Six S's of Sources of Public Health Data

Like all of health care, public health is a data- and information-intensive activity. HIS can provide support for several of six sources of public health data used for public health activities as outlined in Dr. Richard Riegelman's text, *Public Health 101: Healthy People—Healthy Populations*: single case or small series, statistics, survey sampling, self-reporting, sentinel monitoring, and syndromic surveillance.[4(p.43)] For some of these sources, HIS are highly relevant; for others, less so. Looking at each source of data included in the Six S's, HIS opportunities can be identified that illustrate the relationship of such systems to these important data that enable public health informatics, monitoring, and communications to take place. Generally speaking, modern HIS—enhanced with interoperability, mHealth, connectivity, and more—provide opportunities for tremendously positive change in the outreach and information accessibility needed to support public health efforts. Next, we look at the Six S's of Sources of Public Health Data one at a time and describe types of HIS that can provide support to each.

Single Case or Small Series

Alerts to new or increased cases of new, rare, or resistant diseases can be flagged in EHR and other clinical systems at hospitals, laboratories, clinics, and physician practices. Once they are confirmed, notification may be sent electronically to public health agencies for proper reporting and follow-up.

Statistics (Vital Statistics and Reportable Diseases)

The timeliness of certain statistics, which are required to be collected by law, can be improved by HIS set up to report on selected data already housed in EHR systems. Examples include births, deaths and their causes, and infectious and chronic diseases. Once the EHR system or other HIS is programmed to flag the data that are desired for reporting, the actual reporting and communication of those data become part of the computer-supported workflow of healthcare organizations, which can be helpful for public health purposes.

Surveys and Sampling

These sources of data include automated or manual surveys for end users. HIS are typically not set up to perform this type of activity, although many tools exist now for conducting automated surveys enabled by electronic connectivity via the Internet and other communication networks, making this type of data gathering much easier.

Self-Reporting

Although call centers are often used for this type of reporting, the Internet offers another option for reporting side effects or unusual events for those persons receiving vaccines or taking medicines. Automated support will likely improve reporting, but the same issues of self-selection in actually reporting an event are present. Wireless communications, smartphones, mobile devices, and other technologies allow for more self-reporting of data to occur.

Sentinel Monitoring

Collaboration between public health agencies and healthcare institutions can facilitate reporting of early warnings of events or disease outbreaks, such as influenza, through flags set up in EHR systems. Such flagging or reporting does not automatically happen in EHR systems; rather, it must be set up explicitly during the design, programming, and implementation of a new system (or added as enhanced functionality).

Syndromic Surveillance

New diseases or undiagnosed conditions can be detected through analytics, filters, and predictive capabilities from data gathered of flagged in EHR systems and other computers, including via social media. These types of predictive analytics capabilities are shown as Quadrants III and IV in the HIS planning framework, as example systems (BI/CI systems). Such clinical intelligence systems include predictive capabilities based on a number of symptoms or isolated data points, thereby giving an early warning of a potential new epidemic or bioterrorism event.

An encouraging trend being studied by researchers seeks to refine ways for public health officials to access and use the same clinical decision support tools (part of EHR systems) that are being implemented in hospitals, clinics, and medical offices for care of patients. Methods include (1) using secure Internet connections to broadcast public health information through **health alert networks (HANs)** and (2) building public health alerts into EHR systems' clinical support capabilities. HANs create two-way communication paths between public health professionals who have detected an emerging public health threat and clinicians who can then query the EHR system to see if their patients fit those criteria. This can help clinicians zero in on appropriate diagnostics and treatments for their patients based on the public health alerts, such as a chemical spill or water-borne illness that might be the cause of the symptoms they are seeing in their patients.[12] These types of HIS capabilities support collaborations between clinicians and public health professionals; they must continue to be developed and refined to achieve widespread adoption, but examples of them are increasing.

Population Health Management: Goals of Healthcare Organizations and Public Health Converge

The distinction between the goals of health provider organizations (providing care delivered in organizations such as hospitals and other healthcare settings) and the goals of public health is now becoming less delineated: These two domains are converging through their mutual interest in managing the health of a population. Public health's goal is to monitor and improve the health status of the population; a healthier population, in turn, helps healthcare organizations control the cost of caring for each individual. From the viewpoint of a healthcare organization, a population is usually defined as the community of patients otherwise connected to a certain healthcare provider, an insured population, or even the employees of a self-insured healthcare organization. That healthcare organization's goal is to *manage* the health risks of that population while providing for their healthcare needs as cost-effectively as possible, given that the organization (including those participating in an ACO for Medicare patients) is now *at risk* for the quality and cost per insured person for all care needed by and provided to that population. Public health's mission lines up with population health management—the missions from both these perspectives are to improve the health status of at-risk groups and the population overall. They share this goal, with population health management being more connected with specific groups such as insured populations cared for by particular healthcare organizations, and public health being associated more with the overall citizenry population and its demographic (e.g., teenagers, the elderly) and geographic (e.g., inner city, rural) subgroups and less geared toward patient groups.

Clearly, the intentions and purposes of healthcare organizations and public health overlap at this public health leverage point of population health management—preventing injury and illness, managing risk factors for chronic disease (e.g., diabetes) as well as acute illness (e.g., measles), and improving the overall health status of the population. This chapter's theme of convergence of healthcare provider organizations and public health shows this overlap and the area of public health leverage points—areas identified in the population at which provider organizations and public health agencies intervene to accomplish shared goals. Today, when so many health issues are behavior and lifestyle oriented, the leverage arena becomes population health management, which works best when accomplished through the convergence between healthcare organizations and public health. As healthcare organizations strive to help their patients prevent or manage chronic illness and other health risk factors, they intersect with the public health mission to monitor and improve the population's overall health status through prevention. With chronic diseases dominating the health status landscape, the good news is that 80% of chronic illness is preventable.[4(p.99)] The bad news is that chronic illnesses are occurring in increasing proportions of the population, to the point that 70% of deaths in the United States each year are caused by chronic diseases.[13] These statistics highlight the need for a strong relationship between healthcare provider organizations such as hospitals and physician practices, and institutions of public health.

To deal with this crisis, public health agencies and government have stepped up with programs, awareness campaigns, and interventions. When the private sector does not deal with an issue effectively, is not in a position to deal with a health-impacting issue, or creates a problem that harms the public's health (the problem may be biological, systemic, or organizational), public health agencies and government organizations must act. An example of one such public health approach taken by the government is to intervene with comprehensive legislation (think ACA and HITECH) to begin reorienting the current U.S. health system, which is currently centered on medical care and sickness, toward preventive services and wellness. This systemic approach targets the intrinsic problem reflected in the types of health and medical services that healthcare organizations have traditionally focused on—reimbursable services centered on the medical model of treating disease rather than preserving and maintaining health. Surely we need both, but with a much greater emphasis on prevention than currently exists. This is the only way forward to stop the deteriorating overall health status of the U.S. population and reshape the U.S. healthcare system into one that is affordable and sustainable. Our future depends on it!

Because population health management by healthcare organizations focuses on wellness and prevention (previously the domain of public health) in addition to medical care (with its focus on "cure"), connectivity between providers and patients across the continuum of care is essential. Thankfully, the information infrastructure needed to accomplish this approach is now feasible. It does, however, require new types of HIS and skills in using data that healthcare organizations have not developed to date except in rare instances, such as at the Regenstrief Institute in Indianapolis, Indiana. We are at an important juncture in history—a time when healthcare organizations both *see* and *accept* the importance of population health management to improving clinical outcomes and their bottom lines by improving the health status of communities and populations. As the crisis of rampant chronic disease awakens the sleeping giant called the U.S. health system, healthcare organizations and public health initiatives have an opportunity to gain ground through the use of information capabilities that can be tapped into for synergistic public health purposes, such as the clinical decision support surveillance example described previously.

HIS and IT capabilities needed for population health management center on EHR systems, to be sure, but EHR systems are not enough. Also needed are data connections outside the boundaries of healthcare organizations, to the person—at his or her home, office, school, and other places of daily activities, where careful management of risk factors and behavioral habits that influence the person's health status can take place. Meaningful Use criteria for interoperability notwithstanding, commercially available EHR systems are not designed to interoperate or share data with other systems, let alone be open to patient-entered data or integrate with mobile devices from a "quantified self" perspective. Thus the connection between healthcare organizations and "nodes" on a person's daily healthcare "network" does not exist today. Vendors of EHR systems, as well as suppliers of mobile devices, social media sources, wireless connectivity, and web-enabled systems, must also adapt to a new model and enable sharing, securing, and aggregation of these data. Such requirements pose significant challenges to the HIS capabilities of healthcare organizations, whose core clinical and business systems are not built with interoperability or data exchange in mind.

Additional information requirements for the population health management strategy include predictive analytics, to help clinicians, researchers, and public health officials anticipate who might be at risk for chronic conditions such as heart disease or diabetes, and then reach out to those who may not be seeking care even before they have manifested any detectable symptom or sign. This type of predictive analytics capability moves healthcare providers and organizations from the position of being reactive to being predictive and hopefully then preventive, thereby allowing more proactive management of health, risk, and chronic illness.

Such a predictive information capability is being sought by many health systems, but is clearly still in the developmental stages in most organizations, as is the ability of people working within those organizations to use such information to implement and manage a population health management initiative.[14] Ideally, healthcare providers and public health organizations will move from reactive to predictive and ultimately to preventive capabilities as we learn to anticipate and better manage health risks and illnesses among the populations served.

Examples of governmental policies that can have a dramatic effect on healthcare organizations and public health are the policy changes enacted through healthcare reform—namely, the Accountable Care Act (ACA) of 2010 and the HITECH Act, enacted under Title XIII of ARRA of 2009. Among other things, these two pieces of legislation have provided the platform for healthcare reform by shifting the focus of healthcare organizations toward keeping people healthy. They have increased adoption of clinical care's modern tools of automation to improve quality and cost of care. They have also provided major financial incentives for adoption of EHR systems and implementation of interoperability between systems necessary to accomplish the population health management goal. This shift is realigning healthcare organizations to be more in tune with public health objectives and purposes. The aims of these reforms are to reduce overall costs and increase the effectiveness of healthcare dollars spent, by keeping healthy people healthy and helping those who are already chronically ill to better manage their diseases through direct engagement between patients, providers, and healthcare organizations.[15]

Prior to ACA and HITECH, the U.S. government made several attempts to shift the culture and business of the overall healthcare system toward prevention as well as medical care. These initiatives over the years have included establishment of health maintenance organizations dating from the Nixon administration in the 1970s, introduction of prospective payment systems and diagnosis-related groups in 1983, and emergence of capitation and managed care frameworks of the 1990s and current times. Today, as a response to the overwhelming shift in health status of the U.S. population toward greater prevalence of chronic illness—diabetes, obesity, heart disease, and other lifestyle-related illnesses—the government has endeavored to shift the focus of healthcare providers and organizations to prevention and chronic disease management. The ACA and ARRA/HITECH laws reward health provider organizations through financial incentives (in the form of increased Medicare and Medicaid reimbursement) if provider organizations can demonstrate less costly, more effective ways to care for chronically ill patients and address risk factors preventively and proactively. This proactive approach stands in contrast to the practice of waiting for patients to become so ill from their chronic conditions that they must be treated in hospitals in the later stages of these diseases. In turn, provider organizations are reorganizing the delivery of services into service lines and strategically aligning physicians and physician compensation with those services lines to create greater value for patients and better outcomes for dollars spent.[16] Trying to "treat" chronic illness in the hospital setting is neither effective nor efficient, because by the time someone is so sick that he or she must go to the hospital, the condition is likely to be so advanced that most treatments are targeted at controlling symptoms of the disease and only limited measures can be taken to "cure" it. Moreover, medical and pharmaceutical treatments intended to arrest further progression of chronic diseases can be expensive, invasive, riddled with side effects, and difficult to sustain.

The latest government regulations offer incentives to provider organizations to expand their focus to prevention and wellness in addition to the traditional provision of necessary medical care for acute care needs, such as when a patient is acutely ill or injured and needs inpatient care. Providers receive additional payments for demonstrating cost savings and quality improvements in outcomes through this new set of reimbursement mechanisms. Thus, providers are financially encouraged to engage in population health management, the goals of which are to help healthy people stay healthy and help people with chronic medical conditions manage these illnesses effectively through active, ongoing engagement between clinicians and patients.

This new environment of changed organizational goals, a focus on prevention, payment incentives for maintaining health and managing chronic illness, and incentives to implement EHR in concert with other systems to support these initiatives creates compensation metrics centered on quality, access, and patient satisfaction. How healthcare organizations are paid has always significantly influenced the types of services provided. Because the government is the largest payer for health services through Medicare, Medicaid, and other programs, and because its reimbursement policies drive private insurance practices, changing federal reimbursement policies is a very effective way to change practices in healthcare organizations. To remain viable, organizations must maintain positive financial margins to provide sufficient capital to keep facilities updated and invest in new programs

and technologies, as well as pay their employees fairly and competitively. Otherwise, they cannot build new facilities when needed, retain a strong, well-trained workforce, bring the best new technologies for providing modern standards of care into their organization, and maintain a relevant, leading position in their communities. Today, financial pressures exerted by the government are even greater because the U.S. population is aging and the number of patients covered by the Medicare and Medicaid programs is increasing. (Importantly, treating non-Medicare-covered patients differently from Medicare-covered patients is not allowed, meaning providers cannot reduce the types and amount of care received by Medicare-insured patients compared to patients with private insurance, even when the Medicare reimbursement may be less than a private policy might provide.) Because healthcare organizations are realizing their future financial well-being now relies on keeping people healthy and managing chronic illness in less costly settings than hospitals, healthcare providers are changing their ways.

Providers are putting population health management practices into place, with the goal of managing chronic illness more proactively and thus effectively—managing these conditions by controlling risk factors and other preventive measures that are often behavioral in origin. With chronic and behavior-driven illness, it is essential to remember that grandmother was right: An ounce of prevention is worth a pound of cure. Attacking these conditions in their preclinical state, *before* a person is sick enough to require expensive drugs and hospitalization, results in managing these risk factors and conditions more efficiently in lower cost settings such as primary care practices and the home. Care is more effective in an engaged patient–provider relationship that connects clinicians to people in their homes, workplaces, and daily lives. HIS and related technology, analytics, and connectivity through mobile technology and EHR system support may all be marshaled to provide the enabling technology to connect people in their daily lives with providers in ways that fit the profile of today's health and medical conditions.

The impact of policy and regulations on healthcare organizations is pushing them closer to many of the objectives of public health organizations in additional ways. The scope of public health includes education and community-wide activities outside the range of services that typically go on in healthcare provider organizations (dealing, for example, with issues such as climate change and food safety). Public health's national biosurveillance efforts—such as gathering data from numerous data sources or monitoring infection rates at local healthcare organizations—can assist provider organizations in pinpointing air, chemical, or foodborne diagnoses or preparing for response to natural disaster. In this way, one can see the need for collaboration between healthcare provider organizations and public health agencies and initiatives for numerous health and safety issues.

AREAS DESERVING SPECIAL ATTENTION THAT RELY ON HIS MANAGEMENT

Comparative Effectiveness Research

Comparative effectiveness research (CER) is an area of study that can be applied to all three domains discussed in this chapter: research, policy, and public health. This type of research includes (1) studies of collections of evidence about benefits and risks of various approaches to health care, treatments, processes, and clinical services for different conditions, groups, and populations based on currently available published literature, clinical trials, and research studies; and (2) studies that produce new evidence about the effectiveness of treatments, processes, tests, or services.[17]

The goal of CER is to provide the best possible synthesis of research results to clinicians and others in healthcare organizations so that these findings may be put to use.[18] CER results are also helpful to policy makers who build these results into recommendations and criteria such as Meaningful Use criteria or other guidelines. CER is based on comparative effectiveness; the comparative effectiveness of various treatments, processes, and approaches to care is based on assessment of the benefits and risks of one method relative to other methods, not relative to some absolute metric. Existing evidence regarding benefits or risks associated with treatments and methods forms the baseline. Thus, the result of a comparative analysis is a relative value, and is only as good as the methods used for this type of analysis. This is important to remember when interpreting results from CER studies. Such results are just what the name says—comparative; they are based on the best current evidence and metrics, understanding that additional findings will surely emerge with time.

CER relates to HIS and technology on a number of levels. First, data for CER studies often come from HIS used in healthcare organizations, especially EHR systems and patient billing systems. The greater availability of clinical data elements at a granular level from EHR systems now makes this type of research more feasible than it was in the past, when healthcare data consisted of predominantly claims and billing data. The current monumental push associated with ARRA and HITECH to implement EHR systems in hospitals and

physician practices *improves* the availability of clinical data for those entities using data for secondary purposes. It is important to remember, though, that we are early in the EHR systems implementation and adoption curve: Most EHR systems are immature in terms of the types and amounts of data they contain on patients. Additionally, putting new evidence from CER into practice is a challenge—something easier said than done. HIS and EHR systems in particular can be helpful in this regard as well, because guidelines, reminders, choices from drop-down lists, alerts, and other system features can be used to build evidence, checklists, or other means of improvements into the clinical workflow, by making them part of the EHR system's basic functionality.

Thus, HIS play both primary and secondary roles in supporting the accomplishment of CER and bridging the gap from theory into practice. Enacting change in clinical and administrative processes is always a challenge, as busy healthcare practitioners are well trained in doing things in certain ways. Changing the way they do things requires time, effort, and dialogue about evidence supporting the change, as well as collaboration and attentive patience.

Reasons for slowness or incomplete adoption of evidence-based practices emanating from the CER literature in some ways resemble barriers to adoption of EHR systems. These reasons include misaligned financial incentives, in which reimbursement systems reward old or non-evidence-based ways of doing things, such as the fee-for-service reimbursement system paying for invasive treatments when more conservative or educational-based approaches (which are *not* well rewarded by the traditional fee-for-service reimbursement methodology) may be just as effective. Vague results of CER also hamper adoption and may result in lack of consensus about the interpretation and appropriate action based on those diverse interpretations. Additionally, differing methods of thought and belief systems can influence how evidence is interpreted; for example, when marketing for certain drugs has been heavy or educational programs have convinced a clinician early in his or her training that pharmaceutical approaches are best, it may be difficult for that clinician to accept an alternative method, even if the evidence supports that change. Likewise, change can be difficult if the interpreter of this evidence-based approach prefers action responses to inaction or believes that a technology-driven process is inherently better than a non-technology-driven process. CER studies also might not meet the needs of people actually doing the work, whose goals might be different than the goals of those who might benefit from change downstream. A lack of use or non-availability of clinical decision support systems that might support the use of a new evidence-based practice may halt CER implementation: It often requires real-time information inputs to help the clinician assess trade-offs or nuances in any given situation.[18]

Because EHR systems will provide data for many CER studies, it is important to realize that the current immaturity of many EHR implementations and the resulting data issues and limitations may compromise these studies in the near term. Such issues occur in areas such as data definition variability, data inaccuracy, and incompleteness of data populating the EHR system database. Next, we address these issues individually.

Data Definition Variability

Data definition variability occurs when the actual values of a data element with the same name vary between systems. For example, time to medication in an emergency situation might be defined as time from registration to time of medication administration versus time from triage to time of medication administration. Comparing these two times, given that the values represent different metrics but are called the same thing, would lead to inaccurate conclusions regarding this quality measure for emergency care. Data standards for important metrics like this are helpful in creating consistency in how they are measured, but great care must be taken in their implementation to ensure practice matches definition.

Alternatively, data elements with the same purpose coming from different sources may have different names, making it difficult to combine these data elements to study a larger data set representing different types of organizations or settings. For example, the patient name might be contained in a data element labeled "Patient name" in one EHR system, "Member identifier" in another system, and "Patient ID" in yet another system. This type of problem requires normalizing data elements from various systems to ensure that all data elements with like purposes or definitions are combined properly into the total set for that data element.

In another example, data from 10 separate EHR systems might be combined to do a new study on type 2 diabetes. In four of those systems, primary diagnosis might be coded as an ICD-9 code; in one system, it might be an ICD-10 code; in two systems, type 2 diabetes might be designated with a billing code or special research code; and in three systems, it might be coded in combination with other diagnoses. Clearly, normalizing all those data so they are comparable must precede the actual analysis related to type 2 diabetes.

Data Inaccuracy

EHR data are no better than the care with which they are entered by busy clinicians and the ways the EHR system features and functions interface with these knowledge workers. Thus data accuracy is influenced by the clinician's available time and attention to data completeness, accuracy, understandability, consistency, and accessibility as well as the EHR system's handling of those data. For example, for data to be accessible, they cannot be entered into a free-text field that the system is not set up to read and access for alerts or reports. The exception to this concern would be if the healthcare organization has a natural-language processor or IT system (which is rare indeed).

Data Incompleteness

EHR systems do not consistently have data elements recorded or entered by end users into every available data field. Owing to clinician time constraints, urgent clinical situations, and varying interest in data entry tasks, many data fields in a given EHR—unless required by unpopular full stops of the screen progressions that persist until a data field is completed—are likely to be left empty or incomplete. Also, EHRs often do not house the complete clinical picture of a patient's story. The scope of an EHR is often restricted to just the institution that implemented it, such as a hospital or physician practice; that institution's EHR, however, may not include important data about that patient from other settings. Given that each institutional setting typically has an EHR system that records data only from that institution, significant portions of the patient's overall clinical picture may be split into various institutions' EHRs. For example, in a hospital's busy emergency department or surgical suite, just the data absolutely needed to progress through the screens might be all that is filled out on an emergency department registration screen used by the harried registration clerk or triage nurse, or by a surgical nurse during an emergency surgery. Of course, this means there will be "holes" in the data available to clinicians for patient care purposes and secondary uses, such as quality measurement or outcomes research. This issue is just like when one signs up for a new website and certain data fields are required and others are not—the required fields tend to be the only ones filled out when the user is pressed for time.

Other Data Issues

Data are often coded for purposes of billing, not to reflect purely clinical activities; therefore, it may not be valid to use these billing data for clinical research. Often relevant clinical observations or patient-supplied data are not codified for billing purposes because these are tied to a reimbursable item. These EHR data embedded in narrative clinical documentation or in special "notes" fields may not be able to be automatically captured for analysis as discrete data elements. EHR data may also consist of data originating from multiple data sources, which may vary from EHR to EHR, such as laboratory, pharmacy, and radiology management systems. Another potential complication is the level of specificity of EHR data, which may not match the data requirements of the research. Lastly, the needs of research studies may differ from the processes and documentation needs for clinical care, such that while EHR systems may contain the data elements necessary for care, they may not contain the data elements needed to answer the research questions being asked.[19]

It is not the intention of EHR designers and implementers to saddle busy clinicians with these data problems that are experienced by those who are making secondary use of EHR data, but on a practical level, this is often what happens. Clearly, the primary purpose of EHR systems is to support patient care. Moreover, researchers have long been able to figure out appropriate ways to make use of "imperfect" data without compromising the validity and confidence associated with the research results. Nevertheless, many clinicians criticize EHR system designs because the workflows built into these systems require clinicians to perform many of the clerical tasks formerly handled by clerical staff (such as ward clerks). This adds stress and time to the work of clinicians, most of whom are already feeling the pressures of busy schedules and understaffed clinical settings. This clerical burden can also be a source of dissatisfaction for patients when the patient feels the loss of the clinician's attention on account of focusing on the computer system. If a clinician must decide between attending to the keyboard or to a patient who is in pain, bleeding, upset, or otherwise in need of attention, it is always the correct decision to attend to the patient. This, of course, makes EHR data entry difficult. To solve this problem, many organizations are inserting "physician scribes" into the process, staff who enter data as instructed by the physician during the patient interaction so the physician can focus on the patient interaction and examination. Future EHR systems must address these issues of data entry and make the interface between the people using the computers and the EHR system easier and more efficient than typing on a keyboard. It is imperative to do what we can to be more inventive in

our ways of ensuring accurate and complete data in the EHR systems, and not just to satisfy the needs of researchers: Excellent patient care requires a complete, confidential, and accurate patient record for safety reasons, first and foremost.

Ultimately, healthcare organizations and providers, public health organizations, and the entire U.S. health system are striving to become less reactive and more proactive. We will delve further into this notion of proactive versus reactive health care in another chapter, which examines future directions of HIS and technology in the U.S. health system.

SUMMARY

A significant relationship exists between HIS and technology and the outermost sphere of the HIS model: research, policy, and public health. The foundational layer of the HIS model, HIS and management, provides the source systems and data needed to fuel the activities of research, policy, and public health. Conversely, research, policy, and public health provide crucial feedback to HIS and their management so that insights gained and lessons learned from these disciplines can be embedded into the systems that support patient care and the daily transactions of healthcare processes. Thus, a mutual relationship exists between each of the domains of research, policy, and public health and the HIS that support them.

Several types of clinical and outcomes research may be conducted, each of which gets supporting data from a variety of sources. Policy research derives its source data from an equally diverse set of data sources, and public health research relies on data sources from many settings, including healthcare organizations, individual occurrences of reportable events, and population-level views of health and health status.

The interests of healthcare organizations and agencies of public health are converging in their mutual focus on health status and prevention of disease. Healthcare organizations and providers are both the targets and the recipients of new incentives in payment systems from the government and private payers, as the government attempts to stem the rising tide of healthcare costs and preventable disease prevalence. New types of HIS emphasizing EHR systems, CER, and business intelligence/clinical intelligence (BI/CI) are being implemented across the United States to provide essential data, information, and analytics along with hope for improved quality and cost performance, all while changing our approach to health and health care from reactive to proactive and preventive.

KEY TERMS

© Johan Swanepoel/
Shutterstock, Inc.

Discussion Questions

1. Describe the relationship of foundational HIS to the research, policy, and public health layer in the HIS model. In which ways are these two reliant on each other? List at least three ways.

2. Source systems providing data for the domains of research, policy, and public health are found in a variety of settings. What do these settings have in common, and how do they differ? Describe source systems for each area.

3. In which ways are the interests and goals of healthcare organizations and public health converging? How does HIS play a role in supporting these mutual interests and goals?

4. Comparative effectiveness research (CER) is the compilation and meta-analysis of multiple pieces of research in particular areas of study. Do you think it is a good idea to look at all research results and identify the *relative* effectiveness of various treatments and approaches to care? Why or why not?

5. EHR systems provide much-needed clinical data for research, policy, and public health activities. Name several concerns about data provided from EHR systems. Are these concerns well founded? Why or why not? What will improve these problems with this very important source of data for research, policy, and public health questions, analyses, and programs?

REFERENCES

1. American University, Writing Center. (n.d.). Tips for writing a policy analysis. http://www.american.edu/cas/writing/pdf/upload/Writing-a-Policy-Analysis.pdf

2. Medicaid.gov. (n.d.). Information from Children's Health Insurance Program (CHIP). http://www.medicaid.gov/Medicaid-CHIP-Program-Information/By-Topics/Childrens-Health-Insurance-Program-CHIP/Childrens-Health-Insurance-Program-CHIP.html

3. Hospital Compare: The official U.S. government website for Medicare. (n.d.). About hospital compare data. http://www.medicare.gov/hospitalcompare/Data/About.html

4. Riegelman, R. (2010). *Public Health 101: Healthy people–healthy populations.* Sudbury, MA: Jones and Bartlett.

5. McCullough, J. C., Zimmerman, F. J., Fielding, J. E., & Teutsch, S. M. (2012). A health dividend for America: The opportunity cost of excess medical expenditures. *American Journal of Preventive Medicine, 43*(6), 650–654.

6. Agency for Healthcare Research and Quality. (n.d.). Health outcomes research: A primer. http://www.academyhealth.org/files/publications/healthoutcomes.pdf

7. Health Services Research. (n.d.). Impacting health practice and policy through state-of-the-art research and thinking: Instructions for authors and statement of editorial policy. http://www.hsr.org/hsr/information/authors/instrucauthors.jsp

8. Covey, S. R. (n.d.). The 7 habits of highly effective people. https://www.stephencovey.com/7habits/7habits-habit2.php

9. Agency for Healthcare Research and Quality. (n.d.). Outcomes research. http://www.ahrq.gov/research/findings/factsheets/outcomes/outfact/index.htm

10. Chang, D. C., & Talamini, M. A. (2011, February 27). A review for clinical outcomes research: Hypothesis generation, data strategy, and hypothesis-driven statistical analysis. *Surgical Endoscopy.* http://www.ncbi.nlm.nih.gov/pmc/articles/PMC3116115/

11. Khan, I. (2013, August 3). Big Data is healthcare's biggest threat and also its likely savior. http://gigaom.com/2013/08/03/big-data-is-healthcares-biggest-threat-and-also-its-likely-savior/

12. Agency for Healthcare Research and Quality. (2014, January). Public health may benefit from computer-based clinical decision support: Health information technology. http://www.ahrq.gov/news/newsletters/research-activities/14jan/0114RA25.html

13. Centers for Disease Control and Prevention. (n.d.). Chronic diseases and health promotion. http://www.cdc.gov/chronicdisease/overview/index.htm

14. Cassidy, B. (n.d.). The next HIM frontier: Population health information management presents a new opportunity for HIM. http://library.ahima.org/xpedio/groups/public/documents/ahima/bok1_050281.hcsp?dDocName=bok1_050281

15. Lewis, N. (2012, April 30). Population health management requires better IT tools. *InformationWeek.* http://www.informationweek.com/healthcare/clinical-systems/population-health-management-requires-be/232901120

16. Physician compensation models and metrics under population-based reimbursement. (2013, August 29). *Health Leaders Media* webcast. http://links.hcpro.mkt4507.com/servlet/MailView?ms=NjQzODYwNgS2&r=ODk0MTc4MjEzOQS2&j=NzY4MjcxMTUS1&mt=1&rt=0

17. Agency for Healthcare Research and Quality. (n.d.). What is comparative effectiveness research? http://effectivehealthcare.ahrq.gov/index.cfm/what-is-comparative-effectiveness-research1/

18. Timbie1, J. W., Fox, D. S., Van Busum, K., & Schneider, E. C. (2012, October). Five reasons that many comparative effectiveness studies fail to change patient care and clinical practice. *Health Affairs, 31*(10), 2168–2175.

19. Hersh, W. R., Weiner, M. G., Embi, P. J., Logan, J. R., Payne, P. R. O., Bernstam, E. V., et al. (2013, August). Clinical informatics: Caveats for the use of operational electronic health record data in comparative effectiveness research medical care. *51,* S30–S37. http://skynet.ohsu.edu/~hersh/medicalcare-13-caveats.pdf

SECTION VI

New Directions for HIS and Technology

CHAPTER **12**

What Lies Beyond the Current State of HIS and Technology?

UNDERSTANDING THE FUTURE OF HIS AND TECHNOLOGY

As our world rapidly transforms due to advances in technology in noticeable ways in every industry and walk of life, a similar transformation, due to enabling technologies, is occurring in health care and public health—but at the speed of health care. This pace is criticized by some as too slow, but for others it is too fast. In the words of Eric Topol in *The Creative Destruction of Medicine*, the gradual introduction of six major disruptive technologies over the past 40 years

has gotten us to the point where revolutionary change is occurring in medicine and health care (**Figure 12.1**).[1] These disruptive technologies include cell phones, smartphones, personal computers, the Internet, digital/mobile sensors and medical devices, genomic sequencing, and social media or networks.[2]

In the world of health care, we recognize each of these technologies, to be sure; they are used in an increasing variety of ways by clinicians, patients, healthcare and public health workers, researchers, and administrative workers. When something is so pervasive that there is no clear line regarding where, when, by whom, and for what purpose it is used, it is said to have become *ubiquitous*. This is where we are today with technology and health care. This is the **inflection point**, or "hockey stick" moment in the adoption and use of these technologies in health care, medicine, public health, and health.

Interestingly, a second area of transformation is occurring in the actual goals of health care. For the past 50 years, access to medical care has been the name of the game; yet, over these years, the gatekeepers of health insurance coverage were increasingly obstructing this access. What was originally designed as a perk for employees and safeguard for companies to pay for medical care and health benefits became a barrier to the very thing that health insurance is supposed to do: ensure access to health care when needed. This barrier has been gradually erected due to a combination of factors, mostly revolving around attempts to combat accelerated costs associated with the fee-for-service reimbursement method along with the need to maintain profit margins for

FIGURE 12.1 HIS Transformative Technologies and Their Application to Health Care

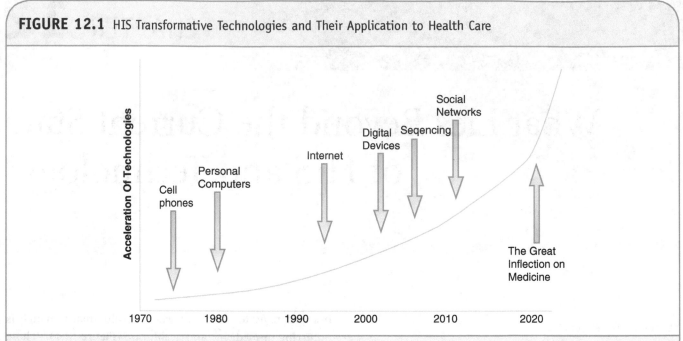

the insurance companies and other entities making up the robust healthcare food chain, including pharmaceutical companies, vendors, suppliers, hospitals, and providers. In this scenario, the financial benefit of the premiums paid to the insurance companies became the guiding principle, rather than what is best for people, patients, and their families.

We have now entered a time in which the rules of this game are starting to change. We are seeing more equitable access to information (a large part of health care and public health) due to changing societal norms and the **ubiquitous availability** of technologies in the hands of most people today, used for myriad purposes of living and learning. What are these technical capabilities and combinations that have had such an enormous effect on the healthcare scene?

Ubiquitous Available Data

"Inflection point." "Tipping point." "Convergence." "Innovation." These terms are commonly used today to indicate the excitement and hope that we are finally *there* in our ability to use new technologies in the modern healthcare and public health arenas, with empowered consumers as patients and people actively connected to clinicians, participating in the management of their health and medical care. Certainly, a great deal of data is floating around in provider organizations, institutions, and homes. In fact, we are awash with data

residing in a staggering number of HIS (many of them still in "silos") in healthcare organizations, personal data stores and access capabilities via the Internet, mobile computing, medical devices, and sensors. We have reached the point where we struggle more with how to make organized sense of all these data than with how to create or gain access to the data, even though access to relevant information that meets the Five Rights (as described elsewhere in the text) remains a problem in many organizations and situations.

Over this same 40 years, healthcare organizations, physician practices, public health agencies, and individuals have hurried to automate, often within a singular domain. The end result has been creation of isolated, disparate data and information silos, lacking perspective, failing at integration, and disregarding the need to coordinate and collaborate in the construction of those systems. This myopic approach to automation has resulted in huge amounts of computing power but very little ability to share those data outside the organizational—or even departmental—boundaries within which these systems were implemented, including a severely limited ability to share a patient's own data with that individual and his or her loved ones.

Add to these the plethora of personalized data created from rapidly emerging mobile devices and sensors, along with Internet-accessible health information, and one can readily see the exponential explosion in the volume of healthcare data. As more data are created, however, we have potentially generated levels of intelligence, specificity, and accessibility inversely proportional to the amount of data available. Better HIS planning, use, analytics, and integration into clinical and business workflows *must* be accomplished to make sense of all these systems and data. This accessibility to myriad sources is sometimes referred to as "Big Data," with an eye being cast toward vast opportunities for new markets, research, improvements in the quality and cost of health care, and development of new knowledge based on intelligence gained from these enormous stores of data. One untoward aspect of the countless, disparate computing systems in health care is the disorganization, disconnectedness, and overall lack of cohesion of health data today.[3] So what does this mean for the future of HIS and technology in health care and public health? A lot!

As we learn how to better coordinate data definitions and implement technical standards, new systems taking a Big Data approach and using flexible "cloud computing" are being developed. This new generation of analytics-oriented HIS, which allows for organizing dashboards and business intelligence/clinical intelligence (BI/CI) systems from a variety of data sources, is emerging with a vengeance. In addition to BI/CI, personal health intelligence is now emerging as part of the "Quantified Self" and digital health movements. As organizations and people become acclimated to ubiquitous technology, they are realizing that these digital resources are the future—and that the organizations that will thrive in the future will be those that best streamline their processes and adapt to these technologies. Cheaper and faster systems; better data, technologies, and devices; more powerful sensors, networks, security, and capacity; advancements in science and medicine such as genomics and nanotechnologies; optimized workflows; virtual care through telehealth and telemedicine; technology-enabled training and education; and personalized health information—these are real opportunities for organizations to innovate, improve, streamline, compete, and ultimately empower and attract people, professionals, customers, businesses, and success. This is now.

Eventually, those who do not adapt in such ways will be outmaneuvered by other businesses and providers, and abandoned by empowered consumers who are experiencing better access and information in other walks of life. This adaptation has already happened in other industries and markets, which in turn is creating demand for those types of capabilities in health care, public health, and personal health. The days of information resting only with the privileged few

with a degree or specialized access to the database or staff of analysts are rapidly becoming the past that, within a few decades, people will talk about incredulously or study in the "history" sections of their coursework.

The future goal of health information is *appropriate access to ubiquitous, personalized, specific information relevant to the situation, available to those who should have access to it, while honoring the privacy, security, and confidentiality of those whose information it is.* Included in this goal is access by patients to data stored in organizations' systems such as electronic health records (EHRs). For example, "open notes" is a hot topic today, where the trend is to let patients see their physicians' notes in their EHR and to support patients in the ability to enter information into their EHR. Patient-provided data is seen as a missing component of current EHR datasets, and this trend embodies true patient engagement. Additional innovations using technology in inpatient settings, such as location tracking, fall prevention, and nurse communications advances, are helping solve long-standing safety and quality of care problems. Service improvement through the use of digital membership cards on which software is running on a smartphone can allow for all sorts of technology integration and consumer-friendly software applications to improve the patient experience. Forward-thinking organizations are using technology to implement service improvements including wayfinding; digital (cell phone) insurance cards; taking copayments online or by a staff member circulating through the admitting and registration areas with mobile credit card receiving capabilities (eliminating the need for patients to stand in lines, and reducing wait times); improving specialty scheduling delays; and other innovations that reduce mistakes, delays, frustrations, and inefficiencies. Through the use of technology, providers are able to place greater emphasis on patient involvement, education, and group therapy help with chronic disease management.

The technology exists today to achieve these improvements and others, but organizations must exert their will to change traditional ways of delivering care and to create, innovate, and make proper use of new information capabilities. How long will it take to make these types of enhanced care and service commonplace? This is difficult to predict. Certainly, we have the software tools and hardware to make it happen today, but inertia can be tough to overcome. Indeed, many of these technologies have been available for decades but have yet to make significant inroads in real-world settings. Thus, until markets and healthcare organizations change, the application of technologies will trundle along in uneven fits and starts of adoption. Once payment mechanisms acknowledge the viability of clinical, business, and personal activities taking place using disruptive technologies such as mobile phones, wireless sensors, and personal monitoring devices, the change will likely happen over a period of years, not decades. Many believe we are approaching the point of inflection in health care and public health—including this author, who has been devoted to this type of work for approximately 30 of those aforementioned 40 years of experience.

The caveat is that professionals who work in these healthcare organizations must learn to work in new ways, and organizations, regulations, and institutions are some of the slowest entities to change.[2] Transforming the healthcare environment may ultimately rely on a generational change. Clearly, realistic expectations must be cultivated and applied when imagining this new vision for health care, public health, and interaction among professionals effectively using health and medical data around the world.

eHEALTH, mHEALTH, SOCIAL MEDIA, AND TELEMEDICINE

eHealth Definition, Progress, and Development

eHealth comprises the technologies supporting an essential shift in methods, attitudes, and actions regarding health and wellness in our society today, often referred to as Health 2.0.[4] As a nation and a world, we are striving to transform our expectations and the healthcare system(s) away from a focus on medicine and "sickness"—of course, necessary at appropriate times—and toward a focus on health. In this "wellness" mindset, people take active roles in managing and maintaining their own health. Health is the essence of what people care about and is ultimately what must be practically managed at the personal level due to its relationship to lifestyle and personal choices. It is also a key to how much medical care individuals eventually need when they reach the stage of vulnerability to chronic illness. More and more, people choose to digest information, including their own health data, interact with providers, and connect through new avenues of technology. Thus a health-oriented organization, the World Health Organization (WHO), defines eHealth as the transfer of health resources and health care by electronic means, encompassing three main areas: (1) the delivery of health information, for health professionals and health consumers, through the Internet and telecommunications; (2) using the power of information technology (IT) and e-commerce to improve public health services, such as through the education and training of health workers;

and (3) the use of e-commerce and e-business practices in health systems management.[5] This wonderful definition encompasses the ultimate goal—a focus on health for people around the world, regardless of their ability to afford insurance or their geographical access to healthcare facilities. It also emphasizes the importance of (1) education, so that people can recognize the relationship between their daily lifestyle habits and their health, and (2) training, to use new electronic means to extend the healthcare workforce and help keep clinical professionals up to date on new information and skills.

eHealth encompasses a broad scope of electronic capabilities used for health and medicine. It includes organizationally based systems such as EHR systems and other HIS and technology, as well as collaboration spaces for researchers to share data and methods, **mHealth**, uses of social media for health and medical purposes, **telemedicine**, and **telehealth**. "Digital health" is another term used to capture these purposes and technologies.

Historically, the major focus has been on medical (or sickness) care, but today's predominant health concerns—which, if left untended, may develop into illness—are more often rooted in lifestyle and everyday behaviors and must be addressed individual by individual, day by day, community by community, where and how we live. This is where eHealth comes in: It provides ubiquitous systems and infrastructure to connect clinicians with people, wherever they are, and when they are healthy as well as sick. One innovative way to adapt healthcare settings to be in closer proximity to where people live is by placing contemporary but small storefronts in retail outlets and at employer sites where people can easily stop in and get non-urgent care. HIS and technology provide the connectivity and necessary information support to make these sites small but viable and convenient healthcare settings. Both good health practices and good medicine are essential to health.

Progress in eHealth is advancing steadily, sometimes carefully through a maze of regulations needed to protect patient privacy. For instance, most medical and nursing schools are training their students to practice their disciplines using electronic systems, such as EHRs. However, this process is hampered by inflexible EHR systems and privacy regulations limiting their use by students.[6] Advances in personalized medicine and patient involvement depend on federal efforts to promote the evolving use of EHRs by revisiting barriers or challenges to individuals' gaining direct access to their health information. Barriers are being removed one by one when appropriate, such as recently overturned privacy legislation that had prohibited direct patient access to lab results.[7] This type of change, which was advocated by patient groups, laboratories, and EHR vendors, will allow patients to play a more active role in their own healthcare decisions.

Many colleges and universities that educate and train health and medical professionals now offer some online coursework in health-related topics. New outreach portals are giving access to information or care in any and all circumstances and settings—urban, rural, local, remote, off-shore, insured, uninsured, rich, poor, and everything in between. The primary limitations to eHealth are people's access to infrastructure such as smartphones, personal computers, the Internet, and other touch points, and access to the health-related programs and professionals who develop and deliver the revolutionary programs supported by these electronic means. While availability of the infrastructure enabling access to the Internet remains a persistent challenge in developing countries, growing proportions of the world population have access to one or more types of infrastructure: 2 billion people have access to the Internet, 6 billion cell phones are in use, and 2 billion personal computers will be in use in 2014.[5]

It bears repeating that the usefulness of eHealth capabilities relies on the discipline of core HIS capabilities, good stewardship, and management of data, just as represented in the HIS model. The ability to know exactly which data are being sent to whom, with confidence in those data's integrity and security, does not get easier with Internet- or mobile-based technologies; the fundamental principles of good data and systems management remain absolutely critical. Bad data means bad eHealth. This extends to ensuring the protection of identifiable health information (PHI) according to standards set in the Health Insurance Portability and Accountability Act (HIPAA), no matter which medium is used to transmit those data.

mHealth

mHealth is the use of mobile technologies for purposes of health care, public health, and health-related activities at the individual level. These activities can be clinical, educational, administrative, or research related: What matters is not the nature of the health activity, but rather the fact that it is enabled through the use of various mobile technologies. mHealth technologies include smartphones, mobile applications using tablets and smartphones, the Internet, **machine-to-machine (M2M)** wireless capabilities, personal computers, sensors and patient monitoring devices, social media, personalized health dashboards, and other applications connecting clinicians and patients or people in new,

efficient ways, bypassing the need to be physically in each other's presence for caring or information sharing to take place. Much as linking computers in healthcare organizations situated in different locations has "taken geography out of the healthcare equation," so mobile computing has removed physical barriers between individuals, individuals and organizations, individuals and information, and organizations and information. The new ways of interacting using mHealth are consistent with the new ways of communicating in other avenues of our lives. These methods—including social networking, business-to-consumer interactions, business-to-business interactions of commerce, and consumer-to-consumer connections—are taking off in health care, public health, and all matters health related. For example, in the United States, the number of adults using mobile phones for health information increased from 61 million in 2011 to 75 million in 2012.[1] Patient beliefs and physician preferences favor adoption of these new technologies to assist in health care in the same way that we are using new technologies in our daily lives.

Additional elements have been encouraging this evolution of health care and public health into mHealth methods and capabilities. In addition to the increasing availability of mobile technologies, these elements include the aging and changing demographics of the population; the increasing implementation of foundational HIS and technology, represented in the systems and management layer of the HIS model (**Figure 12.2**); and the quantified self movement.

- *Changing demographics.* Aging of the population, coupled with chronic illness and the need to manage related risk factors *outside* of institutional settings, has led to a significant shift in the demographics served by health care. The world's population is still growing, but the growth in developed countries such as the United States and Japan is not due to increasing birth rates, but rather increased life expectancy achieved through the control of certain illnesses. In countries and regions where these diseases are not yet well controlled (such as Nigeria), mHealth can assist with the outreach to people living in areas lacking access to care and information. In other areas, such as Japan and Europe, the gradual transition to an older population is leading to concomitant needs for care of an elderly population and increased numbers of chronically ill persons. This set of factors has produced a demographic profile for these countries closer to that of the United States or other developed countries

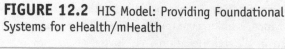

FIGURE 12.2 HIS Model: Providing Foundational Systems for eHealth/mHealth

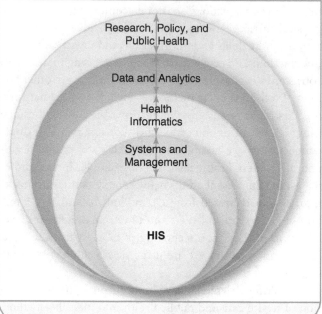

with lower death rates and gradually increasing life expectancy, resulting in greater need to care for people outside institutions.[8]

- *A greater potential role for mHealth.* In Nigeria, for example, outreach to people living in outlying rural areas to communicate important health information and updates regarding disease outbreaks can help those populations avoid contagious disease or get access to precious vaccinations, thus aiding in the control of disease through the use of text messages and cell phones.

  In another example, in Uganda, a UNICEF-sponsored program called mTrac helps health workers use simple texts sent on cell phones to track supplies of medicines and disease outbreaks electronically rather than using paper-based processes. In an area short on hospitals, but with good cell phone coverage and where one-third of the population has cell phones that can send and receive texts, this infrastructure is having a powerful effect on the ability of Ugandans to obtain information about where to access medicine and which places to avoid where a contagious disease outbreak has occurred. This information is shared with townspeople and public health workers to help keep track of what is going on regarding both medicine stock (and needs to reroute

those supplies) and illnesses. A regional dashboard publishes this information along with a hotline from users of healthcare services so that corrections can be made.[9] The mTrac technology initiative is inexpensive and equips citizens with simple but important information that directly impacts their health. Additional funds have been used to train 8000 more healthcare workers, and the same method can be used to track and report other problems, empowering citizens and health workers alike with information to help them protect their health. The possibilities of mHealth and its impact on communication of health information, ability to report disease outbreaks, and access medicine have had a transformative effect on this country and its predominantly rural, poor population.

- *The increasing availability of EHR systems and other HIS and infrastructure that provide a more robust foundation of data for mHealth use, tracking, and communication.* In the HIS model, the first sphere—systems and management—provides foundational systems that organize and house the data created and captured in those core clinical and business systems. These data can then (using proper security and controls for HIPAA compliance maintaining security, privacy, and confidentiality of PHI) be transmitted and used by appropriate parties on each end of the mHealth communication linkages. This secondary use of the HIS data dramatically increases the value and utility of those data for supporting multiple uses and greater efficiency in the delivery of health care and leveraging of the data for public health purposes.

- *Quantified self.* Introduced in 2007 by blogger Gary Wolf, the "quantified self" concept enables individual data to be gathered using mobile devices, smartphone apps, biosensors, and other means, leading to personalized information and customized care. For instance, personal genomic data can be combined with other healthcare information to pinpoint individuals' specific risks, conditions, and appropriate treatments.[10]

Each of these elements is readying healthcare organizations and public health entities for their adoption of new technologies in the mHealth journey, connecting individuals to clinicians, monitoring specific conditions of patients remotely, and streamlining communication of specific, personalized information to improve health, quality of care, and efficiency of processes. mHealth technologies can be used for a multiplicity of increasingly advanced purposes, which in turn move along a continuum of uses (**Figure 12.3**).

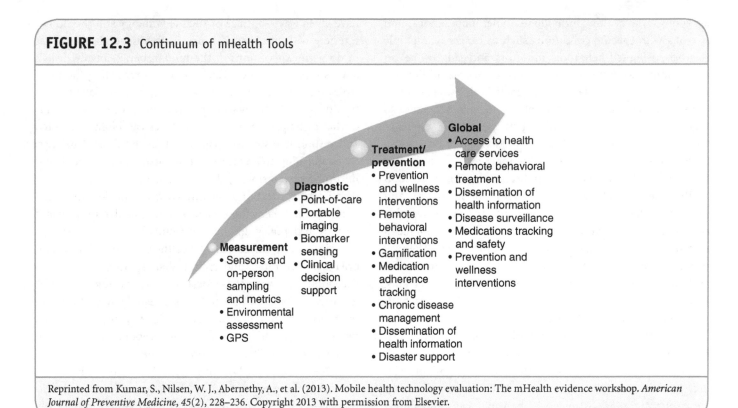

FIGURE 12.3 Continuum of mHealth Tools

Reprinted from Kumar, S., Nilsen, W. J., Abernethy, A., et al. (2013). Mobile health technology evaluation: The mHealth evidence workshop. *American Journal of Preventive Medicine, 45*(2), 228–236. Copyright 2013 with permission from Elsevier.

Social Media and HIS

Social media use in health care and public health is a wide open book at this point. In an area that is actively in what might best be described as a trial and error period, the balancing act between access to one's personal technology and the privacy of what is taking place in the healthcare workplace is being addressed in healthcare organizations, public health entities, and homes alike. The fact that this is an evolving process is important: Where we are today with social media is nowhere near where we were when early social media capabilities, such as MySpace, first began to emerge. Because these early experiences with social media occurred during less technology ubiquitous, pre- and early HIPAA days, the initial policies and practices were rooted in a nonsecure, less "open" world and, therefore, were less facile than attitudes would dictate today. Today, use of social media is being embraced—a major change from earlier years. Healthcare organizations are charged with reaching the ultimate goal of preserving patient privacy, confidentiality, and security of PHI, while still using networking and other technology to create an interactive, engaged patient experience with informed providers. This balancing act requires understanding that the issues involved are partly technology related and partly human behavior related.

How do healthcare organizations use social media? Organizational uses differ from consumer uses of social media, in that organizations focus on marketing and education, reviews, information gathering, and building support communities around specific diseases or processes such as cancer or diabetes. Additional areas of active use include patient education and human interest stories.[11] Facebook, Twitter, LinkedIn, Foursquare, YouTube, Yelp, and other social media capabilities are being used across the United States by healthcare organizations and physician practices to communicate with patients and communities. Physicians, nurses, hospitals, and patient groups may engage one another through these social media platforms and are trusted contributors in the opinions of patients reading the posts. Other parties posting information using social media include other familiar patients, pharmacies, government programs, payers, pharmaceutical companies, alternative healthcare providers, fitness organizations, and other unfamiliar patients. Patients have many topics they like to discuss online, including support for a particular health-related cause; comments about health-related experiences; information sharing regarding particular health-related conditions; reviews of clinicians, treatments, payers, and hospitals; and sharing of images.[11] Enhancing the patient experience for various groups such as young and healthy individuals, older populations, and persons with specific conditions such as cancer or multiple sclerosis, using self-help tools, monitors, and gadgets one can use at home, is a top priority for healthcare organizations.

Key policies and day-to-day practical decisions governing social media use by organizations include adherence to regulations and balancing HIPAA privacy/security adherence with access to and use of social media. Ultimately, social media comprise one more technology, and all technologies must follow overarching policies regarding protection of PHI and patients' rights to privacy, confidentiality, and security of data. Just because some information is available on a new platform (in this case, social media) does not mean it is acceptable to violate those guiding principles. The new technologies are simply additional means of transmitting and communicating information and making connections. Realistically, healthcare organizations should accept both the requirements of HIPAA and the reality of a world that embraces the use of social networking tools. As always, it is up to the human beings who use the technology to work and behave in ways that respect the privacy of patients who are, at that particular moment in their lives, vulnerable. Consequently, those who work in health care and public health must be held to a standard of appropriate behavior and concern for maintaining the privacy, confidentiality, and security of patients' information. Sharing PHI with anyone outside those parties involved in the care and administration of that care is not acceptable behavior, no matter how open a patient or employee prefers to be outside the workplace, either online or offline.

Additionally, when it comes to healthcare employees using social media outlets at their place of work, productivity can be a concern. Clearly, spending time on social media in ways that intrude on a person's work responsibilities is not something that can be left to random or individual attitudes or decisions. A quick email regarding a personal item that allows the employee to continue to attend to his or her duties is probably not a problem as long as it is used appropriately. Organizations are just what their name says: They are *organized*, which means that principles, values, policies, and rules provide structure to the workday. Everyone in the organization must adhere to acceptable norms in that environment. In some cases, organizations originally made the decision to block access to Internet sites other than those related to work. Once social media became ubiquitous, employees did not expect to use those sites at work because they expected that work computers would not be open to non-work-related sites. Gradually, however, these boundaries

have given way—but use of such technology still should not interfere with one's work. Much of this issue, therefore, has to do with expectations of the human beings involved. It is always preferable to educate employees regarding the principles that the organization stands for, and to make protection of patient information paramount. Within the bounds of that principle, behavior and policies can be implemented and responsible workers will maintain the desired balance. By establishing an environment of trust, empowerment, and informed responsibility, deviations from the norm can be seen in the context of a person's typical behavior, and judgments made taking those factors into considerations, based on technical, policy, and human factors.[11]

Ultimately, employees of healthcare and public health organizations must understand that anything posted on Facebook, or Tweeted, or social-media'd in any fashion, is not private. Most of us know this already, having heard on the news or read online about physicians being reprimanded for comments made about cases on Facebook or other social media platforms. That is the bottom line.

Questions about how to handle the use of social media and networking are not unlike the questions that organizations pondered when HIPAA was implemented in the early 2000s. HIPAA, of course, has to do with the protection of PHI; ways to address the security of HIS technology that handles PHI, such as EHR systems; and the behavior of healthcare workers, clinicians, and business people who handle that kind of information all day, every day, so that the privacy and confidentiality of PHI are maintained. These are the same types of issues that arise with the introduction of social media into the mix of technologies available for use in healthcare organizations and throughout health and the population. When HIPAA was originally passed, HIS and technology mattered a lot to that process, meaning organizations had to build HIS to meet HIPAA-level security and technical standards. HIPAA compliance also must take into account the human beings who are handling and accessing the PHI. A major part of implementing HIPAA is education and training of the people involved, so that their decisions and choices as clinicians and business people working with PHI are made while understanding their responsibilities to protect the confidentiality and privacy of PHI. Education and training regarding why and how to protect and properly handle PHI in their daily work is as important as the technical work of the HIS professionals to ensure the security of computer systems and networks storing and translating the PHI.

Before HIPAA was implemented, for instance, systems were accessible to those possessing a password to the system, so patient information was more easily accessed across a broader spectrum of roles, with fewer "need to know" qualifications than are in place today. It was a startling wake-up call to many who worked in health care to realize that they could no longer view PHI unless it was needed for them to do their jobs in caring for or conducting business necessary to the treatment or cure of the patient. Stiff reprimands are handed out if these rules are violated, including termination and, in some cases, legal action for blatant hacking and illegal sharing of private information. Social media outlets are largely the same: The technologies are built to be open, and there is no way to tighten the security technically due to the nature of social media and networking and their basic purpose—namely, open sharing of comments, perspectives, questions, and other interactions between people. The key to protecting patient privacy, then, is education and training of the people involved, so that they know how to regulate themselves and handle preservation of PHI privacy, confidentiality, and security in their daily work and interactions using social media and other platforms. At the end of the day, whether we are talking about HIPAA or use of social media, the greatest risks for breaches of sensitive data are associated with the behaviors and choices of people, much more so than the security of systems.

Telemedicine and Telehealth

Telemedicine and telehealth have many applications and use a variety of technologies discussed in this chapter, including smartphones, Internet, secure email, video transmission, and other telecommunications capabilities. At its core, telemedicine is the remote delivery of clinical services using these types of technologies and the remote delivery of health-related information from one site to another via electronic communications to improve a person's health awareness and access to information in the broader context of health promotion and prevention of illness or harm.[12] WHO adds to that definition by stating that telehealth includes the exchange of valid clinical information in situations where geographic distance is a factor for the purposes of diagnosis, treatment, and prevention of disease and injuries, research and evaluation, and the continuing education of healthcare providers.[13] WHO also describes four key elements of telemedicine—namely, its intent to provide clinical support, overcome geographical barriers, connect users who are in different physical locations using the variety of types of modern information and communication technologies, and improve health outcomes.[13]

New HIS technologies, accompanied by a continuous drop in costs, coupled with these technologies' increasingly ubiquitous availability, are contributing to the current growth of telemedicine and telehealth. These capabilities are increasingly being adopted and refined as useful and cost-effective means of delivering clinical treatments, health services, and enhanced provider-to-provider interactions across distances that were previously challenging, if not infeasible, to surmount. Certainly, telemedicine and telehealth can improve access to medical and health services for those populations currently lacking ready access to health practitioners and information. New adaptations include establishing a telehealth "platform," which includes the virtual care component and video but adds integration with EHRs and workflow optimization.

Barriers to adoption of telemedicine and telehealth solutions include the following issues:

- The complexity of human and cultural factors is a major challenge, including departure from traditional work and communication methods for clinicians, patients, and people receiving the health information. A related barrier is lack of the necessary technical proficiency to connect and use these various technologies to communicate and conduct care processes remotely.
- The cost of sustaining telemedicine and telehealth initiatives originally started with a grant or some seed funding can prove problematic. These ventures often fail for lack of sustaining funding, despite the fact that costs of technologies are consistently declining.
- A shortage of studies evaluating costs and benefits, and a lack of business cases documenting the cost-effectiveness of these telemedicine initiatives, diminishes their viability. Such evidence is needed to win support for establishing the necessary infrastructure and funding program start-up costs.
- Legal issues around the crossing of transregional boundaries may create significant barriers to implementing telemedicine programs. Notably, healthcare providers are challenged by the lack of international law in this area and complexities in differences between interstate laws governing the transmission of healthcare information across national and state lines.
- Technical challenges create barriers to the integration of the various types of systems, devices, and networks needed to conduct telemedicine and telehealth. Many areas that need these types of services are rural or remote, and they may not have the requisite expertise to implement and support the technology platforms.[13]

While telemedicine and telehealth definitions overlap with definitions of mHealth and eHealth, the former terms are typically used to describe various types of uses of HIS and telecommunications to eliminate barriers to care and communication imposed by geography and physical proximity. Telemedicine provides needed medical and health services to patients and citizens separated by distance from the clinicians and healthcare providers. These technologies are also hugely useful in providing connections between providers for purposes of consultation, research, education, and training.

Examples of telemedicine and telehealth include remote radiology interpretations and intensive care monitoring by clinicians for hospitals located remotely or smaller organizations that cannot afford full-time specialists 24 hours a day; clinician–patient consults over live video; and remote patient monitoring for heart disease, diabetes, or other common, chronic conditions that need to be tracked closely but that do not require the patient to be institutionalized.[14] Telemedicine also encompasses education and networking, allowing remote healthcare professionals to earn continuing education credits and giving patients access to online support groups and specialized health information.

EMERGING HIS TECHNOLOGIES AND THE HUMAN–MACHINE RELATIONSHIP

Emerging technologies are only as useful as their practical application and demonstration of value in achieving hoped for results in the form of benefits and creative goals designed into each pilot project or trial testing a new use of HIS. As HIS progresses into its new phases of eHealth, mHealth, telemedicine, and digital health, it is fueled by research, pilot projects, and intentions of improving health outcomes and health care. HIS research and grant projects focus on areas in information and decision support, clinical workflow improvement, care coordination, and understanding the impact of HIS on outcomes. Funding preferences for research currently favor the areas of medication management, outreach care for vulnerable populations, and practice-based research networks. Priority areas identified by the Institute of Medicine (IOM) include medication management, hypertension, diabetes, heart disease, case coordination, major depression, self-management/health literacy, cancer screening, frailty associated with old age, immunization, pregnancy and childbirth, and tobacco cessation treatment.[15] Such research projects reflect key concerns and represent major opportunities for improvement in health status and outcomes, especially in terms of ambulatory care. Insights will be gained and strides taken as a result of these research projects' findings that will steer evolving uses of HIS in new ways, with technologies being coupled with streamlined processes to achieve improved clinical and cost outcomes.[15]

This pioneering work, which is moving outward beyond the existing edge of uses of HIS and technology, is a creative, arduous endeavor not for the faint of heart. But for those with the will to try and a creative spirit, many new applications continue to be developed in the hopes of being woven into a new fabric of healthcare and public health practices as we know them. Intrinsic to this journey is an evolving relationship between humans and the machines or technology they use. The progression circling around the evolving human–machine relationship piques the interests of those studying emerging technologies. As people adapt to new technologies, the focus of this evolution (historically fixated on using computers to replace humans doing work) changes as well. Currently, three main trends are visible in the innovative use of emerging technologies: (1) human work being augmented by technology, such as a healthcare professional using an automatic sign-on computer access device; (2) machines replacing the work of humans, such as a virtual assistant providing automated services to assist a person finding a needed health service in a new community; and (3) humans and machines working together, such as a mobile robot used by a surgeon while performing a surgical procedure. These increasingly refined interactions between people and computers will continue to be applied in ways that improve productivity, transform the customer or patient experience, and improve outcomes from clinical, cost, and competitive perspectives.[16]

In an evaluation of potential benefits and future directions of more than 2000 new technologies, the Gartner Group identified a Hype Cycle for 2013 that describes a phased continuum of adoption and innovation on which new technologies can be plotted (**Figure 12.4**). Many of the technologies on this curve will be meaningful parts of the future in health care and public health; others will not. Technologies that have been the targets of some serious exploration, if not traction or adoption, for use in health care and public health include sensing, three-dimensional (3-D) bioprinting, brain–computer interfaces, prescriptive analytics, biochips, 3-D scanners, mobile robots, Big Data, gamification, wearable user interfaces, virtual assistants, M2M communication, mobile health monitoring, cloud computing, biometric authentication methods, speech recognition, and predictive analytics.

FIGURE 12.4 Hype Cycle for Emerging Technologies

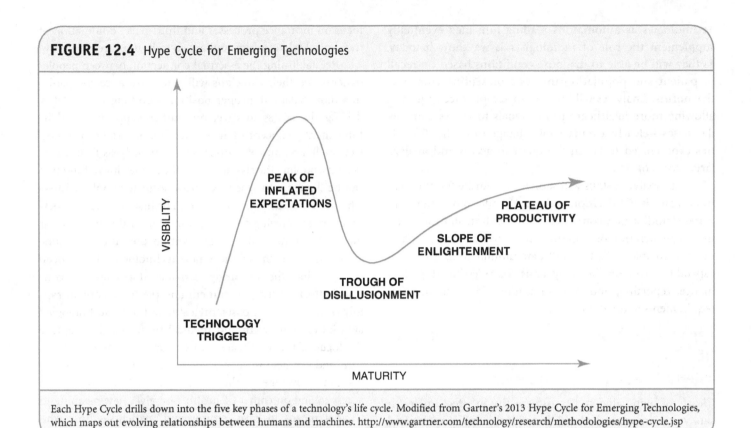

Each Hype Cycle drills down into the five key phases of a technology's life cycle. Modified from Gartner's 2013 Hype Cycle for Emerging Technologies, which maps out evolving relationships between humans and machines. http://www.gartner.com/technology/research/methodologies/hype-cycle.jsp

FUTURE DIRECTIONS IN INFORMATICS, DATA, AND ANALYTICS

Informatics

Considering the interface between clinicians and computers, opportunities for emerging technologies to be integrated into the workflows of clinicians and business professionals are limited only by our ingenuity, our technical prowess, and the boundaries of appropriate care in the essentially human-to-human interactions that compose health care and caring. Reactions—among clinicians and patients alike—to the presence of computers in the clinical exam room have been fierce and varied, with some complaining that this application takes the attention of the clinician away from the human interaction between healer and patient. Specific ways that technology might help clinicians and patients reestablish their human and therapeutic connections will be improvements to the often rudimentary, initial technology adoption that more often than not simply replicates the manual process on the computer.

Forward-thinking organizations are altering outpatient building structures to accommodate such new thinking in ambulatory care, for example. One innovation is to use a centralized, hybrid exam room where the patient stays during the entire visit, and all providers and specialists come to the patient in that room.

In the future, enlightened implementation of technology will move health care away from burdensome technological procedures that relegate some of the most highly trained knowledge workers—namely, physicians, nurses, and other clinicians—to the role of data input clerks. Needed improvements and opportunities lie before us as we seek to refine the integration of technology with the work of these special professionals who devote their working lives to helping and healing others.

Data and Analytics

Greater data availability has proved both a blessing and a difficult curse. The volumes of data and the focus on those data will experience exponential growth in the future.

Technologies as automatons reading film may eventually supplement the role of radiologists as we know it today, as they will be able to diagnose conditions based on recall of patient and population images representing comparative norms. Analytics will mature to accept voice inquiries, allowing more healthcare professionals to access complex databases—clearly a remarkable change from the difficulties experienced today in the quest to access and analyze large stores of data.

Data analytics skills will soon be a requisite for administration and BI/CI decision making. Despite some healthcare workers finding new computer interfaces difficult to adapt to, the next generation of employees must arrive with better and more adaptable skills to avoid data intimidation. Analytical capabilities will be the daily basis for roles-based performance, reporting, and communications for both business requirements and patient care.

THE EFFECT OF NEW TECHNOLOGIES ON PUBLIC HEALTH

mHealth's Impact on Public Health

Clearly of high value and transformative in effect, mHealth can vastly improve isolated individuals' and populations' ability to access health beneficial care, education, information, and professionals. This type of telecommunication and computer connection, whether on a provider-to-patient or provider-to-provider basis, increases efficiency in managing health and chronic illness—important elements as populations age and the prevalence of chronic disease increases.

Prevention Trumps Cure

Amidst this technology revolution, there is some "getting back to basics." The idea of focusing on preventing disease (the wellness or health model) versus curing illness once it occurs (the sickness or medical model) is not a new one. If something can be prevented, that is a much better option than trying to fix it later. Whatever advancements are made using technology in health care should be grounded in principles that allow health care to be more efficient, more effective, and preserving of time and space for caring and compassion. The central relationship between care giver and care receiver can become again what has been often lost in our dependence on administrative, insurance-driven healthcare processes. For this reason, the focus of workflows and processes should be in support of the interaction between a clinician and the patient in health and medical care. At present, we have wandered far afield of that central concept of the unique and intimate conversation between clinician and patient, due to the increased focus on insurance processes and third-party domination of the clinical relationships and access to health care.

Reestablishing the essential connection between people/patients and their clinicians will place insurance companies in a more balanced, proper position—no longer completely driving the access to care, but rather supporting it. The fundamental concept of insurance has always been to collect small amounts of money on a regular basis from many persons, pooling the risk as well as the money into a fund that can be dipped into when expenses occur for pool members who need medical and health care. The insurance tail has definitely been wagging the healthcare dog in this instance for quite some time—interestingly, within the same timeframe as the development of these new technologies. It has been 40 years since the beginning of managed care and the continual efforts of the government and payers to contain rapidly rising healthcare costs. mHealth and other technologies' abilities to help health and medical professionals recapture the focus of the healthcare industry are revolutionary, to be sure, and can help rebalance the respective roles of care and insurance coverage for that care. Using mHealth to improve access to and outcomes of health care gives new meaning to what it means to have "empowered" patients—those who are actively participating in managing and maintaining their health care and health.

ALIGNMENT BETWEEN HIS AND TECHNOLOGY AND THE FUTURE CHALLENGES IN HEALTH CARE AND PUBLIC HEALTH

As we move into the future, tracking the impact of HIS and technology and the overall cost of health care in United States will be important for determining whether we are succeeding in improving the value of healthcare dollars spent. In terms of our current progress, of the more than 85% of eligible hospitals participating in HITECH EHR Meaningful Use (MU) incentive programs, more than 75% had received incentive payments for meeting the MU criteria of EHR systems as of March 2013. Continued progress along the adoption curve of MU functionality and other helpful technologies such as eHealth and mHealth will reveal whether we have accomplished the desired improvements through the massive investments in technology made throughout the healthcare system. Eligible physicians, providers, and hospitals have increased their participation in MU programs and adoption of EHR systems, mHealth, and other new technologies. As of March 2013, approximately 44% of all eligible professionals had received a MU incentive payment.[17] Tracking progress along this path of increasing adoption and MU will be important markers for future directions in HIS and new technologies, as EHR systems provide the foundation for many of the mHealth and digital health capabilities, including the inflection in the application of new technologies.

Other significant statistics to monitor as we move ahead are those reflecting unintended consequences of HIS and technology. As more and improved literature is published from studies of the benefits and risks of HIS, insights will be gained into how we can ensure that the introduction of these new technologies does not hinder progress or introduce new forms of errors. Despite all the good intentions when implementing new technologies in health care, these technologies are disruptive and must be carefully managed and continually evaluated to ensure their effects are positive and not harmful.

The future of the HIS marketplace appears quite dynamic, as new products and services related to HIS and new technologies are being developed with great vigor by inventors, innovators, vendors, and research and development laboratories. Current federal investments and new standards are stimulating the development of many of these new products, as well as spurring the updating or retirement of old products that do not meet the new regulatory and industry requirements. For example, approximately 941 vendors provide more than 1700 unique certified EHR system products in the United States. It will be interesting to see if that number increases or decreases in the next few years, as competitive processes weed out lower-quality products while innovators introduce new ones.

Additional job opportunities have been emerged as a result of this growth in HIS, EHR systems, BI/CI, and other new technologies in health care and public health. Since HITECH was enacted, more than 50,000 HIS-related jobs have been created—and this number does not even count the jobs created in the new businesses developing the many new products described previously. Clearly, tracking the growth, maturation, and improvement of the products, jobs, and roles involved in the development and evolution of HIS will be an exciting adventure.

ISSUES AND ETHICS TO CONSIDER AS THE FUTURE OF HIS AND TECHNOLOGY UNFOLDS

Finding the Balance: Security and Privacy Versus Access to Health Information

A significant issue that arises with the increased availability of HIS and access to data is the flip side of the accessibility coin—*inappropriate* access and violation of personal privacy and security of PHI. The healthcare community is aggressively pursuing interoperability between systems in an effort to facilitate the exchange of data among a variety of organizations to care for individuals more efficiently, as well as to make widespread secondary use of data from those systems. In our rush to "connect the dots" between systems and organizations on behalf of interoperability, we are also challenged with numerous practical and ethical issues. These issues center on finding the balance between access to data and systems and the intentions of "doing good"—with protection of the data and privacy of those whose lives are reflected in the data being a paramount concern. We are a long way from knowing exactly where the fulcrum of that balance should be centered—a balance that will be some right combination of technology and behavior.

Ethical Considerations Regarding Sharing Patient Data in EHR Systems and Health Information Exchanges

Questions abound regarding exactly which information should be shared and under which circumstances. Certainly, common sense is an important guide here: If patients give permission and request their data be gathered from multiple institutions to aid in their care and prevent them from having to undergo repeated diagnostic tests or repeat answers to the same questions over and over again, *and* these data are presented only to those clinicians who need to see them, then that is appropriate use. Conversely, if those same data somehow become accessible without patients' understanding and permission to business ventures whose interests are more aligned with financial gain associated with the secondary use of data for commercial purposes, then we have crossed the line; those types of uses are inappropriate.

HIPAA is intended to prevent the latter circumstance from happening. Regulators are, in fact, levying stiff financial and organizational penalties for inappropriate uses of data and breaches of patient privacy and data security. HIPAA requires organizations to make earnest efforts to comply with this act's privacy and security requirements. Thus, if all organizations comply with the HIPAA requirements, all is well. Unfortunately, as diligently as organizations and individuals strive to thoroughly and properly implement HIPAA (and they are), mistakes are bound to happen and breaches occur. How many mistakes in this area would be too many? Do penalties achieve the kind of impact they are intended to make? Would we avoid these problems if we stuck with paper records? Does it matter, or are we too far down this path to turn back?

The author of this text would answer "yes" to the last question. The world has changed, and information and technology have become integral parts of how we live and work. It is not feasible to imagine that we can turn back, or de-install EHR systems from the many healthcare organizations that have implemented them. In fact, the government has, in effect, mandated their implementation by providing financial incentives and increased reimbursement for healthcare organizations and physician practices that implement these systems according to MU criteria. Ultimately, because the government pays for about half of all medical care in the United States, the net effect is that those healthcare organizations and physician practices that implement EHR systems that have met MU criteria have a much better chance of remaining financially viable and surviving to care for patients into the future. Those that do not "earn" the enhanced levels of reimbursement for having met MU criteria probably have a less rosy fate in store. So onward we must march through the swamps of expensive and difficult issues associated with implementing these systems well and properly protecting the data they contain for the primary purposes of patient care and the secondary uses for research, policy, and public health.

Another transformative development to consider when thinking about the ethical issues associated with use and sharing of data is genomic sequencing and the increasingly affordable availability of personal genomic data. How should genomic data be used? Shared? Stored? Does this type of data deserve special treatment and if so, are currently certified EHR systems actually capable of providing this different level of treatment? Even if the systems are capable of making such distinctions, are organizations and the human beings who handle genomic data using those data in ways that are helpful to patients and properly packaging the data for secondary uses? Which policies, regulations, and practices accompany the creation, use, and availability of these powerfully informative data? Should healthcare organizations automatically make personal genomic data available to insurance companies? What are the ethical and moral considerations of payers in the use of these data and the coverage of the insured populations who pay premiums to those insurance companies for their medical and health care? These are just the beginning of a long list of questions dealing with a topic for which there are far more questions than answers. These issues concern not only the future, but also the present. The purpose of this section is not to try to answer all these questions or to stop interest or work in HIS and technology until all of these uncertainties have been resolved, but rather to get the reader thinking about them and to open up dialogue about what might be the best ways to proceed into a future characterized by genomic data's appropriate and specific use.

Claims Versus Care: What Is Your Priority?

Another practical and philosophical issue related to HIS and technology is the question of whether the construction of EHR systems and other HIS is primarily undertaken to meet financial objectives such as populating insurance claims and patient bills versus for purposes of patient care. The ethos inside the programs and functionality of systems that are used in hospitals and physician practices across the United States reflects the choices made by each organization, the vendors that supply the software, and those who help design and implement the system, as the software may emphasize either the "claim" or the "care." Heretofore, these systems in hospitals and physician practices reflected the financial ethos and were less oriented toward the support of clinical processes; these systems focused more on capturing charges, almost functioning as extensions of the billing system. As strange as this seems, these earlier HIS for clinical areas were marketed as clinical support systems. EHR systems are the first comprehensive clinical systems that have created and captured discrete clinical data elements and documentation as a by-product of supporting actual clinical workflow throughout healthcare organizations. To achieve such goals, however, they must be designed, built, and implemented with these multiple aims in mind. That explains why EHR implementation is such a major priority and has drawn so much attention among healthcare organizations, software vendors, consultants, policy makers, public health professionals, research groups, and the government.

Perhaps the question of whether these systems should be focused more on clinical or financial objectives is easier to answer than some of the questions posed in the previous paragraphs. Philosophically, many still argue about what the priority is—clinical or financial. For this author, because the core mission of healthcare and public health organizations is to care for those persons who need that care and support, the clinical orientation should trump the financial when push comes to shove. Embracing such a perspective forces us to develop processes and systems within organizations that are effective and efficient. Moreover, these two objectives are in no way mutually exclusive; in other words, to accomplish one (clinical) does not negate the ability to accomplish the other (financial). Well-documented, clinician-directed care, efficiently supported by systems and streamlined workflows, can provide billing systems with all the data needed to properly determine billable codes for care through a process called automated charge capture, which, when done correctly, improves the content and quality of data supporting the claims made to insurance companies for reimbursement and the bills sent to patients. A well-implemented EHR system will improve charge capture and claims preparation for the patient accounting processes and should result in better financial performance as well as better clinical quality and patient safety.

Getting Through the Current State of Flux: Moving from Paper to Electronic Processes

Will we ever be paperless in health care? Do we want to be? For the past 40 years, healthcare organizations have been striving diligently to go electronic, under the assumption that when they do so, eventually paper will be eliminated. In fact, in many (if not most) cases, once an EHR system is in place, the amount of paper produced and stored tends to increase, not decrease. This result comes as a surprise to many people, who think such an occurrence is counterintuitive.

In truth, most EHRs are not anywhere near a complete replacement for all paper processes in terms of the functionality they provide. The discipline of redesigning, streamlining, simplifying, and standardizing new processes and workflows is vital. Letting go of old ways of doing work and automating the many paper forms used in healthcare organizations is a very difficult thing to do and is clearly one of the greatest struggles in HIS implementation. The relatively few "paperless" healthcare environments that exist in health care tend to be implementations that were built "from the ground up"—in other words, the systems implemented were part of a brand new building that opened from its first day of operation without paper. This is not the typical scenario for HIS implementations, of course. Most HIS implementations take place during the course of an organization's normal operation and are rather painful transitions from all paper, or old systems, to new automated systems, resulting in a mixture of automated and paper workflows. It is only through an incredibly concerted effort to get rid of the paper, form by form, process by process, that the use of paper can be minimized. And, of course, any paper used in the care or accounting functions of a healthcare entity must be saved, typically forever. Many organizations invest in scanning old medical records into new EHR systems as a way to reduce paper charts significantly, although this process is very expensive and must be factored into the overall cost and effort associated with an EHR implementation project. Moreover, even

if all the paper charts are gone, paper exists everywhere in organizations—in clinical and administrative offices, and nooks and crannies throughout.

Clearly, the days of paperless healthcare environments, while closer, still lie in the distant future. Of course, paper records can be inappropriately accessed just as electronic data can, so the notion that only electronically processed and stored patient charts and financial accounts are subject to the risks associated with inappropriate access and breaches of PHI security, privacy, and confidentiality is false. Paper records also must be protected according to HIPAA standards and requirements.

FUTURE IMPACT OF HIS AND TECHNOLOGY ON RESEARCH, POLICY, AND PUBLIC HEALTH

Data emanate from numerous new electronic sources—from EHR systems going into healthcare organizations across the country, from other HIS, from mobile devices monitoring patient conditions such as diabetes and heart disease, and from sharing of data between many organizations through health information exchanges. Opportunities abound for obtaining HIPAA-compliant data from myriad sources for purposes of research, policy analysis, and public health purposes. As described at length through other chapters of this text in the context of data and business and clinical informatics, opportunities for analytics, access to Big Data, policy analysis, public health data surveillance, reporting, and health status analysis are there for the taking. Certainly, the disciplined management and proper treatment of these data and the challenges associated with normalizing data from many disparate systems lie before us as obstacles to be overcome, but new integration technologies are on the near horizon to help solve these problems.

Healthcare professionals are applying many lessons from the mobile technologies, retail, and telecommunications industries as they enter the wide open healthcare data analytics frontier, and their exciting new solutions will create vast opportunities and wonderful "sandboxes" for researchers, policy analysts, and public health professionals alike. For example, predictive analytics accessing Big Data can improve quality of care immeasurably by sweeping through combinations of data stores to find and address serious and difficult to identify issues such as managing sepsis (a life-threatening blood infection that strikes quickly) before it gets out of control. Sepsis is both deadly and quick in its action: Patients who get antibiotics more than 6 hours after the infection starts have only a 40% chance of survival. In fact, sepsis causes more deaths each year than prostate cancer, breast cancer, and HIV/AIDS combined. By informing clinicians in real time about this condition and enabling them to intervene early in the disease course, HIS and technology could ensure that ineffective treatments that will not work can be changed in time to save the patient.[18]

As seen in this example, Big Data enables clinicians to explore large data sets and identify difficult to find problems and solutions. They can adopt a population health management perspective and gather intelligence regarding how their healthcare organization is performing with targeted conditions, based on real-time analysis driven by intelligent algorithms data and their own reality, not general assumptions or national statistics. From there, clinicians can make changes in real time, can compare their performance to that of peers within their organization, and can benchmark their outcomes against those in other populations. The timeliness of these analytical data queries surpasses that of the traditional retrospective data reporting and analytics, through which trends may be spotted, but only when it is too late to do anything other than identify flawed processes so as to prevent the same problems from occurring again. The possibilities are tremendous in this unfolding arena of near real-time analytics and connecting multiple disparate data sources to find clear areas for improving clinical outcomes and cost performance.

SUMMARY

Summarizing the future of HIS and technology is a mighty task, but if we follow along with the themes of this text, we can track the types of changes in technologies and advancement of opportunities to improve health status, clinical outcomes, cost performance, and the outlook for our future in health care.

The predominant change in HIS and technology going into the future is based on the fact that it is now ubiquitous: IT infrastructure is present in all aspects of our lives in an increasing number of forms, such as mobile devices, sensors, cell and smartphones, Internet access, Big Data analytics, personalized data, and other forms of technology and data. More than ever, as technologies allow for vast data sharing possibilities, sound data management practices and the discipline of data stewardship become essential. Personalized care, therapies, and preventive strategies are all made feasible by the pervasive availability of data, both organizationally and personally. eHealth, mHealth, social media, telemedicine, and telehealth offer new opportunities in health care and public health, capitalizing on technological advancements in other avenues of our lives. The growth of HIS provides

opportunities for eHealth and mHealth to be productively used in the informatics, research, policy, and public health spheres as represented in the HIS model.

Emerging technologies are just beginning to undergo pilot testing in health care and public health, yet the outlook is already very promising. With their ability to improve healthcare services and access to health care and information, these technologies invite citizens around the world to be active participants in their health care and health. The human–machine relationship will become ever more important in such a world, and creative solutions to improving human–machine, machine–machine, and human–human connections must accompany this evolution. The Hype Cycle for emerging technologies highlights a select few among thousands of new tools, all in different stages of development and adoption, and it remains to be seen which ones will stick.

Informatics is evolving in sync with the application of new technologies, resulting in new options and better informed practices of medicine, nursing, other clinical and business disciplines, and public health. Data and analytics are evolving owing to the explosion in data volumes and greater accessibility to such data as a result of widespread adoption of EHR systems and other HIS; such data and analytics have the potential to both inform and revolutionize clinical care, healthcare and population health management, and public health opportunities.

The government's role in health care in the United States is tracking along with progress in the areas of EHR systems and their adoption, incentives for HIS and technology advancements, and goals of the Affordable Care Act. The government's role in HIS and EHR system adoption through HITECH, HIPAA compliance, and public health measures will play an influential part in the continued progress, innovation, and participation in these arenas.

Innovators and entrepreneurs who develop new HIS and technology products are also making key contributions to the progress and evolution in health care. New applications of technologies developed in other industries such as telecommunications are finding exciting places in improving the delivery of health care and the availability of data for analytics and public health advancements in the United States.

The blue sky of inflection of healthcare and emerging technologies is not without clouds: Issues of unintended consequences and ethical considerations, if not outright dilemmas, arise with new uses of HIS and technology. In this age of systems interoperability and data exchange, finding the balance between access to systems and data versus protecting the security of PHI is a continual struggle that must be debated and attended to diligently. This challenge involves not only ensuring the security of systems, but also educating and training the human beings who handle those data and access those systems so their behaviors and choices will protect the privacy of the data. Sharing patient data safely should be part of every healthcare organization's overall data management strategy and responsibilities, whether those data exist on paper or on a hard drive.

The issue of "claims versus care" brings up a key question: What is the organization's priority for the functionality, contents, and capabilities of its HIS? Is the priority clinical care or financial gain? The answer to that fundamental question will often skew the ethos reflected in a system's design and workflows toward either enhancing the financial performance of the organization *or* improving clinical care and quality. While patient safety must always be *the* top priority,

clinical and financial objectives are not mutually exclusive and can coexist successfully and peacefully. Achieving this feat requires that both objectives be discussed openly and creatively during system design and implementation processes, with the organization neither dismissing nor compromising on either objective.

Lastly, the idea of a future without paper remains a long way from reality. How long will it take us to get there? Is this truly the ultimate goal? Diligence in streamlining and simplifying workflows and processes as part of HIS implementations can help organizations gradually eliminate the need to print and maintain partial paper portions of the record alongside EHR systems, thereby improving efficiency and realizing the gains of electronic systems throughout healthcare organizations and public health (and saving many trees in the process).

KEY TERMS

eHealth 242
Inflection point 239
Machine-to-machine (M2M) 243

mHealth 242
Telehealth 242
Telemedicine 242

Ubiquitous availability 240

© Johan Swanepoel/
Shutterstock, Inc.

Discussion Questions

1. What does *ubiquitous availability* of HIS technologies systems mean?

2. Place yourself in an imaginary future time—say, 5 or 10 years from now—and describe health care, the use of emerging technologies, research, and public health scenarios. What are potential improvements in each of those arenas and what are potential problems?

3. Which new technologies will likely have an impact on health care and public health? Consider mobile devices, expanding Internet access, Big Data and analytics, smart/mobile phones, and wireless technologies.

4. eHealth, mHealth, social media, and telemedicine are overlapping but useful labels for capabilities slightly unique from one another. Discuss the scope and impact of each, and challenges in their use in health care and public health.

5. If you were the administrator of a community hospital, would you support the use of social media? Why or why not? What about if you were the chief legal counsel? The vice president of marketing?

6. Use the HIS model to describe ways in what HIS and management support mHealth.

7. Emerging technologies and human–machine relationships go hand in hand. In what ways do improvements in human–machine relationships help the advancement and application of emerging technologies to health care and public health?

8. Where do new technologies used in health care fall today on the Hype Cycle? Which do you think have the most promise?

9. Do you expect the U.S. federal government to keep its money and hand in efforts to advance HIS, especially EHR systems? What are its reasons for stimulating the adoption of EHR systems? Will those reasons persist into the future? Is there a relationship between the government's interest in EHR systems and interoperability of systems and its interest in public health?

10. Describe the most concerning of the issues and ethical considerations described in this chapter. Which of these issues seem solvable, and which do not?

REFERENCES

1. Topol, E. (n.d.). *The creative destruction of medicine: How the digital revolution will create better health care.* New York, NY: Basic Books.

2. dw2. (2012). Smartphone technology, super-convergence, and the great inflection of medicine. http://dw2blog.com/2012/03/25/smartphone -technology-super-convergence-and-the-great-inflection-of-medicine/

3. Mace, S. (2013, August 3). Disconnected health data "beyond absurd," says innovator and patient. HealthLeaders Media. http://www .healthleadersmedia.com/page-3/TEC-294920/Disconnected-Health-Data -Beyond-Absurd-Says-Innovator-and-Patient

4. The quantified self: Counting every movement. (2012, May 3). *The Economist,* Technology Quarterly: Q12012. http://www.economist.com/ node/21548493

5. World Health Organization. (n.d.). Trade, foreign policy, diplomacy and health: E-health. http://www.who.int/trade/glossary/story021/en/

6. Pelletier, S. G. (2014, January). Bridging the gap: Integrating electronic health records into medical education. *AAMC Reporter.*

7. Conn, J. (2014, February 3). HHS issues rule granting patients direct access to lab test results. http://www.modernhealthcare.com/ article/20140203/NEWS/302039958?AllowView=VDl3UXk1TzdDdmVCbk JiYkY0M3hlMEdwakVVZEQrND0=&utm_source=link-20140203-NEWS -302039958&utm_medium=email&utm_campaign=hits&utm_name=top#

8. Riegelman, R. (2010). *Public Health 101: Healthy people—healthy populations* (pp. 196–199). Sudbury, MA: Jones and Bartlett.

9. Luscombe, B. (2012, August 27). Disease can't hide. *Time,* pp. 50–52.

10. Guillemi, A., & Benedict, K. (2013, May). mHealth trends and strategies 2013. ID number NCS05013A. http://www.anypresence.com/ mHealth_Report_2013.php

11. Baum, S. (2013, July 20). Wow of the week: A detailed breakdown of how hospitals are using social media. http://medcitynews.com/2013/07/ wow-of-the-week-a-detailed-breakdown-of-how-hospitals-are-using -social-media/#ixzz2dhgapI7Z

12. American Telemedicine Association. (n.d.). What is telemedicine? http://www.americantelemed.org/learn

13. Telemedicine opportunities and developments in member states: Report on the second global survey on eHealth. (2010). *Global Observatory for eHealth, 2.* http://www.who.int/goe/publications/goe_telemedicine_2010 .pdf

14. Steciw, A. (n.d.). What is telemedicine, and how does it affect health IT? http://searchhealthit.techtarget.com/healthitexchange/healthitpulse/ what-is-telemedicine-and-how-does-it-affect-health-it/

15. Agency for Healthcare Research and Quality. (n.d.). Health information technology ambulatory safety and quality. http://healthit.ahrq.gov/sites/ default/files/docs/page/findings-and-lessons-from-the-improving-quality -through-clinician-use-of-health-it.pdf

16. Gartner. (2013, August 19). Gartner's 2013 Hype Cycle for Emerging Technologies Maps Out Evolving Relationship Between Humans and Machines. Stamford, CT. http://www.gartner.com/newsroom/id/2575515

17. Centers for Medicare and Medicaid Services. (2013, April 23). A record of progress on health information technology. CMS Media Relations. http://www.cms.gov/Newsroom/MediaReleaseDatabase/Fact-Sheets/ 2013-Fact-Sheets-Items/2013-04-23.html

18. Halton, R. (n.d.). Solving sepsis by making information pervasive. http://www.pervasive-health.com/healthcare_saas_article_sepsis_data.html

Glossary

Affordable Care Act (ACA)—Legislation passed by Congress and signed into law by President Barack Obama in 2010, including a "Patient's Bill of Rights."

Accountable care organization (ACO)—A group of physicians, hospitals, and other healthcare providers who come together voluntarily, as part of cooperative frameworks to deliver care in the most effective and low-cost settings in conjunction with the Affordable Care Act and other government-sponsored initiatives, and to give coordinated high-quality care to patients. ACOs coordinate care from primary to acute care, depending on the needs of the patient.

Adoption curve (Rogers' adoption curve)—A theory to explain the adoption of disruptive technology as described by Rogers in 1962 in his landmark book, *Diffusion of Innovations*.

Advisory groups—End-user groups that play a critical part in designing an HIS plan by providing information to developers. These multidisciplinary advisory groups also serve as steering committees throughout the HIS life cycle.

Agency for Healthcare Research and Quality (AHRQ)—One of 12 agencies within the U.S. Department of Health and Human Services. Its mission is to improve the quality, safety, efficiency, and effectiveness of healthcare for Americans. AHRQ sponsors, conducts, and disseminates research to aid in informed decision making and improve the quality of healthcare services. Formerly known as the Agency for Health Care Policy and Research.

Aggregation—The act of combining data points, such as the lab results of patients, with other points of data for the purpose of analysis. Aggregated data enhance healthcare providers' information and knowledge through tracking, reporting, and predicting health status, treatment outcomes, cost ratios and financial performance, and a myriad of other useful analyses.

Alliance for Nursing Informatics (ANI)—Supported by both AMIA and HIMSS, a group that represents more than 2000 nurses and brings together 18 independent nursing informatics groups.

American College of Medical Practice Executives (ACMPE)—A membership association for professional administrators and leaders of medical group practices.

American Health Information Management Association (AHIMA)—A health information management professional association with more than 67,000 members.

American Medical Informatics Association (AMIA)—An association of leading informaticists: clinicians, scientists, researchers, educators, students, and other informatics professionals who rely on data to connect people, information, and technology. This organization holds conferences at which members present findings from studies and reports on informatics development and use of systems to enhance their disciplines.

American Recovery and Reinvestment Act (ARRA)—Commonly referred to as the Stimulus Act. This act's Title IV set Health Information Technology for Economic and Clinical Health Act (HITECH) into place. This act (1) created a strategic plan for a nationwide interoperable health information system, a plan that must be updated annually; and (2) called for a leadership structure consisting of two committees to advise the Office of the National Coordinator, a Health Information Policy Committee, and a Health Information Standards Committee.

Analytics—The process of inspecting aggregated data, looking for patterns and statistics to help improve processes, and creating information ultimately leading to new knowledge that helps improve efficiency and effectiveness of health care, and other goals of health and public health.

Antivirus—Software designed to identify and destroy computer viruses or other malware.

Automation—The use of technology to optimize productivity in the production of goods and delivery of services.

Basic EHR system—An EHR system that has functionality on at least one clinical unit that includes patient demographics, physician notes, nursing assessments, patient problem lists, laboratory and radiology reports, and diagnostic test results, as well as computerized ordering for medications.

Big Data—A recently coined term to describe how data or information is becoming incredibly large. Understanding data/information's relevance to the world and to specific industries is and will become an imperative to optimize performance.

Biomedical informatics—Informatics as applied to health care; an interdisciplinary field that studies uses of biomedical data, information, and knowledge for scientific study, clinical care, analytics, and decision making. Both art and science, it is aimed at improving and transforming health and clinical care, organizations, processes, and research capabilities through the use of HIS and technology.

Business intelligence (BI)—The practice of pulling together or aggregating data from a variety of systems into meaningful and useful information for business purposes.

Canned report—A predefined report from an HIS menu that end users can access regularly. An example would be an accounts receivable report that has been designed with the same information and is updated for use over a repetitive, determined interval (e.g., daily, weekly, monthly).

Centers for Medicare and Medicaid Services (CMS)—A federal agency that administers Medicare, Medicaid, and the State Children's Health Insurance Program; a lead agency in implementing health care and healthcare reform in the United States under HIPAA standards and regulations.

Central data repository (CDR)—A location that serves to store large amounts of information, provides a replication of data from the source systems, organizes the data for extraction for analytics, and may provide an environment for disaster recovery. Also called a data warehouse.

Central processing unit (CPU)—The hardware within a computer that carries out the instructions of a computer program and operating system.

Certified Professional in Healthcare Information and Management Systems (CPHIMS)—A professional certification program for healthcare information and management systems professionals, administered by HIMSS.

Change management—An approach to transitioning employees, departments, and entire organizations toward a future state. In HIS, this refers to helping people transition to the new HIS system and processes.

Change management board (CMB)—A committee that makes decisions regarding whether proposed changes to a software project should be implemented. The CMB is constituted of the organization's project stakeholders or their representatives, and information technology leadership.

Chief information officer (CIO)—The chief executive in charge of HIS and information technology at a healthcare organization.

Chief medical informatics officer (CMIO)—A physician appointed to the HIS department or team who represents the perspective, leadership, processes, workflows, and needs of physicians to shape the HIS architecture and systems.

Chief nursing officer (CNO)—Sometimes called chief nursing executive. An organizational role that also is instrumental in working with the HIS department or team and that represents the perspectives, leadership, processes, workflows, and needs of nurses so as to shape the HIS architecture.

Children's Health Insurance Program (CHIP)—A program administered by the U.S. federal government that provides matching funds to states to provide health insurance to families with children. The program was designed to cover uninsured children in families with incomes that are modest but too high to qualify for Medicaid. Also known as State Children's Health Insurance Program (SCHIP).

Circuit—The pathway by which electronic signals, data packets, or messages between servers and/or clients travel. Copper wire, fiber-optic cable, and wireless transmissions are three of the most common circuit types deployed today; switches, routers, and gateways are devices used to enable circuits to transmit information.

Client—In terms of data structure, the computer, such as a PC, tablet, or laptop, that a user uses to access the server and tap into data.

Clinical data—A more complex set of data, as compared to demographic data, including lab results, previous or ongoing conditions, and so on.

Clinical information system (CIS)—A computerized system that supports clinical diagnosis, treatment planning, and medical outcomes evaluations. It keeps health history, prescriptions, doctor's notes and dictation, and all other information together electronically, and replaces the paper charts of the past. Department-specific CIS systems include laboratory information systems, pharmacy information systems, radiology information systems, medical imaging systems, and long-term care systems.

Clinical intelligence (CI)—Much like business intelligence, the practice of pulling together or aggregating data into meaningful and useful information for clinical purposes.

Commercial off-the-shelf (COTS)—Software that is widely commercially available, sold in large quantities, and not necessarily modified for the user or organization.

Comparative effectiveness research (CER)—Research whose goal is to provide the best possible synthesis of existing research results to clinicians so that these findings may be put into use. CER is based on "comparative effectiveness"—the comparative effectiveness of various treatments, processes, and approaches to care reflects the benefits of one method relative to another method, not relative to some absolute metric. CER studies are mostly based on current evidence and metrics, with the understanding that additional evidence and metrics will emerge over time.

Comprehensive EHR system—An EHR system that includes basic functionality plus 14 other clinical functionalities and is used throughout the entire hospital. The functionalities include patient demographics, physician notes, nursing assessments, problem lists, medication lists, discharge summaries, advance directives, lab reports, radiology tests, medications, consultation requests, nursing orders, clinical guidelines, clinical reminders, drug allergy results, drug–drug interactions, drug–lab interactions, drug dosing support, and many ways to view images, results, and more.

Computerized physician order entry (CPOE)—Also called computerized physician order entry. The process in which a physician electronically enters orders or instructions into an electronic health record system for a patient's care, rather than the orders or instructions being transcribed by a ward clerk or other ancillary personnel from the clinician's hand-written order. This relays information directly from the source (e.g., a physician or nurse practitioner) to the pharmacy or laboratory or other destination to which the order for a test or therapy is directed. CPOE is intended to reduce medical errors by avoiding errors of transcription, and allowing the ordering physician or provider to directly verify the correctness of the order at the point of entry, thus reducing the frequency of needing to catch errors elsewhere in the process path.

Continuous power source (CPS)—A type of flywheel-driven utility power feed for data centers used as backup power. The flywheel is driven by high-speed turbines. Robust and environmentally friendly, CPS systems are more expensive and slower to assume the primary load than UPS systems.

Control Objectives for Information and Related Technology (COBIT)—An information technology governance framework developed in the 1990s by the IT Governance Institute. COBIT is useful for HIS governance, oversight, and process audit, and includes requirements for the control and security of sensitive data.

Current Procedural Terminology (CPT)—A set code maintained by the American Medical Association that describes medical, surgical, and diagnostic services. CPT codes are designed to communicate uniform information about medical services and procedures for administrative, financial, and analytical purposes.

Current state—An organization's current use of technology, systems, data, workflow, and key processes. It includes interviews and documentation of systems' and processes' strengths, weaknesses, opportunities, and failures (threats).

Current systems review—The process of documenting all existing systems in the organization as the baseline for creating an HIS and technology migration plan to take the organization from its current state to its desired future state of automation.

Customer resource management (CRM)—The use of technology to organize and manage an organization's interactions with current and future customers. In health care, CRMs intersect with sales, marketing, customer care, technical support, and billing.

Dashboards—Graphically presented, often-used data sets made available in a central location to provide users with easy access.

Data—Facts and statistics collected together for reference or analysis, the analysis and aggregation of which leads to the creation of information. In health care, data may be general (e.g., gender, age) or clinical (e.g., diagnosis, test result, prescription, allergies).

Data centers—The facilities where HIS are located; they are vital to the successful implementation and ongoing support of providing healthcare applications. Data centers can be remotely hosted, commercially owned co-hosted data centers, or maintained on site.

Data delivery and translation—The art of taking critical information from a database and bringing it to the correct personnel in a format that they understand and can readily apply to their work.

Data dictionary—A directory or database that contains definitions and descriptions of the data elements in the systems of an organization; also referred to as a type of metadata ("data about data").

Data mining—The act of extracting information from a data set for use in data analytics.

Data model—A map or visual representation showing how data are organized according to key aspects of a process and relationships between the various data elements. In healthcare organizations, these key aspects would include patients, providers, employees, and suppliers, among others. A data model is helpful in the systems engineering and programming processes to illustrate data layout.

Data ownership—(1) The determination of whether the HIS vendor or the healthcare organization owns the data collected by the HIS. It is advantageous for the healthcare organization to own its data—a point that should be addressed in the original vendor contract. (2) Within the organization, the answer to the question, "Who is responsible for the information collected?" Typically, this is the process owner of the sanctioned source of each data element. The CIO is responsible for providing leadership for data strategy, management, and stewardship.

Data security—The need for data in general and each discrete data element to be secure in terms of its access and use. In health care, very specific legal requirements and regulations govern the creation, storage, access, and use of data.

Data sharing—Making data available for more than one person to access and use. This sharing process can be for an individual's purpose or it may be for a team or organization. Both technical considerations and security issues arise in regard to the sharing of data.

Data sources—In health care, HIS capture many different types of data from many different sources. These include clinical, personal, transactional, payer, third party, external, and government sources.

Data structures—The methods and formats used to organize data in a computer, often described in terms of records, files, and arrays.

Decision support system (DSS)—A computer-based information system that supports flexible organizational decision-making activities, typically using data from many source systems.

"Dematerialized" information—Information that is distributed electronically, because it no longer has ties to a physical piece of paper in a specific location.

Diagnosis-related group (DRG)—A system to classify hospital cases into one of originally 467 groups. This system of classification was developed as a collaborative project by Robert B. Fetter of the Yale School of Management and John D. Thompson of the Yale School of Public Health.

Disaster recovery (DR)—The process of preparing for and getting data back after they are lost in a system failure.

Distributed antennae system (DAS)—A network of antenna nodes separated by distance and connected to a common source for the purpose of providing wireless service within a geographic area or structure.

eHealth—As defined by the World Health Organization, the transfer of health resources and health care by electronic means, encompassing three main areas: (1) delivery of health information, for health professionals and health consumers, through the Internet and telecommunications; (2) use of the power of IT and e-commerce to improve public health services, such as through the education and training of health workers; and (3) use of e-commerce and e-business practices in health systems management.

Electronic data interchange (EDI)—The transfer of specifically structured information from one machine to another, without human interaction. The information is formatted to communicate specifically with the originator and the recipient, and the machines may vary. Rules and standards for EDI between providers/healthcare organizations and payers (insurance companies or intermediaries) are established by HIPAA.

Electronic document management (EDM)—A major part of the transition from paper to electronic records; a system that involves scanning paper documents and using technology to convert the image to editable text.

Electronic health record (EHR)—A collection of health information accessed, stored, and processed electronically, about individual patients or populations, the goal of which is to replace paper records in healthcare provider organizations. This digital format is theoretically capable of being shared across different healthcare settings, "following" patients wherever they might seek care. EHR systems span multiple care settings, track and store a patient's information over a longitudinal time horizon, and contain functionality that assists in activities associated with maintaining a person's health, as well as information and functionality pertaining to episodes of that person's illnesses and medical treatments.

Enterprise resource planning (ERP)—A cross-divisional, organization-wide system that supports core business functions of an organization in the arenas of finance, human resources, and supply chain management. ERP applications are tied to a common database. ERPs facilitate integration of administrative and business information, and accessibility to that information by those who need it to perform their jobs in those areas. Enterprise-wide ERP systems facilitate business-related information flow throughout an organization.

Executive information system (EIS)—A type of system that facilitates and supports senior executive information needs. It provides easy access to internal and external information relevant to organizational goals.

Extraction, transformation, and load (ETL)—A process that extracts data from outside sources, transforms those data to fit operational specifications, and then loads the results to the end destination (such as a central data repository).

Extranet—A private network that uses Internet Protocol technology and the public telecommunication system to securely interact with or share information or operations with suppliers, vendors, partners, customers, or other businesses.

Five Rights of Clinical Decision Support—A principle to guide and support clinical decisions: right information, to the right person, in the right format, via the right medium or channel, at the right time or point in the workflow.

Five Rights of Health Information Management—A principle to guide and support HIS decisions, much like the Five Rights of Clinical Decision Support: right time, right route, right person, right data, right use.

Future state—An organization's vision of where it wants to be in 5 to 10 years. To begin HIS planning, an organization must know its current state and then develop a vision and HIS architecture for its desired future state.

Hardware—The physical machines that use software to perform their functions. Hardware in an HIS architecture includes computers, servers, tablets, printers, devices, and more.

Health alert network (HAN)—A program under the Centers for Disease Control and Prevention designed to ensure that communities have rapid and timely access to emergent health information on a 24/7 basis. Most state-based HAN systems have access to 90% of the communities they represent.

Health information exchange (HIE)—Communication of healthcare information electronically across organizations within a locale, region, community, state, or nation. The goals of HIE are to improve access to and retrieval of clinical data or other information relevant to a patient's care, to reduce waste, and to provide better and more timely care. HIE is also useful to public health authorities in identifying events or conditions for which they are monitoring and conducting surveillance on behalf of the public's health (e.g., infections such as tuberculosis), or those associated with potential bioterrorism (e.g., smallpox or anthrax).

Health information management (HIM)—A health information and coding department within a healthcare organization.

Health Information Management Systems Society (HIMSS)—A not-for-profit organization dedicated to promoting a better understanding of healthcare information and management systems.

Health information system (HIS)—The information technology that supports healthcare functions. It includes all computer systems (including hardware, software, operating systems, and end-user devices connecting people to the systems), networks (the electronic connectivity between systems, people, and organizations), and the data those systems create and capture through the use of software.

Health information technology (HIT)—See *Health information system (HIS)*.

Health Information Technology for Economic and Clinical Health Act (HITECH)—Part of the $787 billion American Recovery and Reinvestment Act (ARRA) stimulus package, this legislation requires the U.S. government to lead the development of standards that allow for nationwide electronic exchange and use of health information to improve quality and coordination of care. It (1) created a strategic plan for a nationwide interoperable health information system, a plan that must be updated annually; and (2) called for a leadership structure consisting of two committees to advise the coordinator, a Health Information Policy Committee and a Health Information Standards Committee.

Health Insurance Portability and Accountability Act (HIPAA)—Federal legislation aimed at improving the U.S. health system's efficiency and effectiveness by introducing standards governing the use and communication of healthcare information, originally targeting the objective of facilitating movement of people and their information from one insurance plan to another when they changed employment. The HIPAA regulations set standards for electronic data interchange. The HIPAA Privacy Rule protects the privacy of individually identifiable health information; the HIPAA Security Rule sets national standards for the security of electronic protected health information; the HIPAA Breach Notification Rule requires covered entities and business associates (of healthcare providers) to provide notification following a breach of unsecured protected health information; and the confidentiality provisions of the Patient Safety Rule protect identifiable information being used to analyze patient safety events and improve patient safety.

Health services research—Research that examines access to health care, care costs, and care outcomes. The main goals of health services research are to identify the most effective ways to organize, manage, finance, and deliver high-quality care; to reduce medical errors; and to improve patient safety.

HIS architecture—The comprehensive, structured collection of HIS systems and infrastructure within an organization.

HIS governance—The leadership and organizational structures and decision-making processes that make sure the organization's HIS and technology plans and projects sustain and extend the organization's strategies and objectives, are conducted fairly, and make the best use of the organization's resources. Governance is conducted throughout the organization, from the highest levels of decision making at the board of directors, down through executive and mid-level management, and to multidisciplinary advisory committees selecting and implementing systems and representing end users.

HIS planning—The art and management rigor of taking the time to create and architect a plan for an HIS system and its implementation that will support the overall HIS strategy and organization's progress to its "future state," where the organization wants to be in the next 5 to 10 years.

HIS strategy—The art and methods of aligning an HIS plan with an organization's mission, values, strategies, and goals.

Implement/implementation—The act of setting in place (installing) and activating the use by trained end users of the infrastructure, hardware, and software laid out in the organization's HIS plan.

Implementation planning—The process of HIS requirements definition, systems selection, elements of contract negotiation, system specification, documentation of the setting in which the system will be implemented, and development of a step-by-step, milestone-driven implementation plan.

Individually identifiable health information (IIHI)—As defined and protected by HIPAA, information that can be connected to a patient individually. Common identifiers include name, address, Social Security number, date of birth, or ZIP code.

Inflection point—In math, the point on a curve at which the curve changes curvature or direction; used in the worlds of history, technology, and business to describe a significant point or moment of change.

Informaticist—A person practicing the science of informatics, applying informatics to a specific discipline such as medicine, nursing, and other disciplines in health care.

Informatics—The use of information systems and technology to redesign, improve, and recreate the ways disciplines such as the practice of medicine, nursing, medical imaging, and public health do their work.

Information technology governance (ITG)—Structured and formal processes designed to mitigate the risk of failure and increase user satisfaction ratings once HIS are implemented. ITG can be divided into two additional areas. IT demand governance (ITDG) is a decision-making and oversight process by which healthcare organizations effectively evaluate, select, prioritize, and fund their HIS investment—in other words, decide what IT should be working on. IT supply-side governance (ITSG) focuses on making sure the IT organization operates in an efficient and organized fashion—essentially, who in IT should be doing what IT is doing.

Information Technology Infrastructure Library (ITIL)—The most commonly adopted ITG framework in use in healthcare organizations today, ITIL was first developed in the early 1990s by the British government. Its fundamental objective is to describe an integrated set of seven process-oriented best practices for managing IT services.

Infrastructure—The "electronic highway" that carries data, images, voice, and information traffic between the myriad users of the health information systems and technology. It includes data centers, computers, computer networks, database management devices, and software systems. There is nothing more important than a reliable, robust network infrastructure as the foundation of an organization's HIS and technology plan.

Infrastructure-as-a-service (IaaS)—A cloud computing service from vendors that provides virtual machines, servers, storage, network, and other infrastructure-type computing components.

Integration—A system in which two or more products work closely together to combine different functionalities into one product. Integrated data are maintained in one location; this supports clear, high-quality solutions.

Interface—A system in which where two or more separate software products communicate under limited capacity. Data are maintained in multiple locations and therefore require much more administration.

International Electrotechnical Commission (IEC)—An internationally recognized standards-setting organization. ISO/IEC 38500 is an ITG framework that describes six guiding principles for the effective, efficient, and acceptable use of IT: responsibility, strategy, acquisition, performance, conformance, and human behavior.

International Organization for Standardization (ISO)—An internationally recognized standards-setting organization. ISO/IEC 38500 is an ITG framework that describes six guiding principles for the effective, efficient, and acceptable use of IT: responsibility, strategy, acquisition, performance, conformance, and human behavior.

International Statistical Classification of Diseases and Related Health Problems (ICD)—The standard diagnostic tool for epidemiology, health management, and clinical purposes. ICD-10 was endorsed by the Forty-Third World Health Assembly in May 1990. The 11th revision of the classification will continue until 2015.

Intranet—A computer network that uses Internet Protocol technology to share data, information, operational systems, or computing services within an organization.

IT service delivery—An important process area that encompasses the support processes needed to ensure acceptable service. Often, this includes a service desk.

IT service support—An important process area that encompasses the support processes needed to ensure acceptable service. Often, this includes a service desk.

Key performance indicator (KPI)—A type of performance measurement used by an organization to evaluate its success.

Knowledge worker—An employee or worker whose main value is his or her knowledge in specific areas of expertise; a person who "thinks for a living." In health care, this label applies to anyone making patient care, diagnostic, business, or strategic decisions. Knowledge workers are the targets of many information technology and HIS initiatives; these systems create a workplace or platform that supports the integration of data and information and functions to support the work and decisions of the knowledge workers.

Local area network (LAN)—A type of network made of groups of devices located within the same geographic area, such as one or more floors within a building, or multiple buildings in close proximity to each other. LANs are the primary networks used by desktops, servers, and network and other devices to communicate when they are in close proximity with each other.

Logical Observation Identifiers Names and Codes (LOINC)—A database and universal standard for identifying medical observations. It was developed in 1994 by the Regenstrief Institute, a U.S.-based nonprofit organization, and meets the demand for an electronic database for clinical care and management. It is publicly available at no cost.

Machine-to-machine (M2M)—When two machines "talk" to each other without a human intercepting or feeding that information to a second machine; for example, a sensor on a patient feeding medical data to a physician's computer through cloud computing.

Malware—Malicious software; a class of dangerous, destructive software programs that include viruses and spyware. Designed to disrupt productivity, gather information illegally, or gain access to restricted computer systems.

Master patient/person index (MPI)—A database that is used across departments and entities within a health system or health information data exchange by assigning each individual a unique identifier. It connects each patient's/person's information from disparate systems.

Meaningful Use—Also called Meaningful Use criteria. The set of standards and criteria defined by HITECH and used by the CMS (including Medicare and Medicaid programs) that governs the qualification of vendor software products for participation in the Meaningful Use incentive programs by providers and healthcare organizations using those electronic health record software products. Eligible providers and hospitals can earn incentive payments and avoid financial penalties later in the program by meeting specific criteria. The goal of Meaningful Use is to promote the spread of adoption of electronic health records and thereby improve efficiency and quality of health care.

Medicaid—A U.S. government insurance program for persons of all ages whose income and resources are insufficient to pay for health care. This income-based program is jointly funded by the state and federal governments and managed by the states.

Medical administration record (MAR)—The functionality with an EHR system used by nurses and other clinicians to plan, record, track, and report a patient's medications, dosages, and timing; it serves as a legal record of the drugs administered to a patient at a facility by a healthcare professional. Sometimes referred to as drug charts or eMARs.

Medical Group Management Association (MGMA)—Professional organization of medical practice managers.

Medicare—A national social insurance program, administered by the U.S. federal government since 1965, that guarantees access to health insurance for Americans aged 65 and older and younger people with disabilities. Medicare provides recipients with a defined benefit.

Metadata—Data about data.

mHealth—Mobile health; the use of mobile technologies for purposes of health care, public health, and health-related activities at the individual level. mHealth technologies include smartphones, mobile applications using tablets, Internet, machine-to-machine wireless capabilities, sensors and patient monitoring devices, and more.

Milestone payment structure—A payment structure agreed upon by the healthcare organization (the customer paying for software and hardware) and the vendor (the provider and seller of software and hardware products). A milestone-based plan differs in important ways from a payment plan based on dates; the former is advantageous for the organization because it incents the vendor to achieve milestones. Milestone payments should be in the vendor contract.

National Provider Identifier (NPI)—A unique 10-digit number required by HIPAA for all healthcare providers to be used in all transactions by healthcare organizations. Providers include both individual (doctors, nurses, dentists) and organizational (hospitals, health systems, clinics, skilled nursing/long-term care facilities, home health, and other) healthcare providers.

Network infrastructure project—An HIS planning project to lay the foundation, or the "information highway" for new HIS systems and processes, including necessary hardware and software for establishing an entire network and communications between all end users accessing systems and data. The project also includes resources that enable network connectivity, communication, operations, and management of an enterprise network.

Normalization—The process of organizing data to minimize redundancy and dependency. Normalization isolates data so that additions, deletions, and modifications of a field can be made in just one table and then propagated through the rest of the database.

Nursing informatics—The use of computers to support and enhance nursing workflow, documentation, management, analytics, and care processes as well as the use of information for analysis of quality and effectiveness properties of clinical care.

Office of the National Coordinator for Health Information Technology (ONC)—An agency created by HITECH. A staff division of the Office of the Secretary, within the U.S. Department of Health and Human Services, it is primarily focused on coordinating nationwide efforts to implement and use health information technology.

Open Systems Interconnection (OSI) model—Developed in 1984, a model of the process of sending data to a receiving device (data transfer). The OSI model has seven layers: physical, data link, network, transport, session, presentation, and application.

Outcomes research—Research that studies the end results of medical care—the effect of the healthcare process on the health and well-being of patients and populations. Conducted by agencies, research universities, healthcare providers, and others, outcomes research evaluates the results of the healthcare process in the real-life world of the healthcare provider organization.

Pay for performance (P4P)—In contrast to the fee-for-service payment model, a payment model that rewards healthcare providers for meeting certain performance measures for quality and efficiency. Providers are paid based upon pre-established targets for delivery of healthcare services.

Peak volumes—In terms of HIS and technology, the volume of highest usage or traffic that the system will experience. An HIS system must be built for peak volumes.

Personal health record (PHR)—A health record maintained by the patient/person that contains data relevant to only that patient's care/person's health. In contrast, an EHR is maintained by the healthcare organization and includes a comprehensive record of clinical data for the patient cared for at that institution or practice.

Phishing email—Scam email designed to lead users to make their computers vulnerable to malware, often through links in the email.

Picture archiving and communication system (PACS)—A system that manages image storage, local and remote retrievals, and distribution and presentation of PACS image files.

Platform-as-a-service (PaaS)—A cloud computing service from vendors that provides operating system, database, web server, development level, and other platform-type computing components.

Policy analysis—Analysis that produces reports and recommendations for policy makers at local, state, and national governmental levels.

Population health management—An approach to health that aims at improving the health of an entire population, a covered population that a health system or other healthcare organization serves, or a community.

Practice management system (PMS)—Software that deals with the day-to-day operations of a medical practice, including appointment scheduling, maintaining lists of insurance payers, performing billing tasks, and generating reports.

Primary uses of data—The transactions of the systems that support activities of professionals and organizations as work is conducted (e.g., patient care delivery, care management, patient care support processes, clinical care and therapies, financial and other administrative processes, and patient self-management and engagement).

Product life-cycle support—A stipulation in the vendor contract that includes licensing and updates for software for a set period (typically 10 to 20 years). It obligates the vendor to "care" for an HIS system with regular updates, bug fixes, and enhancements.

Project management (PM)—The discipline of planning, organizing, documenting, securing, managing, leading, and controlling resources to achieve specific goals. A project is a temporary endeavor with a defined beginning and end.

Project Management Professional (PMP)—A certification offered through the Project Management Institute.

Protected/personal health information (PHI)—Demographic information, medical history, test and laboratory results, insurance information, and other data that are identifiable to a particular person or patient, and that are collected by a healthcare professional or organization to identify an individual and deliver appropriate care. Healthcare organizations are forbidden by HIPAA to access or use PHI in any ways other than those needed in the direct care and business processes surrounding that care on behalf of the person or patient, without specific written permission from that person.

Public health—The health of the community at large. Public health careers and research focus on improving the health of communities through education, research, and promotion of health lifestyle choices, as well as protecting the safety of the public through surveillance for disease outbreaks and measurement of health status of a population.

Quality management system—A type of HIS that combines data from several different systems (such as electronic health record, laboratory, and patient accounting systems) and gives the healthcare organization a platform for developing and tracking desired quality metrics by which it will measure and report its performance regarding quality of care.

Quantified self—A movement to incorporate technology into daily life, tracking measurable wellness activities, outputs, and states through self-monitoring and sensor devices. Outputs monitored include steps taken, blood pressure, oxygen levels, sleep patterns, exercise performance, and myriad other functions. A helpful component of digital health and personalized medicine. Also called body hacking, life-logging, and self-tracking.

Regional health information organization (RHIO)—A not-for-profit health information exchange or collaboration of providers coming together to share data for the purpose of improving care within that region. Providers may include hospitals and hospital systems, clinics, physician practices, emergency responders such as paramedics, tumor registries, imaging centers, and community clinics.

Regulatory compliance—A section in the vendor contract stating that the vendor guarantees that the system complies with and will be made to continue to comply with all federal and applicable state laws and regulations, including HIPAA, ARRA, and Meaningful Use criteria.

Remote hosting—A computing method by which a computer server remains separate from the organization using the system, from which data and information are accessed via a private or public network. This approach is intended to free the organization from tasks required for day-to-day system management, and the management services are often paid for on a monthly basis.

Request for information (RFI)—A precursor to a request for proposal.

Request for proposal (RFP)—A request issued to vendors by organizations to initiate the bidding process for HIS and technology systems.

Revenue cycle management (RCM)—The process that manages claims processing, payment, and revenue generation.

Roles-based use—An updated and more practical view of systems, which assumes that every employee needs access to data, not just executives. This approach modifies data delivery with regard to the person's position, duties, and personal preference.

Secondary uses of data—The use of data by organizations outside of the original healthcare provider, such as public health groups, policy makers, and research institutions. These third parties use data for the purposes of education, regulation, research, public health, homeland security, and public policy support. Secondary uses of data can reveal ways to improve health care processes, health outcomes, population health status, and overall effectiveness in health care.

Security information event management (SIEM)—A critical technology designed to automate and intelligently analyze system logs for anomalies and inappropriate activity.

Server—A host computer at the center of a computer network that stores data or software and is accessed by clients (the input/output computers that users use). While a server resides at one end of a communication circuit, a client is the input/output hardware device at the user's end of a communication circuit or computer system.

Service level agreement (SLA)—An agreement between a service provider and its customer, wherein service provider performance is tracked and measured for adherence. For example, in a typical healthcare environment, HIS outages can be categorized with critical, high, medium, or low SLAs regarding how much time can transpire before the system must return to an operational state.

Single sign-on (SSO)—A type of log-in system for opening up a secure session with roles-based access to numerous applications by computer system end users (e.g., healthcare organization employees). The user has to remember only a single log-in and password, and the SSO system will automatically log the user into various other applications. SSO is designed to save clinician and administrator time.

Six Aims of *Crossing the Quality Chasm*—Six areas to strive for in terms of patient care as listed in the Institute of Medicine's 2001 report, *Crossing the Quality Chasm*: safe, effective, patient centered, timely, efficient, and equitable.

Six S's of Sources of Public Health Data—Data sources that inform public health; they include single case or small series, statistics, surveys and sampling, self-reporting, sentinel monitoring, and syndromic surveillance.

Software—A unified set of computer programs designed to support related functions and work of end users; any set of machine-readable instructions that a computer uses to perform specific operations. In health care, common software functions include the types of software represented in the HIS planning framework—namely, patient and provider support, institutional processes, and clinical and management reporting and analytics.

Software-as-a-service (SaaS)—A cloud computing service from vendors that provides applications and services, such as CRM, email, communications, enterprise web content management, and other software programs.

Software development life cycle (SDLC)—A methodology designed to ensure that end-state solutions meet user requirements in support of the healthcare organization's strategic goals and objectives. SDLC steps include conceptual planning, planning and requirements definition, design, development and testing, implementation, operations and maintenance, and disposition.

Source data—The origin of information found in computer systems and electronic media, which is often interfaced from source systems, or input by users or other means.

Spyware—Malware that is designed to collect information about a user or from a computer system without the user's knowledge or consent.

Steering committee—A committee internal to the organization, often with cross-departmental representation, with a primary focus on guiding strategic decisions concerning future realization of the organization's investment projects, such as HIS and technology.

Storage area network (SAN)—A dedicated back-end computer system designed to efficiently and cost-effectively store and transfer a healthcare organization's server data.

Strategic initiatives—Prongs of an HIS strategy and plan that can be broken down into phases. A good HIS strategy has three to five strategic initiatives in operation at any given time, with an equal number in the pipeline.

Strengths, weaknesses, opportunities, and threats (SWOT) analysis—A useful tool in HIS planning and determining future and current states.

Subject-matter expert (SME)—A professional who brings departmental or functional expertise to bear in the project planning and implementation processes.

Subsecond response time—A measure referring to the amount of time that passes between the user entering a process on a computer (such as conducting a search, filling in a field, or pressing the Enter key) and the machine/system responding to that action; a gauge of capacity and responsiveness of a server's or system's configuration.

Supply chain management (SCM)—A system that manages delivery of services to clients. In health care, this is healthcare services to patients.

Systematized Nomenclature of Medicine—Clinical Terms (SNOMED)—A systematic, computer-based collection of medical terms that allows a consistent way to index, store, retrieve, and aggregate medical data across specialties and sites of care.

System design—The process of architecting the HIS system. System design is done in concert with overall process redesign, including interfaces required for sharing data between those systems feeding and those receiving data.

Telehealth—The remote delivery of health-related information from one site to another via electronic communications to improve a person's health awareness and access to health-related information.

Telemedicine—The remote delivery of clinical services using technology.

The Joint Commission—Formerly the Joint Commission for Accreditation of Health Care Organizations. Founded in 1951, this independent, not-for-profit organization accredits and certifies more than 20,000 healthcare organizations and programs in the United States. Joint Commission accreditation and certification indicates an organization's commitment to meeting certain quality and performance standards, through a survey process that measures and reports on that organization's adherence to a the standards, and identification of areas of noncompliance that must be corrected to maintain accreditation.

Transmission Control Protocol/Internet Protocol (TCP/IP) model—Also known as the Internet model. This model illustrates the process of sending data to a receiving device (data transfer). The TCP/IP model has three layers: application group, internetwork group, and hardware group.

Trojan—A hacking malware that appears to perform a desirable function yet, after it gains access to a system, causes system harm or steals unauthorized data. Often appears as an email attachment.

Ubiquitous availability—Always accessible, at any place or time. In terms of HIS and technology, this term refers to how increasingly more people and organizations have and use various technologies and hardware, such as mobile phones.

Unified communications (UC)—Technology that involves the integration of real-time communication services, such as instant messaging and presence, VoIP and VoWLAN, video conferencing, and web conferencing.

Uninterruptable power supply (UPS)—A type of battery-supported utility power feed for data centers used as backup power. While less expensive than CPS systems, UPS systems are not "green" and require more regular maintenance and replacement.

Velocity, volume, and variety (Three V's)—The usefulness, amount, and variety of data, all of which are increasing.

Virtual desktop infrastructure (VDI)—A desktop-centric service that hosts user desktop (PC) environments on remote servers, which are accessed over a network remotely. For users, this means they can access their desktop from any location, without being tied to a single client device.

Virus—A malware computer program that attempts to spread throughout application software programs, workstations, servers, and entire networks by replicating itself and replacing other files.

Voice over Internet Protocol (VoIP)—A family of technologies that enables Internet Protocol networks to be used for voice applications such as telephony, messaging, and collaboration.

Voice over wireless local area network (VoWLAN)—A technology that is designed to integrate mobile devices using the WLAN. This is particularly useful as more clinical applications are developed for use with smartphones, tablets, and portable computers.

Wide area network (WAN)—A network built from groups of devices located in diverse geographic areas. WANs connect backbone networks and metropolitan area networks; they can connect devices that are located around the world.

Wireless local area network (WLAN)—A local area network that uses high-frequency radio signals to transmit and receive data over distances of a few hundred feet.

Wireless wide area network (WWAN)—A wide area network that provides service to large geographic areas through separate areas of coverage, referred to as cells. Cell phones, smartphones, tablets, and hot spots are mobile devices commonly used to connect to WWANs.

Worm—Malware that replicates itself in a system; worms are "stand-alone" programs and do not need to attach themselves to another file to spread.

Index

Note: Page numbers followed by *e, f,* or *t* indicate material in exhibits, figures, or tables, respectively.

people–process–technology paradigm, 86f
personal health records (PHRs), 60
pharmacy information system (PIS), 60
PHI. *See* protected health information
PHIN. *See* Public Health Information Network
phishing emails, 101
PHRs. *See* personal health records
physical layer, 63
picture archiving and communication systems (PACSs), 60
PIS. *See* pharmacy information system
platform-as-a-service (PaaS), 69
PMI. *See* Project Management Institute
PMP. *See* Project Management Professional
PMS. *See* practice management system
policy analysis, 225
population health management, 219, 227–230
    center, 228
    opportunities, 225
    strategy, 228
P4P. *See* pay-for-performance
practice management system (PMS), 192
predictive analytics capabilities, types of, 226
predictive information capability, 228
presentation layer, 64
primary use of data, 21, 22f
Privacy Rule, 7
private clouds, 69
problem management, 88
process in health care, 174
product life-cycle support, 128
programmatic reporting system, 225
programming language, 58
project-based organization, 96
project communications management, 98
project cost management, 97
project human resources management, 97
project integration management, 98
project management, 96–99
Project Management Institute (PMI) phases, 97
Project Management Professional (PMP), 105
project procurement management, 97
project quality management, 98
project risk management, 97
project scope management, 97
project stakeholder management, 98
project time management, 97
protected health information (PHI), 6, 100, 153
protection, data, 194–195

public health
    challenges in, 250–251
    convergence of, 221f
    HIS and technology strategy, 45–46
    new technologies effect on, 250
    protection of, 10
    scope of, 229
    social media, 245
Public Health 101: Healthy People—Healthy Populations, 226
public health data sources, 226–227
public health informatics, 177–178
Public Health Information Network (PHIN), 22
public health inquiry and research, 225–226
Public Health Institute, 19
public health management opportunities, 225
public health organizations, 18–19
    external regulatory, reporting, research, and, 20–22
public health reporting systems, 22
public health research, 225

Q

Quadrant I, HIS planning framework, 37f, 38–40, 165
Quadrant II, HIS planning framework, 37f, 38, 40, 166
Quadrant III, HIS planning framework, 37f, 38, 165
Quadrant IV, HIS planning framework, 37f, 38, 166
quality management systems, 50
quality-oriented objectives, 172
quality reporting system, 225
quantified self movement, 165, 244

R

RAID. *See* redundant array of independent drives
RCAs. *See* root-cause analyses
redundant array of independent drives (RAID), 67
regional health information organizations (RHIOs), 19–20
Registered Health Information Administrator (RHIA), 148
Registered Health Information Technicians (RHIT), 148
Registered Record Administrator (RRA), 148
regulatory compliance, 131
relative value unit (RVU), 207
release management, 88
remote hosting, 63
request for information (RFI), 123
request for proposal (RFP), 93, 124
research, types of, 222–230, 222f
resource sharing, 65
revenue cycle management (RCM), 187
RFP. *See* request for proposal